CHILDHOOD

ANXIETY

DISORDERS

CHILDHOOD

ANXIETY

DISORDERS

A Guide to Research and Treatment

DEBORAH C. BEIDEL & SAMUEL M. TURNER

Routledge
Taylor & Francis Group

NEW YORK AND HOVE

Published in 2005 by
Routledge
Taylor & Francis Group
270 Madison Avenue
New York, NY 10016

Published in Great Britain by
Routledge
Taylor & Francis Group
27 Church Road
Hove, East Sussex BN3 2FA

Printed in the United States of America on acid-free paper
10 9 8 7 6 5 4 3 2 1

International Standard Book Number-10: 0-415-94797-9 (Hardcover)
International Standard Book Number-13: 978-0-415-94797-8 (Hardcover)
Library of Congress Card Number 2004030818

Library of Congress Cataloging-in-Publication Data

Beidel, Deborah C.
   Childhood anxiety disorders : a guide to research and treatment / Deborah C. Beidel and Samuel M. Turner.
   p. ; cm.
   Includes bibliographical references and index.
   ISBN 0-415-94797-9
   1. Anxiety in children.
   [DNLM: 1. Anxiety Disorders—Adolescent. 2. Anxiety Disorders—Child.]
   I. Turner, Samuel M., 1944– II. Title.

RJ506.A58B45 2005
618.92'8522—dc22   2004030818

Taylor & Francis Group
is the Academic Division of T&F Informa plc.

Visit the Taylor & Francis Web site at
http://www.taylorandfrancis.com

and the Routledge Web site at
http://www.routledge-ny.com

Contents

There are very few people in this world whose life so positively impacts the lives of many others, be they patients, colleagues, students, or friends. Although we will always miss his gentleness, grace, courage, and laughter, his legacy will continue to enrich those of us who were fortunate enough to have truly known him. This book is dedicated to my co-author, colleague, and very best friend, Samuel M. Turner, who passed away during its final production.

DEBORAH C. BEIDEL

About the Authors

Deborah C. Beidel received her Ph.D. in 1986 from the University of Pittsburgh. After serving as faculty at the University of Pittsburgh and the Medical University of South Carolina, she joined the Clinical Psychology Program at the University of Maryland in 1998. In addition to her appointment as Professor of Psychology, she is the Co-Director of the Maryland Center for Anxiety Disorders (MCAD). She was the 1990 recipient of the Association for Advancement of Behavior Therapy's New Researcher Award and the 1995 recipient of the Distinguished Educator Award from the Association of Medical School Psychologists. Dr. Beidel holds the American Board of Professional Psychology (ABPP) Diplomate in Clinical Psychology and Behavioral Psychology and is a Fellow of the American Psychological Association and a past-president of the Society for a Science of Clinical Psychology. She serves on the editorial board of a number of scientific journals. Her academic, research, and clinical interests focus on child and adult anxiety disorders, including their etiology, psychopathology, and behavioral treatment. Her research is characterized by a developmental focus, and includes high risk and longitudinal designs, psychophysiological assessment, treatment outcome, and treatment development. Along with her colleague, Dr. Samuel M. Turner, she is the recipient of NIMH grants addressing the development and efficacy of behavioral interventions for adults and children with anxiety disorders.

Samuel M. Turner received his Ph.D. in Clinical Psychology in 1975 from the University of Georgia. Following faculty tenures at the University of Pittsburgh and the Medical University of South Carolina, he joined the University of Maryland, College Park, in 1998. He is Professor of Psychology and Co-Director of the Maryland Center for Anxiety Disorders (MCAD), a clinical research center for the study of anxiety in adults and children. Dr. Turner is a Diplomate of the American Board of Professional Psychology (ABPP) in Clinical Psychology and in Behavioral Psychology and a Fellow of the American Psychological Association and the American Psychological Society. In 1997, he was the recipient of the American Psychological Association Award for Distinguished Contributions to Professional Knowledge and the 1998 recipient of the Distinguished Scientist Award from the Association of Medical School Psychologists. He served as

Associate Editor-in-Chief of *The American Psychologist* and is on the editorial board of numerous scientific journals. Dr. Turner's primary academic, research, and clinical interests are in the anxiety disorders, and behavioral theories, behavioral assessment, and behavioral treatment. His program of research includes studies designed to delineate the phenomenology of anxiety states, etiological and developmental parameters of anxiety disorders, and development and evaluation of treatments for anxiety disorders. In addition to these primary areas of focus, he has interest in clinical methodology, measurement, scale development, and racial, ethnic, and cultural factors in the etiology and treatment of anxiety disorders.

Preface

Once thought to be primarily disorders of adulthood, it is increasingly recognized that maladaptive anxiety states are common and debilitating disorders of childhood. Research aimed at understanding their manifestations continues to emerge and efficacious treatment programs are being developed and tested. However, much of this literature has yet to make its way into the hands of the numerous health and mental health professionals who, every day, attempt to manage and treat children with these conditions.

Over the years, we have provided many workshops on treating childhood anxiety disorders and we often are asked for clinical materials (e.g., treatment plans, treatment manuals, sample fear hierarchies, self-monitoring forms) that we use in our clinical practice and in our ongoing treatment protocols. Thus, in this book, we discuss the research efforts of many investigators and also describe our clinical experience in treating children with anxiety disorders. We hope that by including these clinical materials we can make more vivid the scientific descriptions and illustrate the range, severity, and functional impairment that childhood anxiety disorder can impart. In addition, we hope these clinical materials will illustrate the creative process of fitting appropriate treatments to individual cases, the necessity for understanding the nature of the condition and how they affect those who are afflicted, and the necessity for an understanding of the scientific literature. Indeed, it is unlikely, in our view, that these conditions can be effectively and appropriately treated if any of these components are missing. Hence, one objective was to discuss the material presented in such a manner that this would be unabashedly clear. We trust we were successful in this regard.

Because fears are so common in children, we felt that it was important that this book include not only anxiety disorders but also the developmental background necessary to place childhood anxiety disorders in their proper context. Therefore, we have divided this book into two parts. Part I, consisting of the first four chapters, provides an overview of children's fears, children's anxiety disorders, developmental considerations, and etiological factors that cut across specific disorders. Many of the interventions used to treat anxiety disorders in children emerged from the literature on adult disorders, and as such, sometimes are neither developmentally sensitive nor appropriate for children or adolescents. For those just beginning to do research and/or clinical interventions in this area, it is important to have a clear understanding of how these developmental factors affect both clinical presentation as well as the construction and implementation of efficacious treatment plans.

Part II includes chapters on all of the identified childhood anxiety disorders as well as a chapter on medical and dental fears and somatic disorders that may be related to anxiety disorders. This chapter was included because medical and dental fears are common among children and often create significant impairment. Although these data could have been included in the chapter on specific phobia, we chose to include a discussion of recurrent abdominal pain because stomachaches (and other somatic complaints) often are among the primary presenting complaint of anxiety disorders in children. Because all of these children are more commonly seen in medical settings (as opposed to psychological or psychiatric settings), we felt that it was appropriate to devote a single chapter to medical issues.

Throughout the chapters, we have endeavored not only to emphasize the developmental focus but also to present the literature on variations in clinical manifestation by age, gender, and culture. With respect to the latter, available data are quite sparse but we hope that the information presented in these chapters will inspire others to conduct more work in these areas.

As authors, we are responsible for the veracity of the material contained in this book. However, without the assistance of others, its completion would not have been possible. First, we would like to thank our editor, George Zimmar, and our assistant editor, Dana Bliss, for their advice, patience, and support throughout the development of this manuscript. We also want to acknowledge the assistance of Brennan J. Young for conducting the numerous literature searches and for his careful editing of the references. Special thanks to our families and friends for understanding the need for the long hours at our computers in order to produce this book. Finally, to our patients and their parents who never fail to teach and inspire us in so many ways, we owe you our thanks and our gratitude.

PART I

OVERVIEW
OF CHILDHOOD
DEVELOPMENT

CHAPTER 1

An Introduction
to Children's Fears

Joshua is a cheerful 1-year-old baby. Until recently, he would let anyone hold him. But now, whenever anyone other than his parents tries to pick him up, he cries and twists away. He can't be comforted except by his mother or father. Joshua has developed stranger fear.

Four-year-old Sondra refuses to go to bed. She cries and says there are monsters in her closet. She used to sleep in her room with a night-light and a chair barricading the closet door so "the monsters can't get out." Now she insists on sleeping in the same bed as her parents. Sondra has a fear of monsters.

These case descriptions illustrate just two of the myriad of fears that exist among children and adolescents. Fearful reactions are widely recognized as very common (Jersild & Holmes, 1935; Lapouse & Monk, 1959; MacFarlane, Allen, & Honzik, 1954; Ollendick, 1983), and often, certain fears are considered to be part of normal development (Barrios, Hartmann, & Shigetomi, 1981; Fonseca, Yule, & Erol, 1994). For many years fears and anxiety in children were not considered "serious" (Graziano, 1975). As a consequence, parents often were advised by medical and mental health professionals not to worry because children would "outgrow" their fears (Graziano, 1975; Poulton et al., 1997). In fact, many children do overcome some fears with time. However, as will be illustrated throughout this book, not every child outgrows or overcomes fear responses, and, in a number of instances, these "fears" are not minor matters. Rather, they are manifestations of serious and often chronic conditions, or alternatively they may be the harbinger of more serious disorders. When fears are part of a serious condition, they sometime create unreasonable emotional distress and/or resulting functional limitations, such as academic or social impairment (e.g., Woodward & Fergusson, 2001).

A recent meta-analytic study suggests that anxiety in the general population has increased over the past 40 years (1954–1981) and children's average scores on a standard child anxiety inventory, the Children's Manifest Anxiety Scale, have increased by one standard deviation (i.e., an average increase of 5–6 points for both boys and girls; Twenge, 2000). Interestingly, by the 1980s, children who were considered to be without a psychiatric disorder (i.e., normal children) had higher scores on this inventory than did children diagnosed with a psychiatric disorder in the 1950s. Increases in anxiety scores were strongly correlated with increases in divorce rate, birth rate, and the crime rate. There was no relationship between anxiety and economic conditions in general. There was a positive relationship between anxiety and unemployment rates, but a negative relationship with poverty (the author speculated that this was perhaps due to the sharp decrease in poverty levels during the 1960s). Although additional factors probably contribute to these increased scores, the data clearly indicate that anxiety is becoming an increasingly common phenomenon in the general child population.

When reaching the level where they interfere with social, emotional, and academic development, fears and anxiety often are more appropriately termed anxiety disorders. Anxiety disorders consist of many overlapping and inter-related diagnostic categories that are among the most common psychiatric disorders in the United States and throughout the world (e.g., Costello, Costello, Edelbrock, et al., 1988; McGee, Feehan, Williams, et al., 1990). This book will focus on anxiety disorders, their clinical presentation and development, as well as factors associated with their maintenance and treatment. To facilitate an un-derstanding of the anxiety disorders, particularly in children, some background on normal fears, their prevalence, development, and stability is necessary.

WHAT IS FEAR?

Fear is a basic human emotion usually considered to be a response to objects or situations that threaten physical safety or emotional well-being (e.g., Marks, 1969; Miller, 1983). Fear is multi-dimensional consisting of an outer behavioral expression, inner subjective distress, and associated physical or physiological changes (Marks, 1969). In addition to its ubiquitous nature, fearful reactions sometimes are adaptive; serving to keep one alert in dangerous situations (Korte, 2001). Similarly, the word "anxiety" has become part of everyday vocabulary, and can have different meanings depending upon the context in which it is used. Children might use the term "anxious" to represent excitement, for example, when talking about a birthday party. In this instance, the child's interpretation of anxious is one of positive expectation.

To illustrate the relationship between anxiety and optimal performance, examination of the classic anxiety and performance curve will be instructive (Figure 1.1).

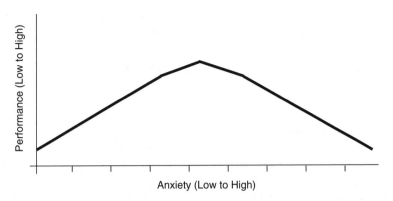

FIGURE 1.1 The relationship between anxiety and performance.

To illustrate how anxiety exerts different effects at different levels of intensity, consider the example of test anxiety. A small to moderate amount of anxiety often enhances motivation and helps one recall answers or concentrate on details required to solve certain problems. When anxiety exceeds a certain point, however, it has the opposite effect. Thus, in competitive situations, a moderate amount of anxiety improves the ability to excel, but severe anxiety interferes with the ability to concentrate and acts to decrease performance. Of course, there are individual differences with respect to the amount of anxiety one can tolerate before performance is affected (McDonald, 2001).

In most cases, however, the word anxiety describes a negative emotional state such as the anxiety that one feels before an important testing situation. During a test, children can be fearful that they will forget the answers, for example, or that their mind will go blank. If called to the blackboard or asked to recite in front of the class, they might worry that they will not know the answer, that they will say the wrong thing, or not be able to talk at all and in so doing will embarrass themselves. In short, anxiety in children most often is a negative emotion and one that they seek to eliminate. The precipitants of anxiety are usually less clear and predictable than for fear. In fact, sometimes anxiety has no easily identifiable cause—it is just an uncomfortable, ill-defined feeling of apprehension. Therefore, although technically, fear sometimes is considered to be the immediate defensive reaction to a threatening stimulus, anxiety, on the other hand, often is defined as apprehension about some future event (Johnson & Melamed, 1979). In reality, however, these terms often are used interchangeably as will be done throughout this book. Throughout each of the ensuing chapters, specific issues with respect to clinical presentation, etiology, maintenance and treatment of specific childhood anxiety disorders will be addressed. We begin with a general review of fears in children.

THE EPIDEMIOLOGY OF FEARS
IN CHILDREN AND ADOLESCENTS

For many years, there was a propensity on the part of parents and professionals to regard most fear responses as part of normal development. Indeed, there is a high probability that any child will, at some time, manifest some type of fearful behavior. In the earliest report on prevalence (Jersild & Holmes, 1935) non-referred children displayed a number of fears. Interviews with mothers of 2- to 6-year-olds revealed that their children displayed between four and five different fears and exhibited a fearful reaction once every 4½ days. In one of the first longitudinal studies (MacFarlane et al., 1954), 90% of the sample demonstrated at least one fearful reaction at some time between the ages of 2 and 14. In a classic study of childhood fears, 43% of children (ages 6 to 12) had 7 or more fears and worries, leading the authors to conclude that fears are quite common at this age (Lapouse & Monk, 1959). In addition, 15% of the mothers reported that their children had three or more anxious behaviors such as nail biting, teeth grinding, and thumb sucking.

Miller et al. (1974) surveyed parents of 249 children selected from the general population. Using the Louisville Fear Survey Schedule, parents rated their child's response to each situation as either no fear, normal fear, or extreme fear. Each specific object or event evoked excessive fear in less than 5% of the sample. For each fear stimulus, 84% of the children showed no fear, 5–15% demonstrated what was judged to be a normal fear, and 0–5% showed an excessive fearful reaction. Furthermore, even in cases where the reactions were judged to be excessive, the fears still were considered to be part of normal development. However, there were a number of specific objects and events for which the distribution of parental ratings more closely approximated a normal curve. This group included snakes, rats, lightning, fire, tornados, being wounded, getting shots, and being seen naked. With respect to social and performance fears, 25% of the children (boys and girls) were rated as having some fear of attending social events due to worries of rejection or embarrassment. Fully 50% of the children were rated as having normal or extreme fears of being criticized, reciting in class, making mistakes or doing something wrong, and tests and examinations, a fear which Campbell (1986) also noted as predominant among school-age children.

More recently, an interview survey of 190 school age children (Muris, Merckelbach, Gadet, & Moulaert, 2000) revealed that 75.8% of the sample reported fear of an object or situation, 67.4% endorsed the presence of worry and 80.5% reported the presence of a "scary dream." The most common fears endorsed by the children included animals, imaginary creatures, being kidnapped, and social threats. The most frequent worries included thoughts of harm, death, performance at school, and being separated from their parents.

The most common content of the scary dreams included imaginary creatures, harm, being kidnapped, dangerous animals, and death.

One limitation of these early studies is that the data were based solely on parental report, and thus it is not entirely clear if the children perceived themselves to be anxious or fearful. There are some data to suggest that the actual incidence of fearful reactions in children may be much higher than parental estimates. A validity study, conducted as part of the Lapouse and Monk (1959) study, indicated that maternal reports underestimate fear prevalence by as much as 41%. Similarly, comparison of mothers' and children's responses on the Fear Survey Schedule for Children revealed only moderate agreement between the mothers' rank-ordered estimates of their child's fears with the child's own estimate (Bondy, Sheslow, & Garcia, 1985). Mothers discerned their child's "main" fear, but could not accurately report on secondary fears. In addition, mothers' overall estimates of their children's general fearfulness were correlated only with their daughters' general fearfulness, not their sons'. Thus, data generated by parental report alone may underestimate the prevalence of fears, and mothers appear to be more accurate in judging fears of their daughters than those of their sons.

Finally, as noted in the introduction, at least some fearful reactions are not stable over time. For example, Eme and Schmidt (1978) assessed the stability of fears in fourth-grade children. One year later, 83% of the objects or events initially identified as fear producing were still regarded as fearful by the children. However, the stability of the relative rank of the feared events within the group was low ($r = .38$). That is, although after 1 year, children still endorsed the same objects or events as fearful, the severity of the fear had changed. In another study of stability, phobic children aged 6–15, were reassessed 2 years after the initial evaluation. Only 7% still had a "severe phobia," while 80% were symptom-free. More recently, Spence and McCathie (1994) reported a 2-year follow-up of Australian primary school children (Grades 3 or 4 at time 1 vs. Grades 5 or 6 at time 2). Among those boys and girls who initially scored above one standard deviation on the Fear Survey Schedule for Children-II, 40% of the boys and 36% of the girls remained highly fearful (above one standard deviation) 2 years later. In contrast, only 6.5% of the boys and 12.8% of the girls who were not fearful at time 1 scored in the highly fearful range at time 2. Thus, both the prevalence and severity of fearfulness is somewhat unstable over time and for any individual child absolute level of fearfulness can wax and wane in intensity.

In one of the few studies to examine fears in adolescents (Poulton et al., 1997), the frequency and content of fears remained relatively stable from ages 13 to 15. However, when viewed as a function of change in age, few adolescents who reported fears at age 13 also endorsed these fears 2 years later. Therefore, although common across all ages, there appears to be substantial instability in any one child's specific fears, even during adolescence. Thus, children may manifest fear at one point in time but not another.

DEMOGRAPHIC CHARACTERISTICS OF CHILDREN'S FEARS

Although a few early studies failed to identify gender differences (Mauer, 1965; Miller, Barrett, Hampe, & Noble, 1971; Nalvern, 1970), the majority of studies consistently find that girls report a greater number of fears compared to their male counterparts (e.g., Croake & Knox, 1973; Lapouse & Monk, 1959; Scherer & Nakamura, 1968; Poulton et al., 1997; Spence & McCathie, 1993). Parents also attribute a greater level of fear to their daughters (Bondy et al., 1985). The higher incidence of fears in girls appears to be a reliable finding, yet why this is so is yet to be determined (Graziano, DeGiovanni, & Garcia, 1979). One explanation is that young girls legitimately experience a greater range of fears than boys. The same observations have been made with adults (Agras et al., 1969). Conversely, cultural and/or gender role expectations may impact how boys and girls report fears, and perhaps how parents judge them as well. Thus, girls appear more fearful than boys because girls are more willing to *report* fears, not because they actually *have* more fears. However, this hypothesis is yet to be confirmed by empirical study.

Although self-reports indicate gender differences, these differences are not always apparent when physiological reactivity is assessed. When taking tests, for example, test-anxious boys and girls show equal increases in blood pressure and pulse rates, both reactions considered indicative of anxiety (Beidel & Turner, 1988). This would suggest that when measures of fear not under a child's voluntary control (e.g., heart rate) are used to determine fear, boys and girls react equally (at least in test-taking situations), even though boys may not admit their anxiety as readily as girls. Thus, these data support the hypothesis that social appraisal and/or role expectations influence the self-report of fear and self-report data collected from boys and girls. Although the gender difference finding appears to be reliable, the reason for the difference remains unclear.

Socioeconomic status (SES) has been associated with the frequency and intensity of children's fears. Among early studies, the most reliable variation relates to fear content. Fears most often reported by lower SES children included events such as violence, whippings, dope peddlers, switchblades, drunks, rats, and cockroaches (Angelino, Dollins, & Mech, 1956; Nalvern, 1970). Children from higher SES groups were more likely to fear heights, car accidents, train wrecks, and more abstract categories of stimuli such as poisonous insects or dangerous animals. When differences were examined in terms of the total number of fears rather than simply examining fear content, lower SES children report a greater number of fears. Graziano et al. (1979) concluded that lower SES children perceived their immediate environment as much more hostile and fearful than higher SES children, which probably reflected their reality. Fear survey schedules often equate total number of fears with fear intensity. Although someone who fears a variety of stimuli is likely to be more generally fearful than someone with a particularly circumscribed fear, the description of the stimuli (as illustrated by the type of fears listed above) undoubtedly affects self-report. Lower SES children reported highly specific categories of fears, while children of higher SES identified more abstract categories of fearful stimuli. Equating number of reported fears with fear intensity becomes even more problematic when children must freely generate the names of objects they fear, rather than endorse a list of items. If indeed this level of abstraction, based on SES, were a reliable finding, the differences in fear intensity would be an artifact of the child's level of abstraction not a valid measure of their overall fear state (Graziano et al., 1979). In summary, differences in childhood fears that are considered to be a function of SES are more likely to result from the vastly different type of environments in which the children live and perhaps the different kinds of educational experiences available to them.

Fears appear to occur consistently across various racial and ethnic groups within the United States as well as internationally. For example, African American and Caucasian children fear similar objects and situations; most commonly they are afraid that they or a family member will be harmed in some way (Neal, Lilly, & Zakris, 1993). Test anxiety also seems to be about equally common for the two groups (B. G. Turner, Beidel, Hughes, & M. W. Turner, 1993). However, African American and Caucasian children rank their fears in a slightly different order, as shown in Table 1.1.

Internationally, children in different countries, including Australia, China, and England, endorse the same fears as American children (Dong, Yang, & Ollendick, 1994). Specifically, 6 of the top 10 fears of Chinese children are also among the top 10 fears of Australian and American children. Fears of physical

TABLE 1.1 Fears of African American and Caucasian Children Ranked by Frequency

African American	Caucasian
1. Not being able to breathe	1. Being hit by a car or truck
2. Being hit by a car or truck	2. Not being able to breathe
3. Falling from high places	3. Bombing attacks—being invaded
4. Getting a shock from electricity	4. Fire—getting burned
5. Germs or getting a serious illness	5. Falling from high places
6. Bears or wolves	6. Burglar breaking into the house
7. Getting lost in a strange place	7. Death or dead people
8. Bombing attacks—being invaded	8. Getting lost in a strange place
9. Burglar breaking into the house	9. Being sent to the principal
10. Strange or mean looking dogs	10. Germs or getting a serious illness
11. Fire—getting burned	11. Getting poor grades

Source: Based on a survey of children between the ages of 6 and 12 (Neal, Lilly, & Zakis, 1993).

danger and safety are very common; so are fears of situations involving people (social fears such as giving an oral report or having to speak to an authority figure such as the school principal; Dong et al., 1994). More recently, fears of Kenyan and Nigerian children using the Fear Survey Schedule for Children-Revised (FSSC-R) have been examined (Ingman, Ollendick, & Akande,1999). Children from Nigeria had a significantly higher level of fear than children from Kenya. Furthermore, both groups appeared to have higher scores on the FSSC-R than those previously reported for British, American, Australian, or Chinese children. However, a direct statistical comparison was not conducted and perusal of the means does not clearly indicate if these differences would be statistically significant. In addition to an analysis by country of origin, Ingman et al. (1999) examined differences based on religion, gender, and age. However, unlike results from other cultures, there was no difference in the level of fear reported by children and that reported by adolescents. Furthermore, there was no main effect for gender, which also is inconsistent with findings from the majority of other studies that used the same methodology and the same assessment instrument.

To explain these disparate findings, the authors suggested that the relatively poorer socio-economic conditions of these African countries may create higher levels of stress and more fears. Furthermore, depending on where these children lived, they might face more everyday dangers. Either hypothesis would be consistent with earlier research on difference in fears among children from various SES groups within the United States (Graziano et al., 1979). Additionally, with respect to gender, the suspected cultural difference that might affect reports in the United States and Europe might not be operative in Africa. For example, Kenyan children show sex segregation in peer groups at an age later than American children (Ingman et al., 1999). Perhaps this later emphasis on gender-specific activities also relates to gender-typical behaviors such as willingness to endorse fears. In summary, the recent study of African children notwithstanding, across a variety of cultures and countries, younger children appear to be more fearful than adolescents, and girls express more fears than boys (Dong et al., 1994; Gullone & King, 1993, 2001, Poulton et al., 1997; Spence & McCathie, 1993). Fear, then, seems to be a universal childhood experience.

Of all the reported normative differences, the most important variable appears to be the age-related nature of children's fears. Not only are different fears more salient at different ages, there also is a normal developmental sequence. In the most widely used research paradigm, investigators administer fear surveys to different aged children or the children's parents, and examine the natural course by extracting those fears most commonly reported for each age group. Fears that are typical at each age are presented in Table 1.2 (Ollendick, Matson, & Helsel, 1985).

Several studies have examined the relationship of age to specific objects or events. There is an overall decline in children's fears with increasing age,

TABLE 1.2 Typical Fears at Specific Ages

Age	Fears
Infancy	Loss of physical support Sudden, intense, and unexpected noises Heights
1–2 years old	Strangers Toileting activities Being injured
3–5 years old	Animals (primarily dogs) Imaginary creatures Dark Being alone
6–9 years old	Animals Lightning and thunder Personal safety School Death
9–12 years old	Tests Personal health
13 years and older	Personal injury Social interaction and personal conduct Economic and political catastrophes

and differing predominant fears associated with each age (Barrios, Hartmann, & Shigatomi, 1981). Young infants are frightened by loss of support, sudden intense and unexpected noise, and heights. One- and 2-year-old children are afraid of strangers, toileting activities, and of being injured. Preschool children fear imaginary creatures, animals, and the dark. Younger elementary school children are fearful of animals, natural events such as lightening and thunder, and report concerns for their own safety. Additionally, school and health related fears become common at this age. Older children are fearful of injury, and economic and political catastrophes. In discussing their developmental nature, Miller (1983) reported that around age 2, fear of the toilet is common. Dogs seem to provoke the most fear at age 3, while fear of the dark is most salient at age 4. At age 6, school related anxiety becomes predominant, then decreases somewhat in intensity until around age 11, when there is another increase. Fears of injury and social anxiety remain stable throughout the life span from the time of their first appearance in early childhood.

Similar to the universality of the range of fear, this developmental sequence also appears to cut across culture. Australian children aged 7–10 years old had higher fear scores than those aged 11–14 or 15–18 years (Ollendick, Matson, & Helsel,1985). Consistent with other studies, younger children reported more fears of animals whereas older children reported more fears of social evaluation and psychic stress. All of these developmental studies consistently demonstrate that younger children fear specific events, particularly those related to physical danger, whereas older children are more likely to endorse social fears and general distress.

From Grades 3 and 4 to Grades 5 and 6, girls reported decreased fears related to getting sick, parental criticism or punishment, the dark, and bears or wolves (Spence & McCathie, 1993). Boys showed decreases in fear of physical injury, parental criticism, the dark, meeting a stranger, and being left at home with a baby sitter. The only fear that increased to any significant degree was "giving a spoken report" which was more frequently endorsed when boys were in Grades 5 and 6 than when they were in Grades 3 and 4. There was an increase in overall fears, as well as social fears, in children initially assessed at age 13 and then again, 2 years later (Poulton et al.,1997; see Table 1.3), based on 17 fearful situations listed in the Diagnostic Interview Schedule for Children (DISC; Costello et al., 1982). Interestingly, the primary fear at both ages was "speaking in front of the class," which increased in prevalence from age 13 to 15. The authors concluded that although the overall percentage of fears increased from time 1 to time 2, this was primarily due to the increase in social fears.

Among 4 to 6-year-old children, fears were reported by 71% of the sample whereas nightmares were reported by 67.7% (Muris et al., 2000). These prevalence rates increased to 87% and 95.7% respectively among 7- to 9-year-olds and then returned to somewhat lower levels (67.8% and 76.3%, respectively) among 10- to 12-year-old children. Worry however, showed a different developmental pattern. Whereas 46.8% of 4- to 6-year-olds reported the presence of worry, the percentage was significantly higher among 7- to 9-year-olds (78.3%) and continued at the same level in 10- to 12-year-old children (76.3%). This different developmental pattern for worry probably reflects children's emerging cognitive development.

TABLE 1.3 Fears in Adolescents

Age and Gender	Percent Experiencing At Least One Significant Fear	Percent Experiencing Public Speaking Fear
Age 13		5.0
Boys	14.4	
Girls	12.1	
Age 15		8.3
Boys	15.0	
Girls	23.9	

Source: Poulton et al. (1997).

This entire developmental hierarchy may, in part, be a function of cognitive development. Vandenberg (1993) compared fears of children with mental retardation to those of children with at least normal intelligence. The fears of children ages 4 through 12 years were classified into one of four categories (fears of imaginary things, fears of animals, fears of events in the physical world, and fears of events involving humans, such as being hurt by someone). Consistent with all other studies of fears in children with at least average intelligence, fears of imaginary things were more prevalent at the younger ages whereas fears of people-related events were more prevalent at the older ages. A comparison of the fears of children with mental retardation and children of at least average intelligence at the same chronological age revealed significant differences in fear content. Specifically, children with mental retardation were significantly more fearful of imaginary things and significantly less fearful of people-related events than children of the same chronological age but with at least normal intelligence. However, fears of children between the ages of 7 and 12 who had mental retardation were not different from the fears of children between the ages 4 and 6 with at least average intelligence. Thus, it appears that the fears of children with mental retardation are more likely to reflect their level of cognitive development rather than their chronological age.

In summary, fearful reactions in children are common and tend to follow a consistent developmental sequence. Younger children are more fearful of physical events and imaginary creatures, whereas older children and adolescents are more fearful of social events. Girls are more likely than boys to express fears, but it remains unclear if this is a true difference or if it reflects cultural and role expectation parameters. Furthermore, although most childhood fears dissipate over time, some fears, particularly those that are social in nature, tend to remain constant.

WHEN DOES FEAR BECOME A PROBLEM?

Even if fear appears extreme, some fearful reactions disappear within a short period of time. For example, children who move to a new neighborhood may be fearful of a new school and initially refuse to go. If they watch a horror movie, they may be afraid of "monsters" for a few nights. However, as noted above, fears involving social situations may not dissipate without professional intervention (Achenbach, 1985; Davidson, 1993). Furthermore, some fears may interfere with a child's or a family's functioning so seriously that waiting for it to dissipate is not an option. If a child needs surgery, for example, a parent cannot wait to see if the child will outgrow a fear of needles or doctors. Therefore, the challenge to parents, educators, and health care professionals is to decide when a fear is a problem, even if it is not acknowledged as such by the child. Following are several points to consider when attempting to determine if a child's fear is abnormal and if intervention is necessary (Miller et al., 1974):

1. Is the fear out of proportion to the demands of the situation? Some anxiety before a final exam would be considered normal. However, fear so severe that it inhibits the ability to study, causes nausea or vomiting on the morning of the exam, or makes the child forget all the answers that were so well known the previous night, would be considered out of proportion to the situation.
2. Can it be explained or reasoned away? A child may hear and even be able to repeat a logical explanation about why monsters do not exist, but that does little to calm the child's fear. Despite parent's best attempts to explain or demonstrate that there are no monsters under the bed, the child still refuses to sleep in her own room. Reason and logical explanations do not make the fear go away.
3. Is the fear beyond voluntary control? Fearful thoughts keep returning despite parental reassurances that these worries are groundless. Similarly, crying, rapid heart rate, or rapid respiration cannot be controlled, no matter how hard the child tries. If telling a child "Just relax" seems useless, the fear is probably beyond voluntary control.
4. Does the fearful reaction persist unchanged for an extended period of time? Many childhood fears disappear within several months after their first appearance. If a fear persists intensely for more than 6 months, intervention may be required (American Psychiatric Association, 1994). However, if the fear involves refusal to attend school or prevents needed surgery or other medical attention, treatment should be initiated much sooner.
5. Does the fear lead to avoidance of the situation? A child whose separation or social fears are so severe that he refuses to attend school would be considered a problem. Similarly problematic would be refusing medical intervention because of a fear of needles.
6. Is the fear unadaptive? As noted earlier, moderate anxiety may enhance performance and help a child adapt to a stressful situation. However, severe fear does not allow a child to adapt. In fact, it prevents adjustment to a changing situation; hence the common expression "frozen with fear."
7. Is the fear connected with a particular age or stage? A 4-year-old child's fear of the dark and insistence on a night-light would not be considered a significant problem (although it may seem that way to other family members at the time). However, it could be problematic for a 12- or 13-year-old.
8. Perhaps most important, does the fear interfere with social, emotional, or academic functioning? This can happen in multiple ways, and some of these may not appear to be obviously related. Excessive fears and anxiety can result in limited academic achievement, poor self-concept, deficient

social skills and inhibited knowledge of social role expectations, extensive social isolation, and restrictions in play activities, loneliness, and depression (e.g., Beidel, Turner, & Morris, 1999; Kovacs, 1998). Anxious children sometimes have difficulties falling or staying asleep. As discussed in chapter 5, anxiety also can result in true physical symptoms such as headaches or stomach pain. These somatic symptoms can further impair or limit functioning and can create or increase emotional distress. Impairment of functioning is probably the most important consideration when deciding if treatment is needed.

As noted above, perhaps the most important question to consider is whether the child's fear interferes with school, social, or emotional adjustment. For example, does a child who is afraid of snakes but lives in New York City have a snake phobia? Although expressing a fear of snakes, the real question is this: Does the fear prevent the child from doing what he/she would like to do? What if the child's grandparents lived in the country and the child refuses to visit because the grandparents once told the child that they saw a snake in the backyard? In this situation the fear might require treatment because it prevents the child from visiting and spending time with grandparents. However, if the child rarely goes to a place where snakes are found, treatment probably is not necessary.

Interestingly, there are few actual data on the relationship of self-reported fears and functional impairment. Among a sample of Australian adolescents, overall, there was a significant relationship between level of fear and level of functional interference as a result of that fear (Ollendick & King, 1994). Across the 10 most common fears (8 of which related to physical danger and 2 of which were social-evaluative fears), 13% reported that their fears created little or no distress, 26% indicated that their fears resulted in some distress, and 61% reported that their fears resulted in maximal distress. Of course, these data are based solely on self-report and as noted by the authors, assessment of functional interference via more objective and standardized procedures would illuminate the relationship more clearly.

The crucial issue is whether the fear creates functional interference. Like adults, children have "work" to do; they must go to school, learn, and participate in activities such as athletic events, dancing school, or groups such as Boy Scouts or Girl Scouts. As often noted, the work of children is play. They should attend parties, have friends, and be comfortable with domesticated animals. The list goes on and on. Why is participation in these activities important? Playing with other children, for example, teaches rules of social interaction. Without socialization experiences, children may not learn the social skills necessary to develop friendships and establish the foundation for adult social behavior. Also, a child without friends suffers from loneliness, which can lead to other social and emotional problems. Treatment is needed if a child's fears prevent participation in or enjoyment of activities appropriate for his peer group, and last for more than a few months.

SUMMARY

Although the prevalence of fears and anxiety disorders in children appear to be quite common, research devoted to understanding and treating these childhood disorders remains sparse. This is unusual because the study of childhood fear was instrumental in the development of theories of general human behavior (Barrios, Hartmann, & Shigatomi, 1981). Freud's analysis of Little Hans' fear of horses (1909, 1962) marked the beginning of child psychoanalysis. Approximately 11 years later, Watson and Rayner (1920) published the case study of Little Albert. This study gave credence to Watson's treatise on behaviorism, and provided an empirical test of a conditioning theory of human behavior. Despite these auspicious beginnings, the scientific study of fears and anxieties in children made little progress for many years; perhaps because fears were considered normal and transient or because it was assumed that interventions developed for adults would also be useful for children. Whatever the reason, until approximately 30 years ago, it was appropriate to say that childhood fears and anxieties remained in the "prescientific era" (Miller et al., 1974). Since that time, there has been an exponential increase in interest regarding childhood anxiety disorders and currently there is a fairly substantive literature regarding the clinical presentation of children's fears and anxieties. Many childhood fears represent a normal reaction to environmental events; others represent what are considered normal stages of development, and still others are clearly maladaptive. Many fearful reactions will dissipate fairly quickly and the challenge to clinicians is to determine the difference between those that are part of normal development and transitory, and those that are maladaptive, likely to be chronic, and part of a more significant anxiety disorder.

CHAPTER **2**

An Introduction to Childhood Anxiety Disorders

Kendra is 9 years old. Two months ago her grandmother died suddenly. Since that time, Kendra has been reluctant to leave her mother's side. She cries about going to school. Kendra's parents cannot leave her with a baby sitter because she cries uncontrollably. Kendra may be suffering from separation anxiety disorder.

Liu was always obedient, but now he refuses to go to school. He even refuses to get dressed and complains of stomachaches and headaches. After his father dresses him and takes him to school, he cries uncontrollably in the classroom. His father must return to the school and take him home. This is creating problems at work for Liu's father and the school is threatening to call the truant officer. Liu's symptoms are characteristic of anxiety-based school refusal.

Fifteen-year-old Hector is getting ready for his first date with Maria. Although he likes Maria a great deal, he is sweating and has butterflies in his stomach. He gets so nauseous that he cancels the date. He desperately wants to socialize, but his parents are worried. He has withdrawn from social situations and does not have any friends. Hector appears to have social phobia.

The "modern" conception of childhood anxiety disorders often is tied to the descriptive cases of Little Hans (Freud, 1909) and Little Albert (Watson & Rayner, 1920). However, in a cogent review of the history of childhood anxiety disorders, Treffers and Silverman (2001) noted that Hippocrates (460–370BC) described fears in young children. Yet, prior to the nineteenth century, little attention was paid to childhood fears. A publication by West (1860) entitled *On the Mental Peculiarities and Mental Disorders of Childhood* appears to be a turning point in the problematic nature of recognition of childhood anxiety disorders (Silverman & Treffers, 2001). Since that time, there has been increased interest, and within the last quarter century, there has been substantial attention regarding substantive issues of psychopathology and treatment. In subsequent chapters in this book, a variety of anxiety disorders will be reviewed in detail. Here, an overview of issues that cut across specific disorders is provided as well as their most prevalent conceptual models. In addition, epidemiology, comorbidity, and functional impairment related to anxiety are reviewed. Finally, general assessment issues to assist clinicians in determining the presence and severity of anxiety disorders will be presented.

GENERAL CONCEPTUALIZATION OF ANXIETY DISORDERS

With respect to the clinical presentation of anxiety disorders, the tripartite model (Lang, 1968) has been the dominant conceptualization for over 30 years. In this model, used with children and adolescents as well as adults, anxiety is conceptualized as consisting of three components: physiological responses, subjective distress (more recently referred to as the cognitive dimension) and behavioral responses. Below each of these three dimensions is reviewed.

Physical and Somatic Distress

The physical aspects of fear encompass virtually any bodily response, although among children, headaches and stomachaches (or butterflies in the stomach) are common complaints (e.g., Beidel, Christ, & Long, 1991). Other physical symptoms include sweating, difficulty breathing, hot or cold flashes, dizziness, numbness or tingling in the hands or feet, chest pains or nausea, muscle aches and pains, and vague physical complaints such as a sore throat. Beidel et al. (1991) examined physical complaints in children who met criteria for an anxiety disorder and a group of peers without a disorder. Children identified a situation that made them feel nervous and then were asked, "What happens to your body when you are in the situation?" A range of physical symptoms were endorsed by both groups, although the anxious children endorsed a greater number of physical symptoms than the children without a disorder. Children with anxiety disorders endorsed significantly higher frequency of hot flashes/cold chills, fearing fainting, and feeling like dying.

It is important to note that each anxious child does not experience every possible physical symptom or even any physical complaints. Among children, just like adults, certain symptoms appear characteristic of specific anxiety disorders. In fact, children with panic disorder or separation anxiety disorder are significantly more likely to report somatic complaints than children with phobic disorders (Last, 1991). Also, older children are more likely than younger children to report somatic complaints. Additionally, even when two children have the same anxiety disorder, they will not necessarily have the same physical symptom profile, although headaches and stomach aches, the most common physical complaints, appear to cut across all disorders.

In addition to broad physical complaints, children react to anxious events or situations with heightened physiological responses. Early studies focused on heart rate reactivity when infants were placed in situations designed to elicit anxious distress. These studies examined heart rate reactivity when infants were in a normal resting state and then when exposed to a fear-producing situation. Infants' heart rates accelerated when placed in several distressful situations: over the deep end of the visual cliff task (Schwartz, Campos, & Baisel, 1973), when in the presence of a stranger (Campos, Ende, Gaenbauer, & Henderson, 1975), or when approached by a stranger in an unfamiliar environment (Sroufe, Waters, & Matas, 1974). In another early study, imagination of idiosyncratic, emotionally arousing scenes (as opposed to resting quietly) was accompanied by increases (over baseline) in heart rate and respiration in a group of asthmatic children (Tal & Miklich, 1976). Thus, even at a very early age, basic physiological reactivity patterns in infants and children are similar to adult patterns.

Initial comparative group studies of children identified as anxious or nonanxious examined dental anxiety. Higher dental fear was associated with higher heart rate (Striker & Howitt, 1965; Venham, Bengston, & Cipes, 1977) and greater galvanic skin response (Melamed, Yurcheson. Fleece, Hutcherson, & Hawes, 1978). Physiological responses also have been studied in test anxiety, another commonly occurring fear (Beidel, 1988). Children self-described as test anxious had significantly higher heart rates (averaging 95.5 beats per minute) when taking a test or reading aloud in front of a small audience in comparison to their non-test anxious peers (averaging 90.7 beats per minute). Additionally, test anxious children had a heart rate response that was consistently elevated across the 10 minute duration of the task. In contrast, non-test anxious children had a brief increase in heart rate at the start of each task that then decreased to baseline by the time of task completion. Most recently, Monk et al. (2001) examined heart rate and heart rate variability in children with either separation anxiety disorder, overanxious disorder, panic disorder/panic attacks, or social phobia compared to normal controls. Children with anxiety disorders had higher heart rates and less heart rate fluctuation during baseline. Additionally, those with anxiety disorders had smaller overall changes in heart rate variability during baseline and during a carbon dioxide inhalation challenge task, although results were not reported separately by diagnosis.

These heart rate variability data are consistent with those reported for infants with behavioral inhibition (see chapter 4) and also for adults with social phobia (Turner, Beidel & Larkin, 1986). Furthermore, the data are consistent with data collected from rhesus monkeys when placed in anxious or stressful situations (Suomi, 1986). Specifically, when placed in an unfamiliar living colony, monkeys bred to be socially anxious reacted with increased heart rate reactivity that did not dissipate during their time in the unfamiliar situation. The consistency of these reactivity data (across rhesus monkeys, behaviorally inhibited infants, test anxious children and adults with social phobia) suggests that it may not be just initial increased heart rate but a persistent increase throughout the task's duration (i.e., the individual does not habituate) that differentiates those with maladaptive anxiety from those without anxiety disorders. In summary, the presence of physical complaints and a pattern of physiological reactivity to anxious or distressing events appear common among children with fears and anxiety disorders.

Cognitive and Subjective Distress

In addition to somatic distress, cognitive features are a prominent part of the clinical syndrome of adult anxiety disorders, and indeed, there has been much theorizing about the role of maladaptive cognitions in the etiology, maintenance, and treatment of anxiety states. In contrast, maladaptive and negative cognitions are not a consistent part of the clinical presentation for many clinically anxious children, and particularly those with phobic disorders (e.g., Beidel, 1991; Bogels & Zigterman, 2000; Kendall & Chansky, 1991; Treadwell & Kendall, 1996). Clinically, children with phobic disorders (specific phobias or social phobias, for example) report that when in a distressing situation, they are so overwhelmed by emotion that they are unable to think. One hypothesis put forth to explain this disparity is that young children's cognitive abilities have not matured to the extent necessary to monitor their own cognitions (i.e., they do not yet have the ability to "think about thinking"). Thus, cognitive features of anxiety states in children may be age related. Negative cognitions may not appear until adolescence, when children reach the age where they can monitor and report their thoughts.

To date, basic studies of cognitive development have had only limited impact on understanding the cognitive dimension of anxiety. For example, children's ability to reflect on their own mental activity increases with age and much of this increased reflection is verbal in nature (Flavell, Green, Flavell, & Grossman, 1997). Furthermore, it is not until ages 6 and 7 that children understand the concept of "talking to oneself" as a mental activity (Flavell, Flavell, & Green, 2001). Children younger than ages 6 or 7 probably are not capable of detecting, and therefore reporting, negative cognitions. Thus, as a result of basic cognitive immaturity, the cognitive dimension of anxiety may be absent in very young children; at least it does not appear to be the same as that of older children, adolescents and adults.

In addition to the basic question of whether negative cognitions exist, the qualitative features of children's cognitions also are a function of physical and cognitive maturation (Graziano et al., 1979; Vasey, 1993). As noted, young children's fears tend to center on physical, external events (dogs, burglars). With increasing age, the child develops the ability to consider the future and thus, they report thoughts of catastrophic events and concerns related to social evaluation. Therefore, with cognitive maturity, fears and worry become more internal and abstract (Vasey, 1993), a reflection of the maturation of basic cognitive abilities (e.g., from concrete operations to more abstract thinking; Piaget, 1970).

When basic cognitive abilities have developed so that negative cognitions and worry are possible, some children with anxiety disorders report excessive worries and catastrophic thoughts. For those with phobic disorders for example, anxious thoughts are usually specific to the feared object or situation and usually occur when the child confronts or anticipates contact with the phobic stimulus. Before performing in a school play, for example, children may worry that they will forget their lines and make fools of themselves, even though they are well prepared. A child who fears dogs may worry that any dog, even a puppy, will bite, creating a need for stitches or hospitalization. Similarly, a child who is afraid of elevators may fear that the elevator will get stuck between floors and that he will be unable to get out. Typical negative thoughts reported by anxious children include concerns that something may happen to their parents, that they themselves may be killed or kidnapped, that their home may be robbed, or that they may do poorly on a test. Thus in most instances, the cognitions or thoughts experienced by anxious children typically are specifically related to the feared object or event.

For some children, however, negative thoughts and worries are not specific to one object or situation. Rather, there are a myriad of worries including future events ("Where will I work?" "Will I get into a good college?" "Will I get married?"), past behavior ("Did I make my best friend mad?"), social or academic abilities ("I m not good enough."), their own health ("Do I have cancer?"), or the health of someone they love ("Were my parents in a car accident?"). Worries are usually associated with both common and uncommon probabalistic events or situations. Although worry may occur among children with any anxiety disorder, it is most often found in children with generalized anxiety disorder and separation anxiety disorder (Prins, 2001).

Despite the fact that worries appear to be common and often even occur in children without anxiety disorders (Bell-Dolan, Last, & Strauss, 1990), to date, there is little research on childhood worry. One study (Last & Perrin, 1997) assessed the construct of worry in children with anxiety disorders, attention deficit hyperactivity disorder, or children without a disorder. There was no difference in the content of the worries endorsed by children in any of the diagnostic groups. However, children with anxiety disorders reported more frequent worrying than children in the other two groups. This finding, that it is the frequency and not the content of worry that seems to specifically characterize children with anxiety disorders is consistent with other investigators who report frequency and severity of the worries, not content, is what distinguishes those with an anxiety disorder (Bell-Dolan et al., 1990; Rachman & DeSilva, 1976; see chapter 6)

Relatedly, some children and adolescents suffer from obsessions, which are specific, persistent intrusive thoughts, often of an unrealistic nature. Obsessions are defined as recurrent and persistent thoughts, impulses, or images that are intrusive, inappropriate and cause marked distress (DSM-IV; APA, 1994, p. 418). Unlike worries, the content of obsessions is highly unusual. For example, a 14- year-old girl with obsessions had intrusive thoughts that her heart would stop beating and that she would die. However, like worries, obsessions cannot be reasoned away and the child's concern usually is much greater than the situation requires. Furthermore, children feel that they cannot exert any control over their thoughts. Children who express worry across many different spheres of functioning are most likely to be suffering from Generalized Anxiety Disorder (see chapter 6), and those with specific and recurrent cognitions likely suffer from Obsessive-Compulsive Disorder (see chapter 11). Here again however, children, and particularly young children, may not be able to clearly articulate the specific thought content associated with what appear to be severe fears. Sometimes children may describe a general feeling that something will go wrong, or that it is "just a feeling." They cannot be more specific about their concern because as noted, children under age 12 may have trouble articulating their thoughts (Alfano et al., 2002). Therefore, some children may not be able to express adequately or clearly their concerns, but only make vague statements about "not feeling well" or express physical complaints such as "a headache."

In summary, cognitions of anxious children may vary in content, severity, frequency, and controllability. Age and cognitive development appear to play a larger role in the cognitive dimension than in the expression of physical symptomatology. In some children, cognitions may be absent. Others may have only vague concerns and some may have thoughts that resemble those found in adults with the same disorder.

Behavioral Response and Avoidance

In children, the behavioral dimension of anxiety is the easiest to observe and behavioral signs may be the first indication that a child is fearful. Because of developmental immaturity, children often express their anxiety differently from adults. For example, they may cry, cling to a parent, or have a tantrum in certain situations. Although less frequent, children sometimes demonstrate anxiety through disobedience or oppositional behavior. For example, they may refuse to follow parental instructions if it involves contact with a feared event or object. In extreme cases, a child may refuse to go to school because of a school-related fear or separation fear (see chapters 8 and 9) or refuse to speak because of social fears (see chapter 10).

Other anxious behaviors may be less recognizable but just as debilitating (Beidel, Neal, & Lederer, 1991). Children may "play sick" on exam day to avoid taking a test. In school, children may avoid eye contact with the teacher in an effort to avoid being asked a question that requires a verbal reply. Other signs may include delay tactics or taking an inordinate amount of time to get ready for an event (in the hope of missing it). Children with social fears may choose to stay inside and read rather than ride bicycles and play outside with other children. Those with performance anxiety may refuse to participate in school plays, recitals, or athletics because they fear performing poorly in front of others (Beidel, 1991). In some cases, fearful situations or events occur suddenly and without warning. For example, on days when a child knows that he or she is required to give an oral report, the child may "play sick" and stay home. If suddenly called on to read in front of the class, the child may still try to avoid the situation by "freezing" or refusing to speak. Thus, avoidance is another behavioral expression of fear.

Children also may express anxiety through repetitive behaviors or rituals (see chapter 11). Common repetitive behaviors include spending extensive periods of time bathing, washing, cleaning, or performing repetitive acts (Thomsen, 2000). A child who fears that burglars will break into the house or that the house will catch fire sometimes spends hours checking door locks, windows, and oven knobs. Although these behaviors may appear nonsensical, they often are a result of a child's attempt to decrease distress about a particular feared event or consequence.

Escaping or avoiding situations often brings temporary relief from anxiety and fear. However, over time, avoidance or escape behavior actually serves to strengthen anxiety and reinforce avoidance through the process of negative reinforcement (Mowrer, 1947). In the short term, avoidance or escape eliminates the fearful reaction and acts as a powerful reinforcer. However, it also strengthens the avoidance response as well as the fear response (Mowrer, 1947). As will become evident throughout this book, the psychosocial interventions that have the most extensive empirical support are those that expose the child to the fearful situation or object. Thus, a primary goal of behavioral treatment is to reverse the pattern of avoidance or escape by exposure to the feared situations.

EPIDEMIOLOGY OF ANXIETY DISORDERS

As noted, anxiety disorders are quite common among children and adolescents. Table 2.1 depicts world-wide prevalence rates. As illustrated, rates increase with age (Costello & Angold, 1995; Essau, 2000) and disorders are more commonly reported among females than males (Essau, 2000). Many of the studies listed in Table 2.1 also provide rates for specific anxiety disorders and these will be addressed in the chapters devoted to each specific disorder.

TABLE 2.1 Prevalence Rates for Anxiety Disorders in Children and Adolescents

Study and Location	Age Range	Subject *N*	Prevalence
Germany			
Essau (2000)	12–17	1,035	8.6%
New Zealand			
Anderson et al. (1987)	11	782	7.4%
Fergusson et al. (1993)	15	961	12.8%
McGee et al. (1990)	15	943	10.7%
McGee et al. (1992)	18	930	12.4%
Newman et al. (1996)	21	961	20.2%
United States			
Costello et al. (1988)	7–11	789	15.4%
Costello et al. (1993)	12–18		17.7%
Costello et al. (after 1994)	9,11,13	4,500	5.7%
Kashani et al. (1987)	14–16	150	8.7%

An important issue in understanding anxiety disorders in childhood is that the disorders rarely occur in isolation (e.g., Costello & Angold, 1995). Rather, many children meeting diagnostic criteria for one anxiety disorder often will display symptoms of other anxiety disorders as well. Furthermore, many children actually meet criteria for a second anxiety disorder and sometimes even more; whereas others may suffer from a different secondary emotional or behavioral disorder. In Table 2.2, rates of comorbidity from several studies are presented. Anxiety disorders often are comorbid with other disorders such as depression or externalizing disorders. Rates of depression and anxiety comorbidity ranged from 15.9% to 61.9% across various studies (Brady & Kendall, 1992). Anxiety frequently is present prior to the onset of depression (Strauss, Last, Hersen, & Kazdin, 1988). Additionally, when both disorders are present, the overall symptom picture and functional impairment is more severe. In contrast, comorbidity rates for anxiety and behavioral disorders such as ADHD or ODD are lower than for anxiety and other internalizing disorders, ranging from 16.7% to 36.4% (Last et al., 1987). An important issue, and one that will be discussed in the ensuing chapters, is the need for clinicians to differentiate between children who have two distinct disorders and those who have overlapping symptoms but only one disorder. For example, if anxious children refuse to do as their parents' request, because of their fear, their behavior may appear oppositional. However, in this case, the oppositionality is part of a pattern of avoidance and fear, not an entirely separate disorder.

It is important to note that comorbid disorders may in part be a function of age. Specifically, several studies report that comorbidity is more often found among older children (Stavrakaki, Vargo, Boodoosingh, & Roberts, 1987; Strauss, Last, Hersen, & Kazdin, 1988). Although Kendall et al. (2001) did not

TABLE 2.2 Comorbidity Rates for Samples of Children Diagnosed
With a Primary Anxiety Disorder

Study	Age of Sample	Overall Percent with Comorbidity	Type and Percent of Comorbidity
Essau et al. (2000)	12–17 years	51	None: 49 Anxiety: 48 Depression: 30.2 Somatoform: 26.6 Substance use: 11.5

Ginsburg & Silverman (1996)
  Hispanic subsample
  Caucasian subsample
	6–17 years	
		91
		83	

Kendall et al. (2001)	9–13 years	79	None: 21 Anxiety: 49.7 Depression: 4.6 Externalizing: 25.4
Silverman et al. (2001)	7–16 years	67	None: 33 Anxiety: 53.2 Depression: 4.8 Externalizing: 9.7
Strauss et al. (1988)	5–17 years	60	None: 41 Anxiety: 31 Depression: 28

Note: All studies used *DSM-IV* criteria except Strauss et al. (1988), which used *DSM-III* criteria.

report age differences in rates of comorbidity, the age range in that sample was more restricted than the others.

Rates of comorbidity also vary across the different anxiety disorders. In one study, children with a primary diagnosis of separation anxiety disorder had higher rates of comorbidity than children with primary social phobia or primary generalized anxiety disorder (Verduin & Kendall, 2003). Overall, 47% of this sample had a comorbid diagnosis of specific phobia, and this disorder was more common among those with primary separation anxiety disorder or primary generalized anxiety disorder than among those with primary social phobia. In contrast, comorbid mood disorders were more common among those with primary social phobia or generalized anxiety disorder than children with separation anxiety disorder and overall, boys were more likely to have comorbid diagnoses of attention deficit disorder and oppositional defiant disorder than girls.

It is unclear if the presence of comorbid disorders has an effect on treatment outcome. Rapee (2000) reported that comorbid externalizing symptoms did not affect treatment outcome for children and adolescents with anxiety disorders. However, symptoms of secondary depression did appear to predict treatment response among another group of children with anxiety disorders (Berman, Weems, Silverman, & Kurtines, 2000). To date, few studies have reported the effect of comorbid *disorders* (rather than *symptoms*) on treatment outcome. Kendall, Brady and Verduin (2001) reported that outcome did not differ among children (treated with cognitive-behavioral treatment) who had only a single anxiety disorder, children with comorbid anxiety disorders, and children with comorbid externalizing disorders. Rapee (2003) reached similar conclusions for children with a singular anxiety disorder, children with comorbid anxiety disorders, and children with a comorbid nonanxiety disorder (mood or externalizing disorders).

As with epidemiological prevalence data, specific comorbidity rates found for each primary anxiety disorder and their effect on treatment outcome will be reviewed within the context of each specific chapter, where other issues to consider when determining the presence of secondary disorders also will be addressed. The issue is raised here to alert the reader that children often present with a myriad of fears as well as other emotional and behavioral difficulties.

In addition to their substantial prevalence rates, further evidence that anxiety disorders in children merit serious attention comes from several longitudinal studies. In one of the earliest studies, 100% of children originally diagnosed with a phobia were recovered or improved 5 years later (Agras, Chapin, & Oliveau, 1972). However, although improved 5 years later, an intermediate assessment at three year follow-up indicated that many still suffered considerable distress at that time (Ollendick, 1979). These data suggest that fears may dissipate, but that a substantial period of time is necessary for remission. Among a New Zealand sample of adolescents initially diagnosed with an anxiety disorder (McGee et al., 1992; Feehan, McGee, & Williams, 1993), less than 40% continued to receive a diagnosis 4 or 8 years later; 7% met criteria for other disorders.

Although not strictly a longitudinal study of anxiety disorders, Cantwell and Baker (1989) conducted a four year follow-up investigation of children (aged 2.3 to 15.9 years) who presented at a speech and language clinic. Among those initially diagnosed with an internalizing disorder (anxiety disorder or depression) at time 1, 66% still had a disorder 4 years later. In comparison, 87% of children originally diagnosed with an externalizing disorder (such as conduct disorder or attention deficit hyperactivity disorder) still had a disorder 4 years later, suggesting many children retained their diagnosis, although the internalizing disorders showed more instability. In further analyzing the children initially diagnosed with either anxiety or depression who remained symptomatic 4 years later, 36% had the same disorder, whereas 64% had a different disorder. Specifically among those initially diagnosed with avoidant disorder, 36% had recovered 4 years later. For separation anxiety disorder, 44% had recovered, whereas for overanxious disorder, 25% had recovered. Although some children recovered from a disorder, to date it is not clear when or how such a recovery occurs. Furthermore, other children continued to suffer, although not necessarily with the same initial diagnosis. Again, factors which predict why the form of the disorder changes in some children are not clear.

Keller et al. (1992) examined the lifetime psychiatric histories of 275 children. Fourteen percent had a lifetime diagnosis of an anxiety disorder (overanxious disorder or separation anxiety disorder). Life table estimates indicated that the cumulative probability of remaining ill 8 years later was 46%, indicating that these were chronic disorders. Among those with OAD who recovered, 31% had a subsequent episode.

In a follow-up study of children with school refusal, 50% of those with either social phobia or avoidant disorder and 40% of those with overanxious disorder retained their diagnoses one year later, even though they had been treated with CBT and some also received imipramine (Bernstein, Hektner, Borchardt, & McMillan, 2001). Similarly, Cohen, Cohen, and Brook (1993) noted that 50% of children and adolescents with severe overanxious disorder still met diagnostic criteria 2½ years later.

Costello and Angold (1995) described the results of five earlier studies that examined the continuity of anxiety disorders in children and adolescents across intervals from 2 to 5 years. Overall, 20–30% of children who had an anxiety disorder at the initial assessment also met diagnostic criteria at follow-up, suggesting a moderate level of continuity, beyond what would be expected by chance alone. More recent studies support these findings of moderate stability for the presence of anxiety disorders. For example, Last and her colleagues (Last, Perrin, Hersen, & Kazdin, 1996) conducted a 3 to 4 year prospective follow-up study of children with anxiety disorders. Overall, 82% of children diagnosed with anxiety disorders at time 1 did not have the same disorder at follow-up. However, 30% of the sample developed a new psychiatric disorder, including 15.5% who developed a new anxiety disorder, 13.1% a new depressive disorder, and 7.1% an externalizing disorder such as ADHD, oppositional defiant disorder, or conduct disorder. Finally, Newman et al. (1996) reported that individuals with an anxiety disorder at age 21 were significantly more likely to have had a history of anxiety disorders (61.5%) than a different type of disorder (such as depression or substance abuse (18.9%) or no previous disorder (19.5%). Therefore, although not all anxiety disorders develop at an early age, many adults with anxiety disorders have a history of disorders as children.

To summarize, anxiety disorders in children and adolescents appear to be stable over substantial periods of time. Although rates vary among the different studies (likely the result of differing diagnostic practices and sample variances), about 50% of children retain their diagnosis across follow-up periods ranging from 6 months to 5 years. Additionally, there is a small percentage of children (ranging from 25–30%) who seem to develop new anxiety disorders at follow-up. As noted above, it is not clear if the different diagnosis at the time of the follow-up reflects a change in diagnostic practices, developmental maturation, or an actual change in the form of the disorder. In any case, the important factor is that the child still suffers from an anxiety disorder. Finally, there is a small percentage of children (about 20–25%) who have no disorder at follow-up. Furthermore, as is the case with gender differences for overall prevalence, it appears that stability of the disorder is much more common among girls than among boys. Overall, these data suggest that, with the exception of specific phobias, there is moderate temporal stability for anxiety disorders, and a high level of stability for the continuing presence of some type of anxiety state.

As noted above, one criterion for the determination of an anxiety disorder is that the fears or anxiety must result in functional impairment. Overall, there is substantial evidence that children with anxiety disorders suffer from social and academic impairment. Children with anxiety disorders often are socially neglected by their peers (Strauss, Lahey, Frick, Frame, & Hynd, 1988). Specifically, children without psychiatric disorders were significantly more likely to be nominated by their peers as "most liked," and children with conduct disorders were significantly more likely to nominated as "least liked." Children with anxiety disorders received few nominations of either type, suggesting that they had limited social impact upon their classmates. They were not most liked or least liked. Rather, it was as if they were invisible to other children in the classroom.

Social impairment also exists among adolescents with anxiety disorders (Essau et al., 2000). Across a 4 week period, 32% reported impairment in their social contacts. Additionally, 35% reported impaired school performance and 41% reported impairment in their leisure activities. Finally, Woodward and Fergusson (2001) examined the life course outcomes of New Zealand adolescents who at age 14–16 were classified as having either one, two, three or more anxiety disorders, or no anxiety disorder. At age 21, these individuals were re-assessed for the presence of psychopathology, educational achievement, and social role attainment (employment and parenthood). As depicted in Table 2.3, there was a significant relationship between number of anxiety disorders diagnosed at ages 14–16 and negative outcomes at age 21. Specifically, as the number of anxiety disorders at ages 14–16 increased, so did the risk for the presence of anxiety disorders, major depression, and illicit drug dependence at age 21. Rate increases were highest for those with three anxiety disorders, and decreased linearly for those with two disorders, and then one disorder. To illustrate, for those with three or more anxiety disorders in mid-adolescence, rates of anxiety disorders at age 21 were 3.5 times higher, depression was 2.0 times higher, and illicit drug use was almost 4 times higher than those without anxiety disorders. In summary, anxiety disorders create significant impairment across various domains of life functioning. Furthermore, these impairments are evident from an early age and continue throughout adolescence and early adulthood. Longer follow-up studies currently are not available except for several studies of shy children, which will be addressed in the chapter on social phobia (chapter 10).

TABLE 2.3 Relationship of Adolescent Anxiety Disorders
to Social Impairment in Adulthood

No. of Anxiety Disorders in Adolescents	Percent of Anxiety Disorders in Adulthood	Percent of Depression in Adulthood	Percent of Illicit Drug Dependence	Percent Entering the University at Age 21
0	17.4	28.5	3.0	34.2
1	28.8	38.2	4.8	26.0
2	43.7	49.2	7.5	19.0
3	60.0	60.5	11.2	13.4

Note: Modified from Essau et al. (2000).

OVERVIEW OF TREATMENTS FOR ANXIETY DISORDERS

Overall, behavioral and pharmacological interventions have received the most empirical support in the treatment of childhood anxiety disorders. As noted several times throughout this chapter, specific literatures will be addressed within the context of a particular disorder. An evidence-based medicine review (Compton et al., 2004) concluded that for anxiety (and depression), there is substantial evidence to support the efficacy of behavioral and cognitive-behavioral interventions. Medium to large effect sizes were reported for symptom reduction across identified primary outcome measures. As noted, these data set the stage for the next wave of intervention studies that should include comparative and combination study designs as well as dismantling studies.

With respect to general treatment implementation, some issues cut across specific diagnostic groups such as the need to educate parents and children about the particular disorder and the expectations regarding treatment, familial psychopathology, parental concerns about the intervention, and specific treatment modifications that might be considered based on the age of the child. Although many of these issues have not been addressed empirically, substantial clinical experience suggests that they contribute to a successful treatment outcome.

Despite the particular anxiety disorder with which a child might present, or the particular intervention that will be used, treatment outcome will be significantly enhanced if both the child and the parent understand, to the best of their ability, the specific disorder and the proposed intervention. Prior to beginning any intervention, time should be devoted to educating the family, including what is known about the disorder (etiology, demographics, clinical presentation), the current available pharmacological and psychosocial treatment outcome data, an overview of the proposed treatment package, the details of the proposed treatment package (including specific procedures and the time commitment) and an assessment of the motivation of the parent and child to participate in the treatment program. Some of these issues may be covered as part of any informed consent procedure but families often are ill-informed about the particular disorder from which their child suffers and thus, the relevance of the intervention for the treatment of a disorder often is unclear.

An important issue is that children with anxiety disorders (or any other disorder) rarely seek treatment on their own. Rather, adults often recognize the child's distress and seek intervention on their behalf. Thus, children may have less motivation for treatment and establishing a therapeutic relationship with a child may be a formidable task. Although the emphasis on the need for a strong therapeutic relationship differs according to an intervention's theoretical basis, the need for the patient to be cooperative with, and motivated to participate in, the intervention cuts across intervention type. In a meta-analysis of the role of the therapeutic relationship in treatment outcome for child and adolescent interventions (Shirk & Karver, 2003), a variety of factors that might influence the formation and strength of the therapeutic relationship were examined. These include patient variables, intervention type, or research design characteristics. Overall, this meta-analyses indicated that there was only a modest relationship between the therapeutic relationship and treatment outcome ($r = .24$), similar to that found for adult patients. Overall, patient factors, mode of intervention, structure of the intervention and the context in which treatment was delivered (individual, group, or family) did not play a role in moderating the effect of treatment outcome. Interestingly, a strong therapeutic relationship did appear to be important for obtaining a positive outcome when the type of problem exhibited by the child was considered. Specifically, a positive therapeutic relationship was more important for treatment outcome when children presented with externalizing, rather than internalizing, disorders. Thus, these data indicate that although a positive therapeutic relationship plays a modest role in treatment outcome, it is not the most important factor.

Familial pathology will be discussed in detail in chapter 4 with respect to its influence upon the etiology of childhood anxiety disorders. However, to illustrate its importance with one example, Last and her colleagues (Last et al., 1991) reported that 40% of parents of children with anxiety disorders also had a lifetime history of an anxiety disorder. Thus, at the time of the child's diagnosis, parents also may be suffering from an anxiety disorder. How does the presence of parental psychopathology play a role in a child's treatment program? In some forms of behavioral intervention for example, parents play a significant role in the treatment plan. Parents may have to assist in their child's homework assignments (e.g., a parent may have to take the child to the park to interact with other children). However, if the parent suffers from agoraphobia, the ability to assist the child in completing the homework may be impaired. Thus, treatment may fail because homework assignments cannot be carried out as prescribed.

Also as will be discussed in depth in chapter 4, some parents of anxious children have a tendency to be cautious, avoid taking risks and to reinforce avoidance (Barrett et al., 1996). Particularly for behavioral interventions, such parental behaviors would be counterproductive to therapeutic procedures that attempt to place the child in contact with fearful or anxiety-producing situations. Silverman has referred to this parental behavior pattern as the Protection Trap (Silverman & Kurtines, 1996) and noted the need to work with parents to assist them in understanding that (a) exposure to the feared situation is necessary if intervention is to be effective, (b) like adults, children's anticipatory anxiety often is more intense than anxiety actually experienced when in the distressing situation, and (c) the anxiety experienced during the exposure sessions is rarely as intense as what parents imagine (particularly if a graduated procedure is used). In the latter case, inviting the parents to observe an exposure session (through a one-way mirror or via a videotape) will help the parent understand the intervention and decrease their concerns.

Within each specific chapter, the literature on effective interventions for that disorder will be reviewed. Here however, it is important to acknowledge the overall state of the literature, and point out some avenues for future directions. Until about 5 years ago, there was a dearth of controlled trials with respect to the psychological and pharmacological treatment of anxiety disorders in children and adolescents. There were many case studies, single case designs, and a wealth of clinical literature which suggested that both medication and behavioral interventions should be effective. During the past 5 years, there has been a significant increase in the number of published controlled trials, both for pharmacological and psychosocial interventions. Yet, there are still many basic issues that are unresolved. First, there is the intriguing issue that many children have a positive response to interventions that were designed as placebos. Rates of response to pill placebo are reported to be as high as 30% (Riddle et al., 2000). As noted by Silverman and Berman (2001), educational support groups (designed as a psychological placebo) also have been reported to be effective for children with phobic disorders. However, prior to drawing conclusions about the efficacy of educational support groups, the authors noted that there is no evidence that educational support groups would be effective for diagnostic categories such as social anxiety disorder or obsessive-compulsive disorder (as opposed to phobic conditions). Furthermore, the issue of functional impairment must also be considered when evaluating the effect of a placebo. Even among a group of children, all of whom meet diagnostic criteria for a disorder, the degree of functional impairment often ranges from quite mild to very severe. It may be that those children who are less severely impaired may benefit from a less specific intervention strategy such as an educational support group. In support of this hypothesis, classes such as those offered by the Dale Carnegie Institute often are useful for adults who have mild speech anxiety but are rarely effective for those with severe social anxiety disorder. Therefore, level of impairment or severity of the disorder might provide an explanation for the placebo response rates reported in the empirical literature. Finally, it should be noted that few studies have attempted to examine the "permanence" of behavioral change as a result of placebo. It may be that placebo effects wear off, returning the child to his/her previous state of distress.

In addition to placebo, Silverman and Berman (2001) address other issues regarding treatment for childhood anxiety disorders. For example, there are few studies that have examined issues of predicting treatment outcome and prescribing treatments. With respect to predicting treatment outcome, demographic variables such as age and gender are an obvious important consideration; although to date, the findings in this area are unclear (see Silverman & Berman, 2002 for a review). Other factors, such as those mentioned (parental pathology, treatment credibility, illness severity) also must be addressed. In short, although it is clear that pharmacological and psychosocial interventions appear to be effective (based on group responses), not every child who is treated benefits from the intervention. Therefore, there is a need to determine the specific factors that predict treatment response. Once identified, they could become an important part of developing future, and even more effective, interventions.

The issue of prescribing treatments in some ways evolves from an understanding of the factors that affect treatment outcome. Additionally, it requires an acknowledgment that certain behaviors, such as social withdrawal or school refusal, represent symptomatic behaviors that may be the product of different etiologies. Social withdrawal for example, may be an indication of social phobia, depression, or early onset schizophrenia, or perhaps just a temperamentally inhibited disposition. Obviously, these conditions require different types of interventions. Our clinic, for example, offers social skills training for children with social phobia. Often however, we interview families where the child may have social skills deficits but the deficiency is the result of oppositional disorders or pervasive developmental disorders such as autism or Asperger's disorder. Although all these children have difficulties with social skills, the specific deficits often differ markedly and thus, the content of the intervention needs to be much different, even if the specific strategy (i.e., social skills training) remains the same. Kearny and Silverman (1999) also addressed the problem of prescriptive treatments with respect to school refusal, another behavior that can result from various etiologies. In this case, the intervention differs depending upon the specific factors that lead to the problematic behavior (e.g., phobic reaction, tangible reinforcement). As noted by Silverman and Berman (2001), the rationale for adopting a prescriptive approach is logical, but to date there are no data to suggest that this approach is more efficacious than any other.

Finally, there is the issue of treatment efficacy versus treatment effectiveness. Some researchers define effectiveness in terms of the transfer of an intervention from the research clinic to a community clinic setting (e.g., Weisz, Donenberg, Han, & Weiss, 1995). One issue that has plagued the transfer of empirically supported interventions from research clinics to clinical settings has been the belief that patients in research settings were not representative of those in traditional outpatient clinics. However, a recent research investigation examining the demographics of children with anxiety disorders (Southam-Gerow, Weisz, & Kendall, 2003) revealed that there were few differences between children recruited in a research clinic compared to those who sought treatment in a community-based service clinic. In fact, there were no group differences on any measure of internalizing symptomatology, although those in the community clinic were reported by their parents to have more externalizing symptoms and diagnoses than those in the research setting. Among the numerous demographic variables examined, only income and family structure differentiated the groups. Specifically, those treated in the community setting were more likely to be from lower income, single parent families. Although differences in treatment outcome were not examined in this report, the available data suggest that at least in terms of patient characteristics, children with anxiety disorders treated in research clinics are very similar to those seeking treatment in community service settings.

Another way to define effectiveness is in the sense of the clinical impact of the intervention upon an individual's overall life functioning. That is, even if an intervention decreases the self-report of a presenting problem (such as anxiety), does this decrease in symptomatology translate into enhanced daily functioning? To use one example, if an intervention results in decreased self-report of anxiety about attending school, does enhanced functioning also occur (the child joins after-school activities requiring her to after school, rather than leaving the school grounds as soon as possible)? Currently, data regarding the effectiveness of empirically-supported treatments are lacking and should be targeted for future research.

SUMMARY

In summary, anxiety disorders appear to be quite prevalent in the general child population. The characteristic clinical presentation of these disorders includes physical symptoms, subjective (cognitive) distress, and behavioral avoidance. Unlike the common childhood fears discussed in chapter 1, anxiety disorders represent a more serious psychological disorder and often they do not dissipate over time without appropriate intervention. Therefore, contrary to the old adage—they will grow out of it—many children with an anxiety disorder do not grow out of their disorder. Moreover, these severe and chronic conditions also have the potential to significantly impair academic, emotional and social development. Thus, as the understanding of these disorders has evolved, the need to recognize and effectively treat these conditions has become more salient. In this chapter, overarching considerations with respect to the conceptualization, assessment, and treatment of anxiety disorders in children and adolescents have been presented. Furthermore, areas of intervention where more research is necessary have been highlighted. Following the chapters on developmental considerations and etiology, the remainder of this book is devoted to various child and adolescent anxiety disorders, their clinical presentation, and effective intervention strategies.

CHAPTER 3

Developmental Considerations

Sara is 7 years old. She speaks only to her mother, father and brother. At home, she is a happy, even boisterous child. However, when anyone other than her immediate family is present (even her grandparents), she runs and hides. Her mother notes that even at 1 year of age, Sara would cry if others tried to make eye contact. She often cries now if others try to talk to her. Sara sometimes carries a small stuffed animal and on rare occasions, the animal will "talk" aloud in a voice that is very different from Sara's own voice.

Charlie is 16 years old. He does not have any friends. He is very polite and soft-spoken. His mother reports that he often hangs around the basketball court, watching the other boys play but never asking if he can join the game. His affect is sad and he has been having trouble sleeping. He has an above average IQ but gets only average grades because he refuses to speak in class or give oral reports.

As noted in the previous chapters, anxiety disorders exist across all ages. The currently accepted diagnostic system, *Diagnostic and Statistical Manual of Mental Disorders–Fourth Edition* (APA, 1994) considers childhood anxiety disorders as downward extensions of adult anxiety disorders (Schniering, Hudson & Rapee, 2000). In this most recent diagnostic system revision, only separation anxiety disorder is listed in the manual's section on Disorders First Diagnosed in Infancy, Childhood and Adolescence, suggesting something unique about this disorder to the time of childhood. Otherwise, anxiety syndromes commonly diagnosed in children are found in the diagnostic manual's general section on anxiety disorders, in recognition that the disorders exist across all age ranges. However, as an acknowledgment to children's developmental immaturity, the criteria sometimes contain specific descriptors for how the disorder might manifest itself in children. Furthermore, as illustrated by the clinical vignettes that opened this chapter, even within childhood and adolescence, the clinical expression of a particular disorder may vary depending upon the child's particular age. Both Sara and Charlie meet diagnostic criteria for social phobia even though their outward expressions are very different. In this chapter, issues of physical, cognitive, and behavioral maturation as they relate to the expression of anxiety disorders in children will be explored.

CLINICAL PRESENTATION

As noted, only separation anxiety disorder is considered somewhat unique, included in the *DSM-IV* section on Disorders First Appearing in Infancy, Childhood and Adolescence and considered to have an onset solely in childhood. However, the diagnostic criteria for several other anxiety disorders do contain descriptors of how the disorder might be expressed in youth. For example, children often display fear in a manner different from that of adults. The diagnostic criteria for social or specific phobia acknowledge these differences by noting that children may display excessive fear and distress by crying, tantrums, freezing, or clinging, behaviors not commonly displayed by adults with phobic disorders. Another example relates to posttraumatic stress disorder where one of the diagnostic criteria is recurrent and intrusive distressing recollections of the traumatic event, including images, thoughts, or perceptions. In young children, the criteria notes that this symptom may be expressed by repetitive play during which themes of the trauma are re-enacted. These examples function to remind clinicians of the need to be aware of developmental factors that might influence how the disorder is expressed across the lifespan.

In addition to the inclusion of individual behavioral descriptors specific to children, certain diagnostic categories acknowledge developmental immaturity by requiring a different number of symptoms necessary to meet criteria for a diagnosis. For an adult to meet diagnostic criteria for Generalized Anxiety Disorder (GAD), three of six symptoms of anxiety and worry are necessary. However, only one of the six symptoms is necessary for the diagnosis to be assigned to a child. It is important to note that although these specific descriptors acknowledge differences in how the disorder might be expressed, there is still the assumption that the same anxiety disorders exist across the lifespan.

Whereas separation anxiety disorder is considered to occur only among children, one anxiety disorder commonly found in adult patients, panic disorder with or without agoraphobia, is rarely diagnosed in youth. Some (Nelles & Barlow, 1988) have suggested that children may experience the physiological symptoms usually associated with panic, but do not possess the cognitive maturation necessary to experience the cognitive component of panic disorder. The "cognitive" aspect of panic found in adults results in the attribution of at least some panic attacks as emerging out of the blue with specific thoughts of losing control, going crazy or dying. These thoughts require the ability to conceive of the future. Young children may not have yet developed the cognitive ability to consider future events (What if I die? What if I lose control?).

Without the presence of these "cognitive" symptoms, some investigators have suggested that children do not experience panic disorder (Chorpita, Albano, & Barlow, 1996). However, the limited number of children diagnosed with Panic Disorder may reflect the "cognitive bias" of clinicians rather than a true lack of prevalence among children.

> Melissa was 5-years-old and a worrier. At school one day, she choked on a hot dog. Later that week, the family was scheduled to fly to California and the morning of the flight, Melissa had heart palpitations, light headedness, and shortness of breath. She told her mother that she thought she would "fall over and die." At age 7, she had similar symptoms before a trip to Kansas. Melissa never worried about the panic attacks although she had a myriad of other worries. At age 9, her worries became severe enough to warrant a diagnosis of GAD.

Melissa's symptoms will be discussed in detail in chapter 6. However, the panic she experienced clearly illustrates that panic features do occur even in very young children. The question remains however, do young children experience Panic Disorder? Interestingly, there is a condition termed "child hyperventilation syndrome" that is described in the pediatric medical literature. The symptoms endorsed by children who experience these hyperventilation attacks include difficulty breathing, dizziness, tingling sensations, headache, chest pain, nausea; symptoms very similar to those reported by individuals with panic disorder. In addition to the similarities in clinical presentation, the interventions used to treat child hyperventilation syndrome also are similar to those for panic disorder. In fact, successful interventions for hyperventilation syndrome include breathing into a paper bag, supportive therapy, and propranolol for the most severe cases. Despite the similarities in clinical presentation and intervention strategies, there do appear to be differences in the cognitive dimension of these syndromes. For example, prior to the age at which children achieve the cognitive developmental stage of formal operations, children diagnosed with hyperventilation syndrome make external attributions for their physical symptoms. The use of external attributions is in contrast to the "out of the blue" phenomenon characteristic of adults with panic disorder. This situation has become even more muddled as a result of the most recent version of the *DSM* criteria (*DSM-IV*). Currently, panic attacks can be (a) situationally bound, (b) situationally cued, or (c) uncued. In fact, children such as Melissa clearly experience panic attacks in relation to specific objects or situations (i.e., situationally bound or situationally cued). However, controversy remains regarding whether children, particularly young children, can meet the current diagnostic criteria for panic disorder.

Another difference in children's expression of anxiety is the recognition that unlike adults, children may not view their fears as unreasonable (APA, 1994). In fact, the decision to seek treatment for an anxiety disorder usually is not that of the child, but that of a parent or guardian, often after the advice of a physician, teacher, relative, or friend.

> Michael is a 14-year-old boy with obsessive-compulsive disorder (OCD). He worries about contracting a fatal disease. He feels that his clothes are never clean enough and washes them constantly. His parents report that he runs the washing machine 16 hours per day and over the past year, they have had to replace the washer three times because of overuse. Michael does not understand the problem and cannot understand why his parents just do not "buy another machine."

Adults with OCD may engage in the same cleaning behaviors and have the same intrusive thoughts regarding germs and death as does Michael. However, they usually clearly recognize the unreasonable nature of their fear. Thus, even though suffering from its effects, some children may not be aware that their behavior is abnormal.

A study of adult recall of the existence of childhood anxiety disorders may be relevant to this issue of symptom recognition. Masia et al. (2003) interviewed adults previously diagnosed with anxiety or mood disorders (approximate average age at initial intake was 9 years). Childhood diagnoses were assigned after a strict diagnostic procedure, suggesting that these disorders were indeed present at the time that they were first assigned. However, when the subjects (now adults) were re-assessed approximately 12.4 years later, recall of the earlier anxiety disorders was poor, with inter-rater reliability coefficients between anxiety diagnoses assigned at the initial assessment and lifetime anxiety diagnoses assigned at follow-up ranging from $r = .30$ to $r = .33$. Sensitivity estimates indicated that only 40–44% of those originally diagnosed with an anxiety disorder recalled that diagnosis at follow-up. Interestingly, inter-rater reliability for mood disorders was moderate ($r = .55$ to $r = .58$) suggesting that it is not gross memory deficit that accounts for the participant's inability to recall the earlier presence of anxiety disorders. As noted by the authors, the inability of adults to recall documented episodes of childhood anxiety disorders poses difficulties for epidemiological investigations. However, the inability of the individual to recall the presence of a previous anxiety disorder may be related to the use of the DSM diagnostic qualifier that among children, it is not necessary to view the fear as unreasonable. That is, if as children, individuals do not recognize that their symptoms are excessive or unreasonable, then as adults, they may not "recall" these episodes. In effect, the child never recognized the existence of the disorder even though its presence was clear to others. These data illustrate the need for multiple informants when assessing anxiety disorders in youth, particularly with respect to (a) determining severity or functional impairment and (b) understanding that children may not acknowledge the existence of a disorder. In addition to increasing the accuracy of the diagnostic process, children who do not acknowledge the presence of a disorder present significant challenges for implementation of a treatment program.

ASSESSMENT OF ANXIETY DISORDERS IN CHILDREN

In addition to similarities in diagnostic categories and the diagnostic process, the general strategies used to assess anxiety in adults also are used with children (Beidel & Stanley, 1993; Fonseca & Perrin, 2001). These include diagnostic interviewing, self-report measures, and behavioral assessment. Substantial attention to developmental considerations also is needed throughout the assessment process. Given the rapidity of physical and cognitive development during childhood and adolescence, assessment strategies appropriate for 8-year-olds may differ from those required for 12-year-olds which in turn, may be different from what is needed for 16-year-olds. Furthermore, given children's potential lack of recognition regarding the presence and seriousness of anxiety disorders, the importance of collateral data collected from adults is inversely related to the age of the child. In the ensuing chapters, measurement strategies and assessment instruments useful for each specific disorder are discussed. General assessment issues that cut across the disorders are presented here.

In a cogent review of developmental factors, Schniering et al. (2000) noted several important issues that merit consideration when assessing anxiety disorders in youth. These include limited parent–child agreement on diagnostic interviews and lack of adequate reliability and discriminant validity for both interview and self-report strategies. Although the reasons for these difficulties in the assessment process are not readily apparent, cognitive maturation probably plays a critical role in the process of accurate data collection.

Assessment typically begins with a diagnostic interview, usually conducted with both the parent and the child. There are several different structured and semi-structured diagnostic interviews available for use when interviewing children and adolescents with psychiatric disorders. The most comprehensive interview schedule for the assessment of anxiety disorders is the Anxiety Disorders Interview Schedule for Children (ADIS C/P; Silverman & Albano, 1996). The ADIS C/P actually consists of two semi-structured interview schedules, one designed to interview the child and the second for the child's parent. The parent schedule is more extensive and is the only version that assesses for oppositional defiant disorder, conduct disorder and enuresis. Each diagnostic section has a series of screening questions and positive responses lead to a more in-depth evaluation of that particular area. The ADIS-C/P has good to excellent test-retest reliability (Silverman, Saavadra, & Pina, 2001) with kappas ranging from 0.61 to 1.00. Wood and colleagues (Wood, Piacentini, Bergman, McCracken, & Barrios, 2002) reported strong convergent validity between ADIS-C/P diagnoses of social phobia, separation anxiety disorder, and panic disorder and the corresponding empirically derived factor scores on the Multi-Dimensional Anxiety Scale for Children (MASC; March, Parker, Sullivan, Stallings, & Conners, 1997). There was no convergence between MASC scores and the ADIS-C/P diagnosis of GAD, suggesting that children with GAD are not easily differentiated from children with other anxiety disorders (see chapter 6 for a fuller discussion of this issue). One reason for the lack of discriminant validity for the diagnosis is that, consistent with most of the extant diagnostic literature pertaining to GAD in children, those in the sample diagnosed with GAD had more comorbid anxiety disorders than other diagnostic groups. Thus, they had a complicated clinical presentation and the reported lack of validity for the diagnosis may be due to "noise" created by the presence of other disorders (or at least the presence of overlapping symptoms) rather than the inability of the assessment measures to distinguish between clearly defined and independent conditions.

A major issue with respect to diagnostic interviewing is poor parent–child agreement. More often than not, parents and children provide different, and sometimes conflicting, information regarding the child's clinical presentation. A thorough discussion of the issue is beyond the scope of this chapter, however, there are several variables that may affect diagnostic agreement (Grills & Ollendick, 2002). These include child variables such as age (younger children are usually less reliable reporters, although adolescents may hide information from their parents), social desirability (the child's attempts to conceal emotional problems), and type of disorder (there is generally better parent–child agreement for externalizing disorders). Parental and familial characteristics that may affect diagnostic agreement include social desirability (parents concealing behavioral problems), parental psychopathology (parents with psychopathology tend to overreport their children's symptoms), impatience/boredom with the interview, and lack of communication and/or familial conflict. Maternal psychopathology and distress potentially influences maternal reports of children's behaviors (Langley, Bergman & Piacintini, 2002) where symptom endorsement regarding their child's behavior was higher than expected. In addition to child and family influences, interviewer and interview characteristics may function to decrease parent–child agreement. Potential factors that may affect validity include the inability of the interviewer to establish rapport, the different interpretations between parent and interviewer with respect to the meaning of a word such as "sometimes," and the structured nature of the interview process. Furthermore, as noted in chapter 1, when evaluating children, clinicians need to be aware of normative development so that "normal fears" are not considered abnormal behaviors (Langley et al., 2002).

There are practical, as well as theoretical, issues to consider when conducting interviews with children. First, as noted above, diagnostic interviews of children and some adolescents require interviews not only with the child but also with one or both parents, or other significant caregiver. In some instances, young children may not be able to give specific factual information such as age at onset, dates of significant life events, or other information that may be relevant to the diagnostic process. In other cases, contradictory data may be provided by parents and children. Parent–child agreement is only modest, ranging from 7.7% for depressive disorder to 32% for GAD (Grills &

Ollendick, 2003). Percentage agreement rates for other anxiety disorders were 25% for separation anxiety disorder, 24.5% for social phobia, and 29.3% for specific phobia. However, these low agreement rates are not specific to anxiety disorders diagnoses. Percent agreement for ADHD Inattentive subtype was 25% and ADHD Combination type was 25.3%. Thus, in general, to arrive at the most valid diagnosis, diagnostic interviewing requires a consensus meeting, followed by the clinician's synthesis and integration of all available information.

A second practical consideration when conducting diagnostic interviews, particularly with adolescents, is placing limits on confidentiality and age of consent, which may vary across states. Specifically, as the age of the adolescent increases, the interviewer must consider whether interviewing the parents is necessary or advisable. Furthermore, the limits of confidentiality of the information disclosed during the interview must be carefully explained to both adolescents and parents. A third consideration is that interviewing itself is an artificial situation, particularly with young children. Some young children prefer to be interviewed in the presence of their parents. Others are more comfortable if, rather than just sitting and answering questions, an activity such as a coloring book and crayons is used to lessen the formality of the interview process. Additionally, using reinforcers (in the form of stickers or another small token) as acknowledgment for participation in the interview can help engender a positive therapeutic relationship.

One of the most popular methods to assess anxiety in children and adolescents is the self-report inventory. Similar to diagnostic interviews, several practical issues must be considered when administering self-report inventories (Beidel & Stanley, 1993). These include: (a) whether the child has the cognitive ability to describe himself or herself as anxious; (b) whether terms such as fear, embarrassment, and worry have the same meaning for a child that they do for an adult; and (c) even if the child can distinguish among these labels, whether the child is able to accurately rate variations in intensity and frequency of these concepts. In general, self-report instruments rarely are administered to children under age 6. More commonly, they have a lower limit of age 8, an age when children appear capable of reading, and responding to, the inventories independently (Beidel & Stanley, 1993). As with diagnostic interviewing, an overall rule of thumb is that the younger the child, the more likely it is that this information will have to be gathered from alternative sources such as parents or teachers. However, parent–child agreement also is poor with respect to scores on self-report inventories (Schniering et al., 2000), thus the same caveats raised with respect to lack of agreement on diagnostic interviews apply to self-report inventories as well.

As is the case for the prevailing diagnostic criteria, most self-report measures are downward extensions of equivalent adult measures (Schniering et al., 2000). In recognition of this issue, developers of child anxiety inventories have given careful attention to the developmental appropriateness of scale content.

Less attention has been devoted, however, to examining the developmental appropriateness of instructions and administrative procedures. Specifically, can the same instructions used for adults when completing of a self-report inventory also be used with children? For example, adults defined "worry" as the frequency of a particular thought. Thus, high scores on adult anxiety scales usually indicate the frequency of an aversive event. Most children's fear inventories ask children to rate fears using a 3-point scale, anchored with words such as "never," "some," and "a lot." In such cases, "a lot" is supposed to reflect frequency of the worry. However, Campbell, Rapee and Spence (1996; cited in Schniering et al., 2000) noted that the most frequent fears and worries of children appeared to reflect very aversive, but extremely low frequency events (e.g., dying, AIDS), suggesting that children, particularly those of children age 10 and younger, may define "a lot" in terms of the *aversiveness of the event*, not how often the fearful thought occurred. They hypothesized that if children, particularly young children, are responding to the instructions of self-report inventories using a definition different from the intention of the scale's constructors then a child's idiosyncratic definition may result in data that reflect something different than the original intent of the scale's constructor. To illustrate this issue, recall that children consistently rate fears of injury, illness, death, and danger as the most feared situations on fear inventories, despite the fact that these are threats that rarely occur (McCathie & Spence, 1991). In fact, in one sample of children, 56.9% reported extreme fear of AIDS despite the fact that most had never been exposed to the virus (King & Gullone, 1990). The inconsistencies of these data led several investigators (King & Gullone, 1990; McCathie & Spence, 1991) to conclude that children's endorsement of a list of potentially fearful events, such as those on the Fear Survey Schedule for Children-Revised (FSSC-R), reflected their opinion of the *aversiveness* of a specific event, not the *frequent occurrence* of fear or worry of these events in their daily life.

To address this issue of whether children define worry as the aversiveness or frequency of a specific event, Muris et al. (2002) assessed children's fears using three different methods of assessment (the standard FSSC-R inventory [Ollendick, 1983], a fear listing procedure, and a daily diary method) to 102 children between the ages of 8 and 12. The authors specifically were interested in the frequency with which five commonly endorsed FSSC-R fears: "not being able to breathe," "being hit by a car or truck," "falling from high places," "bombing attacks or being invaded," and "fire or getting burned" were endorsed using each of these three methods. Based on scores on the FSSC-R, "not being able to breathe," "being hit by a car or truck," "falling from high places," "bombing attacks or being invaded," and "fire or getting burned" were among the 10 most common fears endorsed by this sample. When given a blank piece of paper and asked to write down their fears, the children listed 49 different fears. "Bombing attacks/being invaded," "falling from high places," "being hit by a car or truck," and "fire/getting burned" still were included in the list although they were less prevalent and not as highly ranked as when the children completed the FSSC-R. Finally, children were asked to complete a daily diary, each day writing down whatever they worried about on that day. When daily diary data were examined, only 5.9% of the children reported fearing "not being able to breathe," 7.8% reported fearing "being hit by a car or truck," 2.9% reported fearing "bombing attacks/being invaded," 6.9% reported fearing "fire/getting burned," and 11.8% reported fearing "falling from high places." Interestingly, in most cases, children reported a very short duration of these fears ("just for a moment") and the intensity was rated as only moderate. In summary, these data suggest the need for careful consideration of the wording of instructions, particularly on self-report inventories. Rather than just handing the child the form, it would be advisable to spend a few moments with the child, clearly defining the instructions. The use of several examples may be necessary to assure that children are completing the form in a valid manner.

Keeping the above-mentioned caveat in mind, children as young 2 to 3 years old can describe themselves as anxious, afraid or scared (Bretherton et al., 1986), and children as young as age 6 are capable of making quantitative ratings of anxiety that correlate reasonably well with observers' ratings of the same emotional state (LeBaron & Zeltzer, 1984). Researchers/clinicians often are challenged to find ways to elicit accurate estimates of anxious severity or the frequency with which children encounter anxiety-producing situations. Practically, administering self-report measures in a group format may be inappropriate for 6- or 7-year-olds who often have many questions about the meaning of particular words or may be unable to read a particular word. Individual administration of self-report inventories may be more appropriate for younger children.

Another issue that merits consideration is that many self-report inventories use numerical ratings scales that embody concepts (e.g., descriptors such as "several" or "often") and require making discriminations that may be very unfamiliar to pre-adolescent children. Rating scales that contain more than three anchor points can be developmentally inappropriate for young children, possibly reducing the scales reliability and validity (Ollendick, 1983). For example, during the development of a scale to measure social phobia in pre-adolescent children, reliability and validity were substantially improved when the rating scale was reduced from 4 to 3 discrimination points (Beidel et al., 1995). An alternative or additional method for increasing validity would be the substitution of numerical or verbal descriptors with visual stimuli that illustrate concepts such as "mild anxiety" or "severe anxiety" (LeBaron & Zeltzer, 1984). Visually appealing self-monitoring forms also increase compliance with tasks such as daily diaries (Beidel et al., 1991; see Figures 3.1 and 3.2 for examples of visual format ratings scales useful with children and adolescents, respectively).

In summary, developmental differences exist in children's ability to differentiate anxiety from other affective and nonaffective states. Furthermore, as

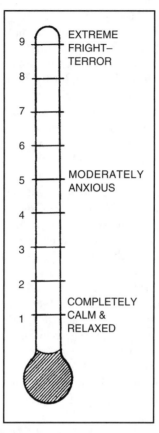

FIGURE 3.1 Self-rating of anxiety.

children's general cognitive abilities mature, so do their abilities to (a) differentiate between cognitions and affect, and (b) apply quantitative concepts such as frequency or severity to accurately describe the extent of their emotional state. All of these issues merit careful consideration in the assessment of children's anxiety disorders.

PUT AN X UNDER THE PICTURE THAT SHOWS HOW SCARED YOU WERE WHEN THIS HAPPENED

FIGURE 3.2

In general, overt (i.e., behavioral) expressions of anxiety are important data in the assessment armamentarium because often they are the first indicators detectable by others that an anxiety disorder exists. Although many researchers and clinicians are aware of developmental differences that may limit children's ability to report subjective distress, fewer are aware of differences in motoric-behavioral maturation that may affect the valid assessment of anxiety. In fact, level of physical maturation will limit a child's range of behavioral expressions. Overall, physical development proceeds in a cephalocaudal and proximodistal manner and thus, children can hold up their heads before they can walk (i.e., they gain control of neck muscles before leg muscles). Furthermore, gross motor behaviors evolve before subtler control is possible and mirroring this, behavioral expressions of fearfulness evolve from gross motoric responses such as crying and running away to more controlled expressions such as gaze aversion (Beidel & Stanley, 1993). Consistent with these findings, the ability of children (ages 5, 9, and 13) to imitate elemental and complex behavioral expressions (fear, anger, happiness, sadness) in humans, increases with increasing age (Ekman, Roper, & Hager, 1980). However, even at age 13, facial actions necessary to produce expressions of fear, sadness, and anger were difficult to imitate.

The inhibition of gross overt behaviors as an expression of fear occurs throughout the developmental maturation of infant and adolescent rhesus monkeys as well as among human subjects (Mineka, Suomi, & Delizio, 1981). Specifically, fearful behaviors in infant rhesus monkeys are characterized by panic, vocalizations, and high activity whereas in adolescents, the typical fearful behaviors are stereotypic activity and silence. Although there are, of course, many differences between rhesus monkeys and humans, these examples illustrate how developmental changes lead to greater impulse control, gratification delay, and the ability to more readily inhibit extreme motoric behavioral responses. Physical maturation and its effect on behavioral assessment of anxiety disorders in children is presented here, with specific attention to the impact of maturation on the construction and utility of behavioral rating scales for use with children.

Actually, differences in cognitive and physical maturation may function synergistically to affect behavioral expressions of fear and anxiety. Among pediatric cancer patients ages 2 to 20 undergoing bone marrow aspiration, a behavioral observation checklist was used to rate anxiety and distress (Jay, Ozolins, Elliot, & Cladwell, 1983). Children between the ages of 2 and 7 were rated as more likely to exhibit overt distress such as crying, screaming, and having to be physically restrained. Age 6 or 7 was the time that distress levels appeared to decrease dramatically, which according to Piagetian theory, is consistent with the age at which children develop a more logical and realistic understanding of medical procedures. The decreased overt expressions of fear exhibited by older children in this study might lead to the conclusion that older children are less fearful, at least according to their scores on the observational checklist. However, if one is not developmentally sensitive to the range of behaviors that children use to express fears, a behavioral checklist could lead to inaccurate conclusions. Specifically, using another sample of children undergoing bone marrow aspiration and a similar behavioral checklist, LeBaron and Zeltzer (1984) confirmed that children between the ages of 6 and 9 were more likely to cry, scream, express verbal anxiety and need physical restraint than children between the ages of 10 and 18. Again, using this checklist, older children had lower scores, which would indicate less distress. However, there were two items, groaning and flinching, which were not on the original behavioral checklist but in this study were coded by the raters anyway. These behaviors were significantly more common in the older children and when the frequency of these behaviors were added to the original checklist scores, group differences in total score on the observational checklist disappeared (i.e., the groups were equally anxious/distressed). Similar findings were reported by Katz, Kellerman, and Sigal (1980) who reported that older children undergoing painful medical procedures displayed fewer overall overt anxious behaviors than younger children but were more likely than the younger children to exhibit muscle tension and specific verbal expressions of pain. Thus, observational scales must be sensitive not only to the behaviors of young children but include items designed to capture the developmentally sophisticated fearful expressions of older adolescents (if the scale will be used across a broad age range).

To summarize, developmental issues play an important role in the assessment of each of the primary dimensions of fear but attention to the role of behavioral, physical, and cognitive maturation is not always considered when researchers and clinicians attempt to assess children's anxious emotional states. These maturational processes do not occur in isolation and thus, improved cognitive abilities, for example, can affect behavioral expressions (Reznick et al., 1986). Furthermore, although the issue of social development was not addressed in this chapter, it must be noted that as children learn societal norms regarding emotional expression (e.g., "boys don't cry," "big girls don't cry"), this in turn may affect responses to fearful events (provided that they have achieved the physical and cognitive abilities necessary to inhibit their behavior). Thus, as noted, these factors likely function in a synergistic fashion to affect emotional expression (Beidel & Stanley, 1993) and therefore, need to be considered in any efforts to accurately assess anxiety in children and adolescents.

OVERVIEW OF TREATMENTS FOR ANXIETY DISORDERS

It is important to re-emphasize that prior to initiating any intervention, clinicians need to be assured that they have differentiated transient or normal fear responses from true disorders. Furthermore, the design of the treatment plan must include information from multiple informants. Children often overlook impairment or interference that results from their disorder (Langley et al., 2002). Thus, even if they admit somatic distress, they may not recognize how the disorder affects their daily functioning. Thus, interviewing parents, and sometimes even teachers, is important in overall treatment planning. Furthermore, at the risk of becoming repetitive, most of the interventions currently developed for children with anxiety disorders also are downward extensions of successful adult interventions and most empirical data exist for interventions that are cognitive-behavioral in approach. However, in children, cognitive interventions are not the sole intervention; rather cognitive strategies are used in combination with behavioral interventions. It is unclear if this is a conscious decision based on knowledge of children's limited cognitive abilities or simply represents (once again) the downward extensions of adult interventions. The latter explanation appears more parsimonious in light of the fact that the basic literature on the content and processes of cognition in children with anxiety disorders have not been thoroughly investigated. In an extensive review, Alfano, Beidel, and Turner (2002) concluded that the evidence regarding the cognitive aspects of childhood anxiety disorders is inconclusive. Among the issues noted are the significant differences with respect to the existence and types of cognitions reported by children with anxiety disorders (when compared with adults), results that are difficult to interpret due to methodological variance across studies and the issue of clinical vs. statistical significance of reported outcomes. Furthermore, nonspecific cognitive assessment procedures do not allow for an assessment of changes in cognitive process (as opposed to cognitive content), which is the goal of cognitive-behavioral treatment. Finally, among 63 studies of CBT, only 9 studies had tried to determine if changes in children's cognitions were instrumental in the therapeutic process (Powell & Oei, 1991). Thus, it is not clear that cognitive-behavioral interventions are changing the cognitive mechanisms that are hypothesized to underlie, and play an etiological role in, child anxiety disorders.

Others also have addressed developmental considerations that need to be considered when selecting an appropriate intervention for children with anxiety disorders. Schniering et al. (2000) noted that there is a body of literature examining stages of cognitive development, particularly with respect to the capacity for introspection. These data indicate that the capacity for true introspection is not fully developed until adolescence (e.g., Harter, 1990) This finding however, raises the issue of whether young children have the capacity to monitor their own thoughts; a key limitation for CBT interventions that require metacognitive skills such as identification, monitoring and modification of negative thoughts. Kendall and colleagues (e.g., Kendall 1994) have used cartoon thought bubbles in order to help children learn to recognize and report their anxious cognitions (see chapter 6 for a detailed discussion of this intervention). Others (Piacentini & Bergman, 2001), also have noted a number of developmental considerations when attempting to implement CBT with young children. For example, in addition to their less well-developed cognitive abilities, children have poorer recognition and understanding of different emotional states, poorer future orientation, and greater variability in motivation for participating in treatment.

With respect to emotional states, children have only a limited ability to identify and differentiate between emotional states (Izard, 1994). In the social skills training program used for pre-adolescent children with social phobia (Social Effectiveness Therapy for Children-SET-C; Beidel, Turner, & Morris, 2000), participants are initially taught to recognize various facial expressions and to relate these expressions to particular emotions (see chapter 10 for a description of SET-C). Other aspects of emotion also have been the subject of investigation. Southam-Gerow and Kendall (2000) examined aspects of emotional understanding (experiential and metacognitive understanding) in children with anxiety disorders (children with generalized anxiety disorder, separation anxiety disorder, and social phobia) and normal controls. Four skills were assessed: knowledge about the cues for emotions, understanding of multiple emotion combinations (Can one be happy and sad at the same time?), knowledge of hiding of feelings, and knowledge about changing emotions (Can one change his/her feelings?). The results indicate that children with anxiety disorders had a less developed understanding of hiding and changing their emotions. As noted by the authors, these two domains are related to the modulation or regulation of emotion, suggesting that certain aspects of CBT, such as replacing negative thoughts with positive coping statements, might be useful in altering the child's anxious emotional state. This type of direct intervention however, need not be the only manner in which changes in anxiety can be produced. Piacentini and Bergman (2001) note that in young children, limited cognitive maturation results in the exclusive use of behavioral strategies. Strictly behavioral interventions such as SET-C also result in high rates of improvement even among children as young as age 8 (e.g., Beidel et al., 2000).

In a meta-analytic study of outcome studies for CBT, 33 studies included at least one measure of cognitive change (Durlack, Fuhrman, & Lampmann, 1991). These studies covered a range of disorders, not simply anxiety disorders. However, the data are instructive for the purpose of this discussion. Interestingly, in these 33 studies, there was no correlation between cognitive change and behavioral change. Thus, despite the theoretical rationale for these studies, the data do not indicate that cognitive change is either necessary or sufficient for positive behavioral outcome.

Development also needs to be considered when designing the implementation of a particular intervention. Overall, graduated (hierarchical) procedures are more commonly used with children. The rationale for intensive procedures often is difficult to explain to young children and sometimes more difficult for parents to accept. Language that both the child and parent can understand will facilitate acceptance of the rationale and heighten motivation to participate in the intervention. Additionally, because children often do not seek interventions on their own, issues of control become very important. Children often are reluctant to engage in exposure activities out of fear or anger at having to see a therapist, or a feeling that "nothing is wrong" with them. Therefore, engaging children in the development of the treatment program and perhaps (within limits) allowing them some choice in the selection of specific exposure targets, goes a long way toward enlisting their cooperation.

Despite the particular anxiety disorder with which a child might present or the particular intervention that will be used, treatment outcome will be significantly enhanced if both the child and the parent understand, to the best of their ability, the specific disorder and the proposed intervention. Prior to beginning any intervention, time should be devoted to educating the family, including what is known about the disorder (etiology, demographics, clinical presentation), the current available pharmacological and psychosocial treatment outcome data, an overview of the proposed treatment package, the details of the proposed treatment package (including specific procedures and the time commitment), and an assessment of the motivation of the parent and child to participate in the treatment program. Some of these issues may be covered as part of any informed consent procedure but families often are ill-informed about the particular disorder from which their child suffers and thus, the relevance of the intervention for the treatment of a particular disorder often is unclear.

Familial pathology will be discussed in detail in chapter 4 with respect to its influence upon the etiology of childhood anxiety disorders. However, to provide one illustration here, Last and her colleagues (Last et al., 1991) reported that 40% of parents of children with anxiety disorders also had a lifetime history of an anxiety disorder. How does the presence of parental psychopathology play a role in a child's treatment program? In some forms of behavioral intervention for example, parents play a significant role in the treatment plan such as assisting in their child's homework assignments (e.g., a parent may have to take the child to the park to interact with other children). However, if the parent suffers from agoraphobia, the ability to assist the child in completing the homework may be impaired. Thus, treatment may fail because homework assignments cannot be carried out as prescribed.

Also as will be discussed in the chapter on etiology, some parents of anxious children have a tendency to be cautious, avoid taking risks and to reinforce avoidance (Barrett et al., 1996). Particularly for behavioral interventions, such parental behaviors would be counterproductive to therapeutic procedures that attempt to place the child in contact with fearful or anxiety-producing situations. Silverman has referred to this parental behavior pattern as the Protection Trap (Silverman & Kurtines, 1996) and noted the need to work with parents to assist them in understanding that (a) exposure to the feared situation is necessary if intervention is to be effective, (b) like adults, children's anticipatory anxiety often is more intense than anxiety actually experienced when in the distressing situation, and (c) the anxiety experienced during the exposure sessions is rarely as intense as what parents imagine (particularly if a graduated procedure is used). In the latter case, inviting the parents to observe (through a one-way mirror or a videotape) an exposure session will help the parent understand the intervention and decrease their concerns.

In summary, developmental factors play an important role in all aspects of childhood anxiety disorders. As illustrated by the descriptions of Sara and Charlie, age affects the clinical presentation and expression of the disorder, the manner in which assessments can be reliably and validly conducted, and how the interventions are conceptualized and implemented. In the ensuing chapters, these issues will be explored as the specific anxiety disorders are examined.

CHAPTER 4

Etiological Factors in the Development of Anxiety Disorders

Some of the most common questions parents ask when a child is diagnosed with an anxiety disorder pertain to causal factors. "How did this condition develop?" "Is it hereditary?" "Is it because of something I did or didn't do?" Although over the past decade there have been considerable advances in understanding childhood anxiety disorders, as well as in the development of successful treatment strategies, there still is no definitive answer regarding questions of etiology. However, in recent years, there has been substantial advancement in understanding the roles of genetics, neurobiological, and psychological factors in facilitating the development of maladaptive anxiety states. At this juncture, what does appear likely is that there are multiple etiological pathways and that different factors, and sometimes various combinations of factors, are important. The same disorder can develop in different ways in different children. In this chapter, those pathways for which there is the most empirical evidence will be discussed.

PSYCHOLOGICAL AND ENVIRONMENTAL PATHWAYS TO FEAR

Although there are a number of psychological theories about the nature of maladaptive anxiety in children (see King, Gullone, & Ollendick, 1998 for a comprehensive review), perhaps the mechanisms enjoying the greatest empirical support are those described by Rachman (1977), who delineated three pathways to fear acquisition. These include direct conditioning (i.e., the experience of an extremely traumatic episode resulting in fear behavior and anxiety), observational learning (i.e., observing someone else experience a traumatic event or otherwise manifesting fear behavior toward certain stimuli), and verbal information transfer (i.e., receiving information that certain situations are dangerous or should be feared). A fourth mechanism through which fears may be acquired, nonassociative learning (Poulton & Menzies, 2002), recently has been proposed to address the widely held view (for which there are some data) that in some cases fears cannot be traced back to a conditioning experience. Nonassociative theory postulates that some fears have an evolutionary basis because they contribute to species survival. Each of these various mechanisms are discussed and evaluated in turn.

Direct Conditioning

> Ten-year-old Mathew has traveled by air on several occasions and never expressed any fear. In fact, he was always eager to fly. On his last trip, however, as he flew with his parents to Miami, the pilot announced during the descent that there was some trouble with the landing gear and that he would try to "bounce" the gear into place. The flight attendant walked through the cabin, instructing everyone to assume a "brace" position in case of a crash landing. There were a few frightening moments while the pilot tried to bring the gear down. Finally, he was able to land, using only the right landing gear. No one was injured, but Mathew refuses to go on a plane again.

When most adults try to understand the development of fears, they assume that, like Mathew, the child must have had a frightening experience with the object or event now avoided or feared. Similarly, psychological theories of phobia acquisition also have invoked primarily mechanisms of classical or associative conditioning, but of course, in many cases the details are not as obvious as the ones associated with Mathew's fear. Specific details of the conditioning experience are important to the development of fear and its subsequent treatment. To illustrate their importance, consider the following example. A child was frightened by a brown German shepherd. The child develops a fear of large brown dogs, but still may be comfortable with the family's white poodle. In cases like this, the child's fear does not include all dogs but is specific to the type of dog involved in the negative experience.

The acquisition of fears through conditioning mechanisms has been the subject of psychological inquiry throughout the twentieth century. The story of Little Albert (Watson & Raynor,1920) is the best known example of fear acquisition. In this now classic study, Watson and Raynor demonstrated how fear of a white rabbit could be acquired through conditioning principles. The subject was 11-month-old Albert, who had never shown fear of white rabbits. In this case, the white rabbit was the neutral stimulus. Through a series of conditioning trials, the white rabbit was paired with a loud aversive noise (unconditioned stimulus). This noise startled and frightened young Albert. After sufficient pairings of the rabbit and the loud noise, Albert would cry as soon as he was exposed to the white rabbit alone, and would avoid any contact with it (i.e., the white rabbit was now a conditioned stimulus capable of evoking fear). As a result of this series of conditioning trials, Albert developed a fear of white rabbits. In other words, the conditioning experience produced a conditioned fear response. Furthermore, his fear generalized to other white furry objects such as a Santa Claus beard. This research was conducted in the 1920s, and although the methods would not meet today's ethical standards for research, it was a powerful demonstration of how the principles of associative conditioning, derived largely from laboratory animal work, were applicable to humans. Moreover, it illustrated the rapidity of the conditioning process and its rapid generalization to many similar stimuli. Similarly, in the case of Mathew, the conditioned fear response was avoidance, accompanied by indices of sympathetic arousal and emotional distress.

Sometimes a fear, such as Mathew's fear of flying, develops after only a single incident. At other times, as in Albert's case, several repetitions of the conditioning event may be necessary. Thus, a child's fear of dogs, for example, may not develop after a single traumatic (conditioning) episode, but result from the additive effects of several smaller but still frightening encounters with dogs. For example, a dog, in the excitement about visitors coming to the house, may jump on a small child who is visiting at the home. Although the dog merely jumps on the child and then runs away, the child is frightened by the dog's sudden movements. After four or five such greetings by the dog, the child becomes tearful upon entering the house, and clings to his mother. Once the fear develops, it frequently leads to avoidance behavior that can persist for an indefinite period of time. Thus, what is illustrated here is the acquisition of an avoidance response through cumulative conditioning rather than a single aversive episode (see LeDoux & Muller, 1997 for a discussion of this issue).

Watson and Raynor's (1920) study illustrated the onset of fear through the process of classical conditioning and a number of subsequent studies supported this mechanism as at least one avenue for fear acquisition (Delprato & McGlynn, 1984). An important extension of this theory was the two factor theory of learning (Mowrer, 1947) which hypothesized that initially, there is an association between a stimulus and an aversive outcome that results in the acquisition of a fear through classical conditioning. Then, the individual learns that avoidance of the stimulus reduces anxiety and fear. Thus, avoidance behaviors are strengthened through the process of negative reinforcement (i.e., avoidance of the negative stimulus terminates fear and hence reinforces the avoidant response), resulting in a behavior that is shaped by both associative and operant conditioning.

Even with the contribution of Mowrer's (1947) two factor theory, it is clear that traditional conditioning theory cannot account for the acquisition of all fears. Several criticisms of this model have been discussed and are well known. First, aversive events are not found in the histories of all patients with fears or anxiety disorders (e.g., King, Eleonora, & Ollendick, 1998). Second, as Rachman (1990) noted, even under circumstances ideal for the acquisition of fear via an aversive event, some individuals fail to acquire the fear (e.g., DiNardo et al., 1988). Third, this model cannot explain the unequal distribution of fears reported in the general population (Agras et al., 1969). For example, a substantial number of individuals endorse fears of snakes or heights, yet few can report an aversive experience with these stimuli. Fourth, the traditional incremental-decremental conditioning model would suggest that after fear acquisition, subsequent nonreinforced presentations of the conditioned stimulus should result in fear attenuation (as demonstrated in laboratory experiments). For example, a spider bites a child and the child acquires a fear. However, there are many spiders in the child's environment and the child is never bitten again (i.e., there are no more aversive events). Yet, the child's fear does not extinguish but actually increases in intensity. To explain this phenomenon, Eysenck (1979) proposed the concept of incubation whereby fear increases over subsequent, nonreinforced presentations of the conditioned stimulus. Fifth, there is substantial evidence that fears can be acquired through observational learning. A recent review of various etiological studies among children illustrate this point (King, Eleonora, & Ollendick,1998). As depicted in Table 4.1, data from retrospective studies indicate that only a certain percentage of fears could be attributed to associative conditioning or an aversive event. Even within the category of specific phobia, the percentage of parents or children who reported that the child's fears began following an aversive event ranges from a high of 91% to a low of 0%. In fact, as noted by these authors, the most common method of fear acquisition among children appears to be observational learning, to which we now turn our attention.

TABLE 4.1 Etiology of Fears Based on Psychological Theories of Fear Acquisition in Children

Study	Sample Size	Type of Fear	Direct Conditioning	Modeling	Information	Unknown
Doogan & Thomas (1992)	30	Dogs	91%	73%	82%	—
King et al. (1997)	30	Dogs	27%	53%	7%	13%
Graham & Gaffan (1997)	36	Water	0%	0%	0%	100%
Menzies & Clarke (1993)	50	Water	2%	26%	0%	72%
Merckelbach et al. (1996)	22	Spider	41%	19%	5%	46%
Muris et al. (in press)	129	10 common fears	61%	50%	88%	
Ollendick & King (1991)	1,092	10 common fears	37%	56%	39%	

DEVELOPMENT OF FEAR THROUGH OBSERVATIONAL
(VICARIOUS) LEARNING

> Several years ago, Michele's older brother had leukemia and had to undergo several medical procedures, including intravenous chemotherapy. Michele's mother wanted to be in the room when he was being treated. Because she could not always find a baby sitter, Michele often saw her older brother crying whenever he had to have an IV needle inserted to receive the chemotherapy. Now Michele is at the doctor's office and needs a tetanus booster shot. As the nurse approaches, she screams and cries uncontrollably.

In addition to conditioning events in which the child directly experiences some kind of aversive event, fears also can develop through vicarious experiences. For example, if a child observes someone acting fearfully, he or she subsequently may react with fear when in a similar situation. In the above example, her older brother's emotional response was quite evident to Michele. However, there also are clinical examples where fears are acquired even when individuals attempt to hide their emotional response.

> Mrs. Smith brought Jimmy to the anxiety clinic because he was afraid of thunderstorms. He would cry uncontrollably even when there were just a few dark clouds in the sky. During the interview, Mrs. Smith confided that she also was terribly afraid of thunderstorms but she had never spoken of her fear to her son. When Jimmy was interviewed alone, however, we learned that he was well aware of his mother's fear because she sat in a darkened hallway during thunderstorms to reduce the chance of seeing lightning.

Just as in Michele's case, nothing aversive happened to Jimmy, or even to his mother; he only observed his mother's fearful behavior. Furthermore, unlike Michele's brother, Jimmy's mother did not exhibit a strong emotional response. She merely sat quietly in a hallway, away from windows, to reduce her chance of seeing lightning. Even so, Jimmy had a fear of thunderstorms.

Some of the strongest data on observational learning comes from a series of studies by Susan Mineka and her colleagues on fear acquisition in rhesus monkeys. Although there are some difficulties in generalizing from animal behavior to human behavior, these data are an instructive model for fear acquisition through behavioral observation. Rhesus monkeys reared in the wild are afraid of snakes, whereas rhesus monkeys reared in the laboratory show no fear of snakes. This suggests that the fear must be acquired, rather than being biologically based. In a series of carefully controlled laboratory studies, Mineka and Cook (Cook & Mineka, 1991; Mineka, 1987; Mineka & Cook, 1988) arranged for laboratory-bred monkeys (who demonstrated no fear of snakes) to observe wild-bred monkeys behaving fearfully in the presence of a snake.

After observation of the wild-bred monkey, the laboratory-bred monkey was placed in the presence of a snake and began to exhibit fearful behavior. In fact, after only 4–8 minutes of behavioral observation, the laboratory-bred monkey demonstrated fear on both a behavioral and an emotional level. These studies demonstrated that not only can a fear be acquired, but that it can be acquired through observation, and in a very short period of time. Importantly, the monkeys not only acquired avoidance behavior but they also acquired emotional responses similar to those characteristic of human anxiety states. This indicates that not only can the behavior response be acquired in this fashion but also the entire emotional complex as well.

Although vicarious conditioning can explain why some individuals develop fears even though they have not experienced an aversive event directly, it does not answer all of the criticisms of the conditioning theory model of fear development (e.g., fears of some objects are more easily acquired than others). For example, using the same observational conditioning procedure described above, Cook and Mineka (1989) demonstrated that fearful reactions were more easily acquired when laboratory monkeys observed wild monkeys behaving fearfully in the presence of snakes or lizards (fear-relevant objects) than when the monkeys were behaving fearfully in the presence of flowers or rabbits (fear-irrelevant objects). In each case, the videotape of a monkey behaving fearfully in the presence of a stimulus was spliced and edited to assure that the "fearful" monkey's reaction was identical; only the object eliciting the fearful reaction (toy snake, toy lizard, toy rabbit or flower) was different. However, acquisition of fear was stronger when the objects were toy snakes and lizards (than when they were toy rabbits or flowers), suggesting that some stimuli are more subject to conditioning than others. However, it is not clear that these findings are readily transferable to humans. For example, humans are exposed to various types of information regarding their environment such that they may have preconceived notions about certain stimuli. For example, humans begin to learn very early about the danger, and indeed the evilness of snakes. This could make them much more prepared to be conditioned to snake stimuli. Also, the notion of biological preparedness (Seligman, 1971) enjoyed a brief period of consideration. This hypothesis simply stated that through genetic transmission humans are predisposed to be fearful of some objects more than others because they are related to survival. However, this hypothesis lost favor because there were few data to support such a conjecture, and importantly, the model had no predictive value for treatment outcome.

In addition to acquiring fears through observation, other data indicate that prior experiences with a specific object or event can *prevent* the acquisition of fear through a process similar to biological inoculation. Mineka and Cook (1986) demonstrated that prior experiences or information (in the form of prior exposure to "nonfearful" models) could inoculate monkeys against acquisition of fear. Laboratory-bred monkeys were first exposed to other laboratory-bred monkeys behaving nonfearfully in the presence of a snake. Then, these labora-tory-bred monkeys observed wild-bred monkeys who behaved fearfully in the presence of a snake, using the paradigm described above. When the observer monkeys were exposed to the snake, they did not behave fearfully. In other words, acquisition of fear did not occur. This is extremely important because it suggests that psychological and environmental factors might serve to produce fearful states but also environmental factors could be important in preventing them.

As a clinical example, imagine two 4-year-old children, Nicole and Adam. Nicole has a dog and has lots of positive experiences with her dog. Adam does not have a dog and only rarely has he been in the presence of a dog. One day when Nicole and Adam are playing in the park, a large dog runs toward another child and jumps on him. The child cries loudly but is not hurt. Adam and Nicole see this event happen. Now, Adam cries whenever he sees a large dog and says "Doggie jump on me." Nicole does not. Why did Adam develop a fear and Nicole did not? One hypothesis is that Nicole had lots of experiences with her own dog (who might have jumped on her on occasion). Therefore, watching this negative event did not have the same effect on Nicole that it did on Adam (i.e., Nicole's positive experiences with dogs "inoculated" her against the development of fear following this event).

As depicted in Table 4.1, a substantial percentage of individuals with various specific fears indicate that the fear began after a vicarious condition-ing experience, and in some cases, it was the primary agent of onset (e.g., Ol-lendick & King, 1991). Of course, conclusions from these studies are limited by the retrospective nature of the reports. However, there are recent data that directly examine the potential transmission of fear via modeling (vicariously). In one study, the extent to which a mother's open expression of her own fears was related to the severity of her child's fear was examined (Muris, Steernman, Merckelbach, Meesters, & Cor, 1996). Mothers rated their fearfulness on a 3-point scale and children completed a standardized self-report measure of fear. There was a positive relationship between mothers' and children's fearfulness, suggesting that the more open the mother was about expressing her own fears, the greater the level of fearfulness in the child. Although intriguing, further stud-ies using more extensive and standardized assessment, particularly of mothers' fears, are needed before these findings can be accepted as conclusive.

To summarize the theory of vicarious fear acquisition, if a parent fears germs, public speaking, thunderstorms, or anything else, and if the child ob-serves the parent's fearfulness (even if it is passive avoidance as in the case of Jimmy's mother) the child may also acquire the fear. However, characteristics of the model can be very important (e.g., Bandura, 1969). In short, observational learning (modeling) is a very powerful method of fear acquisition. Furthermore, it could be an alternative explanation (in addition to biology, see below) for why fears seem to run in families. For example, if several family members have the same specific fear, or are generally fearful, it may not be because of a particular gene that is transmitted from parent to child, but a result of observational learning from a lifetime of vicarious experiences.

The role of observational learning in the acquisition of fear responses both enhances and complicates understanding of the etiology of childhood anxiety disorders. In some cases, children's phobias might result from firsthand aversive experience. However, they also might result merely because the child has observed someone else behave fearfully (even subtle fearfulness). Observational learning also can be a positive force. By observing others who are not fearful but who cope positively in frightening situations, fears might be prevented and eliminated (Bandura, 1969)

Development of Fear by Information Transfer

> Seven-year-old Jennifer has two older brothers who like to tease her. Over the past several weeks, they have been telling her stories about the bogeyman and monsters that come out at night to hurt little girls. They have been so convincing that Jennifer now will not sleep in her room alone; she has nightmares and cries uncontrollably. Her parents have tried to reason with her, but without success.

The provision of information is a third mechanism through which fears and avoidance behavior might develop. In an elegant study of the impact of parents upon the fearful and avoidant behavior of their children, children with anxiety disorders were presented with a series of ambiguous events designed to tap into social or generally anxious situations (Barrett, Rapee, Dadds, & Ryan, 1996). One such vignette asked the child to imagine walking down the street when he sees a group of children playing a "great game." The child is asked what he would do in that situation. Initially, many children with anxiety disorders indicated that they would attempt to join the group of children and participate in the game. Next, these children were presented with the same situation in the presence of their parents. When queried about their response in the presence of their parents, they again initially said yes. Then parents and children were asked to discuss the situation. Verbatim transcripts of the familial discussion revealed that parents made statements such as "maybe they won't let you play" and "you are not very good at games, you know." After hearing these comments, anxious children were significantly more likely to change their answer in a direction indicating social avoidance of the situation than either control children or those with an externalizing disorder (i.e., rather than indicating they would try to join the group, they indicated that they would avoid the group). This study provides data that clearly indicate that parental behavior (in this case, their verbal comments) exerts substantial control over anxious children's behaviors and may serve to shape or maintain anxious responses. However, it should be noted that questions of etiology cannot easily be addressed by this study inasmuch as the children already were suffering from anxiety disorders. Thus, it cannot be determined if the parents' behaviors precipitated, or were the result of, their child's disorder. In the latter case, because the child was fearful, it is not possible to say that the parental behaviors precipitated the fear onset. Perhaps parents developed these "protective behaviors" as a result of the child's fear and as a mechanism to help their fearful child avoid distressing or frightening situations. High risk studies and longitudinal designs are necessary to disentangle these issues.

Although not high risk or longitudinal data, the results of Barrett et al. (1996) are strengthened by retrospective accounts of adults with anxiety disorders who frequently indicate that their own parents often instructed them about fearful and anxious situations. However, because these data are based on retrospective self-report, it is important to look for validation of these reports using other methods of assessment.

A second literature addressing information transfer examines observational studies of conversations between anxious parents and their children. Overall, the findings from these studies indicate that when discussing argumentative or anxiety-laden topics, anxious parents were observed to be highly critical of their child's behavior (Hirshfeld, Biederman, Brody, Faraone, & Rosenbaum,1997). Furthermore, anxious parents showed less positive regard, less affection, smiled less, and were more critical and catastrophizing (Whaley, Pinto, & Sigman, 1999) than parents of children with no disorder. They also were less likely to encourage psychological autonomy which was described as solicitation of their child's opinion, toleration of differences of opinion, acknowledgment of and respect for the child's view, avoidance of being judgmental or dismissive, encouragement of the child to think independently, and use of explanation and inductive techniques; Whaley et al., 1999). These data provide some confirmation for the retrospective accounts of the interactions of adults with anxiety disorders and their parents. However, there is another issue that merits further consideration. That is, it is not clear if these behaviors characterize all parent–child interactions or only those involving highly emotional or conflictual topics. Thus, it is unclear how anxious and nonanxious parents might differ in their interaction with their children around noncontentious issues.

To further examine the behaviors of anxious and nonanxious parents, Turner, Beidel, Roberson-Nay, and Tervo (2003) constructed a semi-structured interview, the Parent Behavior Interview (PBI) to address aspects of "overprotective parenting." The interview consisted of twenty-five questions that assess both the parents' willingness to allow their children to engage in typical childhood activities (skateboarding, playing contact sports, going to overnight camp, going to school unaccompanied) and their level of comfort when allowing their children to engage in these activities. Based on a factor analysis, four dimensions of activities were identified: Separation from parents, physical activities, dangerous activities, and being away from home. Parents with anxiety disorders were no more likely to restrict their children's participation in any of the activities included in these four factors. However, they were significantly more likely to feel anxious when allowing their children to participate in physical activities (contact sports, gymnastics, climbing trees, amusement rides, skateboarding, or going on a field trip) or when they were physically separated from their children (child slept overnight with friends or relatives, attended summer camp, crossed the street alone, or when the child stayed with a baby sitter). A second part of this investigation involved the actual observation of parent behavior when the child played on playground equipment such as a cargo net and a jungle gym. Whereas parents without an anxiety disorder were more likely to join their children in the physical play activities, parents with anxiety disorders were more likely to sit and watch from a distance. Additionally, parents with anxiety disorders reported a higher level of peak distress while observing their child play on the equipment although they did not prevent their children from engaging in the activities. Interestingly, by their own report, the children did not perceive their parent's distress. Thus, these results do not support the retrospective reports of anxious adults who describe a history of "parental overprotectiveness" and criticism; they do provide one of the first behavioral assessments of parenting behaviors of anxious adults in "normal" rather than emotionally charged situations. In short, it appears that by their own self-report and upon direct behavioral observation, anxious parents do not necessarily inhibit the activities of their children even though they feel significantly more distressed when their children engage in these activities.

The need to instruct children about potential dangers, such as poisonous snakes or mushrooms, swimming during a thunderstorm, or sticking a knife into an electrical outlet is clear, and indeed, it has been suggested that most harm avoidance behaviors of this sort are learned primarily through vicarious and verbal mechanisms (Bandura, 1967). But if these cautions are extended to less dangerous objects or situations, children may develop abnormal fears. Parents, brothers and sisters, or others may make statements that lead to the development of fear. If parents say that getting a shot will hurt or that the bogeyman will come if the child doesn't behave, the child could learn that everyday objects and situations are to be feared.

Nonassociative Fear Acquisition

Although the most prominent views of fear acquisition have involved some form of associative conditioning, the various weaknesses associated with this model (e.g., the nonrandom distribution of fears, spontaneous emergence of fear) have led to the conceptualization of nonassociative theories of fear acquisition. Although discussion of nonassociative approaches have appeared in the literature over the years (e.g., preparedness; Seligman, 1971), they have not become prominent because there has not been an experimental base to support the construct, and variables associated with this approach have not proven useful in treatment. The essence of the nonassociative model is that conditioning experiences are not necessary for the development of fear. Rather, fears of some stimuli are biologically determined and passed down through evolutionary processes because they serve survival purposes for the species. Some of the hypothesized fears falling into this category includes fear of darkness, heights, and strangers. These theories largely are consistent with views expressed much earlier by Charles Darwin (see Poulton & Menzies, 2002 for a more complete discussion). In a cogent review of nonassociative theory, Mineka and Ohman (2002) addressed two of the theory's basic tenets. First, nonassociative theory asserts that retrospective reviews of fear onset indicate that a number of individuals do not report a specific conditioning experience but rather that the fear has "always been there." However, just because an event cannot be recalled does not mean it did not occur. Furthermore, there is an extensive literature demonstrating that retrospective recall is an extremely unreliable method of data collection (Mineka & Ohman, 2002). A second tenet of nonassociative conditioning is that many nonphobics recall relevant associative learning experiences as do phobics. However, there again is an extensive empirical literature demonstrating that there are many experiential and personality vulnerability (and invulnerability) factors that may mediate the impact of the conditioning experience (e.g., Mineka & Cook, 1986; see Mineka & Ohman, 2002 for an extensive rebuttal of this tenet).

One variable that is known to be associated with development of fear is environmental controllability/predictability. In essence, when one has the ability to predict, alter, or otherwise impact their environment, the risk of fear development is lower. For example, 6-month-old rhesus monkeys, who were reared from an early age (2 months) in an environment the permitted them to control the delivery of food, water, and treats, displayed less fear and more exploratory behavior than monkeys who received food, water, and treats on a noncontingent basis or those who were reared without access to this broad variety of reinforcers. The results suggest that less fear could be attributed to their experiences with increased control over environmental events. In summary, although there are still many questions to be answered regarding the etiology of anxiety disorders, unlike the other pathways reviewed above, nonassociative theory currently does not rest on an experimental literature that would support its theoretical contentions.

BIOLOGICAL PATHWAYS TO ANXIETY

There is substantial evidence to indicate that anxiety disorders run in families. If one family member has an anxiety disorder, the percentage of relatives who also will have fears and maladaptive anxieties is significantly higher than the percentage found among relatives of a normal control group (Crowe, Noyes, Persico, Wilson, & Elston, 1988). Among patients treated for specific phobia for example, about 31% of the relatives also have specific phobias (Fyer et al., 1995), a significantly higher percentage than the rate of 11% found among the relatives of normal controls. These figures suggest that specific phobias, like other forms of fear, are more common in some families than in others, although they do not explain the reason why these family clusters occur.

Rates of anxiety disorders among relatives are even more substantial when only parents and children are considered (in contrast to studies that include all available relatives). Among parents with anxiety disorders, available data indicate that approximately 38% of their children also have anxiety (Turner, Beidel, & Costello, 1987). In contrast, among children with anxiety disorders, 70% of parents have abnormal fears compared to 21.3% of parents of children without a disorder (Last, Hersen, Kazdin, Orvaschel, & Perrin, 1991). However, it is important to note that some parents in this sample had a lifetime diagnosis of anxiety disorders but did not meet criteria at the time of the interview. Other data also support the hypothesis of a familial relationship for anxiety disorders (Beidel & Turner, 1997; Mancini, VanAmerigen, Szatmari, Gugere, & Boyle, 1996; Weissman, Leckman, Merikangas, Gammon, & Prusoff, 1984). In general, although the number of relatives who meet criteria for an anxiety disorder is somewhat dependent upon the specific disorder, this familial relationship is well supported. As noted, it is not clear if the basis for the familial relationship is psychological, biological, or some combination of the two. A biological explanation is what often is first considered and the fact that these disorders are familial has led to the hypothesis that anxiety disorders are genetically determined. However, it is important to remember that in most studies, even if more than one family member is fearful, the fears expressed by another family member often are not the same as that of the proband.

> Angela had fears of dying by eating contaminated food. She avoided eating many types of foods and felt that she had to wash repeatedly to avoid germs and contamination. Her father did not have these fears, but he suffered unexpected panic attacks. He also had a fear of crowds and airplanes.

Before turning to the literature on genetic studies, several "high risk" investigations have examined the concept of familiality by assessing the psychophysiological reactivity of the offspring of anxious parents. Using this paradigm, children of parents with anxiety disorders, considered a group at high risk for the development of anxiety disorders, and children of parents with no disorder, are exposed to various stimuli hypothesized to be fear-producing (e.g., loud tones, picture of snakes). Across several studies (Grillon, Dierker, & Merikangas, 1997; Grillon, Dierke, & Merikangas, 1998; Turner, Beidel, &

Epstein, 1991; Turner, Beidel, & Roberson-Nay, in press), offspring of anxious parents displayed physiological responses suggestive of hyperarousal. These behaviors were evident during both tonic and phasic conditions. Although the particular physiological response is somewhat dependent upon the stimuli used and the variable selected for assessment, the results consistently indicate differences when the reactivity of these offspring were compared to offspring of parents without a disorder. Furthermore, the results were consistent regardless of whether or not the offspring of anxious parents had themselves been diagnosed with an anxiety disorder; that is, those children with no disorder but who had a parent with a disorder display the same pattern of reactivity as children with an anxiety disorder. One potential limitation of these data is that to date, few psychiatric control groups have been included in the studies. This limits the conclusions that can be drawn regarding the uniqueness of these results to offspring of anxious parents (rather than being more generally characteristic of offspring of parents with a psychiatric disorder). With respect to this issue, preliminary data (Grillon et al., 1998; Merikangas et al., 1999) reported that this pattern of heightened physiological reactivity was not evident in offspring of parents with alcohol disorders.

Twin Studies

Twin studies are very important in trying to understand the role of family factors in the development of anxiety disorders. When the presence of fear is more common among monozygotic (MZ or identical) twins than dizygotic (DZ or fraternal) twins, these data are taken as an indication that the disorder has a genetic component (Andrews, Stewart, & Allen, 1990; Kendler, Neale, Kessler, Heath, & Eaves, 1992). However, as in the case of the family data presented above, often the specific fears or anxiety disorders of one MZ twin is not the same as the fear or anxiety disorder in the other twin. For example, one twin might experience sudden and unexpected episodes of extreme anxiety including shortness of breath, hyperventilation, dizziness, hot or cold flashes, nausea, and chest pains. The other twin might have a strong fear of speaking in public (e.g., Torgersen, 1983). Thus, what the twin study data seem to suggest is that what appears to be inherited is a tendency to develop anxiety disorders rather than the presence of a specific disorder. If this analysis is correct, one inherits a tendency to be anxious and other factors likely determine the specific expression of the disorder. Such a conceptualization helps to explain why members of families with an anxious proband, and both MZ and DZ co-twins, often do not have the same anxiety disorder. To summarize, anxiety disorders do appear to run in families. However, because relatives concordant for "anxiety disorders" often are not concordant for the same anxiety disorder, it is unlikely that each anxiety disorder per se, can be linked to a specific gene (i.e., a "fear of heights" gene). What is more parsimonious (and more consistent with current data) is the concept known as anxiety-proneness; or a general tendency toward fearfulness and anxiety. Although longitudinal outcome data are necessary prior to drawing firm conclusions, the heightened psychophysiological response seen in offspring of anxious parents may be one manifestation of anxiety proneness, and that may be what is inherited. Data addressing the biological components of anxiety disorders are reviewed.

Neurobiological Predispositional Factors

Neuropsychiatric studies represent a relatively new area of investigation into the etiology of childhood anxiety disorders. As knowledge gleaned from adult studies continues to inform child researchers and as assessments in the form of magnetic resonance imaging (MRI), functional magnetic resonance imaging (fMRI), computed tomography (CT), and positron emission tomography (PET) scans become more available, these technologies are being used to further understand childhood anxiety disorders. A thorough review of the neurological and neurobiological bases of emotion and anxiety is well beyond the scope and aim of this chapter. In this section, some of the main findings to date will be highlighted. Readers interested in a more extensive discussion are referred to Sallee and March (2001) and Vasa and Pine (2004).

Studies of the biology of childhood anxiety disorders may be divided conceptually into two broad areas: neuroanatomy and neurobiology. The available literature is quite small for reasons discussed. With respect to neuroanatomy, MRI studies have examined the structure of various areas of the brain including the amygdala, which has long been associated with complex fear states. However, neuroanatomical studies to date have produced quite mixed results. Larger amygdala volumes have been reported to exist among a small sample of children with generalized anxiety disorder (GAD) when compared to children without a disorder (De Bellis et al., 2000), whereas no differences in amygdala volume were found when children with PTSD as a result of child-maltreatment were compared to children without a disorder (De Bellis et al., 1999). With respect to another area of the brain, children with GAD were found to have larger superior temporal gyrus (STG) volumes than control children. Differences were evident for several specific areas including total STG volume, right and left side STG volume and STG white and grey matter (De Bellis et al., 2002b). Differences in STG volume also has been reported for children with PTSD (as a result of child maltreatment) when compared to children with no disorder (De Bellis et al., 2002a). However, children with PTSD had larger STG grey matter asymmetry (right vs. left) whereas children with GAD had larger STG white matter asymmetry (right vs. left). In another MRI study, children with

OCD have been reported to have larger thalamus volumes when compared to children with no disorder (Gilbert et al., 2000).

Thus, in general, studies of children with anxiety disorders suggest some differences in brain structure. However, the areas where statistically significant differences have been identified are not always consistent across investigations or across specific anxiety disorders. The extant studies have several addition limitations as well. First, the number of children with a disorder included in the studies is quite small, raising questions about the representativeness of the sample. Additionally, in several studies, only twelve or thirteen children were included in the clinical group whereas the number of children in the control group was twice or five times greater (De Bellis et al., 2000; De Bellis et al., 2002b). Uneven group membership often presents problems for parametric statistical analyses, potentially leading to inaccurate conclusions regarding the statistical (and clinical) significance of the findings. A better data analytic strategy would have been to match each child with an anxiety disorder to a suitable control subject and conduct the data analyses using equivalent group sizes. A second limitation of the extant literature is that current MRI strategies assess many possible areas of the brain (sometimes as many as twenty areas are examined) and differences are usually detected in only one or two areas (De Bellis et al., 2000; De Bellis et al., 2002b). This raises the question of experiment-wise error rate, a factor that may explain why different studies report different significant findings. In short, conducting a large number of statistical analyses without controlling for the probability of chance outcomes increases the likelihood of statistically significant, but erroneous, outcomes. A third limitation is that abnormalities in brain structure often are not associated with the child's self-rating of anxiety. For example, there was no significant association between clinical anxiety ratings and amygdala volumes among children with GAD (De Bellis et al., 2000), but there was a significant relationship between STG volumes and child report on an anxiety measure among this same group of children (De Bellis et al., 2002b). In summary, MRI, PET, and CT technologies provide exciting possibilities to understand the interplay of brain and emotion. However, the extant literature is small, fragmented, and inconclusive. Thus, much work remains to be done in order to understand the role of neuroanatomy in childhood anxiety disorders.

As noted, a second broad area of investigation relating to the biological aspects of childhood anxiety disorders is an examination of differences in neurobiological functioning. That is, if anxiety disorders are not due to differences in neuroanatomical structure, perhaps the difference lies in neurobiological functioning. In most instances, assessments of functioning have been conducted using physiologic or pharmacologic challenge paradigms, where children with anxiety disorders and their normal control counterparts are administered a substance believed to induce, or be related to, anxiety. As one example of a physiologic challenge, Pine et al. (2000) administered 5% carbon dioxide (CO_2) to children with anxiety disorders (separation anxiety disorder, generalized anxiety disorder, panic disorder, or social phobia) and children with no psychiatric disorder. The objective was to determine whether breathing CO_2 enriched air would precipitate sensations of panic in children with anxiety disorders. The results indicated that 34% of children with an anxiety disorder met investigator-defined criteria for CO_2 induced panic compared to 2% of the control group. Panic ratings were based on specific questions posed to the children during the CO_2 administration and raters were blind to the children's diagnosis. The results suggest there is something different in the manner in which children with anxiety disorders respond to this aversive stimulus (similar to the finding of the "at risk offspring" reported earlier in this chapter).

An important consideration in interpreting these outcome data is that, in many physiologic challenge studies, the two groups often are different at baseline on a number of the crucial dependent variables. In this particular study, for example, the children with an anxiety disorder had significantly higher baseline self-report ratings of anxiety and panic symptoms (both of which went into the composite rating of panic). A close examination of the data indicate that both groups reported increases in panic symptoms when breathing the CO_2 enriched air, but because of their elevated baseline levels, more of the anxious children reached the panic criterion. In fact, it is not surprising that the anxious group was more likely to meet panic criteria as they started at an elevated anxiety level. This same phenomena of baseline group differences was evident for the physiological variables of tidal volume and respiration rate, suggesting that their higher level of baseline arousal might be a factor in their higher likelihood to experience panic. Using covariance analyses to control for group differences would have allowed a stronger test of the hypotheses.

Pharmacological challenges also have been used to examine group differences in reactivity. In some instances however, the responses of children with anxiety disorders have been found to differ from the responses of adults with this disorder, even when both groups are exposed to the same substance. For example, when administered clonidine, adults with anxiety disorders have a blunted growth hormone (GH) response (see Sallee, Sethuraman, Sine, & Liu, 2000 for a review of this literature). However, blunted GH responses are not characteristic of children with anxiety disorders (Sallee et al., 1998). Similarly, clonidine resulted in increased MHPG response in children with anxiety disorders (Pine et al., 1995 cited in Sallee et al., 2000) whereas decreases in MHPG response are characteristic of adults with anxiety disorders. Why responses differ based on age is unclear although several hypotheses have been proposed.

Yohimbine is another pharmacological substance that has been used in challenge studies. When compared to children without a disorder, the administration of yohimbine to children with panic disorder resulted in increases in self-rated anxiety but no child panicked (Sallee et al., 2000). Anxiety was self-rated at various points during the challenge and similar to the CO_2 challenge, the groups differed in anxiety levels even at the initiation of the challenge. Even though anxiety ratings decreased across the time of the challenge for the normal comparison group and increased for the anxious group, the time by group interaction was not significant. Therefore, like the CO_2 challenge, it is unclear that yohimbine alone was responsible for the group differences in self-reported anxiety, because the groups were different prior to administration of the substance. With respect to the neurobiological (rather than emotional) reactivity, there was a group difference in GH response to yohimbine, with blunting being characteristic of children with anxiety disorders in comparison to the normal control group. Unlike previous findings with other substances, in this instance, yohimbine produced identical responses in children and adults with anxiety disorders (both groups experience a blunted response).

In summary, in comparison to other aspects of childhood anxiety disorders, the number of studies addressing neuroanatomy and neurobiology is quite limited. One reason for the small number is that many investigators do not have access to MRI or PET technology. Also, there are ethical issues regarding the use of invasive assessment strategies such as PET, MRI, and CT scans in children for whom the procedures are not medically necessary. Similar concerns are raised regarding "challenge" strategies such as the administration of carbon dioxide or substances such as yohimbine in children. Pine et al. (2000) followed the children in the CO_2 challenge study for several years in order to determine any long term effects of CO_2 administration (and found none). Many IRBs however, prohibit the use of such invasive strategies when there is no specific therapeutic benefit to the individual child.

In addition to the ethical issues, the literature to date is fraught with many contradictions. Differences based on diagnosis have been discussed above. One striking issue is that the outcome for adult samples often is different from that found for children. In some cases, the findings are directly contradictory, and the most parsimonious conclusion would be that these outcomes are simply random findings. However, Sallee and March (2001) offer an alternative, and very interesting, explanation for the disparate findings. In their review of the literature on stress and its effects on brain structure and functioning, they note that repeated stress, as well as severe or prolonged stress can result, for example, in neuronal death, hippocampal atrophy or decreased hippocampal volumes (see Sallee & March, 2001 for a detailed explanation of the effects of stress on brain functioning). In short, responses seen in childhood may be different in adulthood as a result of the chronic nature of untreated anxiety disorders (obsessive-compulsive disorder, generalized anxiety disorder, posttraumatic stress disorder or social anxiety disorder). Their continued presence could exert substantial psychological stress, which in turn results in changes in neuoranatomy and neuropsychiatric functioning, and the differential resultant reactivity seen in children versus adults with the same disorder.

In summary, it does seem clear that biology plays a role in the etiology of anxiety disorders, but cannot serve as the entire explanation. In fact, biology may be more or less important in any one particular instance. As noted above, psychological and environmental factors also play a role, and sometimes may be even more influential than biology. For example, those who develop post-traumatic stress disorder (see chapter 13) do not always have a prior tendency toward anxiety. An adolescent who enjoyed driving might be involved in a serious car accident; after that, he or she may have continuing nightmares about the accident and begin to avoid driving in an effort to reduce the distress. In this instance, the etiological factors are primarily environmental and psychological.

Anxiety Proneness

If genetics, neuroanatomy, or neurobiology does not result in the development of a specific anxiety disorder, what role does biology play? The most likely mechanism through which biology contributes to the development of anxiety disorders is via the child's "personality or temperamental style." Individuals differ on traits such as fearlessness, nervousness, adventurousness, or inhibition (Caspi, Bem & Elder, 1989) and these traits exist even in very young children (Caspi & Silva, 1995). Among researchers, commonly used terms include *trait anxiety, neuroticism, negative affect, behavioral inhibition,* and *anxiety sensitivity,* all of which describe a tendency for one to respond in an overly emotional fashion to certain situations. In this chapter, use of the term *anxiety proneness* is designed to capture the meaning associated with all of these constructs and describe this tendency.

Anxiety proneness is the potential to respond fearfully, become anxious, or feel threatened in situations that others find relatively harmless, or if found initially fearful, rapid habituation or loss of fear occurs. That is, when made fearful, some individuals adjust and adapt to the fearful stimuli whereas others do not. Those high on anxiety-proneness are more likely to become anxious in stressful situations and they are less likely to habituate when they do become distressed. They also have more of the physical, cognitive (thinking), and behavioral characteristics of fear noted in chapter 1. Also the symptoms of fear occur more often in anxiety-prone children than in other children.

Among the very youngest children, the concept of anxiety-proneness often is usually termed "behavioral inhibition" (BI; Kagan, Reznick, Clarke, Snidman, & Garcia-Coll, 1984). One characteristic of children high in BI is their tendency to become uncomfortable in, and avoid, novel situations (Kagan et al., 1984). These children are often reluctant to engage in activities that might seem novel or adventurous, sometimes to the point of overt avoidance. When placed in these situations, they show high fear in laboratory episodes involving interaction with unfamiliar people and objects. In contrast, children who are not anxiety-prone are less easily frightened, thrive on adventure, readily seek new experiences, and consider fewer situations dangerous. In a series of studies, Kagan and colleagues (Garcia-Coll, Kagan, & Reznick, 1984; Kagan et al., 1984; Kagan, Reznick, & Snidman, 1988; Kagan, Reznick, Snidman, Gibbons, & Johnson, 1988) identified a subset of children who demonstrated the above characteristics of BI. Additionally, when placed in a unfamiliar situations, children with BI had higher heart rates and less heart rate variability. Across time, a number of the children with BI (those with high stable heart rates) were significantly less likely to speak spontaneously and were more likely to have anxiety symptoms. Other investigations have addressed the relationship of BI to anxiety disorders. For example, children with BI were more likely to have social anxiety disorder or avoidant disorder than children without BI (Biederman et al., 2001). The relationship between BI to social anxiety disorder appears specific inasmuch as other anxiety disorders were equally likely to occur among children who did not have BI.

Other investigators also have supported a specific relationship between BI in infants/toddlers and social anxiety disorder in adolescence (Hayward, Killen, Kraemer, & Taylor, 1998; Prior, Smart, Sanson, & Oberklaid, 2000; Schwartz, Snidman, & Kagan, 1999). As noted, the same relationship does not exist between BI and other anxiety disorders such as specific phobia or separation anxiety disorder, suggesting there is something unique about the relationship between BI and social phobia. However, it is important to note that BI is not a necessary precursor for the development of social phobia (or any other anxiety disorder). Although persistently shy children were more likely than other children to have anxiety disorders when compared to children who were occasionally or never shy, 88% of children who had an anxiety disorder at ages 13–14 were not persistently shy as children (Prior et al., 2000).

Still, a number of individuals have hypothesized that BI might be a precursor to the development of anxiety disorders. In addition to the child/adolescent data presented above, others have examined the presence of BI among the offspring of adults with an anxiety disorder. In general, rates of BI are higher among offspring of parents with panic disorder than among psychiatric controls (Battaglia et al., 1997; Manassis, Bradley, Goldberg, Hood, & Swinson, 1995; Rosenbaum et al., 1988; Rosenbaum et al., 2000). However, with respect to anxiety diagnoses in the offspring, it is important to note that few of the children had panic disorder even though their parents did. In fact, as noted above, the disorder that was most common among children with BI was social phobia, although some children with BI also had other disorders such as separation anxiety disorder or specific phobia. Thus, BI may represent a general state of anxious temperament but not necessarily predict the later onset of one particular anxiety disorder (see Turner, Beidel, & Wolff, 1996 for an extensive discussion of this issue). Briefly, although children who are high on the dimension of BI are *more likely* than others to develop anxiety, they are not necessarily *destined* to develop maladaptive fears. Thus, even though a child shows this temperamental style early in life, as noted above, some children do become less inhibited as they mature. Currently, it is not possible to determine exactly which children will "outgrow" their inhibitions, although children who were more likely to remain behaviorally inhibited across a 6-year period were those who had high and extremely stable heart rates (Kagan, Reznick, & Snidman, 1988).

In addition to biological predisposition, several researchers have hypothesized that parents may play an important role in the stability of behavioral inhibition. Toddlers who display consistent inhibition across various environmental settings had mothers who were controlling and warm but not responsive to their children during interactions (Rubin, Hastings, Stewart, Hendersen, & Chen, 1997). In contrast, when parents present their shy and behaviorally inhibited children with opportunities for novelty, particularly novel social situations, they become more comfortable around others (Park, Belsky, Putnam, & Crnic, 1997). When these opportunities are combined with parental encouragement, fearful reactions to new situations (and perhaps the severity of the anxiety proneness itself) decrease (e.g., Asendorpf, 1990). In contrast, children whose parents do not encourage their children to socialize with other children, or whose parents do not provide the specific opportunities, do not appear to outgrow their behavioral inhibition. Likewise, although there are not yet data in support of it, helping an anxiety-prone child determine what is dangerous and what is not, could be useful in decreasing the severity of BI or anxiety-proneness. Thus, although some children may have a biological predisposition to BI or anxiety-proneness, environmental and psychological factors determine how this temperamental style, and therefore specific fears, develop.

SUMMARY

Overall, there is no single explanation for the etiology of anxiety disorders. Even though biological factors often play a very important role, no specific genetic contribution has been identified. In fact, popular media explanations (and sometimes academic publications) oversimplify a very complex process (for example, the idea that anxiety results from an "imbalance in brain chemistry").

Psychological and environmental factors also play an important role in the etiology of anxiety disorders. These factors include direct associative conditioning experiences, observation, communication, parenting practices, and perhaps an environment marked by lack of control and predictability (i.e., an unstable environment). In some instances, these mechanisms work in tandem. For example, having a traumatic experience and watching someone else behave fearfully in the same situation could produce a very severe fearful reaction. Also, anxiety disorders do not necessarily develop after a single conditioning event but can develop from multiple experiences over time. Therefore, an anxiety disorder that emerges after a particular event may not have been produced solely by that event, but may be the cumulative result of many experiences. Similarly, an anxiety disorder need not develop simply because one experiences a traumatic event. Importantly, previous positive experiences with the same "traumatic" object or event may inoculate someone against the onset of a disorder in much the same way that a biological vaccine inoculates one against physical disease. Furthermore, as noted, not every child responds to the same object or event with the same emotions and behaviors. Situations that make some children reluctant, insecure, nervous, and apprehensive, exert little influence on others. Some individuals thrive on danger and adventure; others do not. The facts suggest that some children are more anxiety-prone than others. To date, however, there are no specific data that allow one to predict who will develop anxiety disorders. However, ongoing research may someday allow the ability to detect vulnerable individuals before the onset of the frank disorder. Indeed, the recent study from our laboratory (Turner, Beidel, & Roberson-Nay, in press) revealed that both diagnosed and nondiagnosed children of anxious parents had similar psychophysiological responses to various types of potentially fear producing stimuli, responses that were significantly different from offspring of parents without a psychiatric disorder. A longitudinal study will be needed to determine if these variables have predictive value. Furthermore, the role of parenting is not yet fully understood. More specific data could help improve child-rearing practices, and perhaps aid in developing prevention programs that "immunize" children against the development of fears.

At the beginning of this chapter we noted that parents frequently worry that they may be genetically responsible for their children's fears. Family and family history studies indicate that there may indeed be a biological vulnerability that is transmitted from parents to children. However, at this time, there are no known interventions that can alter genetic makeup. Furthermore, it does not appear that biology alone guarantees or prevents the onset of a disorder. In fact, the most parsimonious explanation at this time is probably that of a diathesis-stress model; even if a child is anxiety-prone, the disorder's onset probably is triggered by the interaction of the biological predisposition with environmental/psychological factors. This chapter also discussed how some environmental factors might play a role in inoculating (preventing) a child against the onset of anxiety disorders. Again, environmental factors, particularly parents, can be a positive factor in the etiology or amelioration of anxiety disorders, regardless of a child's biological predisposition. Throughout the remaining chapters, factors relevant to the onset, maintenance, treatment and prevention of specific fears and anxiety disorders will be discussed.

PART II

ANXIETY DISORDERS IN CHILDREN

CHAPTER 5

Dental Fears,
Medical Fears, and
Chronic Medical Illnesses

Louisa is 9 years old. While staying with her grandmother, she fell off a horse and suffered multiple injuries. It was 2 days until her parents, who were out of the country, could return to be with her. During that time, Louisa had several stressful medical procedures. Although improved, she requires more treatment. Louisa sobs whenever her mother mentions a doctor's appointment. At her last visit, she refused to allow a nurse to take her blood pressure. Louisa has developed a fear of medical procedures.

Visiting the doctor or dentist, being hospitalized, or visiting someone in the hospital are common experiences and almost every child approaches some of these events with a degree of trepidation. Mild fear often can be managed with the help of understanding adults. Louisa's parents were not immediately available, so her story is a little different. However, her emotional distress is not unusual for children who are seriously injured or ill. Even when no serious trauma has occurred, severe medical or dental fears may interfere with needed treatment. In other instances, children with chronic and severe medical illnesses suffer anxiety as a secondary complication of their illness. Finally, some children express somatic complaints that defy an organic basis and exhibit anxious symptomatology. It is these fears that will be the focus of this chapter.

DENTAL FEARS

Dental procedures range from simple examinations, cleaning, restorations, to extractions, and oral surgery. Children may be fearful of any or all of these procedures. Among children aged 4–14, fear of choking was the highest ranked dental fear, followed by fears of injections and then drilling (Melamed

& Williamson, 1991). Childhood dental anxiety has been recognized as problematic for more than 100 years (Steen, 1891, as cited in Townend, Dimigen, &
Fung, 2000) and self-reported prevalence of dental anxiety ranges from 5–19.5%
of the general population (Liddell & Murray, 1989; Milgrom, Fiset, Melnick, &
Weinstein, 1988; Milgrom, Manci, King, & Weinstein, 1995; Murray, Liddell,
& Donohue, 1989; Poulton, Thomson, Brown, & Silva, 1998). Age plays a role
in the frequency with which children report dental fears. Generally, younger
children are more fearful (Melamed & Williamson, 1991), although this general
relationship may be mitigated by the child's oral health. Specifically, younger
children (ages 5–8) with none or few dental caries were two times more likely to
be fearful than older children (ages 8–11). However, severity of dental fear did
not differ by age if children had a substantial number of dental caries (Milgrom
et al., 1995; Townend et al., 2000). Also, some studies report equivalent levels
of dental anxiety for boys and girls (Liddell & Murray, 1989; Milgrom et al.,
1995; Ollendick & King, 1994), whereas other studies indicated higher fear for
girls (Bedi, Surcliffe, Donnan, Barrett, & McConnachie, 1992b; Lidell, 1990;
Wright Lucas, & McMurray, 1980). There is some indication that there may be
an interaction between gender and age, with anxiety increasing over this time
period for girls aged 9 to 12, but not for boys (Murray et al., 1989).

However, it is unclear if this gender difference is real or just the greater
willingness of girls to express fear. Whereas one sample of older girls (ages
11–14) reported significantly more anxiety than other groups (girls aged 7–10,
boys aged 7–10, and boys aged 11–14; Townend et al., 2000), there were no
age or gender differences when fear was assessed by direct observation (i.e.,
ratings by the dentist performing the procedure); an outcome also supported
by others (Melamed & Williamson, 1991). Thus, whereas cultural influences,
both directly and indirectly, either encourage girls to or discourage boys from
openly discussing their emotions, gender differences often disappear when
objective measures are used.

One condition commonly comorbid with dental fear is blood-injury-
illness phobia (BII; see chapter 7). In some cases, complaints of dental anxiety
are based solely on fear of needles (associated with restorative dental care).
However, some individuals have either dental fear or BII and some have both
(Poulton et al., 1998). Among an epidemiological sample of 18-year-olds,
4.7% had dental fear but not BII, 14.3% had BII but not dental fear, and 5.6%
had both dental fears and BII. Both groups with dental fear (with or without
comorbid BII) had a significant greater number of dental fillings but only the
comorbid group had a significantly greater number of decayed tooth surfaces
and a significantly longer average time since the last dental visit, suggesting
greater negative impact for those with multiple fears.

In other cases, children with dental anxiety have elevated trait anxiety
(e.g., Bedi et al., 1992b; Liddell, 1990; Murray et al., 1989) and higher scores
on measures of medical fears, fear of the unknown, and fears of injury/small

animals (Liddell, 1990). Sometimes the existence of a more complicated clinical presentation may predict behavioral avoidance of dental procedures. Children who refused to cooperate with dental treatment also had a fear of medical professionals, were intolerant of any pain or discomfort, did not adapt well to novelty or change, had a more negative general mood, and had difficulty playing with unfamiliar peers (Williams, Murray, Lind, Harkiss, & DeFranco, 1985).

Childhood and adolescence appear to be critical times for the development of dental fears. Among adult dental patients, most (67%) had an onset during childhood (Ost & Hughdahl, 1985). Some (18%) develop dental fears during adolescence, and only 15% had an onset as adults. Dental fears appear to be acquired through the same mechanisms as are other fears; 68% through conditioning, 12% through modeling, 6% through information transfer, and 14% could not identify a specific onset (Ost, 1985). In contrast, when children are interviewed directly, mode of onset data are less clear. Conditioning was reported to be the primary acquisition mechanism in several studies (Liddell, 1990; Milgrom et al., 1995) but not in others (Bedi, Sutcliffe, Donnan, Barret, & McConnachie, 1992a; Klinberg, Berggren, Carlsson, & Noren, 1995). One reason for the discrepancy between adult and child populations is that adult data are based on retrospective self-report whereas child data are usually obtained from actual dental records (Townend et al., 2000).

Trait anxiety or anxiety-proneness may make some children more vulnerable to the onset of fear as a result of aversive events. Among children age 12, general fearfulness appeared to be a predispositional factor, but unpleasant and invasive dental experiences appeared crucial to the development of dental anxiety even for those not generally fearful (Liddell, 1990, Townend et al., 2000). Thus, although general fearfulness may predispose a child to develop fear, an aversive event can precipitate dental fear even in those without this predisposition.

In contrast to the role of classical conditioning, data for acquisition of dental fear by modeling or information transfer is more limited. One study (Bedi, Sutcliffe, Donnan, & McConnachie, 1992b) reported that adolescents with high degrees of dental fears knew other dental phobics, suggesting information transfer as a possible mode of onset. Townend et al. (2000), in a review of the literature, noted that many studies report a consistent link between maternal trait anxiety and child dental anxiety, and although this often has been interpreted as supporting vicarious conditioning, none of the studies reviewed provided evidence that the child actually observed the mother behaving fearfully when undergoing dental procedures. In a carefully controlled investigation, Townend et al. (2000) did not find a significant relationship between (a) maternal dental anxiety and child dental fear or (b) maternal trait anxiety and child dental fear. There was, however, a significant relationship between maternal state anxiety (assessed on the day of the child's dental visit) and child's dental fear. However, this distress was not perceived by the anxious children who rated their mother's "worry" as very low (and not significantly different from the ratings made of the non-anxious children). Thus, the role of modeling and information transfer pathways in the onset of dental fears remains very unclear.

In fact, more than one pathway may be involved in the etiology of dental fears. Direct conditioning experiences and parental modeling factors were significant and independent predictors of the child's severity of dental fear and the relationships remained significant even after controlling for gender, age and other sociodemographic variables (Milgrom et al., 1995). In summary, like other fears, the etiology of dental fears is complex. Aversive events often are assumed to be responsible but these data are usually based on retrospective reports and not actual behavioral observation. Furthermore, it is possible that more than one mechanism might be involved. In the next section, we turn our attention to how environmental influences, such as parental and dental professional responses to a child's expression of fear, can influence the manifestation or the severity of the response.

Factors Which Mediate the Severity of Fear

Once established, the presence or absence of various personal and environmental factors may serve to exacerbate or attenuate the fearful response. In the case of dental anxiety, child temperament as well as parent and medical personnel behaviors have been identified as contributory factors.

Although independent observers were able to detect fear behaviors in parents, children with high dental anxiety did not detect their mothers' high state anxiety (Townend et al., 2000). Specifically, in addition to higher state anxiety, these mothers displayed more agitation, were more likely to ignore their children during the dental procedure, were more likely to make empathic gestures and to provide their children with information about dentistry during the procedures. Thus, although clinical lore suggests that anxious parents may influence their children's distress, this study indicated that the exhibition of anxious (nonverbal) behaviors is not necessarily perceived by their children. However, these parental behaviors could still exert influence over the child's emotional state, even if the children do not label their mother's emotional state as "anxious."

Negative dentist behaviors may exacerbate dental fear. Children and adolescents were nine times more likely to be highly anxious concerning dental treatment if they viewed the dentist as brusque and unfeeling (Milgrom, Vignehsa, & Weinstein, 1992; Townend et al., 2000). Criticism also had a very negative effect on the behavior and anxiety of anxious children aged 4–12 (Melamed et al., 1983). Other studies also support the contention that negative behaviors by dental professionals exacerbate dental fears (Berggren & Meynert, 1984; Eli, Uziel, Baht, & Kleinhauz, 1997; Kleinhauz, Eli, Baht, & Shamay, 1992; Moore et al., 1991). Conversely, positive behaviors can alleviate distress at least to some degree. Dentists can elicit cooperation from children if they are exhibit empathy and provide friendly guidance (Weinstein, Getz, Ratener & Domoto, 1982a, b) and if children know that dentists will respond to their signals of pain (Weinstein & Nathan, 1988). Thus, the behavior of dental professionals may exert a significant influence on the child's behavior but it is unclear if these behaviors actually decrease fear.

As noted in the etiology chapter, children with high trait anxiety and/or high anxiety-proneness may be predisposed to fear development. For example, children with dental fears often report more anxiety about other types of medical procedures, more fears of the unknown (novelty), and more fears of injury (Murray et al., 1989). They also often have a tendency to become anxious more easily and about more situations than other children, and to have a lower pain tolerance. Although parental discussion about an upcoming dental procedure did not mitigate moderate to severe fear (Townend et al., 2000), making the situation more familiar, and therefore less novel, might reduce mild levels of fear. When delivered by a professional, several effective interventions for dental anxiety (see below) are based on this rationale.

Assessment and Treatment of Dental Fears

Usually, dental fear is not difficult to detect. Most children will exhibit behaviors such as tearfulness, somatic complaints, reluctance to go to the dentist's office and refusal to cooperate with instructions of dental professionals. In clinical or research settings, there may be a need to quantify the severity of the child's fear. In such instances, self-report instruments such as the Children's Fear Survey Schedule-Dental Subscale and the Child Dental Control Assessment Scale (see Weinstein et al. 1996) appear to be reliable and valid inventories. Behavioral observational coding systems also are used to quantify behavioral distress but these are used primarily in research settings.

With respect to treatment, Reid (1988) suggested that hypnosis could be helpful but noted difficulties associated with its implementation. First, parents often are reluctant for their children to undergo hypnosis. Second, although useful for minor procedures, it is not recommended for surgical interventions. Also useful for mild fears, distraction in the form of reframing (relabeling "pulling" as "helping it fall out") or attention diversion (watching television, listening to music, having a dental assistant make idle conversation) has been recommended (Reid, 1988). Another strategy to decrease mild levels of fear is called Tell-Show-Do (Reid, 1988). Prior to the procedure, the dentist first tells the patient what he will do, then demonstrates, and only then actually performs the procedure.

Several general recommendations useful in preparing anxious children for dental treatment include setting the right environment (e.g., calm, welcoming, perhaps even "child-friendly"), pinpointing the child's fearful behaviors, providing children with appropriate information about treatment, using a friendly (and perhaps very patient) dental assistant and selectively using parents to distract the child (Melamed & Fogel, 2000). Parents of children with dental fears might benefit from specific training in effective distraction procedures (see Table 5.1 Parental Instructions for Helping Children Cope).

With respect to specific psychosocial interventions, McMurray and colleagues (McMurray et al., 1986) examined locus of control and teaching specific coping strategies for children aged 9–12 with moderate to high dental anxiety. Children were either instructed in the use of cognitive coping strategies or were assigned to a placebo control condition. Those who learned coping strategies had significantly reduced dental anxiety in comparison to the placebo group. In addition, those with a higher internal locus of control had greater decreases in physiological arousal than those with external control. Specifically, the coping strategies program was most effective (i.e., decreased physiological arousal as well as self-report of distress) for those children who perceived themselves able to exert some control over environmental events.

The utility of videotape or film preparation in decreasing dental fear has been examined by several different researchers. In one of the earliest investigations (Melamed et al., 1978), the effect of film preparation on 4–11-year-old

TABLE 5.1 Strategies for Helping Children Cope with Aversive
Dental and Medical Procedures

What Does Not Work
- Multiple reassuring comments from the parent ("don't worry")
- Apologies to the child for having to undergo the procedure
- Giving control of the situation to the child
- Criticizing the child for feeling fearful

All of these behaviors draw the child's attention to the procedure or the pain. Thus, these types of statements should be avoided.

The following procedures can be used to help a child cope:
- Instruct the child to use any coping strategies that were learned specifically for that purpose. Just as we sometimes forget to keep breathing when we are exercising, children may forget to use the coping behaviors once the stress of the medical procedure is upon them.
- Gentle reminders in the form of direct commands are helpful. Do not give the command in the form of a question (Do you think you could start your relaxation now?). Use a direct statement (Start your relaxation now, please.).
- Engage in nonprocedural talk with the child. Discuss school, brothers and sisters, friends, an upcoming vacation, anything other than the procedure. Leave procedural talk to the physician or dentist.
- Use humor with the child; it can be another form of distraction.

---

children undergoing dental treatment was examined. Based on self-report, behavioral observation and physiological indicators of emotion, children exposed to a peer-model videotape (rather than a simple procedural demonstration) reported less anxiety and exhibited fewer disruptive behaviors when undergoing treatment. In fact, active participant modeling (the film model prompts the viewer to practice procedures such as controlled respiration and imagery as they watch the tape) is more effective than symbolic modeling (just watching the tape) in decreasing self-report and behavioral observations of fear in children (Klingman et al., 1984). Furthermore, the children in the active participation group obtained more information from the tape and demonstrated greater reduction in respiration rates.

Summary of Dental Fear Literature

In summary, dental fears and behavior in the dental office have long been used as a paradigm for the study of fearful behavior (Melamed & Williamson, 1991). These data have informed clinicians and practitioners with respect to the etiology of fears and their behavioral management. These data have not only impacted the treatment of dental anxiety but as will be evident below, other medical fears as well.

MEDICAL FEARS

As with dental fears, fears of medical procedures have been a source of concern for health care professionals and mental health professionals for at least the past fifty years (see Broome & Hellier, 1987). As noted by Haggerty (1986) and Melamed (1998), pediatric care has evolved over the past 50 years. Many fewer children suffer what used to be considered common childhood diseases such as measles, mumps, rubella, chicken pox, and polio. Today, the bulk of pediatric medical care is emergency treatment or treatment of children with chronic, life-threatening diseases such as asthma, diabetes, heart disease, and cancer. Thus, research in this area has focused on children's understanding of, and response to, various medical procedures, defined in the broadest possible context ranging from standing on a scale in stocking feet, to stethoscopic examination of heart and lungs, to CT or MRI procedures, to surgery and bone marrow transplantation (Melamed, 1998). Although the percentage of children who are fearful in each setting will vary significantly, it is possible that any of these situations may elicit anxiety. Severe anxiety can result in uncooperative behaviors and interfere with needed medical care. In this section, the literature on medical fears will be reviewed.

Fears of certain medical procedures, such as general anesthesia induction, are quite common among children (Lumley, Melamed, & Abeles, 1993). Younger children appear more fearful of medical procedures than older children or adolescents (Melamed, 1998). For example, younger children are more likely to throw a tantrum and had less tolerance for pain, whereas older children were more likely to groan and flinch (LeBaron & Zeltzer, 1984). Better control over the typical outward expressions of fear may not mean that older children are less fearful. It may be that they are better at hiding their fears from others or perhaps that they have learned to cope in a more sophisticated fashion.

Across preadolescence, medical fears do not appear to differ by age (Broome & Hellier, 1989). Among a sample of children aged 4–10 undergoing anesthesia for surgery, 4–6-year-old children displayed more behavioral and physiological anxiety than did 6–7-year-olds. However, 8–10-year-olds also showed more behavioral and physiological distress than did 6–7-year-olds (Lumley et al., 1993). Cognitive maturity probably accounts for these differences. Specifically, it is typical for young children (aged 4–6) to fear separation and masked strangers, whereas older children (aged 8–10), who have greater cognitive capacity anticipate fear of choking, going to sleep, or pain. In contrast, 6- and 7-year-olds have developed autonomy such that separation and strangers are not problematic. However, their cognitive abilities (particularly with respect to considering the future) have not yet fully developed. In short, they no longer have the fears of younger children, but cannot conceptualize the concerns of older children, thus allowing them to cope more successfully than either the younger or older group. Obviously, this explanation merits further empirical investigation; however, it is consistent with studies of basic cognitive development and the contribution of cognitive development to childhood anxiety disorders discussed in chapter 2.

Age also interacts with the specific content of the medical fear. Younger children are more likely to fear the physical events of medical procedures such as shots, restraints, intrusive procedures (otoscopic exam, temperature taking), and the medical instruments, whereas older children are more likely to be fearful of the long-term consequences (e.g., pain or disfigurement) and their bodily integrity (Broome & Hellier, 1987; Melamed, 1998; Steward & Steward, 1981).

More girls than boys verbally express fears of hospitals (Broome & Hellier, 1987), but both genders show equal levels of fear when objective measures (crying, unwillingness to leave a parent, heart rate increases at the start of anesthesia induction) are compared (Lumley et al., 1993). With respect to ethnicity, there were no differences between African American and white children on a measure of medical fears (Broome & Hellier, 1987). Similarly, Hispanic and Anglo children aged 3–15 who were undergoing either a spinal tap or bone marrow aspiration had equal (and somewhat elevated scores) on the state subscale of the State-Trait Anxiety Inventory for Children as well as on observer ratings of anxiety, pain, and cooperation during the medical procedure. Although the data are limited, there appear to be few differences in medical fears based on gender or ethnicity, at least in the United States.

Most children fear highly stressful medical situations such as venipuncture and anesthesia induction (Lumley, Abeles, Melamed, Pistone, & Johnson, 1990). In addition to the possibility of pain, taped interviews with children in kindergarten through Grade 5 revealed four subcategories of medical fears: intrapersonal fears, interpersonal fears, procedural fears, and environmental fears (Broome & Hellier, 1987). Overall, the five items with the highest fear ratings and the five with the lowest are listed in Table 5.2. Other potentially fearful aspects of medical procedures including unfamiliarity with the medical setting or discomfort associated with specific medical procedures (for example, the operating table, the sound of a saw when a cast is removed, having to stay in an unfamiliar (hospital) bed). Finally, children may become squeamish at the sight of blood or needles that are associated with medical procedures (see chapter 7).

With respect to medical settings, many chronically ill children must undergo repeated uncomfortable and invasive medical procedures (such as lumbar punctures). As noted in the chapter on etiology, repeated "aversive" experiences (even those that are mildly aversive) can lead to the development of fear through a process known as fear incubation (Eysenck, 1976). As children undergo repeated necessary but extensive and painful medical procedures, anxiety and fear may develop, particularly if they fail to cope successfully with the initial procedure (Melamed, 1998). Furthermore, anxiety about medical procedures could develop or be exacerbated as a result of aversive conditioning or if adults reinforce (even accidentally) children's expressions of pain or

TABLE 5.2 Five Most Fearful and Least Fearful Medical Experiences

Child's most feared medical procedures; afraid that:

- Family/friends will catch something I have if I am sick and play with them
- I might have to have an operation if I go to the hospital
- I might get a shot
- Being away from my family if I have to go to the hospital
- Having my finger stuck

Child's least feared medical procedures; afraid that:

- Doctor or nurse might look in my ear
- Doctor or nurse listen to my heart
- I might have to have my temperature taken using a thermometer
- I might have to take medication
- I might have to lie down on the table in the doctor's office

Source: Broome and Hellier (1987).

avoidance behavior, thus increasing the likelihood that the child will continue to express (and perhaps feel) pain. Of course, parents cannot be expected to ignore their children's negative feelings and strategies to teach parents to deal more effectively with these complaints are a crucial element of interventions for decreasing medical fears.

Factors That Mediate the Severity of Fear

Once established, various personal and environmental factors may serve to exacerbate or attenuate the fearful response. For example, with respect to their presence during medical procedures, specific parental behaviors may positively or negatively affect the child's expression of fear (see Friedman, Latham, & Dahlquist, 1998 for an extended review of this literature). Briefly, parental characteristics determine whether they can calm a child or exacerbate the situation. Mothers who displayed agitation prior to their child's medical examination were more likely to ignore their children. In turn, these children displayed more distress during the procedure (Bush & Melamed, 1983). In contrast, parents who were not highly agitated were more likely to interact with their children and to keep them from becoming distressed. Other parental behaviors also may affect their children's expressions of pain and distress. Distracting attention away from the procedure generally decreases the child's distress whereas parental comforting behaviors (intended to decrease distress), actually *increase* distress (Manne, Bakeman, Jacobsen, Gorfinkle, & Redd, 1994). Parental statements, rather than overt behaviors, have the same effect. Reassuring comments or apologies increase distress whereas directives to focus on something else decrease distress.

Parental psychopathology (such as anxiety) is a second factor that might affect children's fear. Although parental displays of dental fear can lead to children's dental fears (Milgrom et al., 1995), it is unclear whether parental anxiety has a significant effect on children's medical fears. Some studies indicate that children who had anxious mothers were more distressed during painful medical procedures than children whose mothers were not anxious (Bush & Melamed, 1983; Greenbaum, Cook, Melamed, Abeles, & Bush, 1988) whereas others reported that anxiety in parents does not always affect children's distress (Pfefferbaum, Adams, & Aceves, 1990). For example, Hispanic parents were more anxious than Anglo parents during bone marrow aspiration or spinal tap procedures but there were no differences between the children's distressful behaviors. A crucial factor may be whether or not parents display anxiety during the procedure, rather than whether or not they feel anxious (Melamed, 1998), although, even when maternal behaviors were easily observed by others, their children did not seem to notice. It may be that it is not necessarily the display of maternal fear that elicits fearful behavior in the children, but maternal–child interactions when in the feared situation that reinforce child fearfulness.

The behavior of health care professionals often can attenuate children's fears. Positive behaviors include encouraging trusting relationships (devising signals to indicate that the child needs a rest period), providing emotional support (reassuring physical touches rather that saying, "This won't hurt.") and giving age appropriate information that will assist in developing coping strategies to be used at appropriate times (Melamed, 1998). With respect to age-appropriate information, sensory information (such as how machines might sound or whether something will be "hot" or "cold") appears to be more effective than general information (Melamed, 1998).

For children, several factors that may negatively influence a child's response to medical procedures (Melamed & Ridley-Johnson, 1988) include: (a) a negative prior experience with a medical procedure, (b) age less than 7 years, (c) a punishing parental style, (d) a parent who copes poorly with stress, and (e) an avoidant coping style. Similar to dental fears, prior experience with surgical procedures may actually serve to increase, rather than decrease, anxiety. Most children exhibit behavioral or physiological anxiety during surgical procedures, but a history of prior surgery and maternal prediction of uncooperative behavior were the best predictors of elevated anxiety at a subsequent surgical procedure (Lumely et al., 1993). Furthermore, elevated anxiety prior to and during surgical procedures, coupled with hospitalization after the surgery (rather than same-day discharge) was related to the development of relatively severe behavioral problems (intense separation anxiety, aggression, sleep problems, apathy, and withdrawal) 2 weeks after surgery. Thus, elevated anxiety can not only affect cooperation during the medical procedure but can be predictive of behavior problems afterward.

Children's expectations regarding medical procedures as well as later recall of the event also may influence their conceptualization of the pain and distress associated with a medical procedure (Cohen, 2001). Fourth-grade African American children were randomly assigned to one of three conditions (typical medical care, distraction procedures, or topical anesthetic). Prior to a three injection vaccination series, they provided ratings of distress associated with the injections. Regardless of treatment condition, children's expectation of distress was significantly higher than their reported actual distress. There was no group difference in level of distress prior to or immediately after the injections. However, children in the distraction or topical anesthetic conditions retrospectively rated the intervention as being significantly superior to the control (typical medical care) in alleviating distress (even though their ratings at the time dispute that assertion) leading the author to conclude that the therapeutic interventions prevented the development of negative recollections about the event.

It is important to note that not all adult behaviors that are meant to be soothing are necessarily calming to children. Children undergoing anesthesia induction were classified according to their predominant temperamental style (approaching or withdrawing) and the effectiveness of parental interventions designed to reduce distress (distraction versus information provision) was examined (Lumley et al., 1990). Distraction was more effective in alleviating distress for children whose predominant temperamental style was characterized by withdrawal. Distraction actually increased distress in children who had an approaching temperamental style. In contrast, information provision was very effective for reducing distress in children with an approaching temperamental style and exacerbated distress in children with a withdrawing style. Thus, although both procedures could be effective, they appear to work best when matched to the child's temperament.

Assessment and Treatment of Medical Fears

Assessment of medical fears is essentially the same as for dental fears. Clinically, informal behavioral assessment is used to determine if children are fearful. In clinical research settings, self-report instruments such as the medical subscale of the Fear Survey Schedule for Children-Revised (Ollendick, 1983) often are used to quantify the extent of fears. Formal behavioral observation scales also are used in research settings.

With respect to intervention, medical fears may appear suddenly, as a result of needed medical treatment as the case for Louisa. In these instances, behavioral avoidance is not an option and in many cases, the child's medical status is such that extensive psychological treatment is impractical. Thus, interventions are brief and designed to prepare the children for the necessary procedure. Immediate behavior management goals include decreasing excessive anxiety, improving procedural cooperation, and hastening physical recovery, whereas long-term goals include teaching coping skills of self-control, maintaining respect for health care professionals and advocating preventative health (Melamed, 1998). An important factor appears to be the age of the child. Because younger children are more fearful of intrusive procedures (Broome & Hellier, 1987) and body-instrument interaction (Steward & Steward, 1981), interventions for this age should include discussion of the purpose of and process involved in particular procedures (Broome & Hellier, 1987).

Timing of the intervention also appears to be important in the preparation of children for procedures such as elective surgery. In one of the earliest studies, Melamed and her colleagues (Melamed, Meyer, Gee, & Soule, 1976) evaluated effectiveness of a child model preparing for surgery. Overall, the modeling film was successful in reducing anxiety. Older subjects (7 and above) benefited most when seeing the film one week in advance of hospitalization, whereas younger children (below 7) needed to see the film immediately prior to hospitalization. If younger children were shown the film 1 week in advance, they were more anxious and sweated more profusely during the admission process one week later. Furthermore, the film was most effective when the model was similar in age, gender, and race to the child observing the film. In a similar study, hospital preparation using slides and audiotapes was not effective, and actually seemed to sensitize very young children or those who had previous negative experiences (Melamed, Dearborn, & Hermecz, 1983). Thus, the importance of a visual model and the time of the intervention appear paramount to the success of the intervention.

Distraction during medical procedures appears effective in alleviating children's fears (Manne, Bakeman, Jacobsen, Gorfinkle, & Redd, 1994; Melamed, 1998). Faust and Melamed (1984) examined two versions of a 10-minute film (hospital-relevant and hospital non-relevant) for the surgical preparation of children aged 4–17. Older children retained more information than younger children and those who saw a hospital relevant film retained more information than those who saw the non-relevant film. Viewing the film the day before surgery decreased fears whereas viewing the film immediately prior to surgery increased physiological arousal (as measure by electrodermal sweating). Interestingly, viewing the non-relevant film immediately prior to surgery appeared to serve as a distraction procedure in that it decreased self-reported fear. These data suggest that the hospital-relevant film was effective in providing important relevant information and decreasing physiological arousal, but the timing of the viewing appears to be very important. Specifically, the film should not be shown immediately prior to surgery.

As with dental anxiety, the use of hypnosis in the preparation of children undergoing bone marrow aspiration has been evaluated (Liossi, 1999). Children aged 5–15 undergoing bone marrow aspiration were randomly assigned to either clinical hypnosis or cognitive behavioral coping skills training (CBT). Children who received either hypnosis or CBT reported less pain and less pain-related anxiety than the control condition. The CBT group reported more anxiety and exhibited more behavioral distress than those in the hypnosis group, although the author concluded that both interventions were effective.

In summary, many of the characteristics of children's fears of medical procedures are similar to dental fears. Younger children display more fear and both genders appear to be equally affected. In many instances however, these fears are not unreasonable. Many of the medical procedures children face are in fact, painful. Thus, the goal is to help children manage their fear (and distress) such that needed procedures can be carried out. In the next section, we examine the prevalence of anxiety disorders in children with documented chronic illnesses.

CHRONIC MEDICAL ILLNESSES

> Jill is 14 years old. She was recently diagnosed with leukemia. Her grandmother recently died from breast cancer and Jill is afraid that she also will die. It has been 2 weeks since her diagnosis and she is experiencing intrusive thoughts, sleep difficulty, and reluctance to leave her parents. She cannot stop worrying that she is going to die.
>
> Now, 1 year later, Jill's cancer is in remission. She is back in school, worrying about boys, grades and typical teenager things. Her medical condition remains under close monitoring by her oncologist and although she worries a little on the night before a medical examination, she appears to be her "normal self" again.

Colds or flus are ubiquitous experiences for children and create very little distress unless the child is forced to miss an event such as a birthday party or field trip. However, chronic physical illnesses, such as asthma or diabetes, do not disappear after a few days as do colds or the chicken pox. In addition, unlike a flu where a child may be bedridden for a few days, chronic disorders (like Jill's) may require a different physical regimen, a different lifestyle, and in some cases restrictions on certain physical activities. So, distress, sadness, and sometimes anxiety may be expected as the child copes with the effects of the illness.

Each year, more than 5 million children in the United States undergo diagnostic procedures that require hospitalization (Drotar, 1981). More than 45% of children under age 7 have been to the hospital and approximately 15% of children have a chronic medical illness. The good news is that children now are surviving illness once considered terminal (leukemia, cystic fibrosis), although they require ongoing medical care (Melamed, 1998).

Jill's behavior represents a common response to a significant physical illness. Most of the time, these emotional responses are of a limited nature. However, in some cases, there are some permanent life changes, and the illness can produce a chain reaction of emotional problems remaining long after the actual medical intervention has ended.

Feelings of anxiety and depression appear to be quite common among children with chronic illnesses, particularly during the initial stages of diagnosis. Among a sample of children diagnosed with diabetes, 64% initially reported some sadness and worry regarding their condition (Kovacs, Brent, Steinberg, Paulauskas, & Reid, 1986). In many instances, children are concerned about the illness and its impact on their activities. However, these depressive symptoms are usually temporary. After an initial adjustment (several weeks to several months), only 14–28% still remained dysphoric and an identical pattern was reported with respect to anxiety symptoms in children (Johnson, Riley, Hansen, & Nurick, 1990; Johnson & Tercyak, 1995). Initial symptoms of anxiety following diagnosis of juvenile diabetes dissipated within 3–4 months. Similar initial but temporary anxiety reactions have been reported for children with asthma (Creer, 1998), cancer (Friedman et al., 1998; Kupst, 1992) and pediatric inflammatory bowel disease (Burke et al., 1989). This pattern of initial, but usually temporary, distress appears to be a characteristic initial response to the diagnosis of a chronic disease.

In many instances, after the initial adjustment period, children with medical disorders do not appear different on measures of psychological functioning than children without these disorders. Children with diabetes did not differ from healthy controls on measures of psychological functioning (Johnson, 1995). Likewise, children with Sickle Cell Disease (SCD) had higher general fear scores than healthy controls (but not higher than their siblings), but there was no significant difference in medical fears among any of the groups. Similarly, children whose cancer was in remission at the time of the assessment reported significantly more noncancer related fears than cancer-related fears (Bull & Drotar, 1991). The most common concerns included school and family issues, which were also the issues most often mentioned by the healthy control children. Children with cancer also expressed some cancer-related issues but these were not their most important concerns.

There does appear to be a subgroup of children who do experience continuing emotional difficulties (Friedman et al., 1998) and there is evidence that chronic disease places some children at higher risk for psychological disorders. Some children with chronic disorders, for example, present with anxious symptomatology that is severe enough to qualify for a diagnosis of an anxiety disorder. Among a sample of children (mean age 11.1–13.2 years) with either Inflammatory Bowel Disease (IBD; Crohn's Disease or Ulcerative Colitis) or Cystic Fibrosis, 4–7% met lifetime diagnostic criteria for panic disorder, 10–29% for phobia, 10–14% for separation anxiety and 7–10% for overanxious disorder (Burke et al., 1989). Anxiety disorders also appeared quite common in a second sample of children with IBD including 40% with SAD, 27% with phobias, 20% with obsessions or compulsions, 13% with overanxious disorder, and 7% with panic disorder (Szajnberg, Krall, Davis, Treem, & Hyams, 1993). However, clinician ratings of children's overall functioning was quite high indicating few, if any, difficulties in daily functioning. Thus, if children had these diagnoses, their impact was quite mild because they did not create significant interference. These rates are somewhat higher than those reported in the general population but still suggest that the majority of children with chronic disorders do not have concomitant psychological disorders. Recently, Ortega and colleagues (Ortega, Huertas, Canino, Ramirez, & Rubio-Stipec, 2002) assessed psychiatric disorders in children with asthma and "other" chronic illnesses (cardiac problems, sickle cell anemia, diabetes). The results indicated that having a history of asthma was associated with an anxiety disorder (any anxiety disorder, separation anxiety disorder, simple phobia, or overanxious disorder) but not an affective disorder or disruptive disorder. Chronic illnesses other than asthma were associated with affective disorders and dysthymia but not anxiety disorders. Children with cancer were not included in this comparative sample because of its life-threatening outcomes. Other studies also suggest that anxiety disorders are common among children with asthma (Bussing, Burket, & Kelleher, 1996; Lehrer, Feldman, Giardino, Song, & Schmaling, 2002; Vila et al., 1999; Wamboldt, Schmitz, & Mrazek, 1998). Furthermore, elevated anxiety and depression have been positively related to asthma severity in children (Mrazek, 1992).

Before assuming that these anxiety disorders are the result of medical conditions, it is important to note that the development of increased anxiety within any one particular disorder may be a function of sociodemographic factors and the particular disease process. At first glance, the literature on pediatric AIDS, for example, appears inconsistent with respect to increased anxiety among those with this disease. Whereas two studies suggested that children with AIDS or who are HIV positive have significantly more behavioral or emotional disturbances, a third study did not find difference in anxiety or depression based on scores of standardized measures (see Armistead, Forehand, & Steele, 1998 for a review of this literature). The authors suggested that one way to explain the disparate study findings was that the three samples differed in terms of SES and method of HIV infection. Specifically, the children who had emotional and behavioral disorders were from lower SES backgrounds and had been infected by vertical transmission from their mothers. Vertical transmission results in a faster disease progression than contamination by blood products, for example. Thus, there were sociodemographic and medical status factors that might provide a more parsimonious explanation for why the sample of children had poorer emotional adjustment than normal controls or other samples of children with the same disorder.

Another factor that must be addressed when considering the issue of anxiety disorders in children with chronic illnesses is that treatment of children with chronic medical illnesses often requires medications that can affect emotional state. For example, higher doses of corticosteriods (commonly used to treat children with asthma) resulted in elevated anxiety and depression, particularly among children with pre-existing emotional problems (see Creer, 1998). Similarly, drugs used to treat chronic gastrointestinal diseases such as ulcerative colitis or Crohn's disease also can affect mood (Burke et al., 1989). Therefore, the possibility of medication side-effects must be carefully considered prior to attributing mood disturbances to the presence of the illness itself.

Treatment of Anxiety
in Chronic Medical Illnesses

The interventions designed for treatment of anxiety in medical illnesses are virtually identical to those that have been presented earlier in this chapter for the treatment of fears of dental and medical procedures. Specifically, strategies designed to assist the family in coping with the effects of the illness are most common. Thus, training parents about the influence of their behavior upon their children's reactions to medical procedures and overall adjustment to the illness consistently appear to constitute the first intervention goal for a variety of chronic illnesses. Another common goal is to return the children to their pre-illness functioning (school, activities; Friedman et al., 1998). Furthermore, because these illnesses often affect parents and siblings, intervention in the form of coping skills training is often offered to other family members as well.

In summary, anxiety and dysphoria are common reactions when children are diagnosed with serious and even life-threatening medical conditions. In many instances however, these reactions dissipate as the medical condition improves. Although only minimal data exist, in many cases the prevalence of anxiety disorders in this group is no different than rates for the general population. However, there do appear to be certain instances where rates of anxiety disorders are higher and the specific reason is not clear. A potential contributory factor is the medications that sometimes are necessary to treat the physical illness. In addition, in some cases, anxiety can create physical illness such as headaches and stomachaches.

Recurrent Abdominal Pain

> Bobby is a 12-year-old boy who complains of stomach pain. Bobby had a benign stomach tumor which required several surgeries. In the last 3 years, he had three operations. Although his physical condition has stabilized, he continues to complain of constant pain. His physician cannot find a physical cause for the stomach pain. When he came to our clinic, Bobby was having several problems, including severe, unremitting stomachaches, nightmares about dying on the operating table, increased worry because of the emotional, medical, and financial consequences of his condition, and academic difficulties due to frequent school absences as a result of stomach pain. Bobby tended to minimize his problems when talking to the therapist. His mother, however, told a different story. Although he was always a little nervous, she noticed a large increase in Bobby's anxiety that started with his surgeries. Bobby also complained of headaches as well as stomachaches.

It is necessary to state at the outset that the lack of a physical explanation for stomach pain is not to deny its existence. Thus, the phrase "it's all in your head" is not descriptive of the pain these children feel and is not useful in helping parents and children deal with the effects of the pain (see section on treatment). However, stomachaches are a frequent somatic complaint among children and often no physical cause can be determined. Among school age children, 13–17% experience weekly abdominal pain (Hyams, Burke, Davis, Rzepski, & Andrulonis, 1996). The term Recurrent Abdominal Pain (RAP) is used to describe stomachaches for which no physical cause can be determined. Not only does RAP produce pain, it also results in functional impairment such as missed school days and increased use of health care resources such as hospital stays, diagnostic tests, and emergency appendectomies (Blanchard & Scharff, 2002; Robinson, Alvarez, & Dodge, 1990; Scharff, 1997).

Phenomenology of RAP

Like childhood fear, RAP appears to commonly exist in the general population. Among the 12% of children in a community survey who reported stomach complaints, 90% had no determined organic cause (Garber et al., 1990). Prevalence rates for RAP range from 9–25% of the general population (Scharff, 1997) and occur worldwide (Boey & Goh, 2001; Olafsdottir, Ellertsen, Berstad, & Fluge, 2001; Hyams, Burke, Davis, Rzepski, & Andrulonis, 1996; Robinson, Alverez, & Dodge, 1990). One reason for this broad range of prevalence rates is that there is no agreed upon definition for RAP. The most common criteria are those of Apley and Naish (1958) who defined RAP as at least three episodes of pain occurring within three months with episodes severe enough to affect the child's activities (see Scharff, 1997 for a review).

There do not appear to be gender differences in the prevalence of RAP among younger children, however among adolescents, more girls report RAP than boys (Blanchard & Scharff, 2002; Hotopf, Carr, Mayou, Wadsworth, & Wessely, 1998; Kristjansdottir, 1996; Stickler & Murphy, 1979). The peak age for RAP appears to be pre-adolescence. After that age, the rate decreases more rapidly for boys than for girls (accounting for the higher prevalence among girls after that age). RAP often is comorbid with other somatic symptoms; 33% of children with RAP also had colic during infancy (Burke, Elliott, & Fleissner, 1999). Hyams et al. (1996) reported that 48–58% of adolescents with abdominal pain had weekly headaches and rates of other comorbid physical diagnoses can range from 14–90% (see Scharff, 1997).

Although the prevalence of RAP appears to decrease with increasing age, follow-up studies indicate that many of those with RAP continue to suffer abdominal distress years later. In a review of this literature, Blanchard and Scharff (2002) examined a number of long-term follow-up studies, which indicated that RAP in childhood is related to (a) continued abdominal pain in adulthood or (b) other somatic symptoms such as chronic headache. With respect to continued complaints of abdominal distress, 24–66% of those initially diagnosed with RAP continued to endorse abdominal pain 5–7 years later (see Scharff, 1997). A 10-year follow-up indicated that 50% of a sample initially diagnosed with RAP had no symptoms at follow-up, whereas 25% continued to have gastrointestinal distress and 25% developed other somatic symptoms (Magni, Pierri, & Donzelli, 1987).

Based on 28–29-year follow-up data, Christensen and Mortensen (1975) reported that 11 of the 18 patients initially diagnosed with RAP continued to have abdominal pain and all 11 reported symptoms consistent with the adult disorder known as Irritable Bowel Syndrome. Another study (Walker, Garber, Van Slyke, & Greene, 1995) suggested that at 5- to 6-year follow-up, only one patient with RAP (out of 31) had a diagnosis of an organic disease that probably accounted for the earlier symptoms, whereas the others continued to suffer from functional gastrointestinal pain. Those with RAP also had higher rates of functional impairment, additional somatic symptoms, and higher rates of health care resources than a general community sample. What is most important for this chapter, however, is that in many cases RAP appears to share characteristics of, and in some cases directly linked to, the presence of anxiety and anxiety disorders.

For those who study and treat anxiety disorders, the most intriguing aspect of RAP is its relationship to anxiety. A number of studies, based on descriptive clinical case reports or chart reviews, reported that children with RAP had more anxiety, depression, and physical complaints than children without RAP (e.g., Olafsdottir et al., 2001; also see Scharff, 1997 for a review of this literature). Those psychiatric disorders, like RAP, appear to continue over time. One long-term follow-up study indicated that children with RAP were significantly more likely to have psychiatric disorders in adulthood (Hotopf et al., 1998). This study used the Present State Examination, a semi-structured interview that quantifies severity of psychiatric distress but is not specific with respect to the type of disorder. Thus, these data indicate the presence of psychiatric disorders but not necessarily the range or type of symptoms present in those with the disorder.

Other investigations have attempted to quantify these descriptive reports through the use of standardized assessment procedures. Among a small sample of children and adolescents with RAP, 72% had a comorbid anxiety disorder and 44% had comorbid depressive disorders (Campo et al., 2004). Walker and Greene (1989) compared children with RAP to children with organically-based stomach pain and a healthy control group. Both groups with abdominal complaints had significantly higher scores on anxiety and depression inventories than the healthy control group. Interestingly, based on parental report, children in the RAP group had significantly higher scores on the Child Behavior Checklist (CBCL) internalizing scale than children in the organic pain group (indicating more anxiety and depression), and in turn children with organic pain had higher scores than children in the healthy control group. However, group differences in internalizing symptoms were not reported by teachers using the Teacher Report Form (TRF). With respect to parental psychopathology, mothers of children with RAP had higher levels of anxiety and depression than the control group but not significantly higher than parents of children with an organic basis for their abdominal complaints.

Garber, Zeman, and Walker (1990) assessed psychological symptoms/disorder in children between the ages of 8 and 17 who had abdominal pain of at least 1 month's duration. The children were divided into either an organic group, a RAP group, a psychiatric comparison group, or normal controls. Using diagnostic interviews, 100% of the children in the RAP group met criteria for a psychiatric disorder as did 91% of these with an organic cause for their stomach pain and for both groups, the predominant diagnoses were overanxious disorder, major depressive disorder and separation anxiety disorder (Garber et al., 1990). These rates were higher than for the healthy control group and not significantly different from the psychiatric control group. Because somatic complaints are part of the diagnostic criteria for these disorders, diagnostic rates were recalculated when complaints of somatic symptoms were excluded. Even so, 81% of the RAP group and 77% of the organic group still met criteria for an anxiety disorder. Children with RAP and psychiatric controls had significantly higher CBCL internalizing scale scores than children with organic pain or healthy controls. However, only the psychiatric controls had significantly higher scores on the CBCL externalizing scale, suggesting that the psychiatric distress of those with RAP was specific to anxious and depressive symptoms and not simply broad psychological distress. Interestingly, mothers of children with RAP also were significantly more anxious than mothers of children with organic pain or mothers of healthy controls whereas there were no differences on measures of fathers' pathology.

As well as a family history of anxiety, gastrointestinal symptoms often are found in the parents or sibling of a child with RAP. Burke et al. (1999) reviewed this literature, concluding that gastrointestinal symptoms (including peptic ulcer disease and irritable bowel syndrome) are more common in families of children with RAP than a healthy control group. Children with RAP often have families who are more pain prone. In addition to a family history of somatic complaints, depression and anxiety are more common in the mothers of children with RAP (Burke et al., 1999), consistent with prior research.

Without a known organic basis and because of its association with anxiety symptoms/disorders, the explanation for the etiology of RAP is usually attributed to "stress." As noted by Walker and her colleagues (Walker, Garber, Smith, Van Slyke, & Claar, 2001) initially, stress was operationalized as negative life events. However, the majority of cross-sectional studies did not document increased life events for children with RAP when compared with children with other disorders (Walker et al., 2001), although prospective studies did find that family negative life events predicted the maintenance of RAP symptoms (see Walker et al., 2001 for details). In contrast to the majority of the literature, two studies (Boey & Goh, 2001; Robinson et al., 1990) reported that children with RAP did have significantly higher rates of negative life events than healthy controls. One reason for the different outcomes is that these two studies compared children with RAP to healthy controls but did not include children with an organic basis for their disorder (as in the majority of the other studies). Furthermore, neither of these two studies identified any one specific event as etiologically related to the onset of RAP, and in the case of Boey and Goh (2001), none of the events (death, hospitalization, changes in home or school circumstances and/or environment) occurred at a frequency greater than 25% for the entire sample. Thus, although the rate of events may have been significantly higher than for children without disorders, overall there was not a high frequency of events. Furthermore what is more significant, is that the frequency of life events does not appear higher than for children with disorders for which there is an organic basis (see Walker et al., 2001).

More recently, these authors (Walker et al., 2001) have re-conceptualized stress in terms of minor daily hassles. Using a sample of children ranging in age from 8 to 15, 154 with RAP and 109 healthy controls, children recorded stressful events three times per day (before, during, and after school). Those with RAP reported significantly more stressors at all three times and were more likely to rate the stressors as more severe (although this finding did not reach the conventional .05 level of statistical significance). Consistent with the earlier literature, children with RAP reported significantly higher levels of other types of somatic symptoms such as headaches. These findings are intriguing although their directionality remains unclear. That is, does the presence of abdominal pain make daily events appear more negative, thus increasing their frequency and severity? Or conversely, does the presence of more frequent and severe minor daily stressors serve to maintain or exacerbate somatic symptoms such as abdominal pain or headaches? Longitudinal studies using at risk populations (perhaps mothers who have had histories of RAP) are necessary to address these issues. Furthermore, as noted by Scharff (1997), the crucial differentiation between children with RAP and those without abdominal pain may not be stressful events or psychological distress but the ability to cope with those events. A recently published study addressing coping responses in children with RAP (Thomsen et al., 2002, see treatment section) provides some initial evidence that this may be a crucial factor

Assessment of RAP

First, a child's complaints of abdominal pain require a physical examination to rule out an organic etiology. Second, if no physical cause can be identified, the circumstances under which the child expresses the complaint need to be considered. Does it occur only in response to certain events? Is it only on school days? When separated from parents? Abdominal pains only in certain situations or when anticipating a certain situation could indicate the presence of any of a variety of anxiety disorders. Third, if the pain does not appear to be related to any one specific event, nonspecific abdominal distress may be a symptom of GAD or perhaps no disorder at all.

Treatment of RAP

In all cases, even if the abdominal distress has no organic basis, the pain itself is still real. As with irrational fears, it is ineffective to try and convince the child that it is "just in the head." Clinicians and parents need to help the child cope with the pain, without rewarding the child's constant expression of somatic distress.

The importance of teaching children how to cope with pain was previously discussed. In a recent study of coping strategies of children with RAP, Thomsen et al. (2002) identified three types of coping and their association to stress, pain, somatic symptoms, and anxiety and depressive symptoms. The results indicated that children who used active coping strategies (problem solving, emotional modulation, acceptance, distraction, positive thinking) had fewer somatic complaints and fewer symptoms of anxiety and depression. Acceptance, distraction, and positive thinking also were associated with less pain. In contrast, passive coping (physiological reactivity, rumination about the pain) or disengagement (escape, inaction) was associated with more somatic symptoms and higher levels of anxiety and depression. The crucial findings from this study are that the most effective strategies include distraction (thinking about happy things rather than pain), positive thinking (telling the self that everything will be all right), acceptance (this is the way it is) and cognitive restructuring (thinking that something will be learned from the situation or that something good will come from it). These strategies, apparently used spontaneously by some children, are the key strategies used to control pain during medical procedures and for the treatment of RAP, and appear to be used spontaneously by children with Generalized Anxiety Disorder (Kendall & Chansky, 1991).

An open pharmacological trial of citalopram for pediatric RAP (Campo et al., 2004) revealed that after 12 weeks of treatment, 84% of the children were judged as treatment responders (48% much improved and 39% were absent any symptom impairment). Statistically significant reductions in child and parent ratings of abdominal pain were evident after 2 weeks. Significant reductions in anxiety were evident at week 1 and for depression at week 2. Although the authors indicate that the study design does not allow one to conclude that the medication's efficacy on RAP was secondary to anxiety or depression, the pattern of results also does not allow this hypothesis to be ruled out. Furthermore, the overall rapid improvement suggests the possibility of a placebo response and also suggests that emotional distress indeed plays a role in the maintenance of RAP. The results of the investigation are encouraging although randomized, controlled trials with sufficient long-term follow-up are necessary.

Although controlled trials of pharmacological interventions for RAP, per se, are not available, in addition to the Campo et al. (2004) open trial, a meta-analysis of antidepressant medication trials for the treatment of adult patients with functional gastrointestinal disorders indicates that these medica-

TABLE 5.3 How to Reinforce Behavior: A Guide for Parents

There are four principles to remember when you want to reward (reinforce) your child.

First, reward the child for the behavior that you want to see. Adults often accidentally reinforce children by paying attention to negative behaviors such as fighting or crying. Any adult attention (even yelling) is a powerful reinforcer for children so adults must be careful which behaviors they reinforce with their actions. Reinforcing brave behavior would mean that you pay attention to the child when he or she is not crying. Use statements such as "It's wonderful that you can be so brave."

Second, reinforcement must be delivered immediately after the behavior occurs (or as soon as possible thereafter). During a medical or dental procedure, comment immediately on the child's brave behavior.

Third, rewards must be delivered consistently. If staying up past the regular bedtime is the reward for cooperating with the physician, then the child must be allowed to do so. Do not promise a reward that you cannot or do not want to deliver. Also, rewards for one behavior cannot be taken away because the child does something *else* that is wrong. Punish the child another way.

Fourth, do not ask for large behavior changes at any one time. Use a procedure psychologists call "shaping." This is another term for successive approximation. You might have used this procedure when you were training an animal to do a trick. You did not expect the animal to perform the entire trick correctly the first time it was attempted. Rather, you rewarded the animal for getting closer and closer to the goal each time. This same principle can be used to change a child's behavior. For example, if a child is very fearful and crying, asking the child not to cry for 10 minutes is asking for too large a change in behavior. Make a game out of it by asking the child to first be brave (not cry, sit still) for 1 minute. Then reinforce the child immediately for accomplishing that small goal. Gradually, the length of time that the child should try to be brave can be increased.

tions appear to be efficacious (Jackson et al., 2000). However, as noted by the authors, whether the improvement is independent of the medication effect on depression merits further evaluation. With respect to other somatic interventions, fiber treatment for children who have RAP and associated constipation, has received equivocal support, with two studies suggesting efficacy whereas a third did not (see Janice & Finney, 1999 for a review). At this time, behavioral interventions for RAP have the most empirical support and appear to be the most promising interventions.

Behavioral treatment of RAP has evolved from using strictly operant procedures to those that combine various approaches. Two early investigations (Miller & Kratochwill, 1979; Sank & Biglan, 1974) both using single case designs indicated that ignoring comments about pain and reinforcing non-pain behaviors decreased the frequency of abdominal pain and pain ratings (also see Blanchard & Scharff, 2002 for a review of this literature). These data have influenced current approaches which combine standard reinforcement principles with more recent elements of cognitive-behavior therapy. Case studies (Finney, Lemanek, Cataldo, Katz, & Fuqua, 1989; Linton, 1986) provided some initial positive results and more recently, a comprehensive program to treat RAP has been developed and evaluated in controlled trials (Sanders et al., 1989; Sanders, Shepherd, Cleghorn, & Woolford, 1994). This six-session intervention combines psychoeducation about RAP and pain management procedures, parent training in contingent social attention and token reinforcement, child training in coping skills/stress management strategies such as relaxation training, distraction, cognitive restructuring, and relapse prevention training. In parent management training, the child's first complaint of pain results in parental instructions to the child to practice stress management procedures. Further comments are ignored and children are reinforced for non-pain behaviors. In two controlled trials, between 55.6% and 75% of children treated with CBT were pain free at the end of treatment, compared to 23.8% and 25% of the control groups. Treatment gains were maintained at 12-month follow-up although even among children in the control group, 37% of the children were pain free (by self-report) and based on parent report, 42% of the children in the control group were pain free. Thus, the superior results of the behavioral treatment is evident, although it is equally clear that in a number of cases, the disorder could remit spontaneously. However, identifying who will remit without treatment has yet to be determined.

> Bobby's reaction to his surgeries was common. However, even after the benign tumor was removed, he continued to express feelings of pain and anxiety. Because Bobby's parents questioned him quite often about whether or not he had a stomachache, and allowed him to skip activities (including school) because of his pain, they appeared to be reinforcing his maladaptive behavior. As noted earlier, adult attention can be a powerful reinforcer, even for negative behaviors (such as pain). As part of the treatment, Bobby's parents were instructed to stop questioning him about whether or not he was experiencing pain and to begin reinforcing him for continuing his activities regardless of the presence of a stomachache. Shortly afterward, the pain and anxiety dissipated completely, and full school attendance was achieved.

SUMMARY

This chapter was devoted to fears that, although quite common in children, are rarely discussed in detail in most volumes on anxiety disorders in children. They were included here because they were the first fears, particularly in the case of dental fears, to be the object of sound empirical investigation. Thus, much of our knowledge about the assessment and treatment of anxiety disorders in children has evolved from the study of dental and medical fears. Also included in this chapter was a review of the prevalence of anxiety disorders in chronic medical illnesses. As noted in this review, increased survival rates for medical disorders previously considered terminal means that many more children are living with the effects of chronic disease. Fortunately, it appears that many of these children suffer what appear to be acute stress disorders which remit with time. Finally, some children present with somatic complaints for which there is no organic basis. In the most common instance, RAP, there are distinct parallels between this disorder and anxiety conditions such as GAD. Although the relationship between RAP and GAD has yet to be fully investigated, there are sufficient consistent parallels to suggest that these disorders may share a common etiological basis.

CHAPTER 6

Excessive Worry and Generalized Anxiety Disorder

Melissa is 9 years old. Her mother brought her to the clinic because several days earlier, Melissa told her mother that she was afraid she was going to die. She thinks that she might die from getting sick and she would "lose everything." She also worries that she might have a heart attack when she's older but "not now." She worries that her mother might die and that her father may get sick. She worries that her parents won't come back when they leave home because something may happen to them. She worries about burglars "a little but not as much as about dying." She also worries about vomiting and choking and, according to her mother, she has had two panic attacks.

Melissa has Generalized Anxiety Disorder (GAD), a common, but poorly understood, childhood anxiety disorder. Interestingly, children with GAD often are regarded as well behaved, eager to please, perfectionistic, and overly mature (Ehrenreich & Gross, 2001). Melissa's worries certainly sound mature for her age. GAD is characterized by excessive anxiety and worry that is difficult to control and is associated with a variety of somatic complaints. Although somatic complaints and cognitive worry are the major components of GAD, they also exist independently and quite frequently in the general population. Thus, before discussing the clinical syndrome of GAD, it is necessary to examine the construct of childhood worry.

CHILDHOOD WORRY

Defined as a cognitive process, worry is characterized by negatively valenced thoughts or images related to potential threats or dangers (Borkovec, 1985). In Vasey's (1993) seminal paper, childhood worry is defined as primarily anticipatory, catastrophic, and self-referential in nature. Because it is cognitively based, consideration of worry in young children must first address the issue of basic cognitive development (see Alfano, Beidel, & Turner, 2002). To phrase it succinctly, some aspects of worry (e.g., the ability to consider the future and therefore to anticipate negative events) are dependent upon basic cognitive maturation. Therefore, worry in children, or even the ability to worry, may be different from worry in adults.

At young ages, children's cognitive capacities are limited. Full capacity to imagine and anticipate future events, for example, appears to develop at age 7 or 8. Whereas 5- to 6-year-olds, for example, worried about threats to their physical well-being, among children age 8 and above, behavioral competence, social evaluation, and psychological well-being were more common (Vasey & Daleiden, 1984). Perhaps even more important, children older than age 8 endorsed a significantly greater number and variety of worries than 5- to 6-year-olds, reinforcing the notion that increased cognitive development leads to a greater capacity for worry (Henker, Whalen, & O'Neil, 1995; Vasey & Daleidin, 1994). As Melissa's case indicates, children as young as age 9 can worry about some future-oriented events, such as a heart attack "when I'm older". Interestingly, to date, studies of the specific worries of children diagnosed with GAD have not been conducted, at least not with respect to developmental changes in their content.

Worry is common among children. In one of the earliest studies, more than 70% of primary school children endorsed 10 or more objects/events about which they worried (Orton, 1982). Among children in Grades 4 through 8, 88% reported at least one worry, and the average number of worries expressed by children was 3.9, most frequently encompassing academics as well as health and safety (Henker et al., 1995). In another nonclinical sample of preadolescent children (Silverman et al., 1995), more than 66% of the children reported at least one worry, most commonly health, school performance, and personal harm. Safety and personal injury were the most frequent worries.

Children classified as highly anxious based on self-report could be distinguished from the other children by a significantly greater number of specific worries and a greater number of areas of worry (Silverman et al., 1995). Furthermore, they worried more frequently. Similar results using a large sample of children and a comprehensive assessment strategy provides further support for this important distinction (Muris, Meesters, Merckelbach, Sermon, & Zwakhalen, 1998). Among nonselected school children aged 8–13, 69% reported that they worried "every now and then." Consistent with findings from other investigations (Silverman et al., 1995; Vasey & Daleidin, 1994), the most common worries were school performance, dying and health, and social contacts. For most children, the mean frequency of their worry was about 2–3 days per week. The level of interference and anxiety elicited by their worry was quite low (none to minimal interference or fear), but the children did note that their worries were difficult to stop. To summarize, while worry itself appears to be common among all children, frequency and intensity of worry may be what distinguishes those who have high anxiety from the "normal" worries of the general population. This conclusion, that frequency and impairment are the distinguishing factors, is consistent with data from comparative studies of children with and without anxiety disorders.

Even among children with psychiatric disorders, worry is not unique to children with anxiety disorders diagnoses. Perrin and Last (1997) assessed worry in children with anxiety disorders, attention deficit hyperactivity disorder, and never psychiatrically ill controls. Infrequent worrying was common among all of the children, including those who had never been diagnosed with an anxiety disorder. However, consistent with the study by Silverman et al. (1995), children with anxiety disorders reported more intense worrying than children in the other two groups, but not more types of worries. Thus, based on the available evidence, it appears that what differentiates normal from pathological worry is not simply the existence of worry itself, but the extent and frequency of worry, and its resultant impact upon daily functioning. When worry does interfere with daily functioning or create somatic distress, intervention is usually necessary. Those interventions that have been successful in the treatment of childhood worry will be presented here.

GENERALIZED ANXIETY DISORDER

As noted at the outset of this chapter, Generalized Anxiety Disorder is defined as excessive anxiety and worry that is difficult to control and is accompanied by various somatic complaints (DSM-IV, APA, 1994; see Table 6.1 for the specific diagnostic criteria). The assignation of the diagnosis of GAD in children is relatively new. Prior to 1994, pervasive and substantive worry was the primary descriptor for Overanxious Disorder (OAD), listed in the "Disorders of Childhood" section of the third edition of the *Diagnostic and Statistical Manual of Mental Disorders* (*DSM-III*, 1980). However, there were numerous problems with this diagnostic category including limited reliability, overdiagnosis, inappropriateness of the specific criteria, lack of distinctiveness from other childhood disorders, uncertain relationship to adult disorders, and lack of external validity (Werry, 1991). The most pertinent issues are discussed here.

Part of the issue with respect to the overdiagnosis of OAD stems from the vagueness of the diagnostic criteria. With respect to the specific content of worries, 31% of a sample of children without anxiety disorders worried about their competence, 23% sought excessive reassurance from their parents, 16% worried about their past behavior, 14.5% reported somatic complaints and 9.8% reported excessive worrying (Bell-Dolan, Last, & Strauss, 1990). Furthermore, 16% reported worrying that harm would befall an attachment figure and 10% worried about self-harm. Concerning the issue of discriminant validity, Beidel

TABLE 6.1 *DSM-IV* Diagnostic Criteria for Generalized Anxiety Disorder

A. Excessive anxiety and worry (apprehensive expectation), occurring more days than not for at least 6 months, about a number of events or activities (such as work or school performance).

B. The person finds it difficult to control the worry.

C. The anxiety and worry are associated with three (or more) of the following six symptoms (with at least some symptoms present for more days than not for the past 6 months). *Note*: Only one item is required in children.
    (1) restlessness or feeling keyed up or on edge
    (2) being easily fatigued
    (3) difficulty concentrating or mind going blank
    (4) irritability
    (5) muscle tension
    (6) sleep disturbance (difficulty falling or staying asleep or restless unsatisfying sleep)

D. The focus of the anxiety and worry is not confined to features of an Axis I disorder (e.g., the anxiety or worry is not about having a Panic Attack (as in Panic Disorder), being embarrassed in public (as in Social Phobia), being contaminated (as in Obsessive-Compulsive Disorder), being away from home or close relatives (as in Separation Anxiety Disorder), gaining weight (as in Anorexia Nervosa), having multiple physical complaints (as in Somatization Disorder) or having a serious illness (as in Hypochondriasis) and the anxiety and worry do not occur exclusively during Posttraumatic Stress Disorder.

E. The anxiety, worry, or physical symptoms cause clinically significant distress or impairment in social, occupational, or other important areas of functioning.

F. The disturbance is not due to the direct physiological effects of a substance (e.g., a drug of abuse, a medication) or a general medical condition (e.g., hyperthyroidism) and does not occur exclusively during a Mood Disorder, a Psychotic Disorder, or a Pervasive Developmental Disorder.

Reprinted with permission from the *Diagnostic and Statistical Manual of Mental Disorders*. Copyright 2000. American Psychiatric Association.

(1991) compared children diagnosed with social phobia, OAD, or no disorder on a variety of clinical measures including self-report inventories, daily diary data, and a psychophysiological assessment, determining skills and anxiety when taking a test or reading aloud. Children with social phobia could be distinguished from normal controls across a variety of measures (lower perceptions of competence, higher trait anxiety, higher anxiety during the behavioral assessment, and significant distress and impairment in daily functioning). In contrast, children with OAD differed from normal controls only by their higher scores on trait anxiety. Finally, with respect to functional impairment (Beidel, Silverman, & Hammond-Laurence, 1996), clinic-referred children with OAD were compared to a community sample who also met criteria for OAD on the presence of specific OAD symptoms, general measures of psychopathology and family environment. The results indicated few differences between the two groups and the differences that did exist represented ancillary, rather than core, features. Specifically, mothers of clinic-referred children endorsed a higher number of OAD symptoms, a higher frequency of mother-reported symptoms of being sick from worrying and often being tense, and finally, a higher number of comorbid diagnoses among the clinic sample. However, there were no group differences in functional impairment. Thus, the clinic-referred sample may present with more severe general psychopathology, but overall, the results supported previous research leading to the conclusion that OAD may not be a clinical syndrome but perhaps a prodromal state.

Based on these data as well as others, OAD was dropped as a separate diagnosis from the most recent revision of the *Diagnostic and Statistical Manual of Mental Disorders* (*DSM-IV*; APA, 1994) and subsumed under the diagnostic category of GAD. Two recent studies examining the validity of GAD in children (Choudhury, Pimentel, & Kendall, 2003; Tracey, Chorpita, Douban, & Barlow, 1997) indicated that there was only poor to fair parent–child agreement for the disorder's presence (κ = .22 or .45) and poor agreement between parent and child with respect to the specific symptoms that comprise the disorder (κs ranged from .20 to .39). Only the OAD symptom of stomachaches had fair parent–child agreement (κ = .49). There was good agreement for the presence of clinical worry (actual κ not reported in the paper). Furthermore, all children with a *DSM-IV* diagnosis of GAD also met criteria for the *DSM-III-R* diagnosis of OAD. Thus, although the issue of reliability remains problematic for this diagnostic category, worry remains its prime clinical feature. Finally, because children who met diagnostic criteria for OAD also meet criteria for GAD and because both disorders include worry and accompanying somatic complaints as primary diagnostic features, data on clinical syndrome and treatment outcome for both diagnostic categories will follow.

Clinical Features

One of the major criticisms of the former OAD diagnostic category was that it often could not be distinguished as a distinct diagnosis. Tracey et al. (1997) reported that children with GAD has a significantly higher number of worries, GAD symptoms, and OAD symptoms than children with another anxiety disorder or children with no disorder. This would be expected inasmuch as the children would not have received the diagnosis without expressing worry and somatic complaints. However, children with GAD also had significantly higher scores on a measure of general anxiety (Revised Children's Manifest Anxiety Scale) and depression (Children's Depression Inventory). Thus, in addition to the specific presence of OAD symptoms, children with GAD also have higher levels of general anxiety and depression when compared to children with other anxiety disorders, thus providing some validity for the diagnostic category.

Although OAD/GAD has received the least amount of attention with respect to determining its prevalence and clinical features, the diagnosis of OAD was fairly prevalent in the general population with rates ranging from 2% to 15.4% in the general population and approximately 10% in child psychiatric clinics (Tracey et al., 1997). In Ontario, 3,294 adolescents were assessed for the presence of OAD (Bowen, Offord, & Boyle, 1990). When the diagnostic threshold required the affirmative endorsement of "often" or "very true" for the presence of each diagnostic criterion, the prevalence rate for OAD was 3.6%. However, if the threshold for diagnosis was loosened, such that "often or very true" was necessary only for the essential items of "excessive or unrealistic anxiety" and "excessive or unrealistic worry" and a criterion of "sometimes" was sufficient for the ancillary diagnostic items, the prevalence rate for OAD rose to 15.3%. As indicated, clinician judgment as to what constitutes "often" or "sometimes" will play a significant role in whether a diagnosis is assigned. Furthermore, the lack of functional impairment criteria means that individual clinicians might rely on their own idiosyncratic criteria by which to determine "often." The lack of operationalized criteria may, in fact, explain the broad range of prevalence rates for this disorder. However, 3.6% is consistent with rates reported from various controlled trials and thus, probably provides a reasonable estimate of the disorder's prevalence in the general population.

Few data exist with respect to the natural course of GAD. Studies examining the stability of OAD reveal that this disorder is unstable over time. In an early study (Cantwell & Baker, 1989) revealed that only 25% retained the diagnosis at follow-up (4–5 years later); 25% were judged to no longer have a diagnosis whereas 50% were diagnosed with a different disorder. Thus, OAD did not appear to be temporally stable. However, the fact that 50% of children originally diagnosed with OAD developed a different disorder during the follow-up period indicates that the symptoms conceptualized as OAD/GAD may not represent a distinct disorder but a subsyndromal state that predisposes the individual to the development of other psychiatric disorders.

Cognitive Symptoms

In the Muris et al. (1998) study on childhood worry, 69% of the children endorsed the presence of worry, but only 6.7% of the sample met diagnostic criteria for GAD or OAD. Children with GAD/OAD could be distinguished from the others on a number of worry variables. For example, those with GAD/OAD reported six specific areas of worry, whereas those without a disorder reported only one area of worry. Additionally those with GAD/OAD worried frequently, suffered more interference from daily activities as a result of their worry, had more anxiety linked to the worry, and had more difficulty controlling the worry.

As noted in the section on worry, it is not content but rather frequency, intensity, and functional impairment that differentiated children with high levels of anxiety (as measured by a self-report inventory of anxiety) from those with low anxiety. A similar conclusion can be drawn with respect to worry among children with GAD. Overall, children with GAD reported an average of 5.74 worries, spanning an average of 4.82 areas (Weems, Silverman, & La Greca,

2000). The most common areas included health, school, disasters, personal harm, and future events. Children's most intense worries were in the area of war, personal harm, disasters, school, and family, whereas the most frequent worries were in the areas of friends, classmates, school, health, and performance. Consistent with the data presented in chapter 3 (e.g., Muris et al., 2002), the worries that children report as most intense are not the worries that occur most frequently. Furthermore, developmental differences appear here as well. Older children (aged 12–16) reported more worries about performance, little things, and appearance than younger children (aged 6–8). When children with GAD were compared to those with specific phobia, there were few group differences in the frequency or content of the worries; children with GAD reported more worries about the future and peer scapegoating, whereas children with specific phobias worried more about the health of others and about the family. There were significant group differences in the total number and intensity of their worries; in both cases, the children with GAD had the higher number of worries and more intense worries.

In two studies of Italian children and adolescents with GAD (Masi, Mucci, Favilla, Romano, & Poll, 1999; Masi et al., 2004), cognitive symptoms (broadly defined by the authors) also appeared to be the predominant complaint. Feelings of tension were the most commonly endorsed (98–100% of the sample), followed by apprehensive expectation (94–95%), need for reassurance (83–86%) and negative self-image (74–90%). Physical complaints were the next most common symptoms (72–75%), suggesting however, that 25–27% of the sample received a diagnosis of GAD without expressing the presence of any physical complaints as defined by these authors. However, feelings of tension might well be considered a physical symptom, in which case, nearly every child experienced the physical symptom of tension. The sensitivity and specificity of the GAD diagnosis appears to be enhanced when one of these "associated" physical features in considered necessary for the diagnosis.

Physical Symptoms

> Melissa's physical symptoms sometimes occur in isolation and sometimes combined in the form of a panic attack. She sometimes experiences heart palpitations, feels very light headed, feels as if she were choking, and worries that she is going to "fall over and die." Melissa gets stomachaches several times per week and headaches about once per week. She sometimes worries that she has phlegm in her throat and frequently, when this happens, she feels that she is unable to breathe.

In addition to excessive worry and subjective anxiety, physical or "associated" symptoms (also called Criterion C; see Table 6.1) are characteristic of GAD. In one sample of children and adolescents (Tracey et al., 1997), restlessness was the associated symptom most frequently endorsed (74% of the sample), followed by irritability (68%), concentration difficulties (61%), sleep disturbance (58%), easily fatigued (52%), headaches (36%), muscle tension (29%), and stomachaches (29%). The data indicated that requiring the endorsement of one associated symptoms as necessary for the diagnosis of GAD maximizes sensitivity and specificity of the diagnosis (Tracy et al., 1997).

In an interesting comparison that provides further validity for the diagnosis of GAD (rather than OAD), Tracy et al. (1997) compared the rate of endorsement of OAD symptoms versus GAD symptoms. Using a sample of children without a diagnosis, only one child (5.5%) endorsed any GAD symptoms whereas 6 children (33%) endorsed OAD symptoms. Although this sample of children without a diagnosis was quite small (n = 18), the results suggest that the diagnostic criteria for GAD result in a reduced frequency of false positives, one of the primary difficulties with the former diagnostic category of OAD.

Sociodemographic Influences on the Expression of GAD

Although GAD can be diagnosed at any age, among children the average age of onset appears to be between 10.8 and 13.4 years (Last, Strauss, et al. 1987; Last, Hersen et al., 1987). With respect to developmental differences, 8- to 12-year-old children had a greater variety and complexity of worries, and a greater capacity to extrapolate on the negative outcomes of their worries than 5- to 6-year-old children (Vasey, Crnic, & Carter, 1994). Several studies reported no significant differences in clinical presentation of GAD/OAD symptoms reported by children versus adolescents (Masi et al., 1999; Strauss, Lease, Last, & Francis, 1988). However, Strauss et al. (1988) reported that older children had more symptoms than younger children whereas no difference in the number of symptoms was reported by Masi et al. (1999). Tracey et al. (1997) examined developmental differences in frequency and type of GAD symptoms in children aged 7–17. There was a significant, but moderate, correlation between child report of the number of symptoms and increasing age, but no differences in the frequency of specific GAD symptoms reported by younger versus older children. However, with respect to the OAD symptoms of stomachaches and headaches, the latter was reported more often by adolescents.

There are few data on gender differences for children with GAD. Children between the ages of 9 and 13 appear to be equally affected by the disorder (e.g., Last et al., 1987). In contrast, in adolescence, many more girls than boys are diagnosed with GAD. This difference appears to be due to a decrease in the number of boys with this disorder rather than an increase in the number of girls with this diagnosis (Velez, Johnson, & Cohen, 1989). Finally, Masi et al. (1999) reported a lack of gender differences based on symptom profiles.

Comorbid and Differential Diagnosis

As noted by Silverman and Ginsberg (1995), differential diagnosis of GAD is complex because of the vagueness of the diagnostic criteria "excessive worry (apprehensive expectation), occurring more days than not for at least six months, about a number of events or activities". Among the earliest studies of comorbidity, 57% of a sample of children with a primary diagnosis of overanxious disorder (OAD) had a secondary diagnosis of another anxiety disorder and 18% received two or more additional anxiety diagnoses (Last, Hersen et al., 1987). More recently, 108 children and adolescents with GAD and with (51%) or without (49%) comorbid depression were compared on other clinical features (Masi, Favilla, Mucci, & Millepiedi, 2000). Overall, there were no differences in comorbidity patterns based on age or gender. Whereas those with comorbid depression endorsed an average of 8.6 symptoms of GAD, those without depression reported an average of 7.8 symptoms, a difference which was significantly different, although probably not clinically meaningful inasmuch as both groups were endorsing a high number of symptoms. With respect to differences among the symptoms that comprise GAD, only complaints of irritability were significantly more frequent among those children with GAD and comorbid depression. Finally, children with GAD and comorbid depression had significantly higher scores on the Child-Global Assessment Scale, indicating a greater degree of functional impairment as a result of their comorbid status.

As noted (Strauss et al., 1988), older children had more symptoms than younger children as well as higher levels of general anxiety and depression. Masi et al. (1999) noted that 62% of their sample with primary GAD had a comorbid depressive disorder (58% of children and 64% of adolescents) whereas 53% (63% of children and 48% of adolescents) had a comorbid anxiety disorder; separation anxiety disorder (21%), specific phobia (29%) or obsessive-compulsive disorder (10%). Comorbid externalizing disorders were rare (9%). Separation anxiety was significantly more frequent among children than adolescents, but there were no differences in the prevalence of comorbid disorders based on gender. In a separate study, children with primary dysthymic disorder with or without GAD (Masi, Mucci, Favilla, & Millipiedi, 2001) were examined on a number of clinical features. Although there was no group difference in the total number of depressive symptoms, suicidal ideation was higher in the comorbid group. Other internalizing disorders also were more frequent in the comorbid group, whereas externalizing disorders were more frequent in the group without comorbid GAD. Among the comorbid cases, the onset of GAD preceded the onset of dysthymia in 60% of the sample and followed dysthymia in the other 40% of the cases.

Neurobiology of GAD

Although there is a small amount of literature addressing the neurobiology of GAD among adults (see Jetty, Charney, & Goddard, 2001 for a review), few studies have examined these factors in children. Furthermore, the interpretation of what data do exist is limited by high rates of comorbidity with other anxiety disorders. Thus, the data are difficult to interpret because it is unclear if the findings are related to GAD or other co-existing disorders.

Using magnetic resonance imaging (MRI), De Bellis et al. (2002) examined amygdala volumes in 13 children with GAD compared to 98 healthy controls. The results indicated that there were no differences between specific brain regions (e.g., intracranial, temporal lobe, hippocampal, and basal ganglia regions) in children with and without GAD. However, those with GAD had significantly larger total white matter as well as gray and white matter superior temporal gyrus (STG) volumes. Furthermore, there was more pronounced right versus left asymmetry in total and white STG matter, leading the authors to suggest that this dysmorphometry may represent a vulnerability to GAD. Two studies (Pine et al., 2000; Sallee, Sethuraman, Sine, & Liu, 2000) have examined the responses of anxious children to biological challenges (CO_2 or yohimbine, respectively). As a group, children with anxiety disorders exhibited greater reactivity to these challenges than healthy controls. However, differences were most prominent in the group of children with Separation Anxiety Disorder. Again, if GAD represents a vulnerability to the development of anxiety disorders, rather than a unique disorder, these results may indicate that reactivity does not occur until after the onset of a unique disorder.

Is GAD a Distinct Disorder?

One of the strongest arguments that GAD may not represent a unique disorder is that it rarely exists in isolation. Among one sample of children with GAD, only 13% (16% of children and 12% of adolescents) had GAD as their only diagnosis (Masi et al., 1999). Also, children with GAD did not have significantly higher scores on a general anxiety scale than children with other anxiety disorders (social phobia, specific phobia, or obsessive-compulsive disorder) as would be expected given that this disorder is one of the few characterized by general overall arousal (Tracey et al., 1997). Furthermore, the overlap is not merely concurrent with other anxiety or mood disorders. In some cases, GAD/OAD may exist as antecedent disorders. For example, the odds ratio for OAD and obsessive-compulsive disorder were significantly elevated for anorexia nervosa, whereas OAD and social phobia were significantly elevated for bulimia nervosa. The authors conclude that OAD (along with social phobia) may reflect underlying personality traits that may represent a general risk factor across various anxiety, affective, and eating disorders (Bulik, Sullivan, Fear, & Joyce, 1997).

Consistent with this hypothesis, some have suggested that GAD (like the construct of behavioral inhibition) actually may be the behavioral manifestation of a temperamental disposition such as neuroticism (Turner, Beidel, & Wolff, 1996). Thus, GAD may be merely the temperamental basis through with interactions with environmental, sociodemographic and cultural factors result in the development of psychopathology (Garrison & Earls, 1987). If this is the case, it would explain why the condition appears to so rarely exist in isolation.

Etiology of GAD

> Melissa's mother dated the onset of her daughter's worrying to a summer picnic when Melissa choked on a hotdog. Although she seemed "fine" for the rest of the summer, she began expressing worry about dying when she started school in the fall.

To date, there are no data specifically addressing the etiology of GAD in children. If, as previously noted, GAD represents an underlying vulnerability, then one might expect that it might be best conceptualized as a biological or constitutional predisposition. In such instances, as in the case of Melissa, the worry that appears to be the hallmark of GAD may represent an exacerbation of an underlying temperamental predisposition rather than the onset of a unique disorder. Thus, an anxious temperamental predisposition may make her more susceptible to a traumatic conditioning event. Also, as in Melissa's case, an event such as choking on a hot dog can, in turn, precipitate an increase in worry. In other words, Melissa's temperament might make her more vulnerable to the development of an anxiety disorder. Unlike children without this predisposition, the worry was not limited to choking and did not dissipate with time, as might be expected if no further events occurred. In Melissa's case, her fear exacerbated (perhaps due to the underlying trait anxiety) into a plethora of broader concerns about her own health and that of her family. In summary, the etiology of GAD is a severely understudied area and the general etiological theories presented in chapter 3 most likely apply to this disorder as it is currently conceptualized.

Assessment of GAD

The same strategies used to assess other anxiety disorders also are useful in the assessment of GAD. Assessment should incorporate multiple methods using various informants and examining a variety of contexts (Morris, Hirshfeld-Becker, Henin, & Storch 2004). Except among the very young, assessment must encompass more that parental report. As noted in chapter 2, agreement on symptoms among parents and children may be only in the moderate range. As one additional example to the information presented in that chapter, Mesman and Koot (2000) reported only small to moderate correlations among child, parent and teacher reports of symptoms of anxiety and depression. Correlations of child and teacher reports were higher than the correlation between parent and child. There may be many different reasons for the low to moderate correlations (see chapter 2), however the important point is that assessment should include multiple methods and multiple informants.

Diagnostic Interviews

In earlier chapters, the importance of diagnostic interviews, both structured and semi-structured formats, have been discussed. Furthermore, as previously stated, the reliability of the diagnosis of GAD is only in the moderate range. However, this should not negate the importance of conducting the interview. In fact, children who are described by their parents as "worrying" often describe a more circumscribed constellation of fears more consistent with separation anxiety disorder or social phobia as opposed to the broader pattern of worry that usually accompanies GAD. Thus, diagnostic interviews may function to clarify the symptom picture for the diagnostician as well as the parent and the child.

Self-Report

Prior to the *Diagnostic and Statistical Manual of Mental Disorders* (APA, 1980), children's anxiety was rarely considered in terms of specific disorders. Instead, anxiety was conceptualized along dimensions or in terms of cognitive and somatic symptoms. For example, the Children's Manifest Anxiety Scale-Revised (RCMAS; Reynolds & Richmond, 1978) assesses three factors: physiological arousal, worry/oversensitivity, and concentration. As noted by Strauss (1988), the scale has good psychometric properties and national normative data. Similarly, the State-Trait Anxiety Inventory for Children (STAIC; Spielberger, 1973) is often used to assess "general" anxiety, in terms of state and trait dimensions. The STAIC has good psychometric properties and differentiates children with overanxious disorder from children without anxiety disorders (see Strauss, 1988). One limitation of these instruments is that they can differentiate children with anxiety from children without psychiatric disorders and children with anxiety disorders from those with externalizing disorders but not between children with anxiety disorders and children with affective disorders, or among children with various types of anxiety disorders (Seligman, Ollendick, Langley, & Baldacci, 2004).

More recently, newer measures of "general anxiety" have been introduced. Rather than addressing cognitive and physical symptoms or the state-trait dimension of anxiety, these measures focus on children's anxious complaints that mirror *DSM-IV* diagnostic categories. The Mulitdimensional Anxiety Scale for Children (MASC; March 1997) assesses a range of anxiety symptoms. It allows the calculation of a total score as well as scores on various subscales (physical symptoms, harm avoidance, social anxiety, separation/panic). The scale has extensive normative data, excellent reliability and a range of validity data including factorial validity, discriminant validity and concurrent validity. The Screen for Child Anxiety Related Emotional Disorders (SCARED; Birmaher et al., 1999) is a self-report instrument that has both parent and child versions. It assesses *DSM-IV* anxiety symptoms, has good psychometric properties in both clinical and community samples and appears to be sensitive to treatment effects (RUPP Anxiety Study Group, 2001). Furthermore, the psychometric properties are consistent for African American and European American samples (Boyd, Ginsburg, Lambert, Cooley, & Campbell, 2003).

The most specific self-report measure of the cognitive component of GAD, worry, is a children's adaptation of the Penn State Worry Questionnaire (Chorpita, Tracey, Brown, Collica, & Barlow, 1997). This scale consists of 14 items that children rate on a 4-point Likert scale. Some of the items include "My worries really bother me; I always worry about something; Once I start worrying, I can't stop." The scale has good internal consistency, is unifactorial, and strongly and significantly correlates with the RCMAS Worry/Oversensitivity subscale, and moderately and significantly correlates with the other RCMAS subscales.

Clinician Ratings

Recently, the Research Units on Pediatric Psychopharmacology Anxiety Study Group (RUPP Group) developed and validated the Pediatric Anxiety Rating Scale (PARS). The PARS was designed for clinicians to assess the severity of anxiety symptoms associated with common *DSM-IV* disorders including social phobia, separation anxiety disorder and generalized anxiety disorder in children. Items were generated from the *DSM-IV* criteria and were reviewed by experts in the field until the pool was reduced to the final 50 items. Nine items assess social interactions or performance situations, 10 items deal with separation, 8 items addressed generalized anxiety, 4 items are allocated to specific phobia, 13 items assess physical signs and symptoms, and 6 items are included in a subscale called "other." Each item is scored as present or absent and then rated (using a 6-point scale) on seven dimensions: number of symptoms, frequency, severity of distress, severity of physical symptoms, avoidance, interference at home, interference out of home. A total score also is calculated. Results of the studies to address the scale's psychometric properties indicate no significant differences based on age or ethnicity (Caucasian vs. Hispanics).

The PARS total score was moderately correlated with other clinician and parent rated measures of anxiety. There were weaker correlations between the PARS and children's self-report measures of anxiety. Preliminary evidence indicates that the PARS total score is a sensitive measure of treatment outcome. As noted by the authors, the PARS fills a gap in the armamentarium for the assessment of children with anxiety disorders. Until the development of this measure, there was no clinician rating scale developed specifically for childhood anxiety disorders (other than for obsessive-compulsive disorder) and clinician assessment was based primarily on adult measures such as the Hamilton Rating Scale for Anxiety (HAMA; Hamilton, 1958) and the generic Clinical Global Impressions Scale (CGI; Guy, 1976).

Physiological Measures

Used almost exclusively in research settings, physiological measures such as heart rate may be very useful in determining the severity of the child's distress. Beidel (1991) reported that children with OAD had higher resting pulse rates than children with social phobia. However, studies of the physiology of children with OAD/GAD are very rare, perhaps in part because of the difficulty in finding children who have GAD without comorbid disorders.

Self-Monitoring

Perhaps the most useful assessment method for diagnostic and treatment planning purposes with respect to GAD is the use of self-monitoring/daily diary methods. Although worry about a number of different situations/events is a hallmark characteristic of GAD in children, careful clarification could reveal a more specific pattern of fears. Melissa was asked to record her worries once per day using a simple recording sheet. One week's worth of monitoring revealed the following range and frequency of Melissa's specific worries and fears:

> That I would choke on phlegm (3 of 7 days)
> That I could not swallow (2 of 7 days)
> That I would stop breathing (2 of 7 days)
> That I would turn blind (1 of 7 days)
> That I would throw up (5 of 7 days)
> That the house would catch on fire (1 of 7 days)

As illustrated, Melissa's fears covered a range of situations. Daily diary ratings can be a valuable addition to the assessment of GAD. Although not without drawbacks (children's compliance with completing and returning the forms), they provide a useful day-to-day picture of the child's worries and are useful in designing and monitoring a comprehensive treatment plan.

Treatment of GAD

To date, there are few pharmacological or psychosocial intervention trials specifically directed at the treatment of children with OAD/GAD. Rather, several large-scale intervention trials had addressed the treatment of anxiety disorders in children and adolescents and have included children with various anxiety disorders in the same sample. In some instances, the results have been analyzed separately for those with OAD/GAD.

Pharmacological Treatment of OAD/GAD

In one of the first pharmacological trials, Simeon and Ferguson (1987) examined the effects of alprazolam in children and adolescents with OAD or avoidant disorder in an open, clinical trial. Fifty-eight percent of the children were significantly or moderately improved as a result of 4 weeks of alprazolam therapy and these gains were maintained during a 4-week, drug-free follow-up. However, the results were not examined separately for children with OAD. In a randomized, placebo-controlled trial (Simeon et al., 1992), 30 children (mean age 12.6 years) with either OAD ($n = 21$) or avoidant disorder ($n = 9$) were treated with alprazolam or matching placebo. Alprazolam appeared superior based on global ratings of anxiety after a 4-week period. However, superiority of alprazolam was not evident on posttreatment evaluator ratings using the Clinical Global Impression (CGI) scales. Furthermore, after drug tapering, there was a trend (albeit nonsignificant) for patients treated with alprazolam to relapse whereas those treated with placebo continued to improve. Thus, the open trial's positive outcome was not replicated in the controlled trial. These negative results, as well as the serious side effects and dose-related complications associated with alprazolam, have led a number of researchers to recommend that benzodiazepines should be considered only as a last resort (Kratochvil, Kutcher, Reiter, & March, 1999; Pine & Grun, 1998; Velosa & Riddle, 2000; Wilens, Spencer, Frazier, & Biederman, 1998).

Selective serotonin reuptake inhibitors (SSRIs) are considered the pharmacological treatment of choice for childhood anxiety disorders. The safety and efficacy data indicate that these medications have high tolerance levels, minimal side effects, and lack of the need for blood level monitoring (Kratochvil, Kutcher, Reiter, & March, 1999; Pine & Grun, 1998; Velosa & Riddle, 2000). In general, side effects are minimal and include headaches, nausea, drowsiness, insomnia, jitteriness, and stomachaches (Velosa & Riddle, 2000), although the recent findings of increase incidence of suicidal ideation among children with depression has lead the FDA to issue a "black box" warning on all commonly used SSRIS. It is unclear how this warning will affect the pharmacological treatment of anxiety disorders in the coming years. Common SSRIs include fluvoxamine (Luvox®), fluoxetine (Prozac®), sertraline (Zoloft®), paroxetine (Paxil®), and citalopram (Celexa®).

In a retrospective study, the effects of fluoxetine (mean dose 25.7 mg/day) in 21 children age 11 to 17 years old who were diagnosed with OAD, avoidant disorder, or social phobia was examined (Birmaher et al., 1994). Based on chart review of nurses and patients' mothers, 6–8 weeks of treatment resulted in 81% of the children being rated as markedly improved in anxiety symptoms. In another open trial treating children with various anxiety disorders, children considered nonresponsive to psychotherapy (aged 9–18 years) were administered fluoxetine (Fairbanks et al., 1997). Similar to Birmaher et al (1994), improvement was apparent at 6–9 weeks, and those without comorbid disorders required lower doses of medication. Because of the small sample size (*n* = 16), results were not examined separately by diagnostic group but overall 81% showed moderate to marked improvement. However, 62.5% of the entire sample still met criteria for an anxiety disorder at posttreatment suggesting that a longer trial or perhaps the addition of a psychosocial intervention might have enhanced treatment outcome.

In a 12-week trial (Birmaher et al., 2003), 74 youth with GAD, separation anxiety disorder, and/or social phobia were randomized to either fluoxetine or matching placebo. At posttreatment, 61% of the fluoxetine group and 35% of the placebo group were rated as much or very much improved according to the treating clinician's CGI ratings. Children with GAD treated with fluoxetine were significantly more likely to be rated as much or very much improved than those treated with placebo (67% vs. 36%, respectively). However, even though improved, at least 50% of the children were still symptomatic at posttreatment, (defined by still having at least three symptoms of anxiety). Furthermore, those children with GAD treated with fluoxetine did not have a significantly better functional outcome (defined as a rating of 70 or higher on the Children's Global Assessment Scale [scores range from 0 to 100]) than those children with GAD who were treated with placebo. Therefore, although anxiety symptoms were improved in the case of those with GAD, this reduction did not translate into enhanced functioning.

In the large multi-center controlled trial known as the RUPP Anxiety Trial, 128 youth (aged 6–17 years) with separation anxiety disorder, social anxiety disorder or GAD were randomly assigned to either 8 weeks of fluvoxamine or placebo (RUPP Anxiety Study Group, 2001). Both groups also received supportive psychotherapy. Fluvoxamine was superior to placebo based on children's scores on the Pediatric Anxiety Rating Scale. Clinicians rated 76% of children treated with fluvoxamine as markedly improved in comparison to 29% treated with placebo. In fact, the fluvoxamine and placebo groups were significantly different at week 3, with differences continuing to increase through week 6, and then were maintained but with no further improvement. Treatment response was poorer for those with a diagnosis of social phobia versus those who did not

(RUPP Anxiety Study Group, 2002). Although not clearly presented, it would appear that, by inference, children with GAD had a better treatment response. However, among patients without social phobia, the placebo response rated was 40% (vs. 24% for those with social phobia). Therefore, those with GAD alone or separation anxiety disorder (SAD) alone appeared to respond to placebo at a higher rate than other diagnostic groups. This casts some concern on the response rate reported for fluvoxamine, if as many as 40% of children with these diagnoses respond to placebo along. Importantly, however, 94% of those who initially responded to fluvoxamine maintained their improvement (RUPP Anxiety Study Group, 2002). One limitation of this double-blind study was that treating clinicians, not independent evaluators, rated both clinical outcome and adverse events. Thus, knowledge of side effects could have biased the clinician ratings of outcome. However, this is a large, well-controlled trial and provides important information on the efficacy of SSRIs for various childhood anxiety disorders including GAD.

Recently, two studies have examined the efficacy of SSRIs specifically for children with GAD. Following a 4–10-day placebo washout period, 156 children and adolescents with GAD were randomized to either venlafaxine or placebo for 8 weeks (Khan & Henderson, 2000). At posttreatment, 64% of those treated with venlafaxine were judged as "much improved" or "very much improved" according to clinician ratings on the Clinical Global Impressions-Improvement Scale compared to 40% for placebo, a statistically significant, but perhaps not clinically significant, group difference. In a 9 week, randomized, placebo-controlled trial of sertraline in 22 children and adolescents with GAD (Rynn, Siqueland, & Rickels, 2001), children treated with sertraline had significantly lower scores on the Hamilton Rating Scale (total score, psychic factor score, somatic factor score) and the Clinical Global Impressions Scale severity score than those receiving placebo. However, it is important to note that during the 2–3 week screening period, 18% of the children originally diagnosed with GAD no longer met the entry criteria. This finding that almost 1 out of 5 children who meet diagnostic criteria at any one time did not do so 2–3 weeks later leads to questions about the validity of this diagnosis. Furthermore, it indicates the need to determine, prior to initiating treatment, that the symptoms are long-standing and not merely a temporary reaction to some type of life event.

In summary, SSRIs may be effective for children with anxiety disorders. However, it is unclear for which disorders they might be particularly, or specifically, efficacious inasmuch as to date, sample sizes have been small and of mixed diagnostic status, and the majority of the evidence for positive outcome is based on a one item clinician rating scale . Furthermore, long-term follow-up data are not available and in many studies, the assessment strategy did not include assessment of functioning. Of course, some of these same issues pertain to the studies of psychosocial trials discussed later.

Psychosocial Treatment of OAD/GAD

In one of the earliest examinations of psychosocial treatment, Kane and Kendall (1989) examined a manualized cognitive-behavioral treatment for four children with OAD. The CBT treatment, Coping Cat Program, encompasses 16–20 individualized treatment sessions with four components: recognizing somatic and cognitive reactions to anxiety, clarifying cognitions in anxiety-provoking situations, developing a coping plan (modifying self-talk, determining which coping activities might be successful), and self-evaluation and self-reinforcement. Behavioral training strategies such as modeling, exposure, role-play, relaxation training, and contingent reinforcement were used as part of the intervention. Using a single-case design, the intervention was effective for these four children.

This initial study formed the basis for a series of randomized controlled trials that have examined the efficacy of this intervention for children and adolescents with various anxiety disorders, including many children with diagnoses of OAD/GAD. In the first randomized trial (Kendall, 1994), children aged 9–13 (with diagnoses of separation anxiety disorder, overanxious disorder, or avoidant disorder) were randomized to either Coping Cat (CBT) program or a wait list control group. At posttreatment, those treated with CBT showed significant improvement on self-report measures of anxiety, coping skills, negative cognitions, and depression when compared to those in the wait list control group. Similar posttreatment differences were found for parent and teacher ratings as well as an overall score on a behavioral observation measure where children were asked to speak for five minutes in front of a camera. Furthermore at posttreatment, 64% of those in the CBT group no longer met diagnostic criteria at posttreatment and treatment gains were maintained 3.35 years later (Kendall & Southam-Gerow, 1996).

A replication study using the same treatment design and the same anxiety diagnoses (Kendall et al., 1997) resulted in a similarly positive outcome for those treated with CBT when compared to a wait-list control group. Additionally, at posttreatment, 53% of those treated with CBT no longer met diagnostic criteria compared to 6% of the wait-list control group. Although specific data were not presented, outcome was reported as similar across the different diagnostic groups. Building on these initial successes, a more recent investigation examined administration of CBT (Coping Cat) in a group versus individual format for children with various anxiety disorders. Despite the manner of treatment implementation, children were significantly improved as a result of the intervention. The measurement strategy was similar to those used in prior investigations. The outcome did not reveal changes in children's social functioning however (e.g., social anxiety, friendships, and social activities), which may suggest that this intervention is more appropriate for those children with GAD rather than for those with social phobia, for example. A recently published 7.4 year follow-up (Kendall, Safford, Flannery-Schroeder, & Webb, 2004) indicated that 90.3% of the children/young adults no longer met criteria of their primary diagnosis. However, because 50% of the follow-up sample received additional treatment (primarily outpatient therapy and/or medication), the long-term effectiveness of this specific intervention is difficult to determine.

Using Kendall's CBT intervention, the additive effects of a family intervention component (CBT+FAM) that included training in reinforcement/contingency management strategies, teaching parents coping techniques to deal with their own emotionality, and communication and problem-solving skills was examined (Barrett, Dadds, & Rapee, 1996). Seventy-nine children with diagnoses of separation anxiety disorder, OAD, or social phobia were randomly assigned to one of three groups: CBT, CBT + FAM, and a wait-list control. Both active interventions (CBT and CBT+FAM) were provided on an individual basis and produced results significantly superior to those in the wait list control group. Between the two active interventions, CBT + FAM was significantly superior to CBT alone. Specifically, 84% treated with CBT + FAM did not meet diagnostic criteria at posttreatment compared to 57% in the CBT group. Among children with OAD/GAD, 81% did not have a diagnosis 6 years later (Barrett, Duffy, Dadds, & Rapee, 2001). Another study (Barrett, 1998) compared the effectiveness of these same interventions but utilized a group format. In the total sample of 60 children, 30 had a diagnosis of GAD. The results indicated that group CBT and group CBT+FAM were significantly superior to wait list control. At posttreatment, 55.9% of the group CBT and 70.7% of the group CBT+FAM no longer met diagnostic criteria and these results were maintained at 12 month follow-up. Unfortunately, the results were not reported separately by diagnostic groups, thus the specificity of the treatment for those children with GAD is not clear, although overall, it appears that the intervention was efficacious.

In an extension of this CBT intervention, Shortt, Barrett and Fox (2001) developed the FRIENDS program, which combines traditional CBT interventions (exposure, cognitive strategies, relaxation, and contingency management), a family-skills component (cognitive restructuring for parents, partner support training, and encouragement to build social networks), with an additional emphasis on the establishment of new friendships and specialized training for children in making internal attributions about their accomplishments. Again using a sample of children with one of several different anxiety disorders including OAD/GAD, 69% of those treated with the FRIENDS program did not have a diagnosis at posttreatment, compared to 6% in the wait list control group. Children in the FRIENDS condition demonstrated significant improvement on self-report measures of anxiety (Revised Children's Manifest Anxiety Scale) and mothers reported a significant decrease in internalizing symptoms. Results were maintained 1 year later. More recently, the social validity of the FRIENDS program has been demonstrated in a series of studies examining its acceptability by parents, its utility for children of non-English-speaking background, and for children who are former Yugoslavian refugees (Barrett,

Moore, & Sonderegger, 2000; Barrett, Shortt, Fox, & Wescombe, 2001; Barrett, Sonderegger, & Sonderegger, 2001; Barrett, Sonderegger, & Xenos, 2003).

Silverman and her colleagues (Eisen & Silverman, 1993, 1998; Silverman et al., 1999a, 1999b) also have examined a cognitive-behavioral treatment of children with anxiety disorders. In the initial trial (Eisen & Silverman, 1993), four children with OAD as defined in *DSM-III-R* were treated using a multiple baseline design that consisted of 6 sessions of cognitive therapy, followed by 6 sessions of relaxation training, followed by 6 sessions of the combination treatment. Exposure also was consistently implemented across all 18 sessions. All children showed significant improvement from pre to posttreatment and gains were maintained at six month follow-up. The combined treatment appeared to result in greater improvement although the greatest response appeared to occur when the intervention was matched to the child's particular symptom profile, for example, using cognitive therapy for a child with cognitive symptoms of worry, using relaxation therapy for a child who has a plethora of physical symptoms, and the combined intervention for those with both cognitive and physical symptoms. In a follow-up investigation (Eisen & Silverman, 1998), four children were randomized to receiving either a prescriptive treatment (cognitive treatment for cognitive symptoms, somatic treatment for physical symptoms) or nonprescriptive treatment (cognitive treatment for physical symptoms or somatic treatment for cognitive symptoms). Using a multiple baseline design, each child received 10 individualized treatment sessions. Across a variety of treatment outcome measures, significantly greater improvement and high end-state functioning was evident when the children received the prescriptive treatments, although there also was improvement in symptoms not logically related to the intervention as well (cognitive interventions produced decrements in the physical symptoms as well). As noted, even though children may meet criteria for a particular disorder, it does not necessarily mean that they endorse each particular symptom that is included in the diagnostic criteria. Thus, there is a need for careful assessment of a child's particular clinical presentation to assure that the selected treatment strategy includes the appropriate interventions.

In a randomized controlled trial, Silverman and her colleagues (Silverman et al., 1999a) examined the utility of group CBT (GCBT) compared to a wait-list control group. The samples included children with social phobia, OAD or GAD. GCBT included 12 weeks of gradual exposure, parent–child contingency management, and cognitive self-control training. At posttreatment, 64% of the GCBT group no longer met criteria for their primary diagnosis compared to 13% of controls. The superiority of GCBT also was confirmed by clinician ratings of severity, as well as parent and child report. Furthermore, treatment gains were maintained at 3, 6, and 12 month follow-up. In a re-examination of these outcome data (Pina, Silverman, Fuentes, Kurtines, & Weems, 2003), Hispanic/Latino and European-American youth achieved equally positive treatment outcomes. Furthermore, long-term follow-up also was equally positive for both groups.

Recently, Ginsburg and Drake (2002) adapted the group CBT treatment used by Silverman and her colleagues (Silverman et al., 1999a) to a school setting. Twelve African American children diagnosed with a variety of anxiety and mood disorders (GAD, social phobia, specific phobia, agoraphobia, major depressive disorder; most children had more than one disorder) participated in a school based program that included psychoeducation, relaxation training, cognitive restructuring, and graduated in vivo exposure. Children were randomly assigned to CBT or an attention-support control. After 10 sessions, 75% of the CBT group no longer met criteria for their primary anxiety disorder at posttreatment as compared to 20% of those in the attention support group. Significant decrements in anxiety also were evident on self-report measures. Although the sample size was small, these results are encouraging and merit further study in a larger controlled trial.

Manassis et al. (2002) compared a group vs. an individual CBT format for children with various anxiety disorders. Their intervention was adapted from Kendall's CBT program. Seventy-eight children (aged 8 to 12), 60.2% of whom had a diagnosis of GAD, were randomly assigned to either group or individual treatment, and both interventions included a parental component. Both interventions resulted in maternal reports of decreased anxiety and significantly improved global functioning when rated by a clinician unaware of group assignment. There were no treatment differences based on the intervention modality. However, the mother's actual scores of the child's anxiety at posttreatment were still elevated and neither the father's ratings of the child's anxiety nor children's self-report ratings of anxiety changed as a result of the intervention.

In another trial of group CBT (GCBT), 96 children (aged 7–16) with various anxiety disorders were randomized to either GCBT or a wait list control group (Rapee, 2000). GCBT consisted of 9 sessions over 11 weeks and included the CBT strategies described above. At the same time, parents were trained in child management skills. The intervention resulted in significant improvement across a broad range of child and parent measures when compared to a wait list control. Furthermore, clinicians unaware of group assignment rated 88.3% of those who received GCBT as moderately or markedly improved. This positive treatment outcome was maintained at 1 year follow-up, and a subset of children continued to improve during the follow-up period. Potential predictors of treatment outcome were examined including child psychopathology and parental psychopathology. The only significant correlation with posttreatment outcome was father's level of anxiety however this correlation was quite low in strength ($r = .29$).

Consistent with that negative outcome regarding the additive effects of direct parental interventions to CBT treatment for children with anxiety, the use of a seven session parental intervention did not enhance child treatment outcome (Nauta, Scholing, Emmelkamp, & Minderea, 2001, 2003). Specifically, the use of teaching parents problem-solving skills and disputation of their own negative beliefs regarding their children's pathology did not increase treatment effects when compared to child treatment alone. Thus, perhaps because the role of parents in the etiology and maintenance of child anxiety disorders has not been adequately explored, adding interventions directed at parents with the intent of enhancing child treatment outcome may be premature.

Treatment of GAD—Case Example

As noted earlier, Melissa presented with a myriad of worries. Always a worrier, the incident at the summer picnic, where she choked on a hot dog, appeared to result in a significant exacerbation of her condition. However, her fears were not limited to choking on food. Rather, the pretreatment self-monitoring revealed that her worries covered a myriad of concerns (see Table 6.2).

Melissa's Treatment Plan

Relaxation Training (decrease general arousal). Commonly used to treat adults with anxiety disorder, relaxation training also is used for children with high states of general arousal such as is commonly found in GAD. When implementing relaxation training with children, there are several general recommendations. First, consider the developmental age of the child. Relaxation scripts for adults are usually 25–30 minutes long, which exceeds the attention span of young children. Therefore, relaxation instructions and the session itself, should be shorter in length. Also, because young children sometimes have dif-

TABLE 6.2 Worries at Pretreatment, Posttreatment, and 6 Month Follow-Up

Pretreatment Week	Worry
Day 1	I would choke on phlegm; I would throw up
Day 2	I could not swallow; I would choke on phlegm; I would throw up
Day 3	I would stop breathing; I would throw up
Day 4	I will go blind; I would throw up
Day 5	I would choke on phlegm; I would stop breathing
Day 6	My family will leave me
Day 7	I will throw up; I would throw up

Posttreatment Week

Although Melissa completed a week of self-monitoring forms, she only worried on one day

Day 4	I might get stung by a bee

Follow-Up Week

Again, Melissa completed a week of self-monitoring but only reported worry on one day

Day 2	Moving to our new house

ficulty with instructions to tense and relax various muscle groups, scripts have been written for young children that cast the tension-reduction cycle in terms of familiar objects. For example, rather than instructing children to tense and then relax their neck muscles, a script by Koppen (1974) instructs the child to imagine being a turtle and to "pull your head into your shell." Similarly, children are taught to tense and relax their arm and hand muscles by "Pretend you have a lemon in your left hand and you want to make lemonade. Squeeze the lemon as hard as you can." This script, and one for somewhat older children by Ollendick (1983) are useful for teaching deep muscle relaxation in children. In the case of Melissa, the Koppen (1974) script was used to provide instructions in relaxation training.

A second overall consideration when implementing relaxation training with young children is to always begin with a tension-relaxation script. Although some forms of relaxation training involve simply the imagination of a pleasant place or experience, particularly for young children who may not recognize or understand the concept of muscle tension, actually having to go through the tension-relaxation cycle helps teach the concepts of tension and relaxation. Thus, even if the clinician chooses to eventually use a strictly cognitive relaxation script, it is advisable to begin with a script such as the ones developed by Koppen (1974) and Ollendick (1983).

Third, children will not successfully acquire the skills in just one training session. Relaxation is a skill and like other skills requires repetitive practice. Children should be encouraged to practice relaxation on a daily basis. To assure that the child is practicing the skill correctly, the therapist should make an audiotape of the first training session and give the child the tape to use at home.

Cognitive restructuring. Using cognitive restructuring (Kendall, 1994), an attempt was made to teach Melissa how to examine her worries and substitute positive coping statements for her negative thoughts and worries. Although Melissa tried very had to accomplish this task, she was unable to do so. As noted by others (e.g., Spence, 2000) younger children often have difficulty with the cognitive component of CBT. In Melissa's case, a decision was made to move to treat Melissa's fears with exposure.

Exposure. Given the problems with cognitive restructuring and the difficulty engineering in vivo exposure to events such as vomiting or going blind, a decision was made to conduct exposure through the use of writing "scary" stories. At each treatment session, Melissa was instructed to write a story about one of her worries. She would then read it to the therapist or the therapist would read it to her while at the same time monitoring her distress level using a 5-point subjective units of distress (SUDS) scale (see chapter 3). The session was terminated when Melissa reported no anxiety while reading the story. See chapter 7 for a detailed description of how to conduct exposure. Following each treatment session, Melissa was given a homework assignment. She was instructed to spend 30 minutes per day reading the story at home to her mother. A 30-minute interval was selected because in session data for Melissa indicated that 30 minutes was a sufficient time period for habituation. It has been our clinical experience that habituation intervals are often much shorter in children than in adults.

Melissa's Exposure Story

> We went to the zoo today. We saw elephants and tigers and panda bears. My stomach felt funny. I said, "Mom, I think I am going to throw up." Mom said, "No you are not. You will be OK." And then I threw up right then and there on my mom. It was yellow, brown, white, and orange. It tasted yucky. I smelled really really really really really bad. My mom and I ran to the bathroom. And while I was going to the bathroom I threw up again. But only this time I threw up in my own underwear. And after that we raced home. The End

Melissa was very reluctant to write her first story, which is not unusual for those with anxiety disorders when asked to engage in exposure activities. She described it as "scary," as not wanting to think about throwing up, and needed substantial encouragement, in the form of stickers, to begin the task. She rated her anxiety as a 5 (the highest) when she began. Once she initiated the task, the anxiety quickly dissipated and she began to laugh as she constructed and later read aloud, the story. There were a total of six exposure sessions coupled with daily homework assignments. At posttreatment, self-monitoring data indicated a significant decrease in frequency of worries and degree of distress associated with the worries that did occur. At 6-month follow-up treatment gains were maintained (see Table 6.2 and Figure 6.1).

Prevention of Anxiety Symptoms/GAD in Children

Recently, Barrett and her colleagues have directed their efforts toward prevention trials of anxiety symptoms in children. Delivered in a school setting and using a sample of 489 children (Barrett & Turner, 2001), the FRIENDS program, as administered by either a psychologist or a teacher, was compared to the standard school curriculum. It should be noted that all children whose parents consented to their participation were included in the project. Thus, this was not a sample of children selected for the presence of anxiety symptoms. In addition to examining its efficacy on anxiety symptoms, the study also examined if the intervention could be successfully implemented by teachers rather than mental health professionals. The results indicated that the FRIENDS program, whether

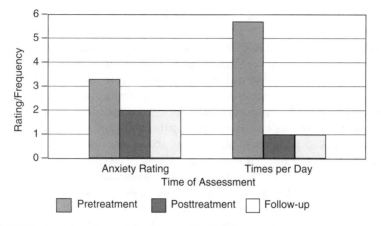

FIGURE 6.1 Anxiety rating and frequency of thoughts per week.

conducted by a psychologist or teacher, resulted in a significant decrease in self-reported symptoms of anxiety. However, some of these differences, even though statistically significant, were quite small and would appear not to reflect clinically significant change. Although the authors attempted to examine the program's efficacy for a subset of children with clinically significant anxiety, the sample size was too small to allow for adequate statistical power. In a second prevention trial, the efficacy of the FRIENDS program on both anxious and depressive symptomatology was examined (Lowry-Webster, Barrett, & Dadds, 2001). Similar to the first trial, the study also examined the efficacy of administration by teachers, and both groups were compared to a "standard curriculum" (no intervention). Again, the FRIENDS program decreased anxiety symptoms across all subjects. Depressive symptoms also decreased but only for children who had high anxiety symptoms prior to participating in the intervention. At 12 month follow-up, treatment gains were maintained. Furthermore, 85% of those treated with FRIENDS and originally considered "at risk" based on elevated anxiety and depression scores at pretreatment, did not meet diagnostic criteria at follow-up. This compared to 31.2% of those in the wait-list group (Lowry-Webster, Barrett, & Lock, 2003). Furthermore, the program appears effective for those in Grade 6 (children) and those Grade 9 (adolescents; Barrett, Johnson, & Turner, in press).

These trials suggest that the FRIENDS program is effective in decreasing anxiety symptoms, and perhaps depressive symptoms, in children who are not necessarily selected because of their clinical status. Longer term follow-up, particularly as children mature and pass through the age of greatest risk for onset of anxiety disorders will allow the further determination of the program's efficacy in preventing anxiety disorders.

SUMMARY

Worry appears to be a common childhood experience and its content covers a broad range of life areas. What appears to differentiate "pathological" from "normal" worry is not content, but frequency and intensity. When based simply on the presence of worry and physical symptoms such as headaches and stomachaches, OAD was an unstable and highly prevalent condition. Based on the latest diagnostic revision, requiring the inclusion of physical symptoms in addition to cognitive symptoms, appears to increase the validity of the diagnostic category now known as GAD. Despite increased diagnostic proficiency, it remains unclear if GAD represents a distinct diagnosis or merely a predispositional state from which more specific disorders emerge. In contrast to many other childhood anxiety disorders, there are few data on its etiology and natural course, and even fewer data on the efficacy of pharmacological or psychosocial interventions specifically for those children with GAD. The majority of the studies reviewed here were comprised of mixed diagnostic groups even though a substantial number of children with GAD were included in the sample. However, based on the data currently available, both SSRIs and CBT demonstrate substantial treatment efficacy but studies using samples consisting solely of children with GAD (rather than mixed diagnostic groups) would further clarify the treatment outcome literature.

CHAPTER 7

Specific Phobia

Joshua is 10 years old. Referred by his mother, he has an extreme fear of injury and death. Currently, his behavior is characterized by hypervigilance and scanning of the environment. Joshua refuses to engage in any activity unless he is certain he will not observe injury to himself or anyone else. He refuses to go to or participate in sporting events because someone might be injured. He refuses to go to the movies unless he knows the entire plot ahead of time because someone might get hurt. He also refuses to watch television, including those shows that he knows are "fake" such as cartoons, because there might be blood or injury. Although his mother reported that he was always a "sensitive" child, the frank onset of this disorder was triggered after watching the movie Godzilla.

Specific phobia (formerly known as simple phobia) is a marked and persistent fear that is excessive or unreasonable (APA, 1994). The fear is elicited by the presence or anticipation of a specific object or event that is not social in nature (social phobia) or is not marked by a pattern of avoidance that is based on the fear of having a panic attack (panic disorder with agoraphobia). In essence, a specific phobia can be related to virtually any other object, situation or event (see Table 7.1 for the diagnostic criteria). There are several aspects of the diagnostic criteria that deserve comment. First, the formal diagnostic criteria contain qualifiers regarding the presentation of the disorder in children. Specifically, as noted in chapter 3, children may express their anxiety by crying, tantrums, freezing, or clinging. A second qualifier pertaining to the diagnosis of specific phobia is that children need not recognize the unreasonableness of their fear. This was the situation with Joshua. He did not see his "need to know everything" ahead of time as unreasonable. For him, it was a protective behavior designed to prevent his distress. So, despite his parents' frustration, he considered his behavior as adaptive, not dysfunctional. Third, for children (i.e., those under the age of 18), the duration of the fear must be at least 6 months. This criterion acknowledges that, in childhood, many fears can be transient. A duration of 6 months decreases the likelihood that treatment will be directed at something that might dissipate without intervention and, as will be illustrated in the treat-ment section of this chapter, children's fears appear to be reactive to nonspecific interventions. A fourth feature of the diagnostic criteria that merits comment is the fact that for the first time, panic attacks are specifically included in the diagnostic criteria for specific phobia, again highlighting that these fears can be quite severe and may be accompanied by a high level of autonomic arousal.

Prior to *DSM-IV*, specific phobia was known as simple phobia. However, careful study of this disorder made it quite clear that phobias often are not

TABLE 7.1 Diagnostic Criteria for Specific Phobia

A. Marked and persistent fear that is excessive or unreasonable, cued by the presence or anticipation of a specific object or situation (e.g., flying, heights, animals, receiving an injection, seeing blood).
B. Exposure to the phobic stimulus almost invariably provokes an immediate anxiety response, which may take the form of a situationally bound or situationally predisposed Panic Attack. *Note*: In children, the anxiety may be expressed by crying, tantrums, freezing, or clinging.
C. The person recognizes that the fear is excessive or unreasonable. *Note*: In children, this feature may be absent.
D. The phobic situation(s) is avoided or else is endured with intense anxiety or distress.
E. The avoidance, anxious anticipation, or distress in the feared situation(s) interferes significantly with the person's normal routine, occupational (or academic) functioning, or social activities or relationships or there is marked distress about having the phobia.
F. In individuals under age 18, the duration is at least 6 months.
G. The anxiety, Panic Attacks, or phobic avoidance associated with the specific object or situation are not better accounted for by another mental disorder, such as Obsessive-Compulsive Disorder (e.g., fear of dirt in someone with an obsession about contamination), Posttraumatic Stress Disorder (e.g., avoidance of stimuli associated with a severe stressor), Separation Anxiety Disorder (e.g., avoidance of school), Social Phobia (e.g., avoidance of social situations because of fear of embarrassment) Panic Disorder with Agoraphobia or Agoraphobia without History of Panic Disorder.

Specify type

Animal Type: If the fear is cued by animals or insects. This subtype generally has a childhood onset.
Natural Environment Type: If the fear is cued by objects in the natural environment, such as storms, heights, or water. This subtype generally has a childhood onset.
Blood-Injection-Injury Type: If the fear is cued by seeing blood or an injury or by receiving an injec-tion or other invasive medical procedure. This subtype is highly familial and is often characterized by a strong vasovagal response.
Situational Type: If the fear is cued by a specific situation such as public transportation, tunnels, bridges, elevators, flying, driving, or enclosed places. This subtype has a bimodal age-at-onset distribution, with one peak in childhood and another peak in the mid-20s. This subtype appears to be similar to Panic Disorder with Agoraphobia in its characteristic sex ratios, familial aggregation pattern, and age at onset.
Other Type: If the fear is cued by other stimuli. These stimuli might include the fear or avoidance of situations that might lead to choking, vomiting, or contacting an illness; "space" phobia (i.e., the individual is afraid of falling down if away from walls or other means of physical support); and children's fears of loud sounds or costumed characters.

simple. Rather they are complex phenomena that may have a significant impact upon the daily functioning of the individual and sometimes of those around them.

> Mallory is 12 years old and is an only child. She is terrified of being kidnapped by aliens during the night and refuses to sleep alone. In fact, Mallory has never slept alone. For her entire life, she has slept in the bed with her parents, or more recently, in a sleeping bag on the floor of their bedroom. She has resisted all of her parents' attempts to make her sleep in her own room. Mallory's parents have never had the privacy of their own bedroom.
>
> Jamal is 15 years old. His brother needs a bone marrow transplant and, luckily, Jamal is a perfect match. Jamal really wants to help but he is terrified of needles. Ever since he was a little boy, he became very upset whenever he had to get a vaccination or tetanus shot and would have to be held down by the doctor, nurse, and his mother. His fear is so severe that he chooses to go without Novocain when he needs dental work, preferring the pain of the dentist's drill to the thought of the needle. He has not been able to sleep well ever since the bone marrow transplant procedures were explained to him.

CLINICAL FEATURES

Although the range of items that may engender fear can be infinite in nature, the current diagnostic schema collapses specific phobias into five types: animal, natural environment, blood-injection-injury, situational, and other (APA, 1994). These categories were developed based on data that suggested that there were categorical differences in age of onset, type of physiological response, and degree of familial aggregation. The characteristics of each type are described along a clinical case description.

Animal Type

The fear is cued by an animal or an insect and the most common age of onset is childhood.

> Randy is 6 years old and has an extreme fear of bees and yellow jackets. He has never had a bee sting but he saw his sister get stung one early autumn. Over the ensuing winter, he did not appear to have any problems, but the following spring, he became fearful of going outside. He needed a great deal of encouragement and his mother noted that he would retreat to the house whenever possible ("I heard thunder, I have to go to the bathroom"). By the beginning of summer, the symptoms had become much worse (he refused a trip to the zoo because bees might be there).

Natural Environment Type

In this category, the fear is cued by objects in the natural environment including storms, heights, or water.

> Leslie is 13 years old and is afraid of the dark, "spooky things," and thunderstorms. Her parents report that she has been fearful for as long as they can remember. She refuses to enter dark places alone. She refuses to sleep alone, insisting that her much younger sister sleep in her room. She also is extremely afraid of thunderstorms and will hide in the closet until the storm is over. If the storm occurs at night, she will hide in the closet of her parents' bedroom. The family tries not to startle her.

Fears of Blood-Injection-Injury (BII) Type

The fear is cued by objects or situations that involve blood, needles, or injury to the body. The onset is commonly in childhood and there is a high familial aggregation.

> Bonnie is 17 years old. She reports a nearly life-long problem of readily fainting at the sight or verbal report of an injury or blood, especially as it pertains to amputation of, or injury to, body parts. When she was 7 years old, she was watching a magician "saw a woman in half." She fainted while watching the magic trick and has been sensitive to such sights ever since that time.

Unique to BII phobias is the individual's physiological reactivity upon exposure to these objects or events (DSM-IV; APA, 1994). As noted in chapter 1, when in contact with the phobic stimulus, increased heart rate and blood pressure is common. However, the physiological response to BII phobias is different; it is biphasic in nature (see Figure 7.1). Specifically, when faced with the feared event (blood, needles, injury), the initial reaction for those with BII is increased heart rate and blood pressure. However, those increases are followed by a sharp decrement in both blood pressure and pulse rate. In fact, in some cases, the decrease is so great that fainting is a distinct possibility. This unusual response makes BII unique and poses some special challenges for conventional treatments (see the Treatment section).

Situational Type

The situations that cue these fears include public transportation, tunnels, bridges, elevators, flying, driving, or enclosed places (DSM-IV; APA, 1994). Unlike the others, the situational type has a bimodal age of onset. Childhood marks one peak age of onset, whereas the other peak occurs in the mid-20s. It

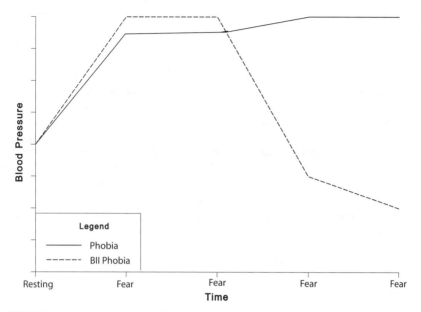

FIGURE 7.1 Blood pressure and BII phobia.

has been suggested that this subtype was similar to Panic Disorder with Agoraphobia based on gender distribution, familial aggregation pattern, and age of onset (APA, 1994). This appears to be the case when the age of onset is in the mid-20s. However, children can suffer from the situational type as well.

> Patricia is 12 years old. She refuses to fly on an airplane. When Patricia was 9 years old, she had been on an airplane that was caught in a wind shear. The plane dropped several thousand feet before the pilot regained control. Ever since that time, she has been afraid to fly. She feels uncomfortable in an airport even if she is just going to greet her father after a business trip. Patricia's mother reported that Patricia also has a life-long fear of heights.

Other Type

When fears are cued by "other" stimuli, they are classified as the other type. This includes fears of choking, vomiting, contracting an illness, or "space" phobias (afraid of falling because of loss of physical support). Phobias in this category can be particularly severe. In some instances, fears of vomiting have been reported to result in weight loss that would meet the criteria for a diagnosis of anorexia nervosa, even when no other symptoms of an eating disorder are present (Manassis & Kalman, 1990) and fear of vomiting was the reason for the restricted eating behavior.

> Edgar is 15. He refuses to go to school because he is afraid that he will vomit. He also avoids any social interactions because of his fear. When he was a toddler, he ingested a poisonous substance and was.given ipecac in order to induce vomiting. Always a "clingy" child, he started complaining of persistent stomachaches and fear of vomiting in the fourth grade.

An important issue to keep in mind is that sometimes, individuals may present at clinics with what appears to be a specific phobia but instead may be an indication of a different anxiety disorder. For example, a "fear of knives" may be indicative of obsessive-compulsive disorder. Similarly, a "fear of tests" may indicate the presence of social phobia. Thus, a careful diagnostic evaluation is necessary to assure that the child's fear is not representative of a different, or perhaps more pervasive, disorder.

Epidemiology

The prevalence rates for specific phobia range from 2.6–4.5% of the general population, with a mean of approximately 3.5% (Ollendick, King, & Muris, in press; see Table 7.2 for available published prevalence rates). Consistent with data presented in chapter 1, specific phobias (like fears in general) exist worldwide and affect a substantial percentage of the general population. Among treatment seeking samples (i.e., children referred to anxiety disorders clinics for treatment), 15–36% met diagnostic criteria for a primary diagnosis of specific phobia (Last, Strauss, & Francis, 1987; Strauss & Last, 1993). Phobic disorders appear to be relatively stable conditions when considered across assessment intervals ranging between 2 and 5 year follow-up (Ollendick & King, in press). Based on the specific time interval used, between 20% and 40% of children

TABLE 7.2 Worldwide Prevalence Rates for Specific Phobia

Study	Country	Age Range	Rate
Anderson et al. (1987)	New Zealand	11 years	2.4%
Bird et al. (1988)	Puerto Rico	4–16 years	2.6%
Costello et al. (1993)	United States	12–18 years	3.6%
Essau et al. (2001)	Germany	12–17 years	3.5%
McGee et al. (1990)	New Zealand	15 years	3.6%
Steinhausen et al. (1998)	Switzerland	7–16 years	2.6%
Verhulst et al. (1997)	Netherlands	12–18 years	4.5%
Wittchen et al. (1999)	Germany	14–24 years	2.3%

diagnosed with specific phobia at time 1 still meet criteria for the disorder at follow-up.

Among one sample of children, specific phobias of the dark and school were most common, endorsed by 29% and 24% of the sample, respectively, followed by phobias of dogs (16%), other animals (8%), heights (8%), insects (8%), elevators (5%), closed places (3%), swimming (3%), needles (3%), drains (3%), and taxidermy (3%; Strauss & Last, 1993). As illustrated, the animal, natural environment, and situational type were most common. BII phobias were less common as were closed places (claustrophobia), perhaps consistent with its much later age of onset.

These subtypes were derived based on data derived primarily from adult studies. However, data support the validity for these distinctions in children as well (Muris, Schmidt, & Merckelbach, 1999). Using a community sample, children rated their fearfulness with respect to fifteen potentially fearful objects and situations drawn from the animal, BII, natural environment and situational types. A factor analysis revealed that the fifteen items loaded on three factors. Animal fears and BII fears loaded on separate, distinct factors. However, the natural environment and situational phobias loaded on the same factor suggesting that those who report phobic symptoms of storms, the dark, and thunder, also report phobic symptoms of flying and heights. Although the results did not perfectly replicate the *DSM-IV* typology, they do suggest some validity for the utility of distinct subtypes.

Sociodemographic Influences

Among a community sample of 1,000 children and adolescents, girls reported a higher level of specific phobia symptoms than did boys (Muris et al., 1999), consistent with the data on fears in general. Also, younger children (age ≤ 13) endorsed a higher frequency of specific phobia symptoms than older children (age > 13). When examined by specific phobia type, again girls and younger children were more likely than boys or older children to report animal phobias, BII phobias, and environmental-situational phobias.

Comorbidity and Differential Diagnosis

Throughout this volume, a recurring theme is that among children, an anxiety disorder rarely exists alone. Rather, most children present with a myriad of symptoms and many children appear to meet diagnostic criteria for more than one disorder. However, the data on comorbidity with respect to specific phobia appear mixed. Among one community sample, the comorbidity rate for the presence of a second disorder was lower when the *primary* diagnosis was a phobic disorder, when compared to comorbidity rates for children who suffer from *primary* panic disorder or another anxiety disorder (Costello & Angold, 1995). However, when comorbidity rates among clinical samples are examined, 64% of children and adolescents with a primary phobic disorder were comorbid for a second disorder, most commonly another anxiety disorder (Last et al., 1987). In another sample of children with specific phobias, 61% were comorbid for a second disorder, most commonly separation anxiety disorder (Strauss & Last, 1993). In comparison to children with social phobia, those with specific phobia were less likely to have comorbid overanxious disorder or avoidant disorder. More recent studies (Ollendick & King, in press; Silverman et al., 1999) report that between 72% and 75% of children with a primary phobic disorder also had an additional disorder. Again, additional anxiety disorders were the most common comorbid diagnosis followed by attention deficit hyperactivity disorder and depressive disorders.

In comparison to those with social phobia, children with specific phobia have an earlier age of onset (7.8 years vs.12.3 years) and were more likely to be prepubertal at the time they were referred for treatment, perhaps because of the earlier age of onset (Strauss & Last, 1993). School refusal was evident in both groups although in differing proportions. Whereas 66% of the social phobic sample expressed distress about school, only 24% of the specific phobic group reported distress regarding school attendance.

Etiology

As noted, most specific phobias appear early in the lifespan. The mean age of onset for animal phobias is age 7 and the mean age of onset for BII is age 9 (Öst, 1987). In contrast, the mean age of onset for claustrophobia is the mid-20s, again suggesting something different about this type of fear, perhaps suggesting the presence of panic with agoraphobia.

Based on available data, phobias appear to develop through one of several learning mechanisms: direct conditioning, social learning (modeling), or information transfer; direct conditioning appears to account for the largest percentage of phobic onsets. However, differences are apparent when examined by subtype (for an extensive review, see Merckelbach, de Jong, Muris, & van den Hout, 1996). Briefly, those with the animal or BII type more often attribute the etiology of their fear to social learning or negative information, whereas those with claustrophobia more often describe a situation consistent with a conditioning episode. Consistent with these data, modeling and information transfer are more often related to an earlier age of onset (Öst, 1987).

More likely than any other specific phobia, the BII type appears to have a familial component. In Bonnie's case, her father admitted feeling "queasy" around needles. Among those with BII phobia, approximately 67% have a relative with BII. This is among the highest rates for a familial relationship for an anxiety disorder, although again, it does not necessarily indicate a genetic vulnerability. Social learning or information transfer by a family member may contribute to the development of that fear in a child.

Assessment

Diagnostic interviews have been discussed in chapter 3 and will not be repeated here. The reader is referred to chapter 3 for an overview of diagnostic interviews and their use with children. The self-report instrument most commonly used (some might say universally used) to assess for specific phobias in children is the Fear Survey Schedule for Children-Revised (FSSC-R; Ollendick, 1983). As noted by Weems and colleagues (Weems, Silverman, Saavedra, Pina, & White-Lumpkin, 1999), the FSSC-R has an extensive body of psychometric data including excellent reliability and validity, a well-validated factor structure, and extensive normative data. Furthermore, the instrument has been validated across a variety of cultures and countries (see Silverman & Hicks-Carmichael, 1999 and Weems et al. 1999 for a more extensive and recent review of the psychometric properties of the FSSC-R). One aspect of the FSSC-R that has received less attention is its discriminative validity, particularly its ability to differentiate among children with different types of specific phobias. Examining the ability of the FSSC-R (both the child and parent versions) to differentiate among children with specific phobias of the dark, animals, shots/doctors, and social fears (Weems et al., 1999) a discriminant function analysis revealed that the children's scores on the FSSC-R were able to classify correctly 62% of the children. Specifically, 50% of those with animal phobias were correctly classi-fied as were 66.7% of those with phobias of the dark, 70% of those with fears of needles, and 55.9% of those with social phobia. Similarly, based on parental ratings, 63.6% of the children with animal phobias were correctly classified, as were 76.5% of those with phobias of the dark, 37.5% of those with needle phobias and 81.5% of those with social phobias. The authors concluded that the FSSC-R could differentiate among children with various types of specific phobias and additionally parental ratings could differentiate those with social phobia from those with specific phobia. Thus, this well-validated instrument is, and should be, a staple in the assessment of childhood fears and phobias.

Behavioral assessments play a significant role in the history of the treatment of childhood phobias, although more recently this strategy appears to have fallen out of favor. For specific phobias, a Behavioral Approach Test (BAT) allows the child to demonstrate his ability (or inability) to approach a feared object or situation. Unlike self-report data, BATs are less subject to social desirability. That is, unlike self-report data where children are free to deny their degree of distress, asking a child who is afraid of heights to ride an escalator or a glass elevator will provide the therapist with a more valid assessment of the child's fear. BATs are quite simple to develop and are limited only by the therapist's creativity. For example, a BAT for fear of the dark might require asking the child to sit in a darkened room for as long as possible. Then, the number of seconds that the child can remain in the room is recorded. When assessing treatment outcome for fear of dogs, Bandura and colleagues (Bandura, Grusec, & Menlove, 1967) timed the number of minutes a formerly fearful child could remain in a pen with a dog. In other instances, the dependent measure is the distance between the individual and a feared object. For example, an individual afraid of snakes may be asked to approach a snake in a cage and to continue the approach until she becomes too anxious to approach any further. Then the distance between the individual and the snake is assessed. At posttreatment, the test is repeated and successful treatment outcome is judged by the individual's ability to get closer to the snake than she did at pretreatment (and hopefully touch the snake). Although conducting a BAT requires more time and effort than simply giving a child a self-report inventory, the resultant data are less confounded by social desirability, expectations of treatment outcome, subject reactivity, or therapist demand.

TREATMENT

Interventions for children's fears are among the oldest established psychological treatments. The now classic demonstration by Jones (1924) that countercondi- tioning (systematic exposure to the feared object in the presence of a response incompatible with fear) was effective in eliminating Peter's fear of rabbits formed the basis for many subsequent studies of fear. Despite this early beginning, until recently, information on the effectiveness of psychological interventions for children's fears consisted primarily of case descriptions. Controlled treat- ment studies of children's fears, particularly group comparison trials, are few in number. However, recent data, based on an extensive review (Ollendick & King, 1998) concluded that imaginal and in vivo desensitization, filmed and live modeling, and cognitive-behavioral interventions all appear efficacious for childhood phobias. Operant procedures, although backed by less literature, also appear probably efficacious. Controlled trials do not exist for other forms of psychosocial interventions. Pharmacological interventions are rarely, if ever, recommended for the treatment of specific phobia. Thus, this review will be limited to the empirical data based on behavioral interventions.

Desensitization

In their review of the treatment literature, Ollendick and King (1998) detailed four controlled group outcome trials examining the efficaciousness of systematic desensitization for "stage-fright" (Kondas, 1967), test anxiety (Barabasz, 1973; Mann & Rosenthal, 1969), and children with various phobic conditions (Miller, Barrett, Hampe, & Noble, 1972). Systematic desensitization is based on a classical conditioning model (Wolpe, 1958) and involves the pairing of a fear producing stimuli (usually presented imaginally) with another stimuli or response that is incompatible with anxiety. The fearful stimuli are arranged hierarchically, from those that are least anxiety-producing to most anxiety producing (see Table 7.3). In most cases, the incompatible response is relaxation, although with younger children food is sometimes used. In the studies cited above, imaginal systematic desensitization was compared to various other active interventions including relaxation training alone, presentation of the fear stimuli in a hierarchical fashion alone (no relaxation), vicarious individual desensitization, vicarious group desensitization, or traditional verbal or play therapy. Each study also included a wait-list control group. Across the four studies, systematic desensitization was more efficacious than the no treatment control condition, relaxation training alone, or presentation of the hierarchy alone. However, vicarious desensitization (group or individual) produced outcomes similar to systematic desensitization.

In fact, currently, systematic desensitization is rarely used to treat children with phobic disorders. One reason might be that children's cognitive immaturity may not allow them to imagine the fearful stimuli in the fashion necessary for a successful desensitization outcome (see chapter 3). For example, in a comparison of imaginal and in vivo desensitization (Ultee, Griffioen, & Schellekens,

TABLE 7.3 Randy's Hierarchy

Situation	SUDS Level
In Session Tasks	
Looking at pictures of bees	1
Touching pictures of bees	2
Watching live bees on TV	2
Touching a dead bee	3
Sitting in a room with a live bee in a jar	3
Listening to bee sounds	3
Holding a jar with a live bee in it	4
Being outside when bees were present	5
At Home Tasks	
Looking at pictures of bees	1
Conducting bee research on the computer	2
Watching live bees on TV	2
Listening to bee sounds	3
Carry a dead bee (encased in clear plastic) with him at all times	4
Keeping a dead bee in a jar in his room	4
Keeping a live bee in a jar in a room	5

1982), water phobic children aged 5–10 were assigned to either eight sessions of in vivo desensitization or to four sessions of imaginal exposure plus four sessions of in vivo desensitization. Eight sessions of in vivo desensitization was superior and according to the authors, one reason may have been that it facilitated familiarity in the water setting, and the acquisition of skill, which would be an important component in assuring fear reduction. However, an alternative explanation is that the young children were not able to successfully imagine the fearful situation, thus attenuating the efficacy of the intervention.

As noted, any response incompatible with anxiety can be used as part of a desensitization strategy, and competing responses other than relaxation have been successful. Kuroda (1969) randomized 58 Japanese children between the ages of 3 and 5 who were fearful of frogs or cats to either group in vivo desensitization or a no treatment control group. Rather than relaxation, the children sang songs about frogs or cats, told stories about frogs or cats, and dramatized the movements of these animals. The results indicated that in vivo desensitization was superior to the no treatment control group.

Another variation of desensitization treatment is emotive imagery (Lazarus & Abramowitz, 1962). In this procedure, the relaxation component is replaced by instructions for the child to imagine an exciting story involving a superhero. Aspects of the fear hierarchy are woven into the story, for example, "Batman comes to you in the middle of the night. He needs your help on a very important mission. But you have to work with him in the dark so that the Riddler does not discover that you are aware of his evil plans..." The rationale is that the positive emotion created by the exciting superhero story serves to counter the child's fear and inhibit the fearful response (Ollendick & King, 1998). However, as noted by these authors, there is only one controlled trial of emotive imagery (Cornwall, Spence, & Schotte, 1997). Twenty-four children aged 7–10 who were afraid of the dark were assigned to either emotive imagery or a wait-list control condition. Emotive imagery resulted in superior outcome on measures of self-report, parental report, and a BAT (a darkness tolerance test).

Modeling

Traditional desensitization and various forms of modeling (Mann & Rosenthal, 1969) were equivalent in terms of efficacy for the treatment of dog fears. Modeling (observational learning) has a long history in the treatment of children's phobias dating back to the seminal work of Bandura (1969), who proposed that extinction of fear would occur through observing a model behave nonfearfully in the presence of a feared stimulus. That is, a child with a dog phobia would observe a child who is not afraid of dogs playing happily with a dog. Additionally, Bandura hypothesized that learning would be enhanced as the patient observed that the model did not experience aversive consequences. There are many variations in the manner in which modeling interventions are conducted. These include live or filmed modeling, observation or participant modeling, multiple modeling versus single-modeling, or highly competent versus average competent models. Bandura and his colleagues (Bandura, Grusec, & Menlove, 1967; Bandura & Menlove, 1968) conducted several controlled, randomized trials examining different presentations of modeling and comparing it to no treatment groups for children with dog phobias. In the first study (Bandura et al., 1967), children were randomly assigned to modeling sessions where the child observed (a) the model behaving nonfearfully in the context of a birthday party, (b) the model behaving nonfearfully in a neutral context, and (c) the dog at the party but without the model. In the control condition, the child attended a party but there was no dog or model present. Both modeling groups were efficacious, and equally efficacious, in comparison to the other two conditions that did not differ from each other. A follow-up study compared the use of filmed modeling in two different modeling conditions: (a) one model interacting nonfearfully with one dog, (b) multiple models interacting nonfearfully with a variety of dogs. The control condition consisted of films without dogs. Both active treatment conditions were superior at posttreatment to the control group based on the posttreatment BAT (the length of time that the child could stay in a pen with a dog). Furthermore, those children who had observed various models and various dogs stayed in the pen with the dog for a significantly longer period of time than those exposed to the single model, thus suggesting some benefit for the use of multiple models and multiple variations of the fearful stimuli.

Bandura's results have been replicated by other researchers. Filmed modeling has been demonstrated to be effective in the treatment of preschool children who were fearful of dogs (Hill, Liebert, & Mott, 1968) and the numerous studies reviewed in chapter 5 indicate the effectiveness of filmed modeling in the treatment of medical and dental fears. In contrast, Lewis (1974) reported that filmed modeling alone was not as effective as either a participation condition (therapist encouraged and then assisted the child to engage in interactive activities at the swimming pool) or a combined filmed modeling/participation condition for children with water fears. In fact, filmed modeling alone did not result in any better outcome than did a control condition, whereas the combined condition exceeded even that of participation alone. It is unclear why filmed modeling alone was not effective in this case. However, it should be recalled that in vivo desensitization was superior to a combination of imaginal and in vivo desensitization for the treatment of children with fears of water (Ultee et al.,1982). Thus, using two different theoretical approaches, imaginal systematic desensitization or filmed modeling alone does not appear as efficacious as an in vivo approach. In the Ultee et al. (1982) study, the superiority of the all in vivo approach was attributed to allowing the children's acquisition of water skills. The same explanation may apply to the Hill et al. (1968) findings cited here.

That is, for water phobias (like social phobia, see chapter 10), the acquisition of skills may be a necessary component of fear reduction and positive treatment outcome.

Symbolic modeling (i.e., story characters behaving fearlessly in the face of fear) has been reported to be effective in the treatment of kindergarten children who were mildly to moderately fearful of the dark (Klingman, 1988). Modeling took the form of five 20-minute story group sessions where single or multiple coping models dealt positively with the dark. Then, there was an unstructured group discussion where children shared reactions and the therapist reinforced positive coping behavior. Both parental and child report indicated that the symbolic modeling was significantly superior to a control condition in terms of decreasing fear and increasing coping statements. However, children with extreme fears of the dark were excluded from this study, thus, the efficacy of this procedure has not been demonstrated in those who have the most severe fear.

Another variation of modeling is participant modeling, where in addition to observing someone behaving fearlessly, the fearful child also engages with the model and the phobic object/situation. Several studies have confirmed that participant modeling is efficacious in the treatment of childhood phobias and in some cases, actually may be more effective than simply live or filmed modeling. In one study, children (aged 5–11 years) who were fearful of snakes were randomized to either live modeling, participant modeling, or a control group (Ritter, 1968). Both modeling conditions were judged superior to the control group; however the participant modeling condition resulted in further significant improvement over live modeling alone. The superior outcome of participant modeling (over imaginal systematic desensitization, filmed modeling, and live modeling) was confirmed in a second study of snake-phobic adolescents and adults (Bandura, Blanchard, & Ritter, 1969) and another study of snake-phobic children (Murphy & Bootzin, 1973).

The important of participant modeling and skill acquisition in the treatment of some childhood fears is reinforced by Jones and his colleagues in their work on fear of fire (Jones, Ollendick, McLaughlin, & Williams, 1989; Williams & Jones, 1989). Williams and Jones (1989) randomly assigned children aged 7.6 to 10.5 years to (a) a fire safety/fear reduction group, (b) a fire safety group, (c) an attention control condition, and (d) a wait-list control condition. The fire safety/fear reduction group included instructions in self-control statements. For example, children were taught that when faced with a fire situation, they should say, "I should relax and calm down. I can take care of myself because I know what to do." The therapist then modeled the use of self-control statements and then stated the behavioral steps in a fire safety sequence (roll out of bed, get into a crawl position, crawl to the bedroom door, etc). Children then verbally repeated each step. The fire safety group consisted of simple instructions to verbalize each fire safety skill. The children were not taught self-control statements. The attention control group consisted of a discussion of fire-related incidents, fire related stories and drawing pictures of fire prevention activities. At posttreatment, both fire safety groups demonstrated significant gains in knowledge of fire safety skills. However, at three month follow-up, the combined fire safety/fear reduction group had higher retention of skill knowledge. However, there was no significant difference across groups for reduction of fear. Although the use of self-instructional procedures were supposed to address fear reduction, the authors hypothesized that the manner in which the instructions were presented (*pretend you see a fire and "really" experience the situation*) may have served to exacerbate fear. The authors likened this situation to an exposure session but because it was not implemented in a gradual fashion or for a sufficient period of time, it likely was ineffective.

Jones et al. (1989) compared the ability of two training procedures (behavior rehearsal and elaborative rehearsal) for the acquisition of fire safety skills and decrement in fear. In addition, a no treatment control group was included. Both groups were initially trained in the skills necessary to safely escape from a fire situation. For the process of behavior rehearsal, the therapist first modeled the sequence of skills, then the children performed each step. Errors or omissions were immediately corrected and children rehearsed the responses again. Immediately after the behavior rehearsal, those assigned to the elaborative practice received additional training that included asking the children questions regarding the procedures they had learned, explaining correct responses to the questions and asking the child to repeat them, summarizing how correct responses would assist in safe evacuation, and providing the opportunity for children to ask questions regarding their training. Those who received behavioral rehearsal but no elaborative practice were given additional fire safety facts to equate for the therapist time. The results indicated that both groups acquired significant fire safety skills when compared to the control group but there were no differences between the two active interventions. However, on a fear of fire inventory and on a general fear inventory, only the elaborative rehearsal group demonstrated significantly decreased fear. Furthermore, those in the elaborative group demonstrated greater understanding of the rationale. The authors concluded that although both methods resulted in improved skill acquisition, the elaborative rehearsal was superior in decreasing fear and long-term skill retention.

Contingency Management

Ollendick and King (1998) noted that contingency management procedures attempt to alter phobic behavior by manipulating its consequences. Their review concluded that reinforced practice, where children are gradually exposed to the fearful stimulus, without benefit of counterconditioning strategies (such as relaxation) or modeling resulted in significant improvement in severe fears of dogs or riding a bus (Obler & Terwilliger, 1970), fears of the dark (Leitenberg & Callahan, 1973; Sheslow, Bondy, & Nelson, 1983), and fears of water (Menzies & Clark, 1993). In each of these studies, reinforced practice was superior to no treatment control conditions. In a study of nighttime fears, graduated practice was compared to a combined condition consisting of graduated practice and training in verbal self-instruction to assist in handling fears of the dark (Sheslow et al., 1983). Another group received only verbal coping skills training. Both reinforced practice alone and the combination group were more efficacious than verbal coping skills training alone or the no treatment control group, again emphasizing the need for direct contact with the phobic stimulus. In another investigation, reinforced practice plus live modeling was superior to live modeling alone and a no treatment control group for children with water phobia (Menzies & Clark, 1993). Furthermore, the combination group did not produce improvements over the reinforced practice condition alone. Again, the limitation of modeling alone for severe fears of water may be related to the need to develop specific skills (e.g., swimming skills) in order for fear to be diminished.

A recent, and controversial, variation to the treatment literature is the use of Eye Movement Desensitization and Reprocessing (EMDR) for the treatment of fears and anxiety. Shapiro (1995) hypothesized that EMDR reduced fear through the neural "reprocessing" of a traumatic event through the use of saccadic eye movements. Essentially an imaginal exposure paradigm, patients are instructed to imagine the feared object or event and then "become aware" of the thoughts associated with that event. As the thoughts and images are "reprocessed," fear is reduced. One of the purported advantages of EMDR is that it works very quickly, sometimes in as little as one 90-minute session. EMDR is extremely controversial and although studies exist either supporting or disputing the claims, there still is little reason to view this intervention as anything other than a form of exposure. Recently, the use of EMDR was examined in the treatment of 22 girls (aged 9–14) with spider phobia. This was an uncontrolled trial although posttreatment outcome was compared to scores of nonphobic girls. Girls received 1.5 hours of EMDR and 1.5 hours of in vivo exposure. At posttreatment, scores on a spider phobia inventory were still elevated in comparison to those who were not phobic. There are several limitations to this investigation. First, this was not a controlled trial, thus it is not possible to rule out the impact of nonspecific factors. Second, the use of both EMDR and in vivo exposure does not allow for a determination of the specific efficacy of EMDR. It is possible that the active intervention was in vivo exposure. Thus, although the contributions of this particular study to the overall treatment literature is limited, it does represent one of the first applications of EMDR to the treatment of childhood phobias.

Applied Tension

As noted, the physical response to BII phobias involves an initial increase in heart rate and blood pressure followed by a rapid and sometimes dramatic decrease, possibly to the point of fainting. Thus, traditional exposure interventions may be contraindicated inasmuch as prolonged exposure to the phobic stimuli (e.g., a needle or blood) could result in fainting. Recently, Öst (e.g., Öst, Fellenius, & Sterner, 1991) developed a strategy to treat BII phobias that involves gradual exposure to the fearful objects or events while assuring that the individual does not faint; thereby assuring their participation in the exposure session. Applied tension teaches the individual to tense certain muscle groups (arms, hands, chest) when faced with the phobic object or situation. By tensing (rather than relaxing) these muscle groups, blood pressure increases and fainting is prevented. Although the initial reaction of most clinicians would be that teaching a child to become tense in the presence of the phobic stimuli is inconsistent with the goal of an intervention designed to eliminate a phobia, it must be emphasized that the tensing procedure is not used to alleviate distress. Rather, its sole purpose is to increase blood pressure so that fainting and loss of consciousness does not occur, thus allowing the individual to participate in the exposure session. Although no controlled trials of applied tension exist in the child literature, the procedure has been used successfully with adults (Öst et al., 1991) and there are clinical reports of its successful use with children.

Cognitive-Behavioral Interventions

Cognitive-behavioral interventions (CBT) have been used to treat childhood phobias. In one of the first investigations (Kanfer, Karoly, & Newman, 1975), children with severe fears of the dark were randomized to one of three conditions: competence ("I am brave and can take care of myself in the dark"), stimulus control ("the dark is a fun place to be"), and neutral (reciting nursery rhymes). At posttreatment, those in the competence group were significantly improved in comparison to the other groups. In another study, the utility of verbal self-instruction to treat severe nighttime fears also was examined (Graziano & Mooney, 1980). The intervention included relaxation training, imagining a pleasant scene and reciting "brave" statements. In addition, parents were given instructions to provide children with verbal reinforcement and bravery tokens for appropriate behavior. When compared to the control group, those treated with the active intervention demonstrated significantly less nighttime fear and the results were maintained up to three years later (Graziano & Mooney, 1982).

CBT also has been used to treat other types of fears. In a large controlled trial, Öst and his colleagues (Öst, Svensson, Hellstrom, & Lindwall, 2001) examined a one session treatment for children with a variety of specific phobias, including animal, BII, natural environment, and the situation type. Children (aged 7–17) were randomly assigned to one session treatment with the child alone, one session treatment with the child and parent present, and a wait-list control group. The exposure session did not exceed three hours. The intervention, graduated in vivo exposure, was conceptualized as a series of behavioral tests from which the child could get new information. By accessing new information, the child could correct false beliefs held with respect to the phobic object or situation. Neither imaginal exposure nor cognitive therapy was part of the treatment. Rather, the therapists merely encouraged the children to examine and draw their own conclusions about their beliefs after the completed session. For those in the child and parent session, the intervention was identical, but one parent was included in the treatment session. Depending upon the therapist's judgment, some parents functioned solely as a support figure, whereas others were able to serve as a model if the child had initial difficulty engaging with the fearful object or situation. Both interventions were equally efficacious in reducing specific fears as well as decreasing self-report of general anxiety, anxiety sensitivity and trait anxiety. Treatment gains were maintained at 1 year follow-up.

In one of the largest controlled trials (Silverman, Kurtines, Ginsburg, Weems, Rabian, & Serafini, 1999), 81 children and their parents were randomized to either self-control, contingency management, or wait list. In the self-control treatment (SC), children were taught cognitive strategies such as self-observation, self-talk, self-evaluation, and self-reward, coupled with graduated exposure assignments. Contingency management (CM) was designed to facilitate graduated exposure. Parents were taught behavioral strategies including positive reinforcement, shaping, extinction, and contingency contracting, which they implemented during the child's exposure sessions. In the Educational Support (ES) group, the therapist provided parent and child with information about phobias including their nature and course, etiology, major theoretical approaches, etc. No specific information was provided about any therapeutic strategy or how the interventions were implemented in practice. At posttreatment, all children, regardless of group, showed significant improvement on self-report measures of fear, general anxiety, depression and negative cognitive errors. Furthermore, all children demonstrated clinically significant improvement and all treatment gains were maintained at follow-up. This was a carefully designed and implemented randomized controlled trial and the results are in contrast to a large literature suggesting that exposure is a key ingredient in fear reduction. It is unclear why the ES condition (conceptualized as a control for therapeutic support) was as efficacious as the two active interventions, although a similar ES group was efficacious for anxiety-based school refusal (see chapter

8). This study was one of the few to include an active control condition rather than a wait list or no treatment control group, and therefore, the outcome highlights an important omission in the current treatment literature. The vast majority of the current literature can be summed up by the statement "Doing something is better than doing nothing."

MEDIATING FACTORS IN THE TREATMENT OF CHILDHOOD PHOBIAS

To date, few studies have examined factors that might accentuate or attenuate the efficacy of these behavioral interventions. Combining two samples of children treated with exposure-based CBT (Berman, Weems, Silverman, & Kurtines, 2000), a variety of possible predictors (sociodemographics, diagnostic characteristics, treatment format, child and parent reported phobic symptoms, parental symptomatology and marital distress) were examined. Higher pretreatment depression and trait anxiety were the strongest predictors of poor treatment outcome. Parental psychopathology, in the form of depression, hostility, and paranoia, also was associated with the child's poorer treatment outcome. When these predictors were examined by the child's age and whether the intervention was delivered in a group or individual format, the impact of parental psychopathology was weaker for older children or when the intervention was delivered in a group format. The finding that higher levels of depression and trait anxiety result in less positive treatment outcome is consistent with findings from studies examining treatments for other anxiety disorders and suggest that intervention programs that are usually capped at 12 weeks of treatment may be insufficient for a subset of phobic children.

Another factor that merits careful consideration is the issue of treatment dropouts. As noted by others (Stanley & Turner, 1995), treatment outcome rates often are inflated because those who prematurely drop-out are never considered when calculating treatment responders. Thus, it is important to examine the characteristics of those who leave treatment early. In a study of exposure-based CBT for children with anxiety disorders (Pine, Silverman, Weems, Kurtines, & Goldman, 2003), noncompleters received only an average of five treatment sessions. However, even though a variety of variables were examined (demographic characteristics, pretreatment scores on various self-report and parental report inventories), few significant group differences could be detected. The authors noted that their findings are consistent with previous studies thus making it premature to offer recommendations about spotting "early terminators" or offering recommendations about how to promote compliance with the treatment protocol.

In an interesting report of children's perceptions of brief exposure treatment for specific phobias (Svensson, Larsson, & Öst, 2002), many of the children who participated in the Öst et al. (2001) brief-exposure trial were interviewed. Children were questioned about several factors related to the treatment including expectations prior to treatment, worry and cognitions before, during and after treatment, perception of the therapeutic relationship, and outcome and satisfaction with the intervention. Interestingly, 83.9% of the children stated that they wanted to participate in the treatment program; 8.9% did not and 7.1% were doubtful. At pretreatment, only 55.4% thought the treatment would work, 25% were not sure, 17.9% did not think it would work, and 1.8% did not recall their expectations. After treatment, 58.2% described themselves as feeling very good and relaxed, 23.9% said they were happy, and 7.5% admitted to feeling tired. With respect to final outcome, 82.1% reported being satisfied with the therapy outcome, 8.9% were disappointed, and 8.9% were unsure if they were satisfied or disappointed. A number of children felt that they needed more treatment sessions and these were the children who demonstrated the least improvement from the single 3 hour session. This study is important because it represents some of the few available data on treatment satisfaction, particularly from the viewpoint of the child. The data indicate that although many adults believe that exposure interventions are too intense for children, these data indicate that many children are eager to participate in treatment, understand the rationale, and do not suffer negative effects as a result of the intervention.

LIMITATIONS OF THE CURRENT TREATMENT LITERATURE

One of the important limitations of the CBT literature is that in most instances, the only comparison was to a wait-list control group. Although these data confirm that CBT is superior to doing nothing, as noted in chapter 2, it remains unclear if these interventions are superior to "psychotherapy placebo" conditions. In addition to the Silverman et al. (1999) study previously cited, other research suggests that children's phobias may be reactive simply to therapist attention and support. For example, 6 children (aged 7-10) with severe fears of the dark were treated with a combination of relaxation training, cognitive self-instruction, and positive reinforcement using a multiple baseline design (Friedman & Ollendick, 1989). Children were instructed in positive self-statements such as "I can take care of myself in the dark" and "I am brave and can take care of myself when I am alone." Reinforcers consisted of tokens that the children could earn for going to bed "with bravery." Tokens were later exchanged for a party. Although the intervention decreased night time fears, the authors noted that a careful examination of the multiple baseline design indicated that changes occurred prior to the onset of the intervention (e.g., during the extended baseline and monitoring phase). Recall also that in chapter 6, 18% of children diagnosed with generalized anxiety disorder did not meet study criteria after the 2 week assessment phase (Rynn et al., 2001). As noted, many studies do not include an extended baseline and thus, changes in children's behavior attributed to the intervention may actually be due to subject reactivity or demand characteristics. The Friedman and Ollendick (1989) baseline condition did include home monitoring of nighttime behaviors and some therapist expectations such as the elimination of night lights, which may have served to affect behavior. However, because ethical considerations required that the children be treated, it remains unclear if the changes that occurred during baseline would have been maintained had no further intervention been available.

CASE EXAMPLES OF TREATMENT FOR CHILDREN WITH SPECIFIC PHOBIAS

Animal Type

As previously described:

> Randy was 7 years old and had an extreme fear of bees and yellow jackets. He had never had a bee sting but saw his sister get stung about 6 months ago. Over the ensuing winter, he did not appear to have any problems, but the following spring, he became fearful of going outside. He needed a great deal of encouragement and his mother noted that he would retreat to the house whenever possible ("I heard thunder, I have to go to the bathroom"). By summer, the symptoms had become much worse (he refused a trip to the zoo because bees might be there) and his mother sought treatment at our anxiety clinic.

The initial evaluation consisted of an interview with Randy and his mother. The interview did not reveal any other significant fears or other anxiety disorders. Because of Randy's age, he was not asked to complete self-report instruments independently, however, with his mother's help, he did complete the Fear Survey Schedule for Children-Revised. Consistent with the interview, no other fears were rated in the severe range. Randy was aware that he was "too afraid" of bees and yellow jackets. Prior to beginning treatment, self-monitoring procedures were instituted. Randy was asked to record his anxiety level whenever he went outside to go to school or when he got off the school bus in the afternoon. Because of his age, monitoring was made simple. Randy was given a series of five pictures of a child that illustrated various levels of distress (see chapter 3). Prior to beginning self-monitoring, the scale was explained to Randy and he was to be given several practice opportunities to assure validity of the report. Randy's mother also provided monitoring data by recording the number of minutes each day that Randy played outside after school.

Graduated in vivo exposure was selected to address Randy's fear. Two hierarchies were constructed: one for in-session tasks and the second for homework assignments. To construct the hierarchy, items associated with Randy's fear were first generated by the therapist, Randy, and his mother. Then the items were arranged hierarchically from least anxiety-producing to most-anxiety producing. Both hierarchies are presented in Table 7.3 presented on page 137.

Implementing in vivo exposure requires contact with the feared object or situation for a time length of sufficient duration so that habituation (feeling comfortable) will occur. If ended prematurely, anxiety could be exacerbated. The session concludes when the child's distress is reduced by 50% from the highest rating reported during the session. This is commonly referred to as within-session habituation (see Figure 7.2). As depicted, anxiety initially is quite high but decreases over time (X axis). The vertical axis is labeled SUDS (Subjective Units of Distress), a Likert rating scale used by the child to indicate subjective distress. In Figure 7.2, a 7-point SUDS scale is used, ranging from 0 (no distress) to 7 (extreme distress), although with younger children, a simpler scale (perhaps 5 points) might be used.

In addition to within session habituation (which should occur at each session), the ultimate goal of exposure is the achievement of between-session habituation. That is, across exposure sessions, peak distress should progressively decrease, and the time to return to baseline should progressively shorten. An example of between session habituation is depicted in Figure 7.3.

Implementing exposure interventions with children requires another important consideration. Whereas adults and older adolescents usually understand that the only way to get over a fear is to face it, younger children do not always understand the logic behind exposure. Taking the time to carefully explain the rationale to parents and children is important. This allows parents

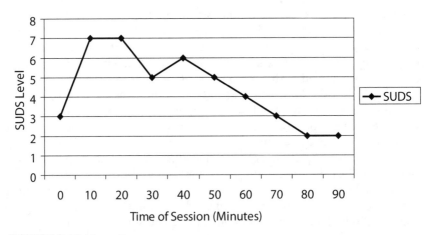

FIGURE 7.2 Within session exposure.

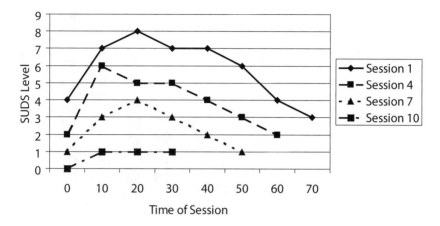

FIGURE 7.3 Between session habituation.

to encourage and reinforce the child's participation in the therapeutic process. Additionally, because children are often reluctant to participate in treatment, external reinforcers to encourage engagement in the in vivo situations may be necessary. Small activities or prizes that can serve as rewards for participation should be available.

In Randy's case, items initially were presented in clinic treatment sessions. No homework was assigned until that item (or a very similar item) did not elicit any distress when presented in the clinic. Consistent with a habituation paradigm, items was presented without the use of any competing response that would serve to minimize the child's distress. Rather, because a graduated hierarchy was used, each item elicited only a minimal degree of distress when it was presented.

When implementing the exposure session, Randy's attention was directed toward the phobic stimulus. Thus, when touching a dead bee for example, Randy was encouraged to describe how the bee looked and felt. In that way, the therapist could be assured that his attention remained focused on the phobic stimulus. Every 10 minutes, Randy was asked to report his level of distress using a 5-point SUDS scale and the session was terminated when, in the therapist's judgment, he appeared relaxed and when he reported two ratings of a "1" indicating no distress. When in session items no longer elicited distress, the item was assigned to Randy for homework.

A total of seven once weekly in vivo sessions coupled with homework assignments resulted in significant decreases in Randy's avoidance of bees as indicated by the self-monitoring data depicted in Figure 7.4. Results were maintained at 3 month follow-up.

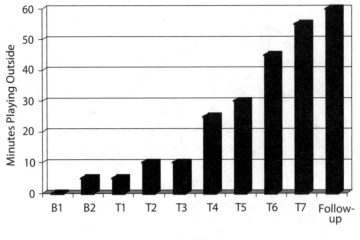

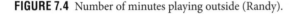

FIGURE 7.4 Number of minutes playing outside (Randy).

Treatment of Natural Environment Type

> Leslie was 13 years old and afraid of the dark, "spooky things," and thunderstorms. Her parents reported that she was fearful for as long as they could remember. She would not enter dark places alone or sleep alone, insisting that her much younger sister sleep in her room. She also was extremely afraid of thunderstorms and would hide in the closet until the storm is over. If the storm occurs at night, she would hide in the closet of her parents' bedroom. The family tried not to startle her.

In addition to these specific phobias, the diagnostic evaluation revealed the existence of some symptoms characteristic of GAD. Specifically, although Leslie did not report specific categories of worry or a significant amount of worry, both she and her mother reported heightened physiological arousal; she was easily startled, complained of headaches and/or stomachaches at least once per week, and often appeared unable to sit still. Therefore, although she did not meet diagnostic criteria for GAD, she exhibited a high level of general anxiety. Leslie did not meet diagnostic criteria for any other *DSM-IV* disorder. In order to determine a baseline level of functioning, Leslie was asked to monitor the frequency of stomachaches and headaches she experienced each day (see Figure 7.5). In addition, part of Leslie's home exposure involved the number of minutes she was able to remain in the dark (see Figure 7.6).

Leslie's case is typical of many children with specific phobias in that there often is the existence of several specific phobias. Thus, the challenge for

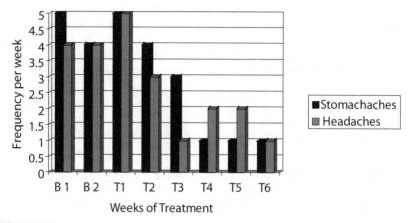

FIGURE 7.5 Frequency of stomachaches and headaches.

clinicians is to consider whether the specific phobias should be treated in a combined or sequential fashion. In the case of Leslie, a decision was made to combine the two situations into one graded hierarchy to be used in the clinic. In addition, a home exposure hierarchy was created (see Table 7.4 for both hierarchies). In vivo exposure was initiated in the clinic. Leslie was required to remain in the situation until she did not report or display any anxiety. She was not introduced to the next step until the previous item did not elicit any

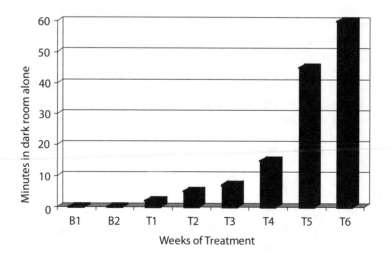

FIGURE 7.6 Time spent in the dark (Leslie).

TABLE 7.4 Leslie's In Clinic and Home Exposure Hierarchies

In Clinic Hierarchy	SUDS
Sit in a room alone with only one desk lamp providing lighting	2
Sit in a room alone without lights but with the door open (thus providing minimal illumination)	3
Sit in a room alone with no lighting at all	4
Sit in a room alone, in the dark, with thunderstorm sounds (on audiotape)	5
Sit in a room alone, in the dark, with "spooky" sounds (on audiotape)	6
Sit in a room alone, in the dark, with thunderstorm and "spooky" sounds (on audiotape)	7

Home Hierarchy

First night: Sit in the dark for five minutes. Each night stay three minutes longer until you can sit in the dark with no anxiety for 30 minutes.

After completing the above, lie in bed for 30 minutes with the light off. Increase by 5 minutes each night.

Rewards for Home Hierarchy Compliance

For every night that Leslie is able to complete her homework, she earns 5 minutes of extra telephone time (on the weekend). The first night she is able to sleep in her bed for the entire night, she earns an extra video rental. When she can sleep in her bed for the entire night for an entire week, she earns a sleep-over party with up to five friends.

distress even upon initial presentation (i.e., between session habituation was achieved for the individual item). As illustrated in the hierarchy, Leslie was exposed to increasing levels of darkness for an increasing period of time. As was the case with Randy, home exposure was not instituted until Leslie was comfortable in the dark in the clinic. As illustrated in Figures 7.5 and 7.6, the intervention resulted in a significant decrease in distress and within 3 weeks, Leslie slept in her own bed for an entire night and by the end of week 6, she had slept in her own bed for an entire week. Additionally, she was able to stay in her room during a thunderstorm. The frequency of stomachaches and headaches decreased in intensity although they did not disappear entirely. Because Leslie continued to demonstrate general tension and headaches, relaxation training was implemented to teach her to deal with her general distress (see chapter 6 for the treatment of GAD).

Treatment of BII

Bonnie is 17 years old and faints at the sight of, or even the verbal report of, blood or injury. Following what appears to be a conditioning event, where a magician "sawed a woman in half," she faints whenever she observes an injury or blood or

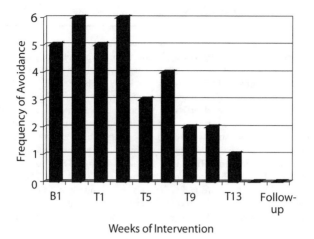

FIGURE 7.7 Avoidance and escape from BII situations.

even when someone is describing these types of events. She avoids using a knife and any other activity where knives or injury scenes were depicted or described (cooking, movies, TV shows, removing herself from friends who may be discussing an injury).

The pretreatment assessment did not reveal the presence of any other anxiety disorder although Bonnie reported that her mother often told her that she "worried too much." However, she did not endorse the presence of any other symptoms consistent with a diagnosis of GAD. Self-monitoring data (see Figure 7.7) indicated daily avoidance of activities involving knives and two fainting episodes.

Because Bonnie fainted easily (and often), she was taught to use Öst's applied tension procedure to prevent fainting during the exposure episodes. Bonnie's age suggested that imaginal exposure might be a useful first step. Additionally, given the need to be extremely careful about direct contact with blood-born pathogens, imaginal exposure eliminates this risk. The imaginal flooding scene is presented in Table 7.5.

As noted, Bonnie was instructed that during imaginal exposure, she should use the applied tension procedure if she began to feel faint. Fifteen imaginal flooding sessions were needed in order to achieve between session habituation. Home exposure also is presented in Table 7.5. After 15 weeks of treatment, Bonnie had stopped avoiding knives and situations that involved sight of or descriptions of blood or injury. Treatment gains were maintained at 6 month follow-up (see Figure 7.7).

TABLE 7.5 Bonnie's Imaginal Scene

It is early on Sunday morning. You and your friends are driving to the ski resort for a day of skiing. You are all sleepy and feel as if you are moving in slow motion. You pull into a fast food restaurant for breakfast. You park the car and everyone gets out. Just as your friend hits the electronic locks and locks the door, you hear your friend Sue screaming. You know it is bad and serious. As you rush over, you see Sue has tears in her eyes and she looks very scared. The door is not fully shut and Sue's hand is stuck in the door. You yell, "Open the door!" Someone finally unlocks the door and Sue's hand is free. But the blood begins to rush out. She is crying and you are getting very nauseous. You take Sue to the bathroom in the fast food restaurant to wash off the blood. After about 30 seconds, Sue passes out on the floor. She hits her head and now blood is gushing from her head and her hand. You yell for help and another friend calls for an ambulance. There is a lot of blood all around Sue. You can see her fingers. The fleshy part of the index finger has been crushed and the nail is hanging off. The middle-joint bone of her middle finger is broken backward so that the tip is pointed sideways at about a 35 degree angle. Another nail is all crushed to pieces. There is blood everywhere. You feel dizzy and nauseous as if you are about to faint. You are lightheaded and sweaty. But you cannot run away. Your friend needs you. She wants you to hold her injured hand. It is all you can do to keep from vomiting as you hold her crushed, bloodied hand in your hands.

Home Exposure

Every day:

Week 1 & 2	Handle a butter knife until any anxiety that is elicited dissipates
Week 3 & 4	Handle a steak knife until any anxiety that is elicited dissipates
Week 5 & 6	Handle a carving knife until any anxiety that it elicited dissipates
Week 7 & 8	Use a paring knife, cut up vegetables (celery, carrots, radishes) until any anxiety that is elicited dissipates
Week 9 & 10	Watch a TV show such as *E.R.* every day
Week 11 & 12	Watch younger sister cut up vegetables
Week 13–15	Observe father shaving

Treatment of Situational Type

Twelve-year-old Patricia refuses to fly on an airplane. When Patricia was 9 years old, she had been on an airplane that was caught in a wind shear. Since that time, she is uncomfortable in an airport even if there is no expectation that she will fly (e.g., going with her mother to pick up her father after a business trip). She also has a life-long fear of heights.

An interview with Patricia and her mother did not indicate the presence of any other psychiatric disorders. Although Patricia did not like being fearful of airplanes, she was very unhappy and embarrassed about having to come to the clinic. Given that her fear was precipitated only when she was at an airport, daily self-monitoring data were not collected. Rather, the outcome of successful treatment was defined as Patricia's ability to fly to Disney World for a family vacation that was scheduled for approximately 4 months from intake. Patricia's hierarchy is presented in Table 7.6. Clinic treatment sessions occurred once per week for 12 weeks. Patricia was able to take the flight to Disney World although

TABLE 7.6 Patricia's Hierarchy

Clinic Hierarchy	SUDS
Riding the elevators alone	2
At the airport but only in the boarding area	3
In the airplane jetway	4
Sitting on the plane, no motor running	5
Sitting on the plane, motor running	6
Flying in the day, ground visible	7
Flying at night	8
Flying in the day, cloudy weather conditions	9

Homework Exposure

Ride escalators for at least 15 minutes at least 4 times per week. Patricia is to ride alone, although for safety's sake, parent should be present and observing the exposure.

she complained of a headache during that initial flight. However, she did not express any somatic symptoms upon the return flight and subsequently, has not been reluctant to fly.

It should be noted that Patricia was treated prior to September 11, 2001, and the airline was able to be much more lenient regarding allowing unticketed individuals to pass through security, thus allowing the items on the hierarchy to be completed in vivo. Given current security restrictions at public airports in the United States, different items (or an imaginal approach) may be necessary although it still might be possible to implement this hierarchy at a private airport facility.

Treatment of Other Type

Edgar (aged 15) refused to go to school because he was afraid that he would vomit. He also avoided any social interactions because of his fear. When he was a toddler, he ingested a poisonous substance and was given ipecac in order to induce vomiting. Always a "clingy" child, he started complaining of persistent stomachaches and fear of vomiting in the fourth grade. Because of his concerns, he had two endoscopic procedures that have not revealed any physical cause for his fear. He avoids eating before social events, avoids eating certain foods (milk, cheese, yogurt, and spicy foods), situations (such as school) from which escape might be difficult if he becomes nauseous, and avoids "hanging out" with his friends. He also had occasional panic attacks at bedtime.

Thus, Edgar also met criteria for panic disorder and separation anxiety disorder. Self-monitoring data included recording the frequency of nighttime panic attacks, stomachaches, number of times that he engaged in "sleep-overs" with his friends.

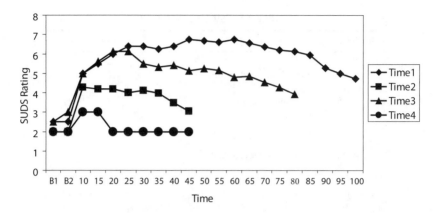

FIGURE 7.8 In vivo exposure: gagging.

For this complicated case (see Roberson-Nay & Turner, 2002 for an extended case presentation) intervention included interoceptive exposure (direct exposure to the cues of vomiting) and in vivo exposure. Specifically, the in vivo exposure consisted of a tongue depressor that was used to stimulate gagging and nausea/vomiting-related sensations. Edgar was asked to place the tongue depressor in the back of his mouth to stimulate the gag reflex. For each session, Edgar had to continue eliciting the gag reflex until he could gag without experiencing any distress. Between session habituation was judged not only by decreases in SUDS across sessions but also by increases in the number of times that he voluntarily elicited the gagging reflex during the exposure session (see Figures 7.8 and 7.9). As depicted in Figure 7.9, Edgar's ability to voluntarily "gag"

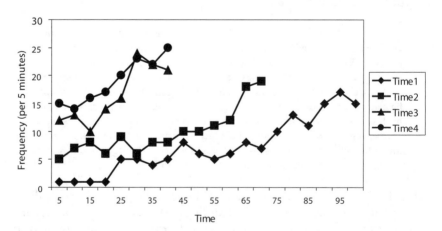

FIGURE 7.9 Gagging frequency.

himself was quite low during session 1, where initially he refused to attempt to elicit the gag reflect. However, by the fourth session, he was able to voluntarily elicit the gag reflex 25 times in a 5 minute period, indicating decreased anxiety with the idea that he would gag and vomit.

A total of five exposure sessions were necessary to achieve between session habituation. In addition to these in clinic sessions, Edgar had homework assignments that consisted of the following: leaving the house once per day for at least 30 minutes, once per day eating one previously "avoided" food such as milk, cheese, yogurt, or a spicy food. Finally, a hierarchy was developed to facilitate re-entry into school (see chapter 8 for treatment of school refusal). Self-monitoring data indicate substantial improvement across all categories of behavior (see Figures 7.10 to 7.12). At follow-up, Edgar was consistently attending school, was spending a great deal of time away from home, stayed at home for four days without his parents, and was gaining weight as a result of eating previously avoided foods.

To summarize, it is evident that behavioral interventions based on exposure paradigms are successful in treating children with a variety of specific phobias. As noted, the literature indicates that the best successes are achieved when the child has the opportunity to come directly into contact with the feared stimulus. Thus, even if a clinician uses one of the other intervention strategies described in this chapter, in vivo exposure (at least in the form of homework assignments) should be included in the overall intervention strategy. Furthermore, given the highly specific nature of these phobias, it is clear that standardized self-report

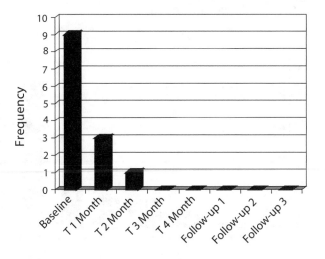

Month

FIGURE 7.10 Panic attacks.

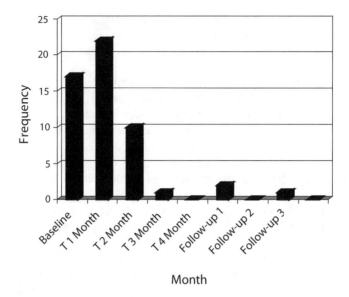

FIGURE 7.11 Stomachaches.

inventories that would be useful for treatment planning or determining treatment outcome do not exist. Thus, clinicians will need to use self-monitoring strategies that identify problematic behaviors and measure changes in those behaviors as a result of the intervention.

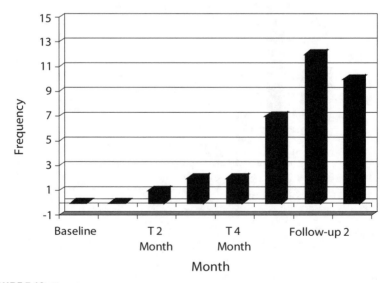

FIGURE 7.12 Sleep-overs.

CHAPTER 8

School Refusal

Mark is 15 years old. He wants to go to school but has not done so consistently for the past 2 years. According to his mother, he misses about two days of school per week, and on the other days, he is late about 50% of the time, sometimes not arriving until noon. Mark is oppositional, and has been verbally abusive and physically intimidating toward his mother, but only when she tries to make him go to school. On some days, he describes feeling anxious and panicky at the thought of having to go to school. On other days, he reports being "just too tired." When he stays home, he is not permitted to watch television or to play with his computer or video games. He is allowed to play with his hamsters and guinea pig, which Mark claims are more interesting than the privileges that are taken away. The situation has become so severe that Mark's mother has quit her job in order to be home with him.

ISSUES OF DEFINITION REGARDING SCHOOL REFUSAL

As a working definition, school refusal can be either (a) refusal to attend or (b) difficulty remaining in school for an entire day (Kearney & Silverman, 1990). School refusal is a complicated behavior inasmuch as children may refuse to go to school for many different reasons. Most important, school refusal must be differentiated from truancy, a distinction initially discussed during the 1930s and 1940s (see Kearney, Eisen, & Silverman, 1995) when school absenteeism was defined as a "clinical behavior" and distinguished from truancy. Truancy, a disruptive behavior, was considered to be an aspect of juvenile delinquency, whereas school refusal described children who desired to go to school but nevertheless were uncomfortable about attendance. In the 1940s, the term "school phobia" (Johnson, Falstein, Szurek, & Svendsen, 1941) was first used (Kearney et al., 1995) to describe the following constellation of behaviors: the presence of child anxiety, maternal anxiety, and an enmeshed mother–child relationship. Specifically, psychoanalytic theory implied that a close symbiotic relationship between mother and child led to an over dependent relationship that resulted in the child's reluctance to attend school. Later, behavioral theory postulated school refusal as a learned reaction to a specific event or situation associated with the school environment (see section on etiology for an extended description of these theories).

Others have forgone linking the refusal behavior to a particular etiological theory. For example, Coolidge, Hahn, and Peck (1957) described school refusal as one of two subtypes: neurotic or characterological. In 1961, Kennedy published a seminal paper on school phobia (school refusal) based on presenting symptoms. Although school phobia was the descriptive term used at that time, this classification system remains the basis for modern studies of school refusal psychopathology. Kennedy (1961) proposed two types of school phobia. Type 1 was a "neurotic crisis" whereas Type 2 was a "way of life" phobia. Both types shared common symptoms: (a) fears associated with school attendance, (b) frequent somatic complaints, (c) a symbiotic relationship with mother resulting in fears of separation and anxiety about many different things, and (d) conflict between parents and school administration. Despite these similarities, Kennedy (1961) listed a number of important differences that are depicted in Table 8.1. As discussed in the section on treatment, these two sub-types show dramatically different treatment outcomes.

Despite Kennedy's re-conceptualization of school refusal by focusing on symptoms instead of potential etiological factors, there remained difficulty with the use of the term school phobia. Specifically, children's self-report often was not consistent with the idea of a phobia. Some children refusing to go to school rated "having to go to school" as "somewhat fearful", not "excessively fearful", as might be expected given their behavioral avoidance (Kearney et al.,

TABLE 8.1 Type 1 and Type 2 School Phobia

Type 1	Type 2
1. Present illness is first episode	1. Second, third, or fourth episode
2. Monday onset, following an illness on the previous Thursday or Friday	2. Monday onset but a minor illness not a prevalent antecedent
3. An acute onset	3. Incipient onset
4. Lower grades most prevalent	4. Upper grades most prevalent
5. Expressed concern about death	5. Death theme not present
6. Mothers physical health in question; she is ill or child thinks so	6. Mother's health not an issue
7. Good communication between parents	7. Poor communication between parents
8. Mother and father well adjusted in most areas	8. Mother shows neurotic behavior; father has a character disorder
9. Father competitive with mother in household management	9. Father shows little interest in household or children
10. Parents achieve understanding of dynamics easily	10. Parents very difficult to work with

1995). Additionally, these children rated fears of nonschool items as high and sometimes higher than their fear of school. Consistent with these data, only 39% of another sample of children with problematic school attendance, reported "a lot" of fear of having to go to school (Barton, Kearny, Eisen, & Silverman, 1993). Other investigators have reported that between 0% and 52.4% of their school refusing samples meet diagnostic criteria for a primary or secondary social or simple phobia which may be related to school avoidance (Bernstein & Garfinkel, 1986, 1988; Last, Francis, & Strauss, 1987; Last & Strauss, 1990). Additional data indicate that negative affectivity (a concept that encompasses both anxiety and depression) also may be characteristic of at least a subset of children with poor school attendance (see Kearney et al., 1995 for a review of this literature). Overall, these data suggest that although fear may drive school refusal behavior in some children, the terms "school phobia" and "school refusal" are not synonymous.

Rather than relying on diagnostic criteria, Kearney and Silverman (1990; also Kearney, 1995) proposed that school refusal results from one of four different motivations: (1) avoidance of stimuli that precipitate negative affectivity (e.g., anxiety or depression); (2) escape from aversive social and/or evaluative situations (e.g., peer relationships, oral presentations); (3) attention (e.g., disruptive behavior to stay home with one's parents); and (4) positive tangible reinforcement (e.g., finding it more rewarding to be at home than at school). Whereas the first two types are considered to be motivated by negative reinforcement, the second two describe school refusal motivated by positive reinforcement (Kearney, 1995). The advantage of this conceptualization is that it allows for a prescriptive approach to treatment planning; a diagnosis describes the child's difficulty, but does not necessarily indicate a strategy for remediation. The functional (or prescriptive) approach allows for identification of the factors that maintain the problematic behavior and thus, indicates avenues for appropriate treatment planning.

To reiterate, truancy refers to those who do not attend school because of lack of interest or defiance of adult authority, whereas school refusal (or formerly school phobia) defines those who desire, but do not attend, school because of emotional distress such as fear, anxiety, or depression. Thus, school refusal is not a clinical syndrome but a descriptive term that may indicate the presence of a variety of emotional disorders. In some instances, no discernable disorder may be present. The focus of this chapter will be on those children who refuse to attend to school because of fear or anxiety.

CLINICAL ISSUES

The characteristic presentation of children with anxiety-based school refusal includes both physical and behavioral symptoms. Upon awakening, children often express somatic complaints such as headaches, stomachaches, or sore throats. Somatic complaints, particularly symptoms related to the autonomic and gastrointestinal systems, also are common among adolescents who refused to attend school (Bernstein et al., 1997). Typically, these physical complaints are more frequent on school days than on weekends or during summer vacations. Sleep difficulties also occur among children with anxiety-based school refusal. In one epidemiological sample (Egger, Costello, & Angold, 2003), 18% of the children reported night terrors, 14% reported nightmares, 32% reported trouble falling or staying asleep, 12% reported fatigue, 8% were reluctant to sleep alone, and 26% got out of bed in the middle of the night to check on family members. Morning tantrums also are common (King & Bernstein, 2001), particularly among younger children whereas adolescents, like Mark, are more likely to "stall" or delay personal hygiene rituals or to simply refuse to get out of bed. Finally, others go to school but cannot stay the entire day.

> Stephanie is 7 years old. She went to school in first grade without any difficulties. However, she is now in second grade and having extreme difficulty with school attendance. She refuses to ride the bus but will allow her mother to drive her to school and escort her to her classroom. Approximately an hour after her mother leaves, Stephanie becomes very agitated and fearful. She cries inconsolably. The school feels they cannot handle her behavior and they call her mother to come and take her home. This has happened every day for the last month. Her mother is seeking treatment for Stephanie because her daily absences from her job in order to pick up Stephanie at school is resulting in negative feedback from her employer.

Whereas some children may beg parents or caregivers to allow them to stay home, others, like Stephanie, will go to school but then disrupt the school environment, causing the school to request the child's removal.

Refusal to attend school has long been related to academic achievement. In one study, about 50% of children who refused to attend school were functioning poorly in the classroom (Chazan, 1962). More recently, learning disabilities and language impairments were significantly more common among an inpatient sample of depressed adolescents who refused school when compared to a matched group of psychiatric controls (Naylor, Staskowski, Kenney, & King, 1994). Furthermore, test anxiety, which may impair academic performance, has been reported to be a common precursor to school refusal (Kearney et al., 1995). Of course, all these data are correlational and do not allow conclusions to be reached regarding etiology. Specifically, it appears that school refusal may be a cause, an effect, or simply a correlate of academic underachievement.

The school environment provides opportunity for more than cognitive achievement. Schools provide an opportunity for children's social development and the establishment of friendships. Children who refuse to attend school miss important opportunities for social development. In one sample of pure anxiety-based school refusal children (Egger et al., 2003), 28.2% reported shyness with peers, 28.9% reported fears of being bullied or teased, 18.9% reported difficulty making friends because of social withdrawal, 17.5% reported difficulty making friends because of aggression, and 27% reported conflictual peer relationships. Again, because these children already were refusing to attend school, it is unclear if these peer problems were the cause or the result of their avoidance behaviors. A prospective design would be necessary to tease out the nature of these relationships. However, it is clear that a percentage of children who refuse to attend school have difficulties in the area of peer interactions.

Strained or poor family relationships also may present as part of the symptom picture (Last & Strauss, 1990). In one sample, two familial factors, single family households and a biological or nonbiological parent being treated for a mental health problem, were associated with anxiety-based school refusal (Egger et al., 2003). Other investigators have examined patterns of family functioning rather than family structure among children who refuse school. Bernstein and her colleagues (Bernstein, Svingen, & Garfinkel, 1989) used the Family Assessment Measure (FAM; Skinner, Steinhauer, & Santa-Barbara, 1983) to examine family functioning in four groups of school refusers (depressive disorder only, anxiety disorder only, anxiety and depressive disorder, no anxiety or depressive disorder). The FAM includes seven subscales: task accomplishment, role performance, communication, affective expression, affective involvement, control, and values and norms. The results indicated a lack of family dysfunction when school refusal was based solely on an anxiety disorder. In other words, family functioning, as assessed by this measure, was in the normal range among children with anxiety-based school refusal This was not the case for children who had both anxiety and depressive disorders (see section on comorbidity). However, family discord may not always appear in terms of the values or dimensions assessed by self-report inventories such as the FAM, and again, correlational studies do not allow for a determination of whether the dysfunctional patterns preceded or followed the school refusal. In Mark's case, marital discord was a result of his school refusal. Therefore, a careful assessment of familial functioning and marital relationships should be a standard part of the assessment battery as they may play a role in the maintenance or treatment of the behavior.

Even parental occupational functioning sometimes is impacted by the child's school refusal. In some cases, as was true for Stephanie's mother, parents are at risk of losing their jobs because of the need to leave work to pick up the child at school. In other instances, such as Mark's, his mother quit her job in order to deal with his refusal. In these instances, school refusal affected not only the child's functioning but also family functioning as well as potentially disrupting the school environment.

School refusal is associated with later adult maladaptive behaviors including agoraphobia, job difficulties, social avoidance, poor school adaptation, and constricted personality development (Burke & Silverman, 1987). A controlled long-term follow-up investigation of Swedish children indicated that those with school refusal suffered long-term social maladjustment (Flakierska, Lindstrom, & Gillberg, 1988; Flakierska-Praquin, Lindstrom, & Gillberg, 1997). At the 20–29 year follow-up interval (participants were at least 30 years old), those who refused school as children had more psychiatric consultations, were more likely to be residing with their parents, and had fewer children than the general population, suggesting that this behavior has the ability to impact long-term outcome even when school attendance is no longer mandated.

DIAGNOSTIC ISSUES

School refusal describes behavior but does not indicate the presence of a particular syndrome. Among children with school refusal treated by private practitioners, the desire to stay at home with parents and desire to avoid aversive social situations were equally common reasons for school refusal (26.1% and 25%, respectively; Kearney & Beaseley, 1994). Less frequent reasons included difficulty with homework or curriculum (12.2%), aversive evaluative situations including tests (10%), fear of specific situations in or related to the school setting (10%), positive tangible rewards (7.8%) and other (6.9%). Thus, even when restricted to anxiety-based school refusal, there are still different anxiety disorders associated with this behavior, including separation anxiety disorder, social phobia, panic disorder and agoraphobia, and perhaps PTSD. The relationship of these disorders and school refusal will be discussed. For an extensive discussion of each disorder, see the individual chapters in this book.

Separation Fears

An early theory regarding school refusal focused on an enmeshed mother-child relationship. Although this particular conceptualization is no longer the most popular explanation, the issue of separation from a caregiver remains a factor for some cases. Among a clinical sample of 63 children aged 7–17 years with school refusal, 38% had a primary diagnosis of separation anxiety disorder, a diagnosis that appears to be more characteristic of younger children (Kearney et al., 1995). Using an epidemiological sample of children with anxiety-based school refusal, 18% reported worry about calamitous separation from parents, 17% reported fear of what might happen at home while at school, and 5% reported worry about leaving home for school (Egger et al., 2003). One might conclude from these numbers that separation from care givers was characteristic of only a small percentage of school-refusing children. However, other results from this epidemiological survey indicated that maladaptive sleep behaviors were present (8% were reluctant to sleep alone, and 26% got out of bed in the middle of the night to check on family members). These complaints could be indications of separation anxiety among a subset of children with school refusal, suggesting that separation fears may be higher among school refusers than some data might indicate.

Social Fears

> Jessica is 16 years old and she loves school. However, she has not been able to go in the last few weeks. She fears being called on in class and giving the wrong answer, causing herself great embarrassment. Now, her anticipation of that possibility is so intense that she wakes up nauseated every morning. When asked about her refusal, she said, "I would love to go to school but I cannot stop vomiting long enough to get on the bus." Her mother agrees, noting that every morning Jessica gets up and gets dressed in an attempt to go to school. However, as the time to leave for the school bus approaches, she runs to the bathroom and begins to vomit.

In the Last and Strauss (1990) clinical sample described above, 30.2% of school refusers had a primary diagnosis of social phobia. Early investigations (Partridge, 1939; Warren, 1948) described children who did not attend school as poorly socially adjusted or timid and sensitive. More recent investigations confirm that social phobia may be a factor in some cases of school refusal (Last et al., 1987; Miller, Barrett, Hampe, & Noble, 1972; Ollendick, King, & Frary, 1989). For example, school absenteeism peaks when children encounter a new school setting (elementary school, middle school, or high school; Grannell de Aldaz, Feldman, Vivas, & Gelfand, 1977), perhaps as a result of a fear of getting lost and appearing incompetent in front of others (Kearney et al., 1995). Other potentially distressing school situations include giving oral reports, writing on the blackboard, taking tests or being reprimanded by a teacher or principal. Having to interact with other children at recess or around group projects also will evoke anxiety among those with social phobia. A less common, although still very significant and functionally impairing social phobia, is that of vomiting in front of others (and being embarrassed by it).

Specific Fears

Among the Last and Strauss (1990) clinical sample, 22% of school refusers met criteria for a primary diagnosis of specific (simple) phobia. This may include fear of riding the school bus, physical education classes, fire or other types of events. In comparison to those with separation anxiety disorder, children with social or specific phobias had a later age of onset, a more severe pattern of school refusal and were less likely to have mothers with a history of school refusal (Last & Strauss, 1990).

Other Anxiety Disorders

Panic disorder, generalized anxiety disorder (formerly overanxious disorder), posttraumatic stress disorder, and obsessive-compulsive disorder also may lead to school refusal behavior although these disorders are less commonly reported in the school refusal literature.

> Susan is 12 years old. She is very fearful of contamination and getting cancer. She is afraid to touch anything that might have been touched by someone who has cancer. There are several children at her school who have been treated for cancer, one of whom is in her class. Susan is refusing to go to school because she is afraid that she will touch something that has been touched by one of the children with cancer. Despite repeated explanations by her parents and her pediatrician that she cannot get cancer by touching something belonging to, or being touched by, a cancer patient, Susan remains very anxious and fearful and refuses to attend school.

As illustrated in our clinical example, panic disorder also may lead to school refusal behavior.

> Mark's school refusal appeared to be related to several underlying conditions. A core feature appeared to be concern with unfamiliarity both with situations and with people. For example, although he will go to malls with which he is familiar, he refuses to go to "new malls" and states that he gets "wobbly kneed" in new situations. He also becomes uncomfortable in and avoids church. He reportedly becomes overwhelmed in crowds and can document panic attacks on at least three occasions: at the mall, at a barber shop, and in a movie theater with symptoms consisting of weakness in his knees, shortness of breath, and a strong desire to escape the situation. Social fears also appeared to play a role. For example, he left a family reunion and it was his mother's impression that he was overwhelmed by all of the unfamiliar people, describing heart palpitations, feeling flushed, and weak-kneed. At school, he has several friends but had difficulty in gym class when the students had to "pair up." He did not have any friends in the class, became very uncomfortable (heart palpitations and feeling flushed) and refused to participate.

Thus, although the prevalence is lower than for other anxiety disorders among children, panic disorder may be a precipitating cause for the school refusal in this case. However, Mark also presents with some degree of social phobia although the severity of this diagnosis was secondary to his panic and depression.

In summary, the prevalence of generalized anxiety disorder, obsessive-compulsive disorder, panic disorder, and posttraumatic stress disorder among school-refusing samples is much lower than for separation anxiety disorder, social phobia, and specific phobia. Because of their lower prevalence, much less information is available on the relationship of these disorders and school refusing behavior. However, it is clear from the case examples that the disorders can be just as impairing as those more commonly associated with school refusal.

Sociodemographic Influences

In their review of the last 10 years, King and Bernstein (2001) noted that approximately 5% of all children manifest school refusal behavior, although rates appear to be higher in urban populations. In a longitudinal study of the development of psychiatric disorders in an epidemiological sample of 1,422 children aged 9 through 16 (Great Smoky Mountain Study; Egger, Costello, & Angold, 2003), the 3 month prevalence of anxious school refusal was 2.0%, whereas the rate of truancy was 6.2%. In an interesting study of clinician referral and practice characteristics, Kearney and Beasley (1994) surveyed practitioners who were members of the American Psychological Association. Six percent of referred children presented with school refusal behavior. Thus, although not an extremely common disorder, children with school refusal behavior are not uncommon among the caseloads of private practitioners.

School refusal is equally common in boys and girls (Grannell de Aldaz et al., 1984; Kearney & Beasley, 1994; Kennedy, 1965; King & Ollendick, 1989) and cuts across socioeconomic status (King & Bernstein, 2001). Among outpatient samples (Kearney & Beasley, 1994), children with school refusal ranged from age 5 to 17, with the highest prevalence rate among 7–9 year olds (31.5%) and the lowest rates among 5–6 year olds (11.2%) and 16–17 year olds (15.2%). In a specialty anxiety clinic, the ages of children with school refusal also ranged from 7 to 17 years with the most frequent age being 13–15 years, followed by age 10 (Last & Strauss, 1990). However, by the time some children are brought to the clinic for treatment, school refusal may be present for several years. Thus, the implied etiological age of onset for a clinic-seeking sample (Last & Strauss, 1990) is consistent with suggestions by others (e.g., Ollendick & Meyer, 1984) that school refusal appears to have certain peak ages, particularly between 5–6 years and 10–11 years. At the younger age, separation anxiety disorder is probably the more common etiological factor, whereas social phobia is more common at older ages (Last, Francis, Hersen, Kazdin, & Strauss, 1987). Thus, these peaks may represent the common clinical conditions found at those ages (i.e., separation anxiety disorder and social phobia).

Another age-related difference is to be in the mode of onset for school refusal. Among younger children, an acute onset is more common whereas an "insidious development" occurs more frequently among older children and adolescents (King & Ollendick, 1989). Among school refusing samples, adolescents usually present with more severe and chronic disturbance, and thus are less responsive to treatment (Burke & Silverman, 1987, also see Treatment section of this chapter).

Several sociodemographic variables, along with clinical and family variables appear to be related to severity of school refusal. Higher rates of absenteeism were associated with older age, less fear (measured by a self-report inventory), and family environments that place less emphasis on out of home recreational activities (Hansen, Sanders, Massaro, & Last, 1998). Less fear among those with the highest rates of absenteeism may seem contradictory, although several factors may have influenced this finding. First, reduced fear may result from more consistent avoidance of the phobic stimulus, in this case, the school (Hansen et al., 1998). That is, if the child succeeds in avoiding the feared situation, they may report only minimal fear. However, a second consideration has to do with the fact that in general, older children have lower scores on fear inventories than younger children (see chapter 1). Thus, lower fear scores among those with higher rates of absenteeism may simply reflect the fact that older children (who also have higher rates of absenteeism) tend to score lower on self-report measures of anxiety than younger children. Future investigations will need to control for the participant's age when examining the relationship between fear and avoidance.

COMORBID AND DIFFERENTIAL DIAGNOSIS

In addition to his anxiety symptoms, Mark reported difficulty sleeping, with both sleep-onset and sleep-continuity problems. He endorsed being depressed, lethargic and irritable, and during the initial evaluation, he was tearful and his affect was blunted. Furthermore, his parents reported the presence of oppositional behaviors such as being defiant and deliberately testing limits. These behaviors occurred primarily around school attendance but also when having to go other public places such as church. Thus, upon admission, Mark met diagnostic criteria for panic disorder and major depression. His oppositional behaviors were viewed as originally secondary to his fears although they recently had increased in scope such that a diagnosis of oppositional defiant disorder was warranted.

In addition to those who refuse school due to the presence of an anxiety disorder, there is a subset of children and adolescents who present with symptoms of both anxiety and depression. There also are those with school refusal who appear to suffer only from depression, but that group will not be discussed here except for comparative purposes (see Kearney, 1993 for a review of depression and school refusal). Among school refusers with anxiety disorders only, anxiety and depressive disorders, depression only, or disruptive behavioral disorders, those comorbid for both anxiety and depressive disorders had significantly higher scores on both mood dimensions (anxiety and depression) than groups with one disorder alone; thus suggesting a more severe symptom picture for this diagnostic group (Bernstein, 1991). Furthermore, in comparison to children with anxiety disorders alone, children with comorbid anxiety and depression, and their mothers, reported decreased abilities to solve problems and respond to crises, less definition and integration of family roles, maladaptive communication styles, and limited agreement about (a) components of the family's value system and (b) the family's adherence to a particular culture (Bernstein, Svingen, & Garfinkel, 1990). A later study (Bernstein, Warren, Massie, & Thuras, 1999) examined family dimensions in school-refusing adolescents with both anxiety and depression. No comparison group was used. Results indicated that 63% of adolescents and 52% of their parents viewed their families as low on family cohesion (i.e., they reported high disengagement). Also, 52% of adolescents and 38% of their parents viewed their families as low on adaptability (i.e., they were quite rigid). Interestingly, their ideal families were conceptualized as more cohesive and flexible than their own real family. Of course, this study did not allow one to determine if these factors preceded or followed the onset of the school refusal behavior. Furthermore, it is unclear if these family factors play a role in treatment outcome.

ETIOLOGY

Even when school refusal samples are limited to those with anxiety-related disorders, there still are many potential etiological factors. Family history may play a role in its onset although the data are equivocal. One study (Berg, Butler, & Pritchard, 1974) did not find a higher incidence of overall psychiatric illness in the mothers of school phobic adolescents, whereas others suggest that children who refuse school also had mothers with a history or school refusal (Berg, Marks, McGuire & Lipsedge, 1974; Last & Strauss, 1990). One recent investigation reported that parent–child concordance with respect to the specific disorder that precipitated the school refusal (Martin, Cabrol, Bouvard, Lepinhe, & Mouren-Simeoni, 1999). Specifically, children with separation anxiety disorder had increased prevalence rates of panic disorder or panic disorder with agoraphobia. In contrast, parents of children who refuse to attend school because of phobic disorders had increased prevalence rates of specific or social phobias. Of course, a family history does not necessarily mean that these disorders are genetically or biologically determined, inasmuch as learning theory also can account for increased prevalence of specific disorders within families. However, it once again suggests that (a) school refusal does not result from one unique etiology, and (b) anxiety disorders are familial.

Certain life events have been associated with the development of school refusal. These include death or illness in a parent or close relative, change of class or school, traumatic events at school, and prolonged absence from school because of personal illness (King & Ollendick, 1989). Although it is unclear how often these events precipitate episodes of school refusal, they appear to be most consistent with children who have Type 1 school refusal.

Learning theory also is relevant for the etiology of school refusal. Classical conditioning, vicarious conditioning, and operant conditioning theories all provide possible explanations for the onset of anxiety-based school refusal. Events such as being embarrassed by a teacher, getting up in front of the class and being unable to speak, or being teased by peers have been related to subsequent school refusal (via classical conditioning). Similarly, if a child observes these events happening to another child who then displays distress, the observing child may develop a fear vicariously. Finally, a child who complains of somatic symptoms and is allowed to stay home thereby escaping from an aversive situation (i.e., negative reinforcement) will develop school refusal as a result of operant procedures.

In summary then, even when school refusal is anxiety-based, its etiology is still multi-faceted. Some children may be predisposed to the development of anxiety or depressive disorders and develop school refusal secondary to the disorder. For other children, school refusal may develop after a traumatic event resulting in the child's refusal to return to the school environment. It is clear that identifying the basis for the disorder is necessary for effective treatment implementation.

ASSESSMENT

Inasmuch as school refusal may indicate the presence of any number of different anxiety disorders or a combination of anxiety and depression (as well as no disorder), the assessment strategy should be broad and inclusive not only for anxiety but also for depression and externalizing disorders. Instruments useful for assessing conditions or factors responsible for school refusal are presented here.

Interviews

The Anxiety Disorders Interview Schedule for Children (ADIS-C/P; Silverman & Albano, 1996) is a general diagnostic interview and also contains a specific section to assess for the presence of school refusal. This interview is administered separately to parents and children and the section on school refusal may provide some preliminary data on the reason for the refusal. Reliability and validity data for the ADIS-C/P have been presented in chapter 3.

Self, Parental and/or Teacher Report

Although many self-report instruments are available for assessing specific anxiety disorders, they will be reviewed in the chapters addressing each of these disorders. Here, self-report instruments designed specifically for school refusal are reviewed.

The School Refusal Assessment Scale (SRAS; Kearney & Silverman, 1990; 1993) and its revision the School Refusal Assessment Scale-Revised (SRAS-R; Kearney, 2002) consists of 24 items assessing four motivating factors: (a) avoidance of stimuli that provoke negative affectivity, (b) escape from aversive social or evaluative situations, (c) attention-getting behavior or traditional separation anxiety, and (d) positive tangible rewards. Six questions assess each factor and there are child and parent versions. The scale has good test-retest reliability, good concurrent and construct validity (Kearney, 2002) and different anxiety disorder diagnoses were associated with different motivations for school refusal (Kearney & Albano, 2004). Specifically, anxiety-related diagnoses were more often associated with negative reinforcement, separation anxiety disorder was more often associated with attention-seeking behavior, and tangible reinforcement was most often associated with oppositional defiant disorder and conduct disorder. As noted, a specific advantage of this scale is that the data can be used prescriptively by the therapist to design an individualized behavioral treatment plan.

The Self-Efficacy Questionnaire for School Situations (SEQ-SS; Heyne et al., 1998) assesses the child's perceptions regarding ability to cope with potentially anxiety-producing school situations. These situations include doing school work, handling questions about absence from school, and being separated from parents or caregivers. Factor analysis revealed two factors: separation/discipline stress and academic/social stress. Although the scale has good reliability, further explication of the scale's validity would be beneficial.

Another self-report instrument designed to assess anxiety in school-refusing children is the Visual Analogue Scale for Anxiety-Revised (VAA-R; Bernstein & Garfinkel, 1992). Similar to the other instruments, the VAA-R has three factors: anticipatory/separation anxiety, performance anxiety, and affective response to anxiety. The VAA-R has good internal consistency and test-retest reliability over a one week period and good concurrent validity.

Commonalities cutting across all instruments include the acknowledgment that a myriad of factors may lead to school refusal. Thus, all of these instruments assess for different anxiety disorders and in the case of the SRAS-R, nonanxiety conditions. These scales allow the clinician to better understand the disorder that results in school refusal and to provide a more targeted treatment plan.

Behavioral Assessment

Daily diaries, completed by parents and children, often provide a valuable source of information necessary for treatment planning. Dependent upon the child's particular difficulty, a self-monitoring plan may include the child's thoughts as well as behaviors, and should include the parent's responses to the child's behaviors as well. Mark's daily diary is presented in Figure 8.1.

A. School Attendance
    Went to school   ____ yes   ____ no
    Went to school on time   ____ yes   ____ no
    Rode the bus to school   ____ yes   ____ no

B. Number of panic attacks that occurred that day   ____

C. Highest level of anxiety experienced that day
  /_____/_____/_____/_____/
  None   A little   Some   Pretty much   A lot

FIGURE 8.1 Mark's self-monitoring (daily diary) form.

In Mark's case, the assessment battery included a diagnostic interview with the Anxiety Disorders Interview Schedule for Children/Parents, the School Refusal Assessment Scale, SRAS, and other self-report measures of anxiety and depression. In addition, both Mark and his mother completed 2 weeks worth of self-monitoring data regarding his school attendance. Finally, a behavioral assessment conducted in the clinic assessed physical symptoms associated with his panic attacks.

The results of the SRAS indicated that one of the primary motivating factors behind Mark's school refusal was avoidance of situations related to negative affectivity. Consistently, the behavioral assessment indicated that the primary panic symptoms included dizziness, increased heart rate, shortness of breath and feeling weak in his knees. Furthermore, self-monitoring data revealed parenting practices that allowed Mark to manipulate the family environment to his advantage.

TREATMENT

The American Academy of Child and Adolescent Psychiatry (AACAP) recommends a multimodal strategy for the treatment of children with anxiety-based school refusal. Specifically, the AACAP recommends consideration of the following components: education and consultation, behavioral or cognitive-behavioral strategies, family intervention, and medication, if warranted (King & Bernstein, 2001). Empirical data in support of these interventions will be examined here.

Pharmacological Intervention

A landmark study on the pharmacological treatment of "school phobia" was published by Gittelman-Klein and Klein (1971). Children refusing to attend school were assigned to either imipramine or pill placebo. At the end of the 6 week treatment, 81% of those in the imipramine group had returned to school compared to 47% of the placebo group, indicating a superiority for the use of imipramine. One limitation of this study was that the sample of school phobic children probably contained children with a variety of diagnostic disorders, such as anxiety and/or depression. Thus, the utility of these findings for a sample of children with solely anxiety-based school refusal is unclear. However a follow-up study of the use of imipramine for the treatment of children with separation anxiety disorder did not show any superiority for imipramine over placebo (Klein, Koplewicz, & Kanner, 1992) and imipramine is no longer considered a "first line" pharmacological intervention, having been replaced by the newer selective serotonin re-uptake inhibitors with their more benign side-effect profile (see concerns about the recent SSRI black box warning in chapter 10).

In an open trial of alprazolam and imipramine for the treatment of school refusal (Bernstein, Garfinkel, & Borchardt, 1989), 17 children (aged 9.5 to 17.0 years; 11 with comorbid depressive and anxiety disorders, 4 with depressive disorder only, and 2 with an anxiety disorder only) were prescribed 1 of the 2 medications. Each child also received a school reentry program and psychotherapy. After 8 weeks of treatment, 67% of those treated with alprazolam were rated as moderately or markedly improved in anxiety and/or depressive symptoms and 55% had returned to school. Similarly, 67% of those treated with imipramine were rated as moderately or markedly improved and 50% had returned to school. The small sample size precluded analyses separately by diagnosis. However, these promising findings led to a double-blind placebo controlled trial of these two pharmacological agents (Bernstein et al., 1989). Twenty-four children with school refusal behavior (mean age 14.1 years) were randomly assigned to either alprazolam, imipramine, or placebo. Ten children had a depressive disorder only, 4 had an anxiety disorder only, and 10 had comorbid anxiety and depressive disorders. In addition to medication, the intervention included a school reentry component that consisted of gradually increasing the number of days that the child went to school, providing a school support person, and attending a classroom for emotionally and behaviorally disturbed students. Additionally, a psychotherapy component consisted of weekly sessions with a child psychologist or a child psychiatry resident. Thus, this intervention might be better considered a multimodal intervention. After 8 weeks of treatment, scores on rating scales suggested that those treated with alprazolam showed the most improvement, with the imipramine group showing moderate improvement, and the placebo group the least improvement. However, baseline scores were substantially different for these three groups and when the pretreatment score was used as a covariate, there were no significant group differences in change scores for anxiety and depression. Similarly, among those for whom school attendance data were available, all subjects in the alprazolam and imipramine groups ($n = 6$ in each group) returned to school with improved attendance (although this term was not fully operationalized). However 5 out of 6 children in the placebo group also met this same criterion. Thus, these data are unclear with respect to the additive specific effects of imipramine and alprazolam on school refusal over psychosocial treatment alone. In fact, the few data that are available indicate that medication alone is not a well-established intervention for school refusal. Furthermore, as we will present, even when medication or multimodal treatment results in statistically significant decreases on measures of anxiety and/or depression, this does not always translate into improved school attendance.

As noted, recent recommendations by the AACAP consider medication to be part of a multi-modal treatment plan for those with anxiety disorders and are not meant to be prescribed alone (King & Bernstein, 2001). Using a multimodal strategy (Bernstein, Borchardt, & Perwein, 2000), 8 weeks of imipramine plus CBT were compared to 8 weeks of placebo plus CBT for the treatment of 63 adolescents comorbid for anxiety and depression and who were refusing school. Anxiety and depressive symptoms improved for both groups although depression improved faster for those treated with imipramine. Using a criterion of 75% school attendance, 54.2% of the imipramine group met this criterion as opposed to 16.7% of the placebo group. Thus, although a number of adolescents were improved, particularly those in the imipramine group, many still were not able to go to school on a regular basis. Furthermore, a naturalistic follow-up (Bernstein, Hektner, Borchardt, & McMillan, 2001) indicated that 1 year later, 64.1% met criteria for at least one anxiety disorder and 33.3% met criteria for dysthymia or major depression, with no differences in prevalence rates between those treated with imipramine or placebo. Additionally 67.5% received at least one pharmacological trial during the follow-up period and 75% received additional outpatient therapy. Rates of school attendance were not available, however it was reported that most children attended school.

In summary, the available data indicate that in most instances, active pharmacological agents are only minimally superior to placebo. Rates of return to school after pharmacological treatment remain variable and sometimes depend upon very study-specific criteria. In some cases, 75% attendance is considered successful whereas more stringent criteria are used in other studies. Furthermore, most of the studies combine pharmacological with behavioral interventions, which are reviewed below. Thus, it remains unclear whether medication really is efficacious for the treatment of this behavior.

Psychosocial Interventions

Similar to the literature for childhood anxiety disorders in general, much of the early literature on the treatment of school refusal was based on case studies and reports. Among clinicians in private practice (Kearney & Beasley, 1994), parent training/contingency management is the most common intervention provided (40.3%), followed by cognitive restructuring (14.4%), contingency contracting (12.2%), forced school attendance (11.6%), imaginal or in vivo desensitization (8.3%), modeling and role play (6.6%), play therapy (6.1%), and pharmacotherapy (0.6%). As will be reviewed below, some of these interventions are more effective than others.

Kennedy's (1961) seminal publication on the behavioral treatment of school refusal examined rapid intervention for children with Type 1 school refusal. As previously discussed, Type 1 has an acute onset, occurs more commonly in younger ages and in intact families where both parents play a role in parenting (see clinical presentation section for a more complete description). Kennedy's intervention was based on behavioral procedures that blocked the child's escape from the feared situation (school) and prevented the establishment of secondary gains. In addition, the child was reinforced for attending school without complaint. Kennedy (1961) reported the success of 50 cases treated with this program whose specific components included establishing good professional relationships, avoiding attending to somatic complaints, forcing school attendance, and educating parents. This last component has several subcomponents including portraying optimism, emphasizing success, and presenting the treatment plan which consisted of the following: (a) no discussion of school attendance on the weekend; (b) getting the child ready to go to school on Monday escorted by the father in a matter of fact fashion (without questions or comments about school); (c) reinforce the child on Monday evening for going to school despite somatic complaints or fears; and (d) repeating the procedure for Tuesday and Wednesday. By Wednesday, it was expected that the child's fear would be virtually eliminated. The results indicated that the intervention was successful with all 50 children with no remission at follow-up. As noted by the author, the evaluation of the intervention was based solely on self-report data and school attendance data. Diagnostic interviews were not part of the investigation. Furthermore, no control group was available for comparison. Thus, it is not possible to determine if some of the children would have returned to school without intervention. Additionally, the program's success in treating Type 2 (rather than the Type 1) cases was much less impressive. Despite these limitations, this study has been considered the landmark study for the behavioral treatment of school refusal. Furthermore, the approach, based on sound behavioral principles, is still used in treating many children with anxiety-based school refusal.

An initial group comparative trial (Blagg & Yule, 1984) compared behavioral intervention to inpatient hospitalization to a homebound instruction and psychotherapy group for children with school refusal. The behavioral condition included: (a) stimulus desensitization through humor and emotive imagery; (b) blocking the avoidance response through forced school attendance;

(c) positive reinforcement both at school and at home for school attendance; and (d) extinction of negative behaviors (somatic complaints, fearful expressions). It should be noted that children were not randomized to these conditions. Rather, preexisting data were analyzed. Thirty children were treated with the behavioral treatment approach (BTA), 16 were treated with inpatient hospitalization (HU) and 20 received home instruction and psychotherapy (HT). Most were between the ages of 11 and 16 and there were no differences on sociodemographic variables. Using the Type I or Type II classification system, about 50% of those treated with BTA, 75% of the HU group and 25% of the HT group were classified as Type II school refusal. After a year of treatment, 93% of those in the BTA group were judged as treatment successes compared to 37% of the HU group and 10% of the HT group. When school attendance rates (defined as school attendance on 80% of the days) were examined, 83% of the BTA group met this criterion compared to 37% of the HU group and 10% of the HT group. Furthermore, not only was the BTA intervention more effective, it also was more efficient. The average treatment length was 2.5 weeks for the BTA group compared with 45.3 weeks for the HU group and 72.1 weeks for the HT group. These results are quite impressive although limitations include the lack of a control group and the lack of randomization to the treatment assignments. One might expect that those requiring inpatient hospitalization represented more severe psychopathology. However, the study was crucial in promoting the use of behavioral procedures for this disorder both in terms of treatment efficacy and cost-effectiveness.

King and his colleagues (King et al., 1998) randomized 34 children aged 5–17 with school refusal behavior to either a 4 week cognitive-behavioral intervention (CBT) or a wait-list control group. The majority of the children met diagnostic criteria for an anxiety or phobic disorder. CBT consisted of coping skills, exposure, and contingency management. In comparison to the wait-list control, those treated with CBT exhibited significant improvement and 88% achieved at least 90% school attendance. Only 29% of the wait-list control met this criterion. CBT also increased children's confidence in coping skills and decreased their anxiety. At 3 to 5 year follow-up, 13 of the 16 treated with CBT (and who could be contacted) were attending school regularly and had not had any further school refusal incidents. Among the three children who relapsed, two had been having problems academically and one was expelled for "uncontrollable behavior." One limitation of this study was the small sample size and the lack of an extensive clinical interview at follow-up (that might have detected the presence of other clinical conditions). Despite this limitation, the 4 week CBT intervention appeared to have remarkable long-term effects for a majority of the children.

In one of the few studies to compare CBT to an attention-placebo control group (Last, Hansen, & Franco, 1998), 56 children with anxiety-based school refusal were randomly assigned to 12 weeks of CBT or an educational support group. CBT included graduated in vivo exposure, cognitive restructuring, and coping self-statement training whereas educational support included educational presentations, supportive psychotherapy and a daily diary of thoughts and fears. There was no encouragement for "facing your fears" in the educational control group. Although the educational support group was designed as a placebo control, the results indicated that both groups demonstrated marked improvement in school attendance, anxiety and depression, and global improvement. Similarly, at posttreatment, 65% of those treated with CBT and 50% of those in educational support no longer met criteria for an anxiety disorder. Treatment gains were maintained at 4 week follow-up. Nevertheless, the authors reported that not all children benefited from 12 weeks of CBT. Thirty-five percent of the children assigned to CBT did not achieve 95% school attendance and 60% had difficulty attending school during the next year. These data are important inasmuch as they indicate that perhaps a more extensive intervention or an additional treatment strategy may be necessary at least for a subsample of the population.

Kearney and Silverman (e.g., Kearney & Silverman, 1990) have been at the forefront in promoting a functional model of treatment for school refusal. Based on their studies of psychopathology and the identification of four patterns of school refusal behavior, their treatment approach has been to tailor the intervention strategy, not merely to the school refusal itself, but to the particular behaviors and clinical symptoms that appear to maintain this particular behavior. In the initial investigation (Kearney & Silverman, 1990), 7 children and adolescents with difficulty attending school were treated with "prescriptive" behavioral treatment (developed specifically for their particular fears). Thus, some children received (a) modeling and cognitive instruction (for social fears category), (b) systematic desensitization and relaxation training (for specific fears category), (c) shaping and differential reinforcement of other behaviors (inappropriate attention seeking from parents), or (d) contingency contracting (tangible rewards category). At posttreatment, 6 of 7 children had returned to school on a full time basis (the seventh decided not to return to school but began work with parental permission) and at 6 month follow-up, 5 of the 6 continued to attend school regularly. Inasmuch as this was a preliminary trial, the results are limited by the lack of a control group (either a wait-list control or children who were randomly assigned to treatment, rather than matched based on their specific clinical profile). However, like the Blagg and Yule (1984) study, this report provides the initial impetus for further investigation in this area, particularly for more tightly controlled clinical trials.

In summary, the psychosocial treatment outcome literature is in much the same status as the pharmacological treatment data. There are only a few controlled trials and although uncontrolled trials indicate substantial treatment success for behavioral interventions, a large randomized controlled trial did not indicate that the behavioral intervention was superior to an attention placebo control condition. Further clinical trials are necessary to clearly establish the efficacy of the interventions for school refusal.

Predictions of Treatment Success

Several factors appear to be related to positive treatment outcome. In the Last et al. (1998) investigation, those children who were younger and had higher levels of school attendance at baseline were most improved. Similarly, Layne and colleagues (Layne, Bernstein, Egan, & Kushner, 2003) reported that higher rates of school attendance at baseline and combined treatment with CBT and imipramine (as opposed to CBT and placebo) were predictive of positive treatment response among 41 anxious-depressed adolescents with school refusal behavior. Interestingly, in this same study, negative treatment response was predicted by the presence of comorbid separation anxiety disorder or avoidant disorder. In combination, these four variables accounted for 51% of the treatment outcome variance. However, the small number of patients included in this sample preclude drawing broad conclusions from these analyses.

The consistency of these findings with those of Last et al. (1998) and Kennedy (1961) suggests the importance of treating children with school refusal as quickly as possible. Unlike other fears in children, where parents are often advised to wait 6 months or so and see if the child might "outgrow" their distress, when the clinical syndrome includes school refusal, intervening quickly appears to be the empirically supported approach. As noted, children with the comorbid disorders of avoidant disorder and separation anxiety disorder responded poorly to this intervention. The CBT program used by Layne et al. (2003) was based on the treatment manual used by Last et al. (1998) and it may be that the CBT procedures included did not specifically address the unique fears of those with these comorbid conditions.

School Personnel Participation

As noted by Kearney (1995), the atmosphere surrounding cases of school refusal is often stressful, sometimes reaching "crisis-like" dimensions. Thus, as the treatment plan is implemented, daily (or near-daily) contact with parents, child, and the school is necessary. Because much of the behavioral program's implementation will occur at the school setting, daily contact with the school allows for program "trouble-shooting" and gives school personnel the reassurance that the therapist is available to assist whenever necessary. This would be particularly important in cases where children's distress in school, has in the past, resulted in their removal from the school setting. Therapists should be willing to initially meet with school personnel to present and discuss the treatment plan. Furthermore, the therapist's physical presence at school on the first day of the child's return assures that the program is being implemented by the school in the manner in which it was designed by the therapist. The investment of a few hours of clinical time on the first day often eliminates the need for "backtracking" at a later date when it become apparent that the program was misunderstood and/or not implemented correctly.

Obstacles to Treatment Success

Although in certain instances there may be a need for a graduated approach to treatment, King and Ollendick (1989) note that rapid treatment has gained widespread acceptance among researchers and clinicians. Rapid treatment minimizes the possibility of "secondary treatment gain," one of the major impediments to successful treatment outcome. Basic principles of learning can be used to explain secondary gain. Specifically, if the child experiences fear in anticipation of school attendance and is therefore allowed to remain at home, the child's fear dissipates (i.e., avoidance is negatively reinforced). Thus, staying home eliminates distress. Additionally, at home the child often is allowed (at least initially) to watch television, play computer games, or engage in other pleasant activities. So, positive reinforcement also plays a role in the secondary gain phenomena. Staying home results in the opportunity to engage in enjoyable activities rather than attending school, which may not be so enjoyable. Therefore, the more quickly the child returns (or is returned) to school, the less likely that secondary gains may complicate the intervention strategy.

Kearney (1995) presented a cogent review of some common obstacles to the successful implementation of treatment for school refusal. Some of the obstacles noted, such as poor clinic attendance, hostility from a family member, noncompliance with treatment procedures, comorbid disorders and psychopathology in the parents, are common obstacles for any type of intervention. One often overlooked impediment to treatment is simply the inability to attend clinic sessions. For example, among families where there is a child who refuses to attend school, approximately 25–40% of families do not arrive for their initial visit and the rate of "no shows" increases as the school year progresses (Kearney, 1995). One factor may be the high spontaneous remission rate associated with school refusal and the second is the parent's inability to bring the child in for the evaluation session. This is consistent with the parents' inability to make the child go to school. Overcoming this latter obstacle often is a matter of parent training and it is possible that initial sessions may need to be conducted without the child being present.

Other obstacles not often addressed in the empirical literature but faced every day by clinicians treating school refusal behavior include the child's reluctance to attend school due to having fallen behind academically. Children also often express reluctance to return to school because they do not know how to explain their absence to their classmates. Children's concerns about these issues appear to increase as a function of the number of days that they have been absent from school, again emphasizing the advantage of early intervention. Although there is no single strategy to deal with these anxieties, there are several guidelines that we have found useful. With respect to the academic issue, tutoring or sending school work to the home might allow most children maintain their academic status (see also the section on homebound instruction). With respect to the issue of what to say to their peers regarding their absence, social skills training could be useful (King & Ollendick, 1989).

Relapse prevention also is crucial in the successful treatment of school refusal. Minor relapses may occur following long weekends or extended vacations (Kearney, 1995). Returning to school after summer vacation is another crucial time when relapse may occur. Booster sessions may be needed at these times in order to consolidate treatment gains.

The Issue of Homebound Instruction

One of the major hurdles with respect to the treatment of school refusal is the issue of homebound instruction. As previously noted, children who have refused school for a number of weeks tend to fall behind academically. This in turn, places additional pressure on the child with respect to returning to school. Not only is the child faced with questions from peers regarding his absence but is also faced with "making up" all of the school work that has been missed. Conversely, engaging a homebound instructor for the child, even during the time during which behavioral intervention occurs, can lead to decreasing the child's motivation to return to school. There appears to be no universal way to handle this issue, rather decisions must be made on an individual basis. Our practice has been to base our decisions on the length of time that the child has been absent from school. If it has been only several weeks, we rely on assignments being sent home by the teacher in order for the child to maintain academic progress. If school absence has been more extensive and it is our opinion that one aspect of the child's concern regarding returning to school is the issue of academics, we negotiate with parent and child regarding a recommendation of a brief period of homebound instruction. That is, we support the request for homebound instruction provided it (a) is only for a limited (usually one month) period of time and (b) it does not interfere with other aspects of the treatment plan.

TREATMENT OF SCHOOL REFUSAL—CASE EXAMPLE

As noted, Mark's clinical presentation was quite complicated. In addition to panic attacks and social anxiety, Mark was depressed, oppositional, and even

TABLE 8.2 Mark's Treatment Plan

Problem Area	Intervention

School Refusal/Oppositionality	1. Parent Management Training
	2. Transfer of Responsibility for School Attendance to Mark
	   (a) Reward successes
	   (b) End morning negotiations
	   (c) Strict bedtime rules

Depression	1. Medication 2. Increase pleasant events
Anxiety/Panic	1. Social Effectiveness Therapy for Children 2. Interoceptive Exposure

disrespectful of his mother's authority. Thus, the treatment plan (presented in Table 8.2) addressed the various aspects of his clinical presentation including school refusal/oppositionality, depression, and anxiety/panic. Specific strategies were developed to deal with each of these issues. In this chapter, only the portion of the plan addressing school refusal is presented.

School Attendance Plan

The goal of this aspect of the treatment was to increase the time in school such that Mark achieved full-time school attendance in six weeks. To accomplish this, Mark and his mother were given specific instructions and contingencies for certain behaviors, and rewards were established. In order to provide ongoing assessment and reward intermediate achievements, both short-term and long-term goals were established. The long-term goal, getting a dog, was something that Mark had wanted for some time but that his parents were unwilling to provide, given Mark's baseline behavior. However, they were willing to agree to a dog, given the contingencies set forth in the contract.

Because at baseline, Mark was attending school 3 days a week, arriving at about 11:00 a.m., this was chosen as the target goal for the first week. This provided the opportunity to "troubleshoot" the contract and to allow Mark and his mother to become familiar with earning and providing rewards without adding in the need to increase his school attendance in the first week of the program. The specific school contract is depicted in Table 8.3.

School attendance was monitored on a daily basis and three specific data points were collected: (1) total number of days per week that Mark was able to adhere to the contract, (2) total number of days per week that he went to school but arrived late, and (3) total number of days that he did not go at all. As depicted, Mark initially had trouble adhering to the contact. In addition, although there was an opportunity for Mark to complete the contract and earn

TABLE 8.3 Mark's Weekly School Contract

Overall Guidelines

1. For each day that Mark meets the week's school attendance goal, his mother will spend up to an hour accompanying him to get a video game or movie. (Mark can use the video game or movie once his nightly homework is completed.)

2. Each week that Mark meets his weekly goal, the calendar will be marked with a point at the end of the week. In addition, at the end of 7 weeks if Mark has stuck to the plan (attends school on time, stays in school for the entire day for 3 weeks at weeks 5, 6, and 7), then Mark will earn a pet dog.

3. Mark will have to earn all 7 points in order to get the dog. Keeping the dog will depend on Mark taking care of the pet (cleaning up after it, walking it when not in school) and staying in school full-time. If Mark does not stay in school, the dog will be taken away.

4. For each day that Mark is disrespectful to his mother or father (example: saying shut up, grabbing, shoving, banging the wall, cussing, calling Mom an idiot or anything else that Mom considers disrespectful), an extra day will be added to the final 3 weeks of full-time school attendance before Mark can have his dog.

Week 1

Goal for the week: Mark gets himself to school by __11__ a.m. on 3 days
To accomplish this:

1. Mark will be responsible for waking himself at _____. He will get ready for school on his own. Mom can make breakfast for Mark and it will be ready at _____. If Mark is not ready to eat, the breakfast can remain there but cannot be heated up by Mom. Mark can do it himself if he desires. Mark will be ready to leave for school at _____ in order to be there by __11__ a.m.

2. If Mark does not go to school at all or goes late, he will not be allowed to play with his pets, watch TV, listen to the radio, play video games, use the computer, play with friends, or interact with his parents during school hours. After school hours, his parents can interact with him as usual. However, there will be no discussion about school or attendance.

3. If Mark goes above and beyond the expectation of the week (extra day of school attendance at or before the time selected on point days), he will get an additional rental from the video store.

Week 2

Goal for the week: Mark gets himself to school by __10__ a.m. on 3 days
The contingencies for Week 1 are still in effect

Week 3

Goal for the week: Mark gets himself to school by __9__ a.m. on 3 days
The contingencies for Week 1 are still in effect

Week 4

Goal for the week: Mark gets himself to school by __8__ a.m. on 4 days
The contingencies for Week 1 are still in effect

Week 5, 6, 7

Goal for the week: Mark gets himself to school by __8__ a.m. on 5 days

Ultimate Goal

After full-time attendance all week for three weeks (Weeks 5–7), then he will have earned the dog. If Mark does not stay in school full-time, he will not be able to keep the dog. Also, if Mark does not care for the dog it will be taken away.

Mark's Signature Date	Mother's Signature Date	Father's Signature Date

the dog within a seven week time period, the length of the contract had to be extended for an additional six weeks because of his oppositional behaviors. That is, when Mark was disrespectful or physically intimidating to his mother, additional days were added to the length of the contract. Mark was aware of this contingency before it was implemented but of course, simple awareness does not assure compliance.

The basic rules of contingency management would dictate that required behaviors and rewards should be one-to-one. That is, if Mark went to school at the appropriate time, he should receive the reward. However, in this case, part of the contract was he had to leave for school in an appropriate, respectful fashion. In other words, it was not acceptable for him to curse at or physically intimidate his mother regarding his school attendance, even if he then got to school on time. Thus, in this case, the required behavior was not simply school attendance; it was going to school in a behaviorally appropriate manner.

Several aspects of the weekly contract deserve comment. First, a behavioral assessment of the morning interactions between Mark and his mother indicated two large areas of conflict. First, although Mark would set his alarm, he would not get out of bed. Mark's mother would make numerous trips to his room in an attempt to encourage him to get out of bed. This attention by the mother was viewed as reinforcing Mark's refusal to get out of bed inasmuch as staying in bed elicited substantial attention from his mother. Thus, the contract made Mark responsible for getting out of bed. The second area of contention between Mark and his mother involved breakfast. Specifically, Mark would ask his mother to make breakfast for him but then by the time that he would get to the kitchen, the breakfast was cold and he would demand that it be heated up again. Clearly, this is one illustration of his disrespectful behavior. Therefore, in the weekly contract, the time that breakfast would be ready was noted, allowing Mark to plan his morning routine appropriately. If he was late, he had the option of re-heating breakfast himself. Third, Mark craved his parents' attention and when he did not go to school, he would talk to his mother all day. Thus, even if his anxiety was important in the etiology of his school refusal, tangible reinforcement obviously was playing a role in maintaining the behavior. Thus, in addition to taking away the usual reinforcers (TV, video games), tangible reinforcement in this case included taking away interaction with his mother during school hours.

Other parts of Mark's program included interoceptive conditioning (see chapter 12) and Social Effectiveness Training for Children (see chapter 10).

SUMMARY

As is evident from the data presented, school refusal is a complicated behavior. Many disorders and conditions may result in school absence and the first action on the part of parents or therapists is to develop a clear understanding of the

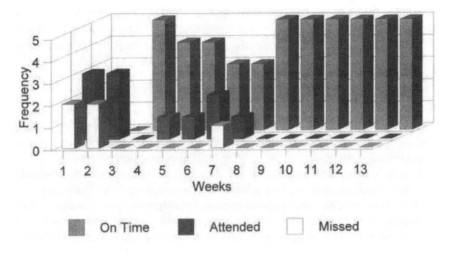

FIGURE 8.2 Mark's school attendance.

underlying motivation. Even when the avoidance appears to be anxiety-based, there are still many possibilities potentially responsible for eliciting this behavior. Diagnostic assessments, self-report measures, and self-monitoring data all may assist in establishing the proper diagnosis and suggesting the appropriate intervention strategy. It is important to note that, as in Mark's case, school refusal may result from one disorder and yet be maintained by additional factors. Thus, refusal may be precipitated by anxiety but yet maintained by other factors such as depression. Furthermore, oppositional behaviors may play a role simply as a result of parental attempts to force the child to go to school or as part of a more general pattern of oppositionality. In either case, parent management training often is a necessary component of a comprehensive intervention program

With respect to specific strategies, both pharmacological and psychosocial interventions have been reported in the literature. Pharmacological interventions have been the subject of several controlled trials and although results sometimes have been positive, the American Academy of Child and Adolescent Psychiatry recommends the use of pharmacological agents as part of a multi-model treatment strategy. There is some evidence that the combination may be helpful although further controlled trials are needed. With respect to psychosocial interventions, there is a rich clinical history suggesting that behavioral interventions are effective in the treatment of this disorder. Starting with the initial work of Kennedy (1961), a rapid response to initial school refusal appears advantageous. Although there are many instances where behavioral interventions appear to be efficacious, some of the recent controlled trials have been disappointing suggesting that they may be no more effective than attention-placebo control groups. The reasons for this are unclear although it may be that the intervention programs have not taken advantage of the relevant research on the psychopathology of this disorder. Specifically, whether school refusers are classified according to types or diagnostic criteria, "one size treatment" may not fit all. That is, given the data presented by numerous authors, and most recently by Kearney and his colleagues, closer attention needs to be paid between the factors behind the school-refusing behavior and the specific intervention. Thus, future investigations may need to pay more attention to functional analyses and matching symptom presentation to a specific intervention strategy.

CHAPTER 9

Separation Anxiety Disorder

Leslie is 10 years old. For the past 6 months, she has refused to go anywhere but school unless accompanied by one of her parents. She was fearful in "unfamiliar places" (her words), including soccer practice, playing at her friend's house, or even taking out the garbage at night. Leslie has no prior history of separation anxiety disorder. In fact, she is quite distressed by her fear and embarrassed by her inability to be away from her parents. Furthermore, she does not like to have to go to therapy and wishes that she was in school instead.

Separation anxiety disorder (SAD) is a severe and unreasonable fear of separation from a parent or caregiver. Most prevalent among young children (aged 5–7), it can occur at any age during childhood or adolescence. Children with SAD are extremely worried that, when apart from a parent or caregiver (sometimes called an attachment figure), harm will occur to that person or to themselves. The anxiety can be so intense that children refuse to separate from their parent or caregiver; in many cases, refusing to go to school. In the most severe cases, the children may be reluctant to be in a room separate from their parents, even in their own home. This sometimes results in children sleeping with their parents well beyond the accepted age.

The construct of SAD is rooted in concepts of psychoanalytic theory and attachment theory. Bowlby (1973) described attachment as a bond between mother and infant that is selective, warm, and biologically motivated and expressed in infant behavior such as maintaining physical contact and proximity. The predisposition to become attached is considered a survival mechanism and protest results when separation from the survival figure occurs. Although on the surface, there are apparent similarities between the separation protests of attachment theory and the protests exhibited by children with SAD, many questions remain regarding the relationship between these concepts. A full exploration of these issues is beyond the scope of this chapter, but one very relevant question is the relationship of these biologically based (and therefore

187

theoretically universal traits among children) and the relatively few children who go on to develop SAD. To date, there has been little empirical data to address this issue.

It is important to distinguish between "normal" separation anxiety and SAD. As noted in chapter 1, "stranger anxiety," common among children between 1 and 2 years of age, is characterized by expressions of distress (usually crying or turning away) whenever anyone other than the child's parents (or primary caregiver) attempt to hold or engage the child in some type of social activity. Although much has been hypothesized about why children behave in this fashion, empirical data regarding the basis for the fear are very rare. In fact, because stranger anxiety is considered a typical developmental stage, there has been very little research into motivations behind this particular fear reaction. However, SAD is distinguishable from "stranger fear" on many dimensions including age of onset, degree of emotional distress, and degree of functional impairment. The remainder of this chapter will address SAD, first introduced into the diagnostic nomenclature in 1980 with the third edition of the *Diagnostic and Statistical Manual of Mental Disorders* (*DSM-III*; APA, 1980). As currently defined in the fourth edition of the *DSM* (*DSM-IV*; APA, 1994) SAD is a severe and excessive of separation fear from an attachment figure (caregiver) that results in significant distress and substantially impairs daily functioning. See Table 9.1 for the *DSM-IV* diagnostic criteria for SAD.

CLINICAL FEATURES

Given that SAD is considered to be a common childhood disorder (Silverman & Dick-Niederhauser, 2004), it is remarkable that there are so few carefully controlled trials examining SAD's psychopathology. Perhaps one limiting factor is that for many years, the terms "school phobia" and "separation anxiety disorder" were used interchangeably. In many instances, reviews and empirical investigations purporting to examine the psychopathology of separation anxiety disorder used samples of children who refused to go to school. As discussed in the chapter on school refusal, children who refuse to go to school suffer from many different psychiatric disorders and therefore the terms school phobia/refusal and SAD, and their related literatures, are not interchangeable.

With that caveat in mind, school refusal is a common feature of many children with SAD. Particularly at earlier ages, school is one of the few activities where children are traditionally expected to separate from their parents and where attendance is mandatory. Among one sample of children with SAD, 73% presented to the clinic with school refusal (Last, Francis, Hersen, Kazdin, & Strass, 1987). Thus, although a very high percentage of children with SAD will avoid school, as illustrated by Leslie, not all children with SAD will refuse

TABLE 9.1 Diagnostic Criteria for Separation Anxiety Disorder

1. Developmentally inappropriate and excessive anxiety concerning separation from home or from those to whom the individual is attached, as evidenced by three (or more) of the following:
   a. Recurrent excessive distress when separation from home or from major attachment figures occurs or is anticipated
   b. Persistent and excessive worry about losing, or about possible harm befalling, major attachment figures
   c. Persistent and excessive worry that an untoward event will lead to separation from a major attachment figure (e.g., getting lost or being kidnapped)
   d. Persistent reluctance or refusal to go to school or elsewhere because of fear of separation
   e. Persistently and excessively fearful or reluctant to be alone or without major attachment figures at home or without significant adults in other settings
   f. Persistent reluctance or refusal to go to sleep without being near a major attachment figure or to sleep away from home
   g. Repeated nightmares involving the theme of separation
   h. Repeated complaints of physical symptoms (such as headaches, stomachaches, nausea, or vomiting) when separation from major attachment figures occurs or is anticipated

2. The duration of the disturbance is at least 4 weeks.

3. The onset is before age 18 years.

4. The disturbance causes clinically significant distress or impairment in social, academic (occupational), or other important areas of functioning.

5. The disturbance does not occur exclusively during the course of a Pervasive Developmental Disorder, Schizophrenia, or other Psychotic Disorder and, in adolescents and adults, is not better accounted for by Panic Disorder With Agoraphobia.

Specify if: Early Onset: if onset occurs before age 6 years

Reprinted with permission from the *Diagnostic and Statistical Manual of Mental Disorders*. Copyright 2000. American Psychiatric Association.

to go to school (see also Silverman & Dick-Niederhauser, 2004 for a discussion of this issue).

An interesting paradox is that although 3–5% of the population may be diagnosed with SAD, it is among the least stable of the anxiety disorders. One of the first longitudinal investigations examining the stability of psychiatric disorders in children (including anxiety disorders) used a sample referred to a speech and language clinic (Cantwell & Baker, 1989). Initially, 9 children were diagnosed with SAD. At 4 year follow-up, only 11% of the children still had SAD and an additional 44% had a different disorder. The other children (45%) did not have any disorder. When compared to other diagnostic categories in the study, SAD had one of the highest recovery rates. In other words, it was one of the least stable diagnostic categories and that presents some constraints for treatment outcome investigations (see section on treatment).

Among an epidemiological sample of 8–17 year old twins (Foley, Pickles, Maes, Silberg, & Eaves, 2004), 80% of those with a diagnosis of SAD at time 1 had remitted an average of 18 months later. Among children, persistent SAD at time 1 and time 2 had significantly more symptoms of oppositional defiant disorder and more impairment associated with symptoms of attention deficit hyperactivity disorder. Among adolescents, more symptoms of SAD at time 1 were associated with the persistence of SAD at follow-up. Additionally, 59% had no psychiatric diagnosis at follow-up, whereas 26% had a different diagnosis at follow-up, the majority of which (62%) were not present at time 1. Overanxious disorder was the most common "new" disorder (43%) followed by minor or major depression (33%), attention deficit hyperactivity disorder (14%), conduct disorder (10%), and phobia (10%).

High recovery rates were also characteristic of another sample of children with SAD referred to an anxiety disorders treatment clinic (Last, Perrin, Hersen, & Kazdin, 1996), where 96% of those initially diagnosed with SAD recovered by 3–4 years later. Similar to Cantwell and Baker (1989), among those who no longer met SAD diagnostic criteria, 25% had developed a new psychiatric disorder. In the most recent investigation, diagnostic instability also was reported in a longitudinal study of 27 children originally diagnosed with SAD at age 3 (9 with SAD and 18 with subclinical SAD; Kearney, Sims, Pursell, & Tillotson, 2003). Three and one-half years later, among the 9 children originally diagnosed with SAD, only 2 children still met diagnostic criteria; 5 had subclinical SAD and 2 had no disorder. Among the 18 originally categorized as subclinical SAD, 1 was diagnosed with SAD at follow-up, 4 had subclinical SAD and 13 had no disorder. The results of these investigations suggest that SAD is not a stable disorder, but a subset of children may present with other disorders at a later date, and that many will have no diagnosis. Part of this instability may relate to neglect of strictly enforcing the functional impairment criterion when determining the diagnosis. Thus, as discussed in the chapter on Generalized Anxiety Disorder, "normal" worries may be over interpreted as a true disorder (see chapter 6). Some degree of concern about a parent's well-being is probably normal, particularly for young children. Severity and impairment are what distinguish "typical" from "pathological" fear. Also, it may be that the current diagnostic criteria are not stringent enough and/or perhaps incorrect. Another possibility is that what has been termed separation anxiety may be a transient condition under the control of changing environmental factors. Finally, this instability creates difficulty for treatment outcome studies. Without proper control groups, inaccurate conclusions about the efficacy of the intervention may result.

It is important to note, however, that among those who do have a chronic course, the long-term impact of SAD can be significant. A 20–29 year follow-up investigation compared 35 individuals with SAD treated for school refusal at ages 7 to 12 years with 35 nonschool refusal psychiatric patients and 35 children from the general population (Flakierska-Praquin, Lindstrom, & Gillberg, 1997). Children with SAD had more psychiatric consultations, were more likely to live with their parents and had fewer children than both of the comparison groups. Thus, SAD, particularly when coupled with school refusal, can impact upon long-term social development.

RELATIONSHIP TO ADULT PANIC DISORDER

Over the past 30 years, there has been continued controversy regarding the relationship of childhood SAD to adult panic disorder. Klein (1964) was the first to examine this relationship, noting that severe separation anxiety was prominent in the histories of patients with panic disorder and that panic attacks often started after a major personal loss (Klein, 1995). Klein (1964) proposed that "spontaneous panic attacks" could be a sign of the "protest-despair" response to separation, and that SAD in childhood may be a developmentally immature form of panic disorder/agoraphobia in adulthood. With respect to this linkage, there are three lines of research that address this issue: (1) similar drug treatment response, (2) family concordance for SAD and panic disorder, and (3) history of childhood SAD in adults with panic disorder/agoraphobia. Each is discussed here.

Initially, pharmacological interventions for both panic disorder and school phobia (presumed to be precipitated by SAD) found that imipramine was efficacious for both disorders (see Gittelman & Klein, 1984 for a review of this literature). However, a later investigation using a sample of children with a primary diagnosis of SAD (rather than school phobia) did not find imipramine to be more effective than placebo (Klein, Koplewicz, & Kanner, 1992; see Treatment section for discussion of this issue). Thus, data on equivalent treatment response for panic disorder and SAD are equivocal.

The second line of data relates to family history. In the initial publication (Klein, 1964), 50% of panic patients described an early history of SAD. However, recent data are more conflictual. Weissman and colleagues (Weissman, Leckman, Merikangas, Gammon, & Prusoff, 1984) reported a higher prevalence of SAD among offspring of parents comorbid for depression and panic disorder. However, when these same children reached adulthood and were re-interviewed directly, no relationship was found (Mufson, Weissman, & Warner, 1992). So again, no definitive conclusions can be drawn.

The third line of evidence examines the history of SAD in adults with panic disorder. With respect to one of Klein's (1964) initial observations that "spontaneous panic attacks" could be a sign of the "protest-despair" response to separation, several investigations examined the prevalence of separation/trauma events in the childhood histories of patients with panic disorder. As was noted above, the data are conflictual; some retrospective data suggest that a history of SAD is significantly more common among female, but not male, patients with agoraphobia (when compared to patients with social phobia or specific phobia; Zitrin & Ross, 1988). SAD also was more common among patients with panic disorder when compared to a group of medical/surgical patients (Battaglia et al., 1995) but not when compared to the childhood histories of patients with other types of anxiety disorders (Lipsitz et al., 1994). Interestingly, a childhood history of SAD was more common among those patients with two or more anxiety disorders as adults (regardless of the type) than those who had only a single disorder. This could suggest that SAD may indicate the presence of severe anxiety (as indicated by the presence of multiple anxiety disorders) rather than predict the presence of one particular anxiety disorder (Lipsitz et al., 1994). Interestingly, a history of traumatic separation *events* are not more common in the childhood histories of those with agoraphobia when compared to adults with specific phobia (Thyer, Nesse, Cameron, & Curtis, 1985). Again, the data remain conflictual and inconclusive.

Three longitudinal studies have examined the relationship of SAD in children and panic disorder/agoraphobia in adults. Two investigations did not find a higher prevalence of adult panic disorder among children previously diagnosed with SAD when compared to children with other anxiety disorders (Aschenbrand, Kendall, Webb, Safford, & Flannery-Schroeder, 2003; Craske, Poulton, Tsao, & Plotkin, 2001). A third study (Klein, 1995) examined the prevalence of anxiety disorders among adults who previously were treated as children for SAD. The probands with a prior history of SAD were compared to a normal comparison sample and the results indicated that adult panic disorder was the only anxiety disorder that distinguished the two groups. However, the prevalence rate for panic disorder among the SAD probands was only 7% (compared to 0% among the comparison group). Given the other findings reported above, the lack of a psychiatric control comparison group limits the conclusions that should be drawn from this investigation.

More recently, there have been research efforts to examine the continuity of SAD in childhood/adolescence and SAD in adulthood. Clinical evaluations and self-report data indicate that some adults report symptoms consistent with *DSM-IV* derived criteria for SAD (Manicavasagar & Silove, 1997a; Manicava-sagar, Siilove, & Curtis, 1997; Manicavasager, Silove, Curtis, & Wagner, 2000) and many retrospectively endorsed the presence of these symptoms as children. As noted by Silverman and Dick-Niederhauser (2003), although intriguing, these data are based on retrospective reports and self-report instruments with only limited psychometric properties. Thus, although suggestive, the validity of a relationship between child/adolescent SAD and adult SAD remains inconclusive as does the relationship between childhood SAD and adult panic disorder.

EPIDEMIOLOGY

Among all of the childhood anxiety disorders, SAD is one of the most common. However, an important consideration is that even when past the "typical age" for developmentally appropriate fears, as suggested earlier in the chapter, many children endorse thoughts of separation. In fact, when functional impairment is not considered, up to 50% of 8-year-old children express separation fears (Kashani & Orvaschel, 1990). Thus, as discussed in chapter 6, many children express thoughts associated with anxiety disorders. However, for most children, these concerns do not impair their daily functioning or their social/academic development, and therefore they would not be considered to have a disorder. This issue is raised as a consideration for clinicians and parents when attempting to determine the severity of a child's fear. A simple expression of fear does not necessarily mean that a disorder is present. Fear plus impairment is necessary to substantiate the presence of an anxiety disorder.

SAD is considered to be a common psychiatric disorder and prevalence rates in the general population range from 3–5% (see Silverman & Dick-Niederhauser, 2004 for a review). The prevalence rate among the general adolescent population is slightly lower (2.4%; Bowen, Offord, & Boyle, 1990). Among children referred to a general outpatient psychiatric clinic, 9.9% had SAD and an additional 2.8% were comorbid for both SAD and Overanxious Disorder (Westenberg, Siebelink, Warmenhoven, & Treffers, 1999). Few data are available for specialty clinic samples although one study reported that 33% of children referred to a childhood anxiety clinic had a primary diagnosis of SAD (Last, Francis, Hersen, Kazdin, & Strauss, 1987).

SOCIODEMOGRAPHIC INFLUENCES

With respect to gender, some studies report that SAD is more common among girls than boys (Anderson, Williams, McGee, & Silva, 1987; Bowen et al., 1990; Costello, 1989; Last, Francis et al., 1987; March, Parker, Sullivan, Stallings, & Conners, 1997) whereas others report equal prevalence rates (Bird, Gould, Yager, Staghezza & Canino, 1989; Francis, Last & Strauss, 1987; Last, Perrin, Hersen, & Kazdin, 1996). Among boys and girls diagnosed with SAD, specific symptoms do not differ based on gender (Francis et al., 1987).

As suggested above, the peak age of onset is between 7 and 9 years of age (Bird et al., 1989; Last et al., 1992; Pruis et al., 1990), although SAD also may develop during adolescence (Bowen et al., 1990; Last et al., 1992). However, SAD is more common among children than adolescents (Breton et al., 1999; Kashani & Orvaschel, 1988, 1990; McGee et al., 1990). In addition to differences in prevalence rates, age differences also have been reported in SAD symptom expression (Francis et al., 1987). Young children with SAD (5–8 years old) were significantly more likely than older children (9–12 years old) and adolescents to endorse nightmares about separation. Excessive distress upon separation was common among the younger and older children but not among adolescents. Interestingly, physical complaints were endorsed by 100% of the adolescents, but only among 58% of the younger children and 69% of the older children. Thus, age appears to be an important consideration in the symptomatic expression of SAD.

Several studies have reported that 50–75% of children with SAD are from the lower SES strata (Last et al., 1992, Last, Francis et al., 1987; Velez, Johnson, & Cohen, 1989) although the reason this might be so is unclear. With respect to populations within the United States, rates of SAD are similar for European American children, African American children, and Hispanic American children (Ginsburg & Silverman, 1996; Last & Perrin, 1993). An interesting cross-cultural study compared Japanese and U.S. preschoolers (4–5 years old) on measures of security, sensitivity, and separation of mothers and children (Mizuta, Zahn-Waxler, Cole, & Hiruma, 1996). After settling the child in a playroom, the mother left the room and returned 60–90 minutes later. Mother and child behaviors surrounding separation and reunion were coded for anxiety, physical proximity, and affection. The results indicated that there were no group differences in overall levels of security or sensitivity upon separation or reunion. However, upon reunion, Japanese children displayed more desire for bodily closeness with their mother (a Japanese concept known as *amae*). Although *amae* was positively correlated with internalizing symptoms among U.S. children, there was no correlation among Japanese children, suggesting again the importance of considering culture when assessing behavior. In this case, physical contact with mother is a signal of separation distress and anxiety for children raised in the United States but the behavior does not have the same meaning for their Japanese counterparts.

COMORBIDITY AND DIFFERENTIAL DIAGNOSIS

As with the other anxiety disorders, children with SAD are likely to present with a variety of comorbid diagnoses, primarily other anxiety disorders. Among one sample with primary SAD, 92% had a concurrent anxiety or affective disorder (Last, Francis et al., 1987). Fifty percent of the children with SAD had a comorbid anxiety disorder (primarily overanxious disorder or school phobia) and 33% had a comorbid affective disorder. Illustrating the influence of age, the percentage of those with SAD and a comorbid diagnosis drops to 35% when the sample is restricted to adolescents (Bowen et al., 1990).

Depression also is common among children with SAD (Keller et al., 1992; Kovacs, Gatsonis, Paulauskas, & Richards, 1989; Last et al., 1987; Ryan et al., 1987) and in most cases, appears after the onset of SAD. In some instances, the prevalence of depression may depend upon the complexity of the child's anxiety disorder. For example, in a sample of adolescents with SAD plus Overanxious Disorder, the prevalence of depression with or without an externalizing disorder was 63% (50% had depression alone and 13% had depression plus at least one externalizing disorder; Bowen et al., 1990). However, among those adolescents with SAD alone, only 13% had comorbid depression (9% had depression alone and 4% had depression plus an externalizing disorder). These data again illustrate that it may be the prevalence of a more complex anxiety state, rather than any one particular disorder, that increases the likelihood of co-occurring nonanxiety disorders.

ETIOLOGY

Although there are many theories, there are few empirical data addressing the etiology of SAD. With respect to biology, twin data (Eaves et al., 1997; Topolski et al., 1997) did not find a genetic component for this disorder. In fact, the heredity estimate for SAD was only 4%, whereas the shared environment estimate, particularly family factors, was 40%. Other data have suggested that the biologically based concept of behavioral inhibition (BI; see chapter 4) might be a risk factor for the development of SAD. However, all available data indicate that although some children with BI may be diagnosed with SAD at a later date, by far BI is more specifically related to social phobia than to any other anxiety disorder including SAD (Biederman et al., 1993)

Among parents of children with SAD, 68–83% of mothers had a lifetime anxiety disorder and 47% had a current anxiety disorder (Last, Francis et al., 1987; Last, Hersen et al., 1987). Among parents with panic disorder or panic disorder plus depression, the offspring are three to ten times more likely to have SAD when compared to offspring of parents with depression alone or parents with no psychiatric disorder (Leckman et al., 1985; Weissman, Leckman, Merikangas, Gammon & Prusoff, 1984). It is important to emphasize that even though anxiety disorders run in families, it is not always the same disorder in parent and child. Also, familial relationships need not imply biological (genetic) transmission. Psychological and environmental factors may plan a role.

ASSESSMENT

The assessment of SAD has not been the subject of much investigation. A recent study (Foley et al., 2004) suggested that there is only poor agreement between parents and children on the presence of SAD in children, again raising concerns about the validity of the diagnosis. However, these data were from a large community sample of twins. It is likely that there may be higher agreement on the presence of SAD symptoms when a clinic or treatment seeking sample is used. In general, the assessment strategies used with other anxiety disorders are also relevant for the assessment of SAD. The Anxiety Disorders Interview Schedule for Children/Parents (ADIS-C/P; Silverman & Albano, 1996) is perhaps the most relevant and valid of the diagnostic interviews. Its psychometric properties have been reviewed in chapter 3. There are no self-report instruments specifically designed to assess the symptoms of SAD, although the Multidimensional Anxiety Scale for Children (MASC; March, 1997) and the Screen for Anxiety Related Disorders (SCARED; Birmaher, 1999) both contain subscales for SAD. Both instruments have established validity for the assessment of SAD (Birmaher 1999; March, 1997). In controlled trials, behavioral assessment rarely has been used for the assessment of SAD. Later in this chapter, the use of a behavioral assessment to gauge treatment outcome is presented in the case example.

TREATMENT

In 1997, the American Academy for Child and Adolescent Psychiatry recommended psychological interventions as the first line treatments for childhood anxiety disorders. Pharmacological interventions are conceptualized as adjunctive treatments for "treatment-resistant" cases, a recommendation reiterated by Masi and colleagues in 2001 (Masi, Mucci, & Millepiedi, 2001). In fact, there are few randomized controlled trials specifically examining pharmacological or psychological interventions for children with SAD. In the majority of instances, children with SAD have been included among larger samples of children with various types of anxiety disorders. Below, the available literature on treatment of SAD is reviewed

Overall, psychological interventions in the form of behavioral and cognitive-behavioral interventions appear to be successful in the treatment of children with anxiety disorders (Barrett, Dadds, & Rappee, 1996; Flannery-Schroeder & Kendall, 2000; Kendall, 1994; Kendall et al., 1997; Silverman, Kurtines, Ginsburg, Weems, Rabian, & Serafini, 1999; Silverman, Kurtines, Ginsburg, Weems, Lumpkin, & Carmichael, 1999). These interventions, which include exposure, cognitive restructuring, contingency management, self-statement training, and parent training among others, were reviewed in detail in chapter 6, "Excessive Worry and Generalized Anxiety Disorder," and will not be reviewed again here. It is important to note, however, that none of these investigations found a differential treatment effect for children with SAD in comparison to those with Overanxious Disorder (now Generalized Anxiety Disorder). In some studies, treatment outcome based on diagnosis was not examined. In other instances, no difference in outcome based on diagnosis was noted. Thus, in these studies, the positive improvement reported for the entire group appears to reflect the outcome for SAD. As noted (Silverman & Dick-Niederhausen, 2004), one conclusion that can be drawn from these outcome data is that perhaps a specific intervention for SAD is not necessary. However, given the high spontaneous remission rate for SAD, more carefully controlled, randomized trials using solely SAD patients and including sufficient long-term follow-up are necessary to definitively address the outcome of behavior therapy and cognitive-behavior therapy for SAD.

With respect to pharmacological treatment, the data also are quite sparse. There are few randomized, controlled trials examining pharmacological interventions for children with anxiety disorders and even fewer examining the efficacy of these agents on children with SAD. In one of the few trials to specifically examine anti-depressant treatment for SAD, imipramine was administered to 21 children with SAD (Klein et al., 1992), in an attempt to replicate an earlier successful outcome for imipramine treatment of school refusal. Unfortunately, the earlier positive findings could not be replicated in this new sample although the reason for the negative outcome was unclear. It should be noted however, that the sample in this study also was nonresponsive to a behavioral intervention and thus, may represent a particularly refractory group. Another trial (Ryan, Last, Birmaher, et al., 1995) also did not find any significant improvement with imipramine for children with SAD resulting in school refusal, suggesting that this particular medication may not be useful for treating SAD.

With respect to the newer pharmacological interventions, the SSRIs, there are no interventions that used a sample consisting solely of children with SAD. Several recent investigations have examined the use of fluoxetine and fluvoxamine for children with anxiety disorders (Birmaher et al., 1994; RUPP Study Group, 2001) and children with SAD were included in these samples. In each of these investigations, the outcome for those treated with medication was superior to that found for placebo. However, the results were not examined separately for children with SAD. Two investigations (Birmaher et al., 2003; Fairbanks et al., 1997) have examined the use of fluoxetine for children with anxiety disorders, and have examined its efficacy for SAD specifically. In an open trial (Fairbanks et al., 1997) 16 children nonresponsive to psychotherapy (defined as 4 weeks of behaviorally oriented psychotherapy and supportive therapy) were treated with fluoxetine. At the end of the 9 week trial, all 10 children with a diagnosis of SAD were rated as clinically improved (4 rated as improved and 6 were rated as much improved). These data are quite promising, however, this was an open trial with no control group. A more recent investigation (Birmaher et al., 2003) consisted of a 12 week, randomized controlled trial. Thirteen patients with SAD were randomized to fluoxetine and 22 patients were randomized to placebo. Outcome was based on blinded clinician ratings and revealed that the clinical response for those children with SAD was not significantly different for those treated with fluoxetine (54% improved) versus those treated with placebo (41%). Thus, as has been noted throughout this volume, initial positive results from open treatment are often not confirmed by follow-up controlled trials. In this particular trial, placebo was just as effective as fluoxetine for the treatment of SAD, and it is noteworthy that only slightly more than half of the sample treated with fluoxetine had a positive treatment response.

In an investigation of the use of anti-anxiety agents, 11 children completed a double-blind placebo crossover trial consisting of 4 weeks of clonazepam and four weeks of placebo (Graae, Millner, Rizzotto, & Klein, 1994). At the end of the 8 week trial, 50% of the children no longer met criteria for an anxiety disorder but there was no order effect, meaning that positive treatment response was equally likely to occur with placebo as with clonazepam. Furthermore, there were no differences between clonazepam and placebo on clinician ratings when rates of improvement were compared to baseline. Although the sample size was small, as noted by the authors, the crossover design should have allowed for the detection of a beneficial medication effect, thus leading the authors to conclude that clonazepam (in doses up to 2 mg./day) are not effective for the treatment of anxiety disorders (specifically SAD) in children and adolescents.

To summarize the treatment literature on SAD, data on the psychopathology and assessment of this disorder are so limited that judgments of improvement are based primarily on self-report of anxiety or clinical evaluations of global improvement. Thus, whether these interventions target and alleviate the specific concerns of children with SAD or only result in a better sense of general well-being remains unclear. Furthermore, the natural history data discussed earlier in this chapter indicates that SAD often remits without intervention and thus, appropriate study designs with appropriate control groups and long-term follow-up data are needed before the effectiveness of psychological and pharmacological interventions for SAD can be appropriately determined.

CASE EXAMPLE OF TREATMENT
FOR SEPARATION ANXIETY DISORDER

As presented at the beginning of this chapter, Leslie is a 10-year-old girl who came to the clinic with her mother because of a 6 month history of separation fears.

Assessment

A diagnostic interview was conducted with Leslie and her mother. Both endorsed significant separation fears with the primary worry being that something "bad" would happen to Leslie if she was away from her parents. A review of her behavior indicated that her definition of "unfamiliar places" was anyplace other than school where she was not accompanied by her parents. An important element of Leslie's clinical presentation was that the onset of her fears was much later than the typical age of onset for SAD. Thus, examining environmental factors that could have been associated with the onset of her fears was considered paramount. The diagnostic interview revealed that the onset of her fears coincided with a medical illness. Specifically, Leslie contracted severe bronchitis approximately 7 months ago and after that infection cleared up, she developed asthma that was currently being treated by oral medication and inhalers. She was under good control with only minimal need for emergency inhalers. Interestingly, despite the fact that she was receiving excellent care for her asthma, her medical condition had not been explained to her by her parents or her physician. Another important element of her presentation was that because Leslie was highly embarrassed by her fear, she was motivated to participate in (and end) treatment. In many instances, children do not understand the negative impact of their disorder and much time is spent engaging their cooperation in the treatment program. This was not an issue in Leslie's case.

As noted above, there are no measures developed specifically and solely for SAD. However, her score on the MASC separation anxiety subscale was in the clinically significant range. Because there are so few specific separation anxiety measures, we conducted a simple behavioral test to assess the severity of her condition and to establish baseline values by which to determine the effect of the intervention. This assessment was conducted outside of the office. Specifically, while her mother stood at the entrance to the building, Leslie and the therapist began to walk away from her mother. Leslie was instructed to continue walking until her anxiety was a 5 (severe) on a 5-point subjective units of distress (SUDS) scale. She also was instructed not to turn around and look at her mother as she was walking away. Leslie was able to walk only a short distance (50 yards) before she indicated that her distress level was at the maximum rating of 5. Furthermore, she stopped and looked back at her mother eight times as she was walking that distance.

Treatment Program

In determining Leslie's treatment plan, both in vivo and imaginal exposure options were considered. However, given Leslie's age, imaginal exposure was not considered to be a viable option. Therefore, the treatment program consisted of education, graduated exposure, and parent training in the implementation of a home-based treatment program. Leslie's parents were firmly committed to helping their daughter and her mother, in particular, was enthusiastic and available to assist in the treatment program. Thus, this was an instance where using a parent to participate in the intervention represented a positive factor.

With respect to education, the onset of Leslie's fears coincided with her illness and subsequent asthma diagnosis. Given her lack of prior anxiety disorders or even lack of a history of substantial fears, it appeared that this illness played a major role in the onset of her SAD. However, no one had talked to Leslie about her asthmatic condition and its actual impact upon her daily functioning. Thus, providing her with a full explanation of her medical condition constituted the first phase of the treatment program. Leslie's parents were asked to contact her pediatrician, who met with Leslie, talked to her about asthma, answered her questions, and practiced the use of her inhalers with her. Leslie had several questions for the pediatrician about her health and the likelihood that she would die from an asthma attack, and whether adults other than her parents could help her if an attack occurred. Clearly, her separation fears were related to her misunderstanding of her medical condition. Following the pediatrician consultation, Leslie demonstrated good understanding of her asthma and how to control it through the use of inhalers. However, a repeat of the behavioral assessment demonstrated no increase in her ability to leave her mother, a phenomenon characteristic of anxiety disorders. Specifically, knowledge and insight alone do not eliminate the fear. Thus, it was necessary to proceed with the behavioral intervention.

As the family lived several hours away from the clinic, massed therapist assisted exposure sessions were not possible. Therefore, it was clear that a large part of the exposure program would have to be conducted by her parents. Prior to initiating a home in vivo exposure program, the second phase of the treatment program trained Leslie's mother in the proper implementation of the graduated exposure program. The elements of the parental training sessions are depicted in Table 9.2.

The graduated exposure program (Phase 3) consisted of both home and clinic in vivo exposure sessions. At the clinic, treatment sessions also focused on separation of Leslie from her mother. Specifically, Leslie's mother was instructed to drop her off at the clinic and then leave without telling Leslie how long she would be away (5 minutes, 20 minutes, 1 hour) or where she was going. During that time, Leslie engaged in activities in which children might engage in at home (do homework, play computer games, watch television). The object of the sessions was for Leslie to be in an unfamiliar environment (the clinic) without the presence of her mother. Allowing Leslie to engage in typical child activities simulated what many children would do if they were home (appropriately supervised) and parents were away running errands, for example. Her SUDS

TABLE 9.2 Elements Included in the Parental Training Session

1. Mother trained in use of SUDS rating scale
2. Mother presents exposure task to Leslie in positive fashion
3. Mother encourages Leslie's attempts at the task
4. Mother ignores Leslie's complaints
5. Mother reinforces Leslie's completion of the task
6. Mother instructed to call the clinic when Leslie completes the task three times without distress

TABLE 9.3. Leslie's At Home Hierarchy

Activity	SUDS Level
Take out the trash at night	1.5
Go to a friend's house in the daytime	2.0
Ride bike—every day increase the distance from home	2.5
Go into a store alone	2.5
Eat in a restaurant with friends	3.0
Go to a birthday party	3.5
Go to after school activity without parent	4.0
Sleep over at a friend's house	4.5
Go on overnight camping trips without parents	5.0

level was assessed every 10 minutes and she was not allowed to know that her mother had returned to the clinic until her anxiety habituated. Her at home hierarchy is presented in Table 9.3. Each item had to be successfully completed three times with a rating of 0 distress prior to moving to the next item. Thus, Leslie was receiving exposure sessions at the clinic and at home.

It took approximately 2 months to complete all of the hierarchy items with no distress. Upon completion, a posttreatment behavioral assessment, identical to the pretreatment assessment, was conducted. In contrast to pretreatment where Leslie was able to walk only 50 yards away and looked at her mother 8 times, at posttreatment she was able to walk 500 yards (including turning a corner so that she could no longer see her mother) and never attempted to look back. In fact, because Leslie turned the corner, meaning that visual contact with the therapist was lost, the therapist had to pursue her and halt the assessment at 500 yards. Seven years later, Leslie contacted the clinic to tell her therapist that she had not had any further episodes and had just been accepted to a very prestigious Ivy League university 3,000 miles from home.

SUMMARY

SAD is a very intriguing anxiety disorder. One of the most prevalent disorders, it can exert substantial interference with academic and social development and significantly impact many aspects of parental and family functioning. For a few children, SAD can continue to affect their lives as adults. However, it also appears to be a disorder that often remits without intervention, although at this time, it is impossible to determine which children will outgrow the disorder. The fact that the disorder is not very stable in a majority of children presents a challenge for evaluating the efficacy of pharmacological and psychological interventions. One of the most pressing studies at this time is to examine the natural course of SAD particularly over the short term. Until that happens, the most conservative treatment recommendation is that children with SAD should receive treatment, particularly if there is functional interference in the form of school refusal. To date, behavioral and cognitive-behavioral interventions and SSRI medications appear to have the most empirical support although it should be pointed out that in no case has there been a treatment trial examining these interventions with a specific and sufficient sample of children with SAD. Perhaps such trials will be forthcoming.

CHAPTER 10

Social Phobia and Selective Mutism

Jessica is 9 years old. She refuses to read aloud in class and at recess she stands on the sideline watching the other children play games. Outside of school, she interacts only with her immediate family, her cousins, and one friend. When people, even her grandparents, come to the house to visit, Jessica hides in her room. She will go to dancing lessons but refuses to perform on stage in the year-end dance recital. She also refuses to go to birthday parties or join the neighborhood soccer team.

Nick is 17 years old. He was accompanied to the evaluation by his parents but they were late because Nick tried to stall the family from coming to the appointment. His parents note that he has always been shy and it has affected his academic achievement. Their motivation to seek treatment at this time is that Nick will leave for college next year. His parents are afraid that Nick's social anxiety will interfere with his college success.

Jessica and Nick are but two examples of the many children and adolescents who suffer from social phobia, one of the most common childhood anxiety disorders. Previously, those who were anxious in social interactions were considered "just a little shy." However, data are now emerging to suggest that social phobia, although related to shyness, is a much more severe and disabling condition (Heiser, Turner, & Beidel, 2003).

SOCIABILITY AND SHYNESS

The term shyness describes behaviors that are commonly recognized by most individuals. Although definitions of shyness have evolved recently into descriptions of low level anxiety states that precipitate social avoidance, shyness initially described withdrawal from social encounters regardless of the motivating factors. It is important to distinguish shyness from sociability, which is a preference for affiliation and companionship rather than solitude (Buss & Plomin, 1984). In fact, these two constructs might be considered orthogonal in nature. Some children are low on the dimension of sociability; they choose not to interact with others, but show (or feel) very little emotional distress when forced to do so. To the contrary, most children desire social contact and among this group, most feel comfortable during social interactions. However, there is a subset of children who strongly desire social interaction but become very distressed when engaged in these encounters (e.g., Coplan, Prakash, O'Neil, & Armer, 2004). In the child developmental literature, these children are described as shy.

Empirically, shyness can be detected at a very early age and appears to be stable across periods of developmental change (Bromberg, Lamb, & Hwang, 1990; Kagan, Reznick, Clark, Snidman, & Garcia-Coll, 1984). In the United States, childhood shyness among elementary school children is associated with higher levels of trait anxiety and loneliness and lower levels of global self-worth (Fordham & Stevenson-Hinde, 1999; Rubin & Asendorpf, 1993). Shy children are described by their teachers as less prosocial and more behaviorally withdrawn and upon behavioral observation, display more reticent behavior and more parallel (rather than interactive) play (Coplan et al., 2004). Additionally, early shyness may lead to long-term social consequences. Longitudinal studies suggest that persistently shy children are more likely to have anxiety disorders in adolescence (Prior, Smart, Sanson, & Oberklaid, 2000), and generalized social anxiety in particular (Schwartz, Snidman, & Kagan, 1999). However, most shy children did not develop an anxiety disorder and most adolescents with anxiety disorders were not especially shy as children (Prior et al., 2000). Thus, there may be a relationship between shyness and social phobia but it is one that is quite complicated.

The developmental literature on shyness is quite extensive and a complete review is beyond the scope of this volume. This discussion is meant simply to illustrate some overlap between the constructs of shyness and social phobia and to caution that these conditions do not exist along a continuum. Although the data on childhood shyness might prove instructive in some cases, it is important to remember that there are many children who are described as shy. In contrast, social phobia (characterized by extreme fear and also by functional impairment) affects a smaller proportion of the population, and it is to this disorder that we now turn our attention.

SOCIAL PHOBIA

Social phobia is characterized by pervasive social inhibition and timidity. Descriptions of social phobia have existed since the time of Hippocrates (Marks, 1985). Modern portrayals of social phobia were discussed by Marks (1970) and appeared in the American psychiatric nomenclature with the third edition of the *Diagnostic and Statistical Manual of Mental Disorders* (*DSM-III*; American Psychiatric Association, 1980). Social phobia, particularly among children, initially was understudied, in part because of the belief that shy children subsequently "outgrow" this condition (e.g., Bruch, Giordano, & Pearl, 1986). Additionally, until *DSM-IV*, children fearful of social interaction could be diagnosed with social phobia, but also other disorders. Specifically, descriptions of overanxious disorder in *DSM-III-R* also included social-evaluative concerns as part of the diagnostic criteria and avoidant disorder of childhood described children who withdrew from others. Only during the last 20 years (Beidel, 1991; Beidel & Turner, 1988, Francis, Last & Strauss, 1992; Strauss & Last, 1993) has childhood social phobia been studied as a distinct diagnostic entity.

CLINICAL FEATURES

The *DSM-IV* diagnostic criteria for social phobia are depicted in Table 10.1, several aspects of which deserve further mention. First, a child with social phobia must have the capacity for age-appropriate social interactions, thereby differentiating this disorder from autism or Asberger's disorder, where there is a preference for social avoidance. Second, the physiological reactions and behavioral signs of distress in children with social phobia differ from those of adults. Children may express their distress by crying, tantrums, freezing, or shrinking from social encounters. Clinically, parents of children with this disorder will report that if a stranger comes to the house, the child will run and hide. Third, as noted elsewhere, because of limited cognitive abilities, children need not necessarily recognize that their fear is excessive or unreasonable. Fourth, the fears must exist for at least a 6 month period to avoid temporary distress as a result of adjustment to a new neighborhood or a new school.

As depicted in Table 10.2, social phobia can result in distress across a broad range of interpersonal encounters (Beidel et al., 1999; Strauss & Last, 1993). Children endorse distress when engaged in performance situations (speaking or reading in front of a group, writing or eating in front of others) or in more informal social encounters (speaking to other children, talking on the telephone, talking informally to adults). For those with social phobia, distressful events occur approximately every other day, significantly more frequent than for children without a psychiatric disorder (Beidel, 1991). School is a commonly feared social situation (Beidel et al., 1999; Strauss & Last, 1993) and when in that setting, unstructured peer interactions (e.g., having to talk to another child) were most frequently endorsed (Beidel et al., 1999). Other common anxiety-provoking situations included taking tests, performing in front of others, and reading aloud. Consistent with the data for preadolescent children, informal speaking/interaction tasks were the most frequently-occurring fear-provoking situation for adolescents with social phobia (Hoffman et al., 1999). Therefore,

TABLE 10.1 Diagnostic Criteria for Social Phobia

1. A marked and persistent fear of one or more social or performance situations in which the person is exposed to unfamiliar people or to possible scrutiny by others. The individual fears that he or she will act in a way (or show anxiety symptoms) that will be humiliating or embarrassing. *Note*: In children, there must be evidence of the capacity for age-appropriate social relationships with familiar people and the anxiety must occur in peer settings, not just in interactions with adults.

2. Exposure to the feared social situation almost invariably provokes anxiety, which may take the form of a situationally bound or situationally predisposed panic attack. *Note*: In children, the anxiety may be expressed by crying, tantrums, freezing, or shrinking from social situations with unfamiliar people.

3. The person recognizes that the fear is excessive or unreasonable. *Note*: In children, this feature may be absent.

4. The feared social or performance situations are avoided or else are endured with intense anxiety or distress.

5. The avoidance, anxious anticipation, or distress in the feared social or performance situation(s) interferes significantly with the person's normal routine, occupational (academic) functioning, or social activities or relationships, or there is marked distress about having the phobia.

6. In individuals under age 18 years, the duration is at least 6 months.

7. The fear or avoidance is not due to the direct physiological effects of a substance (e.g., a drug of abuse, a medication) or a general medical condition and is not better accounted for by another mental disorder (e.g., Panic Disorder With or Without Agoraphobia, Separation Anxiety Disorder, Body Dysmorphic Disorder, a Pervasive Developmental Disorder, or Schizoid Personality Disorder).

8. If a general medical condition or another mental disorder is present, the fear in Criterion A is unrelated to it, e.g., the fear is not of stuttering, trembling in Parkinson's disease, or exhibiting abnormal eating behavior in Anorexia Nervosa or Bulimia Nervosa.

Specify if:

Generalized: if the fears include most social situations (also consider the additional diagnosis of Avoidant Personality Disorder)

even though public speaking is the most universally feared social situation, interpersonal conversations are the most frequently occurring feared situation. When in a distressing situation, both children and adolescents respond with negative coping behaviors such as physical complaints, crying or oppositionality and behavioral avoidance (Beidel, 1991; Essau, Conradt, & Peterman, 1999).

> Matt was ten years old. When asked if he knew why he was at the clinic, he looked the interviewer straight in the eye and said, "Dr. Beidel, all I want in the world is to have one friend."

Although a diagnosis of social phobia can be assigned without evidence of functional interference in life areas such as academic or social development, the

TABLE 10.2 Percentage of Children and Adolescents with Social Phobia who Express Moderate Fear in Common Social Situations

ADIS-C/P Situations	Percentage of Children With Moderate–Severe Distress	Percentage of Adolescents With Moderate–-Severe Distress
Answering questions in class	46	75
Reading aloud	71	91
Asking a teacher a question	44	87
Taking a test	48	76
Writing on the chalkboard	51	76
Working/playing with others in a group	45	75
Gym class	37	76
Walking in the hallway	16	76
Starting or joining a conversation	59	87
Using public bathrooms	24	74
Eating in public	10	68
Group or team meetings	36	75
Answering or talking on the telephone	13	75
Musical or athletic performance	61	87
Inviting a friend to get together	24	81
Speaking to adults	59	86
Speaking to new people	58	86
Attending dances or parties	50	91
Having your picture taken	32	71
Dating[1]	NA	90

[1]Only asked of adolescents.

disorder often does result in immediate and long-term consequences including depression (Perrin & Last, 1993), school impairment and school refusal (Essau et al., 1999; Last et al., 1991).

> Nick's IQ test indicated above average intelligence. However, his grades were C's, D's and F's primarily because he would never ask the teacher for help and he avoided turning in his homework if it involved the need to interact with his teachers.

Social phobia also results in social isolation and loneliness (Beidel et al., 1999; Essau et al., 1999).

> Suzanne was 12 years old. As her mother related during the interview, "Suzanne is the kind of child that one year later, none of the other children even remember that she was in their class."

Interestingly, cultural differences may mediate the consequences of social phobia. For example, among Chinese children, those labeled as shy-inhibited were more likely to be accepted by peers than "average" children, and were more likely to be considered by their peers for honorship and leadership positions

(Chen, Rubin, & Li, 1995). Furthermore, they were rated by their teachers as the most competent in school. Thus, the consequences of social phobia encompass many different areas of life functioning.

Although there are no prospective investigations of social phobia's long-term outcome, a retrospective study using an epidemiological sample reported that about 50% of those with social phobia later "recovered" from the disorder (DeWit et al., 1999). The strongest predictor of recovery was a later age of onset of social fears. That is, those whose symptoms occurred after 13 years of age were 8.59 times more likely to recover from the disorder than those who reported the onset prior to the age of 7 (DeWit et al., 1999). Similarly, Davidson (1993) reported that an age of onset prior to age 11 predicted nonrecovery from social phobia in adulthood. With respect to other potential long-term consequences, longitudinal studies of shy and behaviorally inhibited children are instructive (Caspi, Elder, & Bem, 1988; Kerr, Lambert, & Bem, 1995). Shy boys marry and become parents later than do nonshy boys, whereas shy girls are less likely to attend college than are nonshy girls. Similarly, as adults, behaviorally inhibited children had a less positive and active social life and were less likely to move away from their family of origin (Gest, 1997). In summary, although some children with social phobia may outgrow their disorder, this is most unlikely for those with an early age of onset. Furthermore, in addition to the immediate consequences of social phobia, there are data suggestive of possible long-term consequences as well.

Physical Symptoms

> Jeremy blushed profusely whenever he had to interact with, or perform in front of, others. As he stated in his interview, "The only time I was ever able to be in a school play was when we all wore masks. Because then no one would see me blush."

Among adults with social phobia, physical symptoms associated with the beta-adrenergic system (heart palpitations, sweating, trembling and blushing) are the most commonly experienced (Gorman & Gorman, 1987). Few data are available for socially phobic children and adolescents, but those that do exist indicate that heart palpitations (70.8% of the sample), shaking (66.7%), flushes/chills (62.5%), sweating (54.2%), and nausea (54.2%) are most frequently endorsed (Beidel, Christ & Long, 1991).

Cognitive Symptoms

Those with social phobia worry that others will perceive their behavior as "dumb" or "stupid" and that they will be embarrassed or humiliated. When examining cognitions in children with social phobia, it is important to distinguish between cognitive content and cognitive process. With respect to cognitive content, the issue is whether children with social phobia have cognitions that differ in type or frequency from children with no disorder. That determination sometimes depends upon the particular assessment method. Thus, children with social phobia reported significantly greater frequency of negative cognitions than normal controls (Alfano, Beidel, & Turner, 2002) based on the cognitive items on the Social Phobia and Anxiety Inventory for Children (SPAI-C; Beidel, Turner, & Morris, 1995). However, when negative cognitions are assessed during actual social interactions (rather than a global paper and pencil measure) group differences have not been consistently documented (Beidel, 1991; Bogels & Zigterman, 2000; Treadwell & Kendall, 1996). For example, children with social phobia had fewer total thoughts during a social interaction than normal control children, but they were significantly more likely to report the presence of negative cognitions (Spence et al., 1999). However, the actual average number of negative thoughts reported by the socially phobic and normal control children was 4.33 and 3.56, respectively. Therefore, although the difference was statistically significant, the clinical significance remains unclear. One hypothesis for the low frequency of reported thoughts and the often cited lack of significant group differences is that when the children are engaged in these social interactions, they are so overcome by anxiety that they cannot think. Later, they may report worries or anticipatory anxiety when asked to retrospectively recall their thoughts. To summarize, when differences in cognitive content between children with social phobia/anxiety disorders and those with no disorder are reported they tend to occur: (a) prior to the onset of a specific task rather than during the task itself or (b) when children use paper and pencil inventories rather than when using thought listing or video-mediated recall procedures (see Alfano et al., 2002 for a full discussion of this issue).

With respect to cognitive processes, children with social phobia expect their performance to be less successful than children with no disorder during social and performance situations (Spence et al., 1999). Interestingly, their actual performance in those situations does not differ from children without a disorder. Thus, their expectations do not match their performance. Furthermore, children, particularly preadolescent children, often confuse emotion with cognition. Using video-mediated recall procedures to assess cognitions during an anxiety-provoking task, preliminary data from our clinic suggest that younger children frequently report emotional feelings when asked about specific thought content. For example, a child is asked, "What were you thinking when you were reading aloud?" The child responds, "I was very nervous." In fact, the ability to think about thinking requires metacognitive skill, a cognitive ability not present in young children (see Alfano et al., 2002). In certain instances, the pattern of "negative thoughts" reported by children with social phobia are not thoughts at all, but the presence of negative emotional states. In summary, research on the cognitive aspects of childhood anxiety has produced confusing and divergent findings, and this statement is applicable for the even smaller literature on childhood social phobia. In the attempt to modify adult theories of this disorder, some investigators have paid scant attention to basic developmental factors that may inhibit a child's ability to perform complex cognitive functions. Additionally, limited attention has been paid to the issue of assessment methods and how or why the different strategies produce different outcomes. In summary, although the role of negative cognitions in childhood social phobia cannot be discounted completely at this time, much further work is needed to establish their presence and their potential role in its psychopathology.

Behavioral Symptoms

> Suzanne sought to minimize her anxiety around others by refusing to make eye contact. As she told the therapist, "The only way that I recognize the other children in my class is by their shoes. I've never looked at their faces, but I associate their voices with their shoes."

Avoidant behaviors are characteristic of children with social phobia. Among preadolescent children, responses to distressing situations often consisted of some type of behavioral avoidance (Beidel et al., 1999). Furthermore, the effects of this disorder often extend to greater reluctance to engage in typical social activities such as conversing with others, attending social events, and participating in class than children without social anxiety (Ferrell, Beidel, & Turner, 2001), a group difference that becomes more pronounced after age 10.

A controversy in the literature concerns the presence of social skills deficits in those with social phobia. Although clinical lore suggests that at least some children with social phobia possess good social skills, empirical data indicate that social skills deficits do exist among this population (Beidel et al., 1999; Spence, Donovan, & Brechman-Toussaint, 1999). Behavioral raters blind to diagnostic status rated children and adolescents with social phobia as displaying significantly poorer social skill and significantly more anxiety in both social interactions and public performance situations when compared to age-matched, nonanxious peers (Beidel et al., 1999; Beidel et al., 2004). Similarly, Spence et al. (1999) reported that children with social phobia showed significant social skill deficits (when compared to children without a disorder) whether assessed by self-report, parental report, or direct observation. Coupled with the fact that interpersonal encounters are the most frequently occurring distressful situation, the presence of these deficits indicates that treatment of social phobia should include attention to acquiring appropriate social skill as well as decreasing social anxiety and distress.

Social environment awareness is an aspect of social skill often only implicitly addressed in most studies of social skill deficits. In order for social interactions to be successful, children must be able to recognize cues that the interpersonal partner is interested in a social interaction. Therefore, correctly recognizing facial affect is an important, but often overlooked, social skill. Among socially phobic children and adolescents, two studies suggest that those with social phobia are less accurate in recognition of facial affect. Children and adolescents with *DSM-IV* social phobia were less accurate in the identification of adult facial affect, particularly expressions of happiness, anxiety, sadness, and disgust (Simonian, Beidel, Turner, Berkes, & Long, 2001). Those with social phobia also reported more anxiety during the facial affect recognition task. Similarly, a community sample of Italian children identified as highly socially anxious had lower rates of accuracy when asked to identify various facial affects of boys and girls (Battaglia et al., 2004). Both boys and girls were most likely to misidentify anger as disgust. Furthermore, girls' neutral expressions were often misclassified as sadness. Although certainly more studies are necessary, these studies suggest that attention to facial affect must be an important part of social skills training for children with social phobia.

Subtypes of Social Phobia

Among adults, about 70% of youth with social phobia are of the generalized subtype, a term used to describe those individuals with social anxiety across a broad range of interpersonal situations (Turner, Beidel, & Jacob, 1994). Among samples in the United States, 89% of children (Beidel et al., 1999) and 45.5–92% of adolescents were assigned the generalized subtype (Beidel et al., 2004; Hofmann et al., 1999). Among German adolescents (aged 14–17), 33% were assigned the generalized subtype (Wittchen, Stein, & Kessler, 1999). However, in that study, test anxiety was included as a social phobia, a situation inconsistent with the *DSM-IV* criteria. A large number of adolescents in that study had only testing fears and therefore were classified as nongeneralized social phobics. Thus, the sub-typing strategy used by Wittchen et al. (1999) differed from the other studies and that may account for that sample's lowered prevalence rate for the generalized subtype.

Although among children and adolescents, the subtype distinction remains controversial, several studies have examined group differences based on subtype. Overall, the generalized subtype is characterized by more severe symptomatology. Adolescents with the generalized subtype had an earlier overall age of onset, higher rates of comorbid diagnoses (depression, specific phobia, posttraumatic stress disorder), higher overall symptoms and in particular, more severe fear of humiliation (Wittchen et al., 1999). However, a higher rate of comorbid diagnoses among the generalized subtype was not reported by Hofmann et al. (1999), thus, the controversy remains.

Sociodemographic Influences

As discussed elsewhere (Beidel, Morris, & M. W. Turner, 2004) prior to *DSM-IV* (APA, 1994), prevalence rates for social phobia average about 1% of the general child population (Anderson, Williams, McGee, & Silva, 1987; Kashani & Orvaschel, 1990) but this figure likely is an underestimate. Prior to *DSM-IV*, children with social fears were diagnosed with social phobia, avoidant disorder of childhood or overanxious disorder. For example, using *DSM-III-R* criteria, 8% of a clinic sample of children with anxiety disorders had social phobia but when *DSM-IV* criteria were applied, 40% met criteria (Kendall & Warman, 1997). With the *DSM-IV* revisions (APA, 1994), all children with social fears now are assigned a diagnosis of social phobia, raising the prevalence rate to approximately 3% of the general population (Beidel & Turner, 1998). Among German adolescents, the prevalence rate ranges between 1.6–4% of the general population (Essau, Conradt, & Petermann, 1999; Wittchen, Stein, & Kessler, 1999) and prevalence increases with increasing age (Essau et al., 1999; Kashani & Orvaschel, 1990; Wittchen et al., 1999).

Based on child and adolescent samples, the average age of onset for social phobia ranges from 11.3 to 12.7 years (DeWit, Ogborne, Offord, & MacDonald, 1999; Last, Perrin, Hersen, & Kazdin,1992; Strauss & Last, 1993) but the disorder is common even in children as young as age 8 (Beidel & Turner, 1988; Schneier, Johnson, Hornig, Liebowitz, & Weissman,1992). The gender distribution is approximately equal among preadolescent children (Beidel, Turner, & Morris, 1999) but becomes increasingly more female among adolescents (5.5% vs. 2.7%, respectively) both with respect to overall rate (Essau et al., 1999; Wittchen et al., 1999) and distribution based on subtype (Wittchen et al., 1999). Both Caucasian and African American children have a similar clinical presentations (Beidel et al., 1999) and similar rates of positive treatment outcome, although sample sizes are small (Ferrell, Beidel, & Turner, 2004).

Comorbid and Differential Diagnosis

Similar to the situation for other anxiety disorders, many children and adolescents with primary social phobia present with additional comorbid conditions. Among one sample, only 29% of children with primary social phobia did not have a comorbid condition and 19% received three or more comorbid diagnoses; overanxious disorder was most common (43%) followed by simple phobia (26%)

and mood disorders (19%). Among preadolescent children (Beidel et al., 1999), 60% had a comorbid disorder including generalized anxiety disorder (10%), specific phobia (10%), selective mutism (8%), separation anxiety disorder (6%), obsessive-compulsive disorder (6%), attention-deficit/hyperactivity disorder (10%), depression (6%), panic disorder (2%), and adjustment disorder with anxious and depressed mood (2%). Among adolescent clinic samples, 57.1% had an Axis I comorbid diagnosis, the majority of which (74.1%) was GAD (Beidel et al., 2004). Other diagnoses included specific phobia, obsessive-compulsive disorder, separation anxiety disorder, and selective mutism. Mood disorders were present in 11.1% of the sample. Among an epidemiological sample of German adolescents, 41.2% were reported to have a somatoform disorder, 29.4% had a depressive disorder, and 23.5% had a substance abuse disorder (Essau et al., 1999). Conduct and oppositional behavioral problems, as well as substance abuse/dependence also exist among some adolescents with social phobia (Clark, 1993; DeWit, MacDonald, & Offord, 1999; Essau et al., 1999). It is important to note that sometimes, the presence of oppositional behaviors does not indicate the presence of a distinct disorder but rather a symptom of the severity of a child's anxiety and distress. For example, when teachers attempted to force Nick to talk in front of the class or to engage in social interactions with peers, he often would get angry and "storm" out of the classroom. He would seek out his guidance counselor with whom he had good rapport and ask her to intercede with his teachers to stop making those types of demands on him. Thus, comorbidity is common but there is a need to use a broad perspective to avoid assuming that every behavior necessarily represents a distinct comorbid condition when in fact, they may be part of the primary disorder (in this case, social phobia).

Neurobiology

With advances in assessment technologies such as Positron Emission Tomography (PET), Magnetic Resonance Imaging (MRI), and Functional MRI (fMRI), investigators have begun to examine the neurobiology of social phobia, including neurological structure and function and the neuroendocrine systems of individuals with social phobia. However, to date there is no evidence for a clear neurobiological abnormality in adults with this disorder (Bell, Nalizia, & Nutt, 1999). With respect to children, there are even fewer studies, the work has been preliminary and exploratory, and neuroendocrine studies have used chemical challenges more typically used when examining those with panic disorder (Argyropoulos, Bell, & Nutt, 2001). Based on what does exist, there do not appear to be any neurological structural abnormalities associated with social phobia (Argyropoulos et al., 2001; Potts, Davidson, Krishnan, & Doraiswamy,

1994). Functional abnormalities show that those with panic disorder can be reliably differentiated from those with social phobia (Argyropoulos et al., 2001 Coupland, 2001), but it is unclear how often those with social phobia can be differentiated from those with other anxiety disorder or normal controls. As suggested by Stein (1998), what may be necessary to finally determine neurological abnormalities is the use of neuroimaging to study neurobiological functioning while the patient is engaged in "disorder-relevant neuropsychologic tasks" such as processing facial affect. Although it is possible that such data may prove more informative on the potential role of neurobiology in social phobia, at this time there is no evidence that neurobiology plays a distinctive role in this disorder.

Etiology

Among the etiological pathways to social phobia, direct conditioning experiences account for 44–58% of adults with a social phobia diagnosis (Ost, 1985; Stemberger, Turner, Beidel, & Calhoun, 1995). When examined by social phobia subtype, traumatic conditioning events were reported by 40% and 56% of those with the generalized and specific (nongeneralized) subtypes respectively, whereas 20% of adults without social phobia also reported past events consistent with traumatic conditioning. These data are important for several reasons. First, about 50–60% of adults with social phobia cannot recall a specific conditioning event. Second, some individuals experience traumatic social events yet never develop the disorder. Therefore, conditioning experiences occur but are not necessary or sufficient for the onset of social phobia.

Social learning also has been hypothesized as an etiological factor in the development of childhood social phobia. Adults with social phobia describe childhood family environments where at least one parent was shy or avoidant (Bruch, Heimberg, Berger, & Collins, 1989). Socially reticent parents also are characteristic of children with social anxiety (Bogels et al., 2001) and selective mutism (Brown & Lloyd, 1975). Other family studies, assessing the presence of social phobia among relatives of someone with a disorder, often are used as evidence of a genetic or biological predisposition. Those studies are presented in the section on biological etiology although it should be noted that social learning theory, in addition to genetics, also may account for higher rates of disorders among the relatives of an individual with a disorder.

Information transfer has been correlated with the onset of social phobia in a limited number of cases. Three percent of adults with social phobia reported that their fears were acquired through this modality (Ost, 1985). Although limited by the retrospective research design, adults with social phobia sometimes describe family communication patterns emphasizing shame, social isolation and concern about the opinion of others (Bruch & Heimberg, 1994;

Bruch et al.,1989). Of course, retrospective data are subject to the veracity of recall that may be affected by passage of time or perceptions of an individual with a disorder.

Parental characteristics such as parental overprotection and parental rejection also have been reported to be associated with social phobia in children, adolescents, and young adults (Bogels, van Oosten, Muris, & Smulders, 2001; Caster, Inderbitzen, & Hope, 1999; Lieb et al., 2000). Among children in Grades 7 though 11, there was a positive relationship between high levels of child social anxiety and perceptions of parents as restricting their children's social interactions (i.e., they were more socially isolating of their children), less socially active themselves, more concerned about others' opinions and more concerned about the child's social anxiety and poor performance; Caster et al., 1999). However, the relationship of these parenting practices to social distress may not be specific to parents with social phobia. Rather, the association between parental rejection and adolescent social phobia is significant irrespective of the specific type of parental psychopathology. A limitation of many family investigations is that the data are based on self-report, which may be colored by the presence of a diagnosis.

In one of the few observational studies in the area of family interactions among children with social phobia (Hummel & Gross, 2001), parent–child interactions were observed when the parents and children (mean age 11.8 years) were engaged in solving a jigsaw puzzle. This study is remarkable for assessing father–child interaction, mother–child interaction, and mother–father–child interaction. The results indicated that parents of children with no disorder used significantly more explanations and suggestions and significantly less negative feedback than parents of children with social phobia, again suggesting a certain degree of negative parent interaction when the child has social phobia. Overall, parents of socially anxious children engaged in significantly fewer verbal exchanges with their children. Interestingly, the analysis of child verbal interactions indicated that socially anxious children used significantly fewer explanations, less positive feedback, and fewer questions when compared to the nonanxious peers. Furthermore, they were significantly more likely to use negative feedback and commands than their nonanxious peers, suggesting that these familial communication patterns are reciprocal among parents and children. However, it is not clear if (a) these behaviors preceded the onset of the disorder and (b) the behaviors are specific to social phobia or characteristic of children with any type of disorder.

Biological factors also may play a role in the etiology of social phobia, although what appears to be inherited is probably "anxiety proneness" and not a specific disorder. For example, the familial aggregation of agoraphobia, social phobia, situational phobia, and specific phobia was consistent with "phobia proneness" but the conclusion was that the genetic contribution was "by no means overwhelming in the etiology of phobias" (Kendler et al., 1992,

p. 279). Similarly, social phobia and avoidant disorder were significantly more prevalent among the first-degree relatives of anxious children compared to normal controls, but not more prevalent than among parents of children with attention-deficit/hyperactivity disorder (ADHD; Last, Hersen, Kazdin, Orvaschel & Perrin, 1991). More specifically, among parents with social phobia, 49% of the offspring had at least one *DSM-III-R* anxiety disorder, most commonly overanxious disorder (30%), social phobia (23%), and separation anxiety disorder (19%; Mancini, Van Amerigen, Szatmari, Fugere, & Boyle, 1996). These results must be interpreted cautiously because at least some children diagnosed with *DSM-III-R* overanxious disorder might have been diagnosed with social phobia if *DSM-IV* criteria had been used. Additionally, child assessors were not blind to parental diagnosis thus there is the possibility that these rates could be inflated based on prior knowledge of parental disorder.

More recent investigations are conflictual with respect to a familial relationship between social phobia in parents and children. For example, a positive correlation was reported between parental and child social anxiety (Bogels et al. 2001). Similarly, whereas 2.1% of offspring (aged 14–24) of parents with no disorder had social phobia, 9.6% had social phobia if their parents also had social phobia, significantly higher than the 2.1% for the normal control group (Lieb et al., 2000). However, rates of social phobia were also significantly higher in the adolescent offspring of parents with other anxiety disorders, depression, or alcohol use disorders, suggesting that the relationship of elevated social phobia in adolescent offspring is not specific to parents with social phobia but exists across various diagnostic groups.

Behavioral inhibition is another predispositional construct that appears to have some relationship to social phobia. For example, social anxiety disorder (defined here as the presence of either a diagnosis of social phobia or avoidant disorder) was significantly more common among behaviorally inhibited young children (17%) than uninhibited children (5%; Biederman et al., 2001). Furthermore, as noted in chapter 3, behavioral inhibition in early childhood may be a precursor of later anxiety disorders, particularly social phobia. Childhood behavioral inhibition (social avoidance) was significantly associated with adolescent generalized social anxiety (Schwartz et al., 1999) and adolescent social phobia (Hayward, Killen, Kraemer, & Taylor, 1998). No such relationship was found for behavioral inhibition and specific fears, separation anxiety disorder, or performance anxiety (Schwartz et al., 1999), suggesting some predispositional specificity for social phobia.

In summary, there are many avenues that potentially address the etiology of social phobia in children. In addition to biological and psychological theories, familial interaction patterns have been implicated in the etiology of this disorder. However, some of the established familial relationships may not be specific to social phobia but may be the result of any type of parental psychopathology. Thus, further study is needed to elucidate the nature of this relationship.

Assessment

As with other disorders discussed throughout this volume, assessment of social phobia should be multi-dimensional and developmentally sensitive (Morris, Hirshfeld-Becker, Henin, & Storch, 2004). To be specific, assessment instruments and strategies used for adults or older adolescents need to be modified for use with younger children. For example, when designing behavioral assessment paradigms, impromptu speeches, often used to assess social fears in adults, are not appropriate with young children because this is not a situation that they commonly encounter. A developmentally appropriate alternative would be reading aloud in front of a group, something that children do regularly in a school setting. Below methods for the assessment of childhood social phobia are reviewed.

Diagnostic Interviews

As recommended in other chapters, the most appropriate semi-structured diagnostic interview for the assessment of childhood social phobia is the Anxiety Disorders Interview Schedule for Children for DSM-IV-Child/Parent (ADIS-C/P; Silverman & Albano, 1996). The ADIS-C/P has been reviewed in chapter 3 and the reader is referred there for its psychometric properties.

Self-Report

There are two commonly used self-report inventories for children and adolescents with social phobia. The Social Anxiety Scale for Children-Revised (SASC-R; LaGreca & Stone, 1993) consists of 22 items rated on a 5-point Likert scale (not at all, hardly ever, sometimes, most of the time, and all of the time). The SASC-R has three subscales: Fear of Negative Evaluation, Social Avoidance and Distress with new or unfamiliar people (SAD-New), and generalized Social Avoidance and Distress (SAD-General). Along with a similar scale for adolescents (SASC-A), the SASC-R has been demonstrated to have good reliability and validity (Morris et al., 2004) for the assessment of social anxiety.

Another self-report inventory, the Social Phobia and Anxiety Inventory for Children (SPAI-C, Beidel, Turner, & Morris, 1995) assesses social anxiety across a range of interpersonal and performance situations using a 3-point Likert scale (never or rarely, sometimes, most of the time or always). The scale also assesses the presence of physiological symptoms and negative cognitions that sometimes accompany this disorder. Additionally, some of the items assess distress with three different interpersonal partners—adults, boys, or girls that I know, boys or girls that I don't know. The SPAI-C was designed for clinical, as well as research purposes. Clinically, the SPAI-C can be useful in treatment planning by assisting in determining the specific situations that can be used to develop graduated exposure programs. The SPAI-C has excellent psychometric properties including high reliability (Beidel et al., 1995), excellent concurrent validity (Beidel, Turner, & Morris, 1998) as well as good external and discriminant validity (Beidel, Turner, Hamlin, & Morris, 2000). It is appropriate for children aged 8–14. Above that age, the adult Social Phobia and Anxiety Inventory (Turner, Beidel, Dancu, & Stanley, 1989) is recommended.

Clinician Ratings

The Liebowitz Social Anxiety Scale for Children and Adolescents (LSAS-CA; Masia, Hoffman, Klein, & Liebowitz, 1999) is a clinician rating scale that uses a 4 point Likert rating system and consists of two subscales: social and performance situations. Each item is rated for fear and avoidance. The scale has good psychometric properties including good reliability and convergent validity with self-report measures and judgments of the presence or absence of an anxiety disorder (Storch, Masia, Pincus, Klein, & Liebowitz, 2001). The scale is sensitive to treatment effects (Masia, Klein, Storch, & Corda, 2001).

Behavioral Assessment

Behavioral assessments for childhood social phobia usually involve one or both of the following tasks: role play with an interpersonal partner or performance in front of a group (reading aloud or giving a short speech). The tasks are usually videotaped and ratings of skill and/or anxiety are obtained by raters blind to group assignment. Behavioral assessments provide important data on the social skills and anxiety of children with social phobia. Although they are powerful assessment tools, they are under-utilized, often in favor of easier to administer self-report measures.

Self-Monitoring

Like behavioral assessment, self-monitoring (behavioral diaries; Beidel, Neal, & Lederer, 1991) can provide important information on children's daily social functioning. The caveats for self-monitoring presented in the chapter on obsessive-compulsive disorder also are relevant here. Specifically, the form should be easy to complete both in terms of the data collected as well as the time it takes for completion. For children with social phobia, for example, a simple form might include a daily distress rating, the number of times that a child found him/herself in an anxiety-producing event that day, and their response to that event (avoidance, physical ailment, etc.).

Treatment

The literature on efficacious treatment for childhood social phobia is quite limited when compared to that for adults with this disorder. An important recent trend is that both pharmacological and psychosocial trials are moving away from including socially phobic children among large samples with various types of anxiety disorders and toward samples composed entirely of children with social phobia. Furthermore, comparative trials (psychosocial vs. pharmacological interventions) are underway as are treatment studies examining new types of treatment modalities and approaches. In the following section, the empirical evidence for both pharmacological and psychosocial interventions for children with social phobia is examined.

Pharmacological Treatment

Prior to *DSM-IV*, children with social fears were given various diagnoses, including social phobia, avoidant disorder of childhood, overanxious disorder, and selective mutism (Beidel, Ferrell, Alfano, & Yeganeh, 2001). Thus, when relevant, this review includes several studies examining children with some of these alternative diagnoses. In general, treatment outcome has been mixed for these early trials using children with "related" disorders. For example, 30% of children (aged 8–16) with overanxious disorder or avoidant disorder of childhood treated in a 6-week open trial with alprazolam (Simeon & Ferguson, 1987) had moderate clinical improvement. However, in a follow-up double blind placebo controlled trial, alprazolam appeared superior to placebo on global ratings of anxiety, but not on Clinical Global Impression (CGI) ratings (Simeon et al., 1992). Following tapering, there was a trend for the alprazolam group to relapse whereas the placebo group continued to improve. Thus, the initial positive outcome for alprazolam was not replicated. Coupled with potentially serious side effects and other dose-related complications, benzodiazepines should be considered only after all other medications have failed (Kratochvil et al., 1999; Pine & Grun, 1998; Velosa & Riddle, 2000; Wilens, Spencer, Frazier, & Biederman, 1998).

The majority of published pharmacological trials have evaluated selective serotonin reuptake inhibitors (SSRIs), considered first line agents because of their high tolerance levels, minimal side effects, and the lack of need for blood level monitoring (Kratochvil, Kutcher, Reiter, & March, 1999; Pine & Grun, 1998; Velosa & Riddle, 2000). Common SSRIs include fluvoxamine (Luvox®), fluoxetine (Prozac®), sertraline (Zoloft®), paroxetine (Paxil®), and more recently, citalopram (Celexa®). Initially, minimal side effects such as headaches, nausea, drowsiness, insomnia, jitteriness, and stomachaches have been reported (Velosa & Riddle, 2000). However, recent data indicate that some children treated with SSRIs have increased suicidal ideation when compared to those on placebo. Although to date, suicidal ideation has been documented only among children and adolescents with depression, the United States Food and Drug Administration (FDA) has ordered a "black box" warning be placed on these medications, leaving it unclear whether they will continue to be widely used to treat children with anxiety disorders.

To return to the available outcome data, 81% of children with social phobia, overanxious disorder, and separation anxiety disorder exhibited marked improvement after 6–8 weeks of treatment with fluoxetine, based on retrospective chart review (Birmaher et al., 1994). In an open prospective trial (Fairbanks et al., 1997), 16 children (aged 9–18 years) with various anxiety disorders considered nonresponsive to psychotherapy, were treated with fluoxetine. Outcome was rated by parental and clinician report, the latter including change scores on the CGI Severity scale. Similar to Birmaher et al. (1994), treatment gains were realized at 6–9 weeks, and lower doses were efficacious for children who had only one anxiety disorder. Eighty percent of those with social phobia (8 out of 10) were clinically improved and similar percentages were reported for other diagnostic groups. Even though clinically improved, 62.5% of the entire sample still met criteria for an anxiety disorder at posttreatment, indicating a continuing degree of impairment.

In the multi-center Research Units on Pediatric Psychopharmacology (RUPP) Anxiety Trial, 128 children with separation anxiety disorder, social anxiety disorder, or generalized anxiety disorder (aged 6–17 years) were randomly assigned to either 8 weeks of fluvoxamine or placebo accompanied by supportive psychotherapy (RUPP Anxiety Study Group, 2001). Using the Pediatric Anxiety Rating Scale, fluvoxamine was superior to placebo in reducing anxiety symptoms. Additionally, 76% of the fluvoxamine group and 29% of the placebo group showed marked clinical improvement as measured by the Clinical Global Improvement Scale. Significant between group differences were detected by week 3 and increased through week 6. At that point, group differences were maintained but no further improvement occurred. An examination of potential moderators and mediators of treatment outcome revealed a significant interaction effect for social anxiety disorder and type of treatment (RUPP Anxiety Study Group, 2003). Among fluvoxamine responders, there were no response rate differences for children with a primary or secondary diagnosis of social phobia versus children without a diagnosis of social phobia (79% vs. 71%, respectively). In contrast, the placebo response rate was 25% for children with a primary or secondary diagnosis of social phobia versus 40% for children without this diagnosis. Therefore, children who had an anxiety disorder other than social phobia were more likely to respond to placebo. Although the number of children with social phobia as a primary diagnosis was quite small, these results suggest that fluvoxamine may be efficacious when a diagnosis of social phobia is present, although it is unclear how the presence of other comorbid disorders may affect treatment response. Furthermore, the results indicate that children with a diagnosis of social phobia may be less responsive to placebo than children with other anxiety disorders. At 6 month follow-up, 94% of those children and adolescents who initially responded to fluvoxamine maintained their improvement (RUPP Anxiety Study Group, 2002). As indicated by the authors, the results of the RUPP trial must be interpreted cautiously because although this was a double-blind study, treating clinicians (not independent evaluators) rated both clinical outcome and adverse events. Thus, knowledge of side effects may have created bias regarding clinician judgment of outcome. Additionally, for the purposes of determining the efficacy of fluvoxamine for social phobia, the outcome was not examined separately for children with primary social phobia.

Most recently, Birmaher et al. (2003) conducted a randomized, placebo controlled trial of fluoxetine for 74 children and adolescents (aged 7–17) with generalized anxiety disorder, separation anxiety disorder, and/or social phobia (54% had a diagnosis of primary or secondary social phobia). At posttreatment, 76% of children with social phobia treated with fluoxetine were rated as much or very much improved on the CGI in comparison to 21% who were placebo responders. Furthermore, 45.5% of those with social phobia achieved a positive functional outcome, defined as a score of 70 or higher on the Children's Global Assessment Scale (scores range from 0 to 100) compared to 10% in the placebo group. However, as noted by the authors, even with this improvement, at least 50% of the sample remained symptomatic (defined as still having at least three symptoms of anxiety at posttreatment). In effect, the assessment strategies used in pharmacological trials lead to a judgment of improvement but can be misleading inasmuch as many children, although improved, remain symptomatic.

Following four 1 hour sessions of cognitive-behavior therapy (CBT) that did not result in significant improvement, Compton et al. (2001) administered sertraline to children and adolescents with social phobia. Treatment outcome was assessed based on: (a) CGI Severity and Improvement ratings assigned by an independent evaluator, (b) scores on the Social Phobia and Anxiety Inventory for Children (SPAI-C; Beidel et al., 1995), and (c) ratings of distress when the children were engaged in two behavioral tasks; an 8 minute speech and a one-on-one conversation with a confederate. At the end of the 8 week trial, 36% of the children were treatment responders and 29% were partial responders. SPAI-C scores improved significantly from pre to posttreatment, and posttreatment scores were in the range reported by children who never had a diagnosis. Ratings of distress on the behavioral tasks likewise showed significant improvement. Side effects (nausea, headache, trouble sleeping, restlessness) were characterized as mild or moderate and all were controlled by decreasing the dosage. The results of this trial are very promising, although as noted by the authors, the study is limited by the small number of patients

($n = 14$), the lack of a placebo control group, no randomization, and the possible carryover effects of the brief CBT trial. Interestingly, the authors noted that at the debriefing, several patients attributed their improvement to the combination of the two interventions rather than to either one alone. Despite these limitations, follow-up using a double-blind placebo controlled design is worthy of investigation.

Finally, in a multicenter, randomized, double-blind placebo-controlled investigation, 322 children and adolescents with social phobia were randomized to either paroxetine or placebo (Wagner, Berard, & Stein, 2004). The benefits of paroxetine were first evident at 4 weeks and after 16 weeks, 77.6% of those treated with paroxetine (vs. 38.4% of those treated with placebo) were defined as much improved or very much improved according to the Clinical Global Impressions Scale. Similarly, those treated with paroxetine had a significantly greater reduction on the Liebowitz Social Anxiety Scale for Children and Adolescents than those in the placebo group. However, only 34.6% of those treated with paroxetine (compared to 8% of those treated with placebo) met remission criteria and these percentages were the same for both children (38.6% vs. 8.9%) and adolescents (33.0% vs. 7.6%). Thus, although the authors conclude that paroxetine is significantly superior to placebo on all of the measures, there are two very significant limitations to this investigation. First, all of the outcome measures were based on clinician ratings, rather than using a broad array of assessment measures including self-report, behavioral assessment, and self-monitoring. Additionally, the percentage of children in each group who no longer met diagnostic criteria was not reported. Second, even thought children and adolescents treated with placebo had outcomes that were significantly worse than those treated with paroxetine, very few children treated with paroxetine met remission criteria, indicating that these children were still suffering from social phobia.

In summary, there currently is some promising evidence that SSRIs are effective for the treatment of childhood anxiety disorders, although their future is unclear given the new "black box warning" recently issued by the FDA. SSRIs may be appropriate specifically for those with social anxiety disorder when compared to children with other disorders, although at this time, the majority of the evidence is indirect and limited to small sample sizes. Furthermore, long-term follow-up data are not available and in most cases, studies have not assessed outcome in terms of specific social functioning. Of course, some of these same issues pertain to the studies of psychosocial trials as discussed here.

Psychosocial Treatment

The psychosocial treatment literature for children with social anxiety disorder is somewhat ahead of its pharmacological counterpart. Following initial studies where children with social phobia were included among a larger group with various anxiety disorders (Barrett, Dadds, & Rapee, 1996; Barrett et al., 1998; Flannery-Schroeder & Kendall, 2000; Kendall, 1994; Kendall et al., 1997; Manassis et al., 2002; Rapee, 2000; Shortt, Barrett, & Fox, 2001; Silverman et al. 1999a; Silverman et al., 1999b), there now are several randomized, controlled studies using samples consisting solely of children and adolescents with social phobia. Studies using multiple diagnostic groups were reviewed in chapter 6 and will not be repeated here. Studies using samples composed solely of children with social phobia are reviewed.

The first treatment program designed specifically for adolescents with social phobia (Albano, Marten, Holt, Heimberg, & Barlow, 1995) was a group intervention, Group Cognitive- Behavioral Treatment for Adolescents (GCBT-A), and consisted of psychoeducation, skill building (such as social skills, problem-solving, and assertiveness training), cognitive restructuring, behavioral exposure, and parental involvement. In the initial investigation, 5 adolescents (aged 13–17) with social phobia were treated with GCBT-A using a single case design. At posttreatment, social phobia symptoms had decreased to subclinical levels in 80% of the adolescents. The results of this investigation were promising and larger, controlled trials followed.

A comparison of CBGT-A with or without family involvement revealed that both interventions were significantly efficacious in reducing social anxiety among adolescents with social phobia (70% did not meet diagnostic criteria at posttreatment) when compared to a wait list but that family involvement did not increase the efficacy of the intervention over the original treatment alone (Tracey et al., 1998). In a second trial, Hayward et al. (2000) randomized 35 female adolescents with social phobia to CBGT-A (without parental involvement) or a no treatment control group. After treatment, 45% of the CBGT-A group no longer met diagnostic criteria for social phobia compared to only 4% of the no-treatment group. However, despite improvement, residual symptoms remained at post treatment, and at 1 year follow-up, there were no significant group differences in the frequency of social anxiety disorder diagnoses or self-report of social anxiety severity. It is unclear why these follow-up results were less favorable than those reported for adult populations utilizing a similar treatment protocol (Heimberg et al., 1990) or the initial single case design study (Albano et al., 1995). However, some of the adolescents had comorbid depressive symptoms and this may have attenuated treatment outcome and/or promoted relapse.

Whereas CBGT includes cognitive interventions as well as some social skills training, Beidel, Turner, and Morris (2000) recently developed and examined the efficacy of a multi-component behavioral treatment, Social Effectiveness Therapy for Children (SET-C), in comparison to an active, nonspecific intervention designed to remediate test anxiety. SET-C includes 12 weeks of group social skills training, peer-generalization experiences, and individual in vivo exposure (see Beidel, Turner & Morris, 2004). One session per week is devoted to group social skills training and a peer generalization session. The second weekly session focuses on individualized in vivo exposure. SET-C does not include a cognitive component because as noted above currently there is insufficient evidence that negative cognitions play a major role in the clinical presentation of childhood social phobia (Alfano et al., 2002). The comparison intervention, Testbusters, is a study-skills and test-taking strategy program designed to reduce test-anxiety and promote good study habits. It has strong face validity given that many children with social phobia endorse anxiety in testing situations. Testbusters also includes both group and individual sessions. Sixty-seven children, ages 8 to 12 years, were randomly assigned to one of the two groups. At posttreatment, 67% of the SET-C group no longer met criteria for social phobia, compared to 5% in Testbusters. Across various outcome measures, those in the SET-C group were less anxious, less avoidant of social situations, more skillful in their social interactions, and more engaged in social discourse based on child and parent report as well as independent evaluator ratings. At 6 month follow-up, those treated with SET-C showed continued improvement; 85% no longer meeting criteria for social phobia. These results are particular encouraging because unlike the designs of previous investigations, SET-C was compared to an active, nonspecific control treatment, and not a wait- list control. It remains unclear whether SET-C would be equally effective for socially-phobic adolescents, although such a study currently is underway (see summary and future directions).

A 5 year follow-up of SET-C efficacy is halfway complete. Twenty-nine children have completed a 3 year follow-up (Beidel, Turner, Young, & Paulson, in press) and thus far, treatment gains are maintained, and in some cases, even enhanced. For example, 72.4% of treated children continued to be without social phobia at follow-up. Whereas 3 children (17.6% of those in the follow-up sample) relapsed during the follow-up interval, 6 children who still had a diagnosis at posttreatment (20% of the follow-up sample) did not have a diagnosis at follow-up. There were 5 children (17.2% of the sample) who had a diagnosis at both assessment points (posttreatment and follow-up). These same variables will be examined at the five year follow-up point.

In one of the first transcultural treatment studies (Olivares et al., 2002a; Olivares et al., 2002b), 59 Spanish adolescents, ages 15–17 were randomly assigned to a psychosocial intervention that included distinct elements of traditional cognitive therapy (Therapy for Adolescents with Generalized Social Phobia; Olivares et al., 2002a), CBGT-A, a version of SET-C for adolescents, or a wait list control. At posttreatment, all treatments were significantly superior to the control group and at follow-up, there were few differences among the three active interventions in terms of decreases in social phobia symptoms, improved social skills, and enhanced self-esteem. Although the number of adolescents randomized to each condition was somewhat small (approximately 15 per group), these results are promising and suggest that the interventions are effective across cultures.

The effectiveness of a different CBT program (social skills training, relaxation techniques, social-problem solving, positive self-instruction, cognitive challenging, and exposure) was examined in children with social phobia ages 7 to 14 (Spence, Donovan, & Brechman-Toussaint, 2000). The children were randomly assigned to either group CBT with parental involvement (CBT-PI), group CBT with no parental involvement (CBT-PNI), or a wait-list control group. Parental involvement focused on teaching proper modeling and reinforcement of children's newly acquired social skills, and encouragement of participation in outside social activities. Following treatment, parental reports indicated that 87.5% of the CBT-PI group and 58% of the CBT-PNI group no longer met diagnostic criteria for social phobia, compared to 7% of the wait-list control. Similar outcome resulted when child report was used with no significant differences between the two CBT groups. The interventions did not appear to affect the children's total number of peer interactions, parental report of competence with peers, or independent observer ratings of assertiveness during behavioral observation from pre to posttreatment. However, a treatment interval longer than 12 weeks may be necessary to detect this magnitude of change. Treatment effects were maintained at 6 and 12 month follow-up and both active treatment conditions were associated with improved social skills from pretreatment to 12 month follow-up (based on parent report).

Combination and Comparative Treatments

Clinical trials are beginning to emerge using comparative and combination treatment designs. Chavira and Stein (2002) combined psychoeducation and citalopram for 12 children and adolescents (aged 8–17) with generalized social phobia. Over the 12 week pharmacological trial, children and parents also attended eight 15 to 20 minute psychoeducational sessions conducted by a clinical psychologist. The program consisted of an initial session of psychoeducation, two sessions of instruction in construction of anxiety hierarchies, three sessions constructing graduated exposure tasks and teaching basic social skills and cognitive challenges. The final session was a review of progress and relapse prevention. At posttreatment, 10 of the 12 children (83.3%) were judged as improved; 41.7% as much improved and 41.7% as very much improved. Significant improvement also was found on self-report measures of social anxiety and depression, and parents ratings of social skill. However, even though scores were significantly decreased at posttreatment, the children remained somewhat impaired according to the SPAI-C scores (Beidel et al., 1995). These results are promising, but as with other open-label trials using small sample sizes, they require replication with a larger sample and a randomized, placebo controlled design.

There are two multi-center trials currently underway. In a large, 4 year multi-center trial for the treatment of anxiety disorders in youth (Albano, personal communication, 3/31/03), children and adolescents (aged 7–16) with either generalized anxiety disorder, social phobia or separation anxiety disorder will be randomized to either fluvoxamine, CBT (Coping Cat Program; see chapter 6), the combination of fluvoxamine and CBT, or pill placebo. This will be a 12 week acute trial, followed by a 6 month treatment maintenance program for responders to the three active interventions. This will be the largest study of the treatment of childhood anxiety disorders to date, but it is unclear how many children with social phobia will be included in the final sample.

A second ongoing two site trial is comparing fluoxetine, SET-C, and pill placebo for children and adolescents (aged 7–16) with social phobia (Beidel, Turner, Sallee, & Ammerman, 2004). The project will evaluate the efficacy of SET-C across an expanded age range of adolescents as well as children, will compare fluoxetine to a pill placebo control and SET-C, and will determine the long term (1 year) durability of both active interventions. This study will be the first to compare a pharmacological and psychosocial intervention specifically for children with social phobia.

Recent Innovations in Psychosocial Treatments

Masia and her colleagues (Masia, Klein, Storch, & Corda, 2001) investigated a 14 session group treatment program for 6 adolescents with social phobia. Conducted at school, this intervention included social skills training and in vivo exposure. There was significant improvement on clinician severity ratings, but self-report of social fears did not decrease significantly. Based on these pilot data, there now is an ongoing randomized controlled trial (Masia-Warner, Klein, Albano, & Guardin, 2003). Treatment is conducted in groups and consists of psychoeducation, training in realistic thinking, social skills training, exposure, and relapse prevention. In addition, there are two brief individual meetings, two meetings with the adolescent's teacher, two sessions with the adolescent's parent, and four social activities that include the use of peer assistants. The preliminary results indicate that the intervention is quite efficacious in comparison to a wait list control, with significant improvement across clinician and self-report measures.

Treatment of Social Phobia–Case Example

Prior to presenting the specifics of Jessica's treatment, there are a few general treatment recommendations to consider. First, as with other disorders, children often need encouragement to participate in the treatment program. In the case of social phobia, children often realize that because of their fears, they are missing out on "fun" things to do and that they do not have friends like other children. So, most children have some motivation to participate in treatment. However, they are going to be asked to do things that create significant distress, and their attempts at facing their fears should be acknowledged and rewarded. Second, the program requires homework and in order for the child to comply with most assignments, parental compliance also is necessary. That is, parents must be willing to take children to places necessary for them to complete their homework and assume responsibility for homework completion, particularly for preadolescent children. Thus, homework assignments must be devised so that compliance is maximized.

Following a comprehensive assessment, Jessica was assigned to Social Effectiveness Therapy for Children (SET-C; Beidel, Turner, & Morris, 2004). She participated in both group social skills training and peer generalization sessions as well as individual exposure sessions. In addition to the standard verbal content that is part of the SET-C social skills training, Jessica's individual skill deficits (depicted in Table 10.3) also were targeted for remediation during the group sessions. For example, while learning the skills to initiate a conversation, the group leaders also attended to the need for Jessica to make proper eye contact while using the appropriate verbal content. Of course, all children need to make eye contact. However, in Jessica's case, she needed constant reminders for several weeks to keep her head up and look at the other person. Similarly, in order to increase her voice volume, Jessica was required to repeat her responses until she was able to speak loudly enough to be detected by a decibel meter set at 60 db. Other children in the group had similar individualized treatment plans that were implemented within the group social skills context.

Table 10.4 depicts the tasks used for Jessica's individual exposure sessions and when possible, the corresponding homework assignments. Homework is always assigned and in cases where an appropriate corresponding homework assignment cannot be developed for a particular in vivo task, other homework assignments, such as "say hello to ten people per day" may be used. Homework assignments are an important part of the generalization process and should never be overlooked. In Jessica's case, small external reinforcers (costume jewelry, stickers) were used to increase compliance with both clinic exposure sessions and homework assignments.

At posttreatment, Jessica no longer met criteria for social phobia and her SPAI-C score was 16.9, below the cut-off usually considered indicative of social phobia, although still reflecting some level of social distress. This is not uncommon for intensive, but short-term interventions such as SET-C. Often,

TABLE 10.3 Jessica's Social Skills Deficits

One word answers
Barely audible voice volume
Flat tone
Minimal eye contact
Tearful in interactions

TABLE 10.4 Range of Jessica'a Fears and Associated Exposure Tasks

Fear	Clinic Exposure Task	Homework Assignment
Reading aloud in front of a group	Read aloud in front of others	Read aloud to family every night
Speaking to adults	Ask questions of store clerks in shopping mall	Answer the telephone at home
Joining in with a group	Ask children at arcade to join in a video game	Invite 2 children to "sleep over"
Performing in front of others	Play her flute in a public setting	Go to Sunday School and participate
Ordering food in a restaurant	Order food in fast food restaurants	Order food for family at restaurants
Writing on the blackboard	Take a test in public using an easel pad	Play drawing game with friends

children continue to improve for several months following treatment if they continue to practice the skills they acquired during the treatment program. At 3 year follow-up, Jessica had maintained her treatment gains.

SELECTIVE MUTISM

> Charlie is six years old. When he was three years old, he did not want to go to pre-school. His mother forced him to go. At the end of the first week, his teacher told his mother that Charlie had not spoken a word for the entire week. His mother became quite upset and begged Charlie to talk at school. Charlie refused and since that time has not spoken to anyone except his parents.

Selective mutism (SM) was first described as "aphasia voluntaria" (Kussamaul, 1897; cited in Dummitt et al., 1997). Tramer (1934) was the first to use the term "elective mutism" to describe a boy who despite speaking at home, would not speak at school. In most instances, children with SM will speak freely at home, but less so to their family when they are in public, and hardly at all, if ever, to unfamiliar adults and children. However, it is an error to assume, as some people do, that children with SM are noncommunicative. Such is not the case. Although they do not speak, children with SM, will communicate with gestures, nodding, pulling or pushing (Krysanski, 2003) or even by e-mail.

Clinical Features

The *DSM-IV* criteria for selective mutism are depicted in Table 10.5. Rates of speaking to different individuals vary by child but in general, those with SM are more likely to speak to peers than to teachers or other adults at school (Berg-

TABLE 10. 5 *DSM-IV* Criteria for Selective Mutism

A. Consistent failure to speak in specific social situations (in which there is an expectation for speaking, e.g., at school) despite speaking in other situations.

B. The disturbance interferes with educational or occupational achievement or with social communication.

C. The duration of the disturbance is at least 1 month (not limited to the first month of school).

D. The failure to speak is not due to a lack of knowledge of, or comfort with, the spoken language required in the social situation.

E. The disturbance is not better accounted for by a communication disorder (e.g., stuttering) and does not occur exclusively during the course of a pervasive developmental disorder, schizophrenia, or other psychotic disorder.

Reprinted with permission from the *Diagnostic and Statistical Manual of Mental Disorders*. Copyright 2000. American Psychiatric Association.

man et al., 2002; Steinhausen & Juzi, 1996). Children with SM have significantly higher rates of psychopathology, especially social anxiety, when compared to children with no disorder (Andersson & Thomsen, 1998; Elizur and Perednik, 2003; Steinhausen & Juzi, 1996; Yeganeh et al., 2003). Among one sample, the disorder's course was chronic for 53% of the children, whereas symptoms decreased for 35% of children, and fluctuated for the final 8% (Steinhausen & Juzi, 1996). In an excellent review of the SM literature (Freedman, Garcia. Miller, Dow, & Leonard, 2004), it appears that the majority of children with SM may outgrow the disorder but it is not clear whether some degree of social fears remain. As noted however, the disorder often persists for several years prior to remission and thus, interventions may be useful in shortening its course.

Sociodemographic Influences

Epidemiological data indicate that although SM is not an extremely rare disorder, it is still uncommon with world-wide epidemiological rates ranging from .18% to .76% of the general population (Bergman, Piacentini, & McCracken, 2002; Elizer & Perednik, 2003; Kopp & Gillberg, 1997). Interestingly, among a sample of kindergarten through second graders diagnosed with SM (Bergman et al., 202), 58% were in kindergarten, 17% were in first grade and 25% were in second grade. At follow-up 6 months later, children with SM showed significant improvement in terms of anxious symptomatology, even though impairment was still evident when compared to the control group. A closer examination of the data indicated that children who were female and in kindergarten made the most improvement, confirming earlier clinical observations that indeed some children may "outgrow" this disorder. Furthermore, given that kindergarten may be the first structured educational experience for many children, some children (perhaps those with milder fears) may overcome their mutism once the novelty of the situation lessens.

Becky is six years old. Her mother reports that she appeared to have had anxiety at six months of age. Even at that age, whenever someone tried to make eye contact with Becky, she would avert her eyes.

SM is an early-occurring disorder with the reported mean age of onset for several samples ranging from 3.4–5 years (Dummitt et al., 1997; Steinhausen & Juzi, 1996). In some instances, the onset has been described as insidious in some cases (like Becky), but when it starts abruptly, the mean age was 6.3 years (Andersson & Thomsen, 1998). Girls are more likely to present with this disorder than boys (see Dow, Sonies, Scheib, Moss, & Leonard, 1995 for a review), although boys tend to exhibit their pathology at an earlier age (Steinhausen & Juzi, 1996)

In several investigations, children whose families had immigrated to another country had higher rates of SM when compared to overall epidemiological data (Elizur & Perednik, 2003; Steinhausen & Juzi, 1996). The rates among immigrant families remained significantly higher even when the children themselves were born in the adopted country (Elizur & Perednik, 2003).

Comorbid and Differential Diagnosis

Although the full extent of its relationship is not yet clear, most children with SM also meet diagnostic criteria for social phobia (Black, & Uhde, 1994; Dummit, Klein, Tancer, Asche, & Martin, 1996). Furthermore, children have additional comorbid disorders including separation anxiety disorder (26%), overanxious disorder (14%), and simple phobia (34%; Dummitt et al., 1997). Other samples have reported high comorbidity with developmental disorders or delays, ranging from 18–68.5% across various samples; Kristensen, 2000; Steinhausen & Juzi, 1996). Depression appears to be less common as is hyperactivity (Steinhausen & Juzi, 1996)

One controversial issue with respect to SM is whether children with this disorder have speech, language, and learning disabilities. One etiological theory of SM is that mutism results from the presence of articulation and expressive language disorders that result in the child's reluctance to speak. However, the actual prevalence of these disorders in children with SM is quite variable, ranging from 11–50% of various samples (Andersson & Thomsen, 1998; Dummitt et al., 1997; Kristensen, 2000; Steinhausen & Juzi, 1996). Interestingly, in one study that used a comparison group (Andersson & Thomsen, 1998), 27.2% of children without a psychiatric disorder also had delayed speech development, suggesting that these types of disorders are common among children. In one comparative study, children with SM and comorbid for social phobia scored significantly lower on discrimination of speech sounds than those with social phobia alone (Manassis et al., 2003). However, there were no differences on five other measures of language and thus the clinical significance of this one statistically significant finding is unclear. Therefore, although children with SM may have speech and language difficulties, so do a substantial number of children with no psychiatric disorder, and it is not clear if the rate is significantly higher than is found in the general population. At this time, there is little evidence to suggest that such difficulties are etiological in nature for the majority of children with SM.

> Sasha is eleven years old. In the clinic waiting room, he talks loudly to his mother and his sister. The minute that he sees the therapist approach, he makes eye contact with the therapist, stops talking, presses his lips together, and folds his arms across his chest.

A very controversial area in the SM literature are the clinical reports suggesting that at least a subset of children with SM display oppositional behavior (Beidel & Turner, 1998) and recent data suggest that children with SM may display elements of oppositionality. For example, in comparison to normal controls, children with SM were rated by their parents as more "stubborn, sullen, or irritable" (Elizur & Perednik, 2003). The actual rates of opposition-defiance/aggressive behavior was 21% in one sample of children with SM (Steinhausen & Juzi, 1996). In a different sample, children with SM plus social phobia had significantly higher scores on the Delinquency subscale of the Child Behavior Checklist than children with social phobia alone (Yeganeh et al., 2003), although the scores were not in the clinically significant range. In an interesting comparison, Andersson and Thomsen (1998) noted that 27% of their selectively mute sample was described as aggressive, sulky, and stubborn at school, whereas 67.5% were noted to exhibit these same behaviors when they were at home.

These data suggest that some degree of oppositional behavior may be present in at least a subset of children with SM but it is often subtle. Furthermore, oppositionality may function as an avoidance strategy to deal with social distress, rather than as an independent disorder. Like SM itself, oppositional behaviors may be cued by specific environmental factors or internal triggers such as severe social anxiety. Another important consideration is the observation that oppositional behaviors are more likely to be found among samples of children with SM who were older and clinically referred as opposed to younger, epidemiological samples (Elizur & Perednik, 2003). A number of individuals and self-help goups who promote SM as simply the most severe form of social anxiety or social phobia do not want these children to be portrayed as having externalizing disorders such as Oppositional Disorder. What fails to be understood by these groups however, is that oppositional *behavior* is not the same as oppositional *disorder*. As noted in the beginning of this chapter, children with social phobia may express fear by freezing or tantrumming. Thus, oppositional behaviors may be a result of fears and not a deliberate attempt simply to defy a parent or other authority figure.

An alternative hypothesis related to our discussion of oppositionality is that SM develops in those with high social anxiety through operant mechanisms. That is, these children learn that they can control their environments by not speaking. Indeed, in our experience, parental behavior clearly functions to maintain the disorder. This is not to say that parents are responsible for the disorder. Their behavior could be in response to the child's condition and simply represents the results of ineffective parenting styles.

Etiology

> Becky is in first grade. During the course of the interview, Becky's mother confided that she understood how Becky felt because she, herself, was selectively mute until she was in third grade.

There are numerous etiological explanations for SM including unresolved family conflicts, negatively reinforced patterns of learning, social phobia among family members, faulty family relationships, or a reaction to traumatic events (Krysanski, 2003). With respect to the latter hypothesis (traumatic events), although 36.4% of one sample reported that some form of patient/family trauma had occurred (Andersson & Thomsen, 1998), there are no empirical data to suggest that the onset of SM is the result of traumatic events (Black & Uhde, 1995; Steinhausen & Juzi, 1996). Furthermore, when trauma does result in mutism, it is not specific to certain social situations but occurs universally across all settings. It is important to emphasize the nonrelationship between SM and trauma because as noted by Freeman et al. (2004), evaluation of children with SM by mental health workers and school systems often results in accusations of parents about presumed abuse. Thus, it cannot be over-emphasized that despite an occasional report of SM caused by hospitalization or trauma, data from controlled investigations do not indicate that SM is a reaction to, or result of, trauma.

One way of conceptualizing SM is that these children suffer from significant social anxiety. Refusing to speak is an avoidance behavior, designed to decrease distress in social situations, in much the same way that refusal to enter high places prevents distress associated with height phobia. An interesting and key question is why some children with social phobia continue to speak and others do not. If SM is the result of extreme social distress, then these children should be at the extreme end of the social phobia continuum, with the highest scores on measures of social anxiety. Only recently have several investigations directly compared children with SM and social phobia (SM+ SP) and children with social phobia but no SM (SP) on various measures of psychopathology in order to test this hypothesis (Manassis et al., 2003; Yeganeh et al., 2003). The results indicate that SP+SM children and SP children are not significantly different on self-report measures of social anxiety or general anxiety (Manassis et al., 2003; Yeganeh et al., 2003), suggesting that children with SM+SP did not report higher levels of social distress than children with social phobia alone. Mean scores for both groups were in the moderate range.

Interestingly, clinician ratings of social distress were significantly higher for children with SM+SP than children with SP alone (Yeganeh et al., 2003). However, this may have been due to the fact that children with SM+SP did not respond to the interviewer's questions, thus it was not possible to keep the clinicians blind to group assignment. Similarly, children with SM refused to speak during the behavioral assessment of social skill and anxiety. Therefore, children with SM+SP were rated as having significantly fewer social skills and significantly higher social distress during both role-play social interactions and reading aloud in front of a group (Yeganeh et al., 2003) probably because of their nonresponse. Interestingly, consistent with their SPAI-C scores, children's self-ratings of distress during these behavioral interactions did not differ between groups, and again, mean scores for both groups were in the moderate range. In essence, although clinicians and behavioral raters judged the group with SM+SP as significantly more impaired, the children themselves did not report heightened distress. In summary, although children with SM exhibit social anxiety, extant self-report data do not indicate that their self-reported level of distress is different from children with SP alone. Clinician and behavioral observer ratings do differ between the groups but it is difficult to discount the fact that the children's mutism may have influenced the severity ratings.

Assessment

The specific origin of SM remains unclear and therefore careful assessment is necessary to rule out other causes for lack of speech. Behaviors not characteristic of SM (e.g., not talking to immediate family, absence of speech in any environment) may indicate the presence of a different disorder (aphasia, autism; Dow et al., 1995). Other atypical language problems could indicate Asberger's disorder or any number of neurological problems or learning disabilities. Speech and language difficulties should be specifically queried and if parents report abnormalities, a speech and language assessment may be necessary. Although difficult to accomplish in person, speech and language clinics sometimes can glean important information by watching videotapes of children with SM engaged in conversation with family at home. Furthermore, nonverbal tests of receptive language abilities can be administered (see Dow et al., 1995 for a review of this literature).

As noted, children with SM are not necessarily totally noncommunicative. Therefore, it is possible to interview children by using nods, gestures, and pointing. For example, changing all questions to that the child can nod "yes" or "no" and allowing the child to point to a visual scale depicting various levels of distress will allow a substantial amount of information to be gathered. It allows the child to communicate directly with the therapist and begins to break the pattern of always having someone else communicate for the child. It also allows the therapist to set expectations for the therapeutic relationship.

Self-Report

There are few self-report measures of selective mutism and it is probably one of the few conditions where clarification of the disorder by behavioral observation rather than self-report is easy to achieve. Recently, the Selective Mutism Questionnaire (SMQ) was developed to assess severity, scope and functional impairment (Bergman, Keller, Wood, Piacintini, & McCracken, 2001). The SMQ is designed for use in clinical and research settings and has three subscales: school, home/with family, and public (nonschool) items. The scale has good internal consistency. Other psychometric properties are currently under investigation.

Behavioral Assessment

Because of the operant factors that appear to be an important component of SM, assessment should include observation of parent–child interactions designed to elucidate behaviors that might serve to reinforce the mutism. For example, parent and child might be asked to work on a word puzzle and then have a stranger come in and try to in engage the child in conversation. Observation of the parent during this interaction may reveal important behaviors that serve to maintain the child's mutism.

Treatment

Psychodynamic, family systems, behavior therapy, and pharmacotherapy have been used to treat SM. The literature on psychodynamic and family systems therapy is descriptive and retrospective in nature, making it difficult to evaluate the treatment outcome (Anstendig, 1998). With respect to family systems approaches above, SM no longer is conceptualized as resulting from family pathology (Dow et al., 1995) except that certain family members' behaviors may serve to maintain the disorder. Thus, family therapy no longer is the treatment of choice for SM even though in many cases, families still need to be integrally involved in the treatment plan.

Behavior therapy is the most commonly reported intervention and has the strongest empirical data base. Furthermore, multimodal behavioral approaches appear more efficacious than a single behavioral intervention (Anstendig, 1998). Pharmacological interventions are more recent with mixed outcomes reported. A review of pharmacological and behavioral treatments follows.

Pharmacological Treatment

Two trials (1 open and 1 double blind) have examined the use of fluoxetine with SM children. In an open trial (Dummit et al., 1996), 78% of children (mean age 8.2 years) with SM (also comorbid for either avoidant disorder of childhood or social phobia) had decreased anxiety and increased speech at posttreatment. Using a double blind, placebo controlled design (Black & Uhde, 1994), SM children (aged 6–12 years) comorbid for either social phobia or avoidant disorder were significantly improved over the placebo group according to the parental Clinical Global Impression (CGI) rating. However, there were no group differences using clinician or teacher ratings. Furthermore, overall treatment effects were viewed as modest and most fluoxetine patients were still symptomatic at posttreatment. Thus, in contrast to the open clinical trial, this placebo-controlled trial resulted in only moderate support for fluoxetine. Currently, there are no controlled trials of combined pharmacological and behavioral interventions in the literature, but we agree with others who recommend that combination treatments may be appropriate for children with SM who are older and/or treatment refractory (Freeman et al., 2004).

Psychosocial Interventions

Data on psychological treatments for SM are restricted primarily to case descriptions or single case designs. Behavioral procedures that have been reported to be successful include positive reinforcement, stimulus fading, shaping, and contingency management (i.e., operant strategies, Krysanski, 2003). In many of these investigations, outcome was based on behavioral data collected through observational strategies and therefore, the data are not comparable ether across other psychosocial intervention investigations or to the results of pharmacological trials. In a review of 33 individual case or uncontrolled group investigations (Cunningham, Cataldo, Mallion, & Keyes, 1983), reinforcement procedures were most successful when a minimal level of speech already existed. When there was no baseline speech, stimulus fading procedures were most effective. Response cost contingencies improved the efficacy of both of these interventions and longer interventions resulted in more positive treatment outcome. Across follow-up intervals, only one child showed deterioration of speech at the time of the follow-up assessments.

Many of the behavioral procedures in the above paragraph were discussed in other chapters within this book, but a brief explanation of stimulus fading is included here. Stimulus fading is the "transfer of stimulus control through the attenuation of the discriminative stimulus" (Krysanski, 2003, p.35). In the case of children with SM, this involves the gradual introduction of others into an environment where the child already speaks. For example, in the clinic setting, the child may be placed in a room with the parent alone, where is it likely that the child may talk. Then a stranger may be gradually faded into the room using a fear hierarchy such as those discussed in other chapters within this book. Such a hierarchy may include the stranger (a) standing in the doorway to the room and wearing earmuffs, (b) standing in the doorway without earmuffs, (c) standing just inside the room, not wearing earmuffs but also not looking directly at the child (perhaps reading a book), and so on. Items on the hierarchy would continue, adding in additional people until the child is speaking comfortably in a variety of situations. For another example of a treatment hierarchy, see the case example for Charlie.

In a randomized controlled trial (Calhoun & Koenig, 1973), 8 SM children were randomly assigned to either a treatment or control group. Outcome was determined by the number of words that the child spoke in a 30 minute interval. Treatment consisted of teacher and peer contingent reinforcement for verbal behavior by the SM child. At posttreatment (5 weeks later), those in the treatment group had significantly more vocalizations than the control group but there was no difference at 1 year follow-up.

In a very recent innovation, a seven-year-old child with selective mutism was treated using an Internet Web-based version of CBT (Fung, Manassis, Kenny, & Fiksenbaum, 2002) that included a child workbook as well as parent/teacher manuals. The format followed that used in other CBT programs with 8 sessions devoted to skills training and 6 sessions to practice and application. In this second phase, the child has the opportunity to record short messages via the computer that could be replayed by the therapist during the following treatment session. The use of the recording and playback in the presence of the therapist was aimed at desensitization of social fears. In other words, it allowed the opportunity for others to hear the child speak without the child having to actually produce speech. Such desensitization procedures often are used by behavior therapists when treating children with selective mutism (although the use of a computer is a novel, and perhaps extremely engaging, variation on this strategy). Pre and posttreatment ratings of anxiety by the child, parent and teacher indicated some improvement as did the selective mutism questionnaire. The results of this case description are interesting and given the refractory nature of selective mutism suggest that larger scale interventions are necessary.

Treatment of Selective Mutism—Case Example

Returning to Charlie, the results of the behavioral assessment revealed several factors that were important in constructing his treatment plan. First, his mother reinforced his mutism by speaking for him or laughing/smiling when he would not respond to someone else. Thus, his mother had to be instructed in principles of reinforcement and given practice in not reinforcing Charlie for mute behaviors. Second, with respect to the construction of the exposure hierarchy,

TABLE 10. 6 Charlie's Exposure Hierarchy

Item	SUDS
Whisper aloud to Mom and Dad so that David or Sarah can hear	0
Talk aloud to Mom and Dad so that David or Sarah can hear	1
Whisper directly to David	2
Talk aloud to David	3
Talk aloud to David and Sarah together	3
With Mom and Dad present, say one word to an unfamiliar adult	4
With Mom and Dad present, say one sentence to an unfamiliar adult	5
Say "Hello" to next door neighbor outside of the presence of Mom and Dad	5
Say "Hello" to teacher at school	6
Say "Hi" to a classmate	6
Using the walkie-talkie, stand in a different room and talk to the teacher and class (so they can hear your voice)	7
Talk to teacher without the walkie-talkie	8

consideration included the following factors: (a) Charlie had two friends (David and Sarah) in whose presence he would speak, even though he would not speak to them directly, (b) school and teachers were the hardest situations for him, (c) Charlie was very interested in mechanical toys and electronic equipment. The in vivo exposure program was developed with these factors in mind (see Charlie's exposure hierarchy in Table 10.6).

Because of the presence of oppositional behaviors and the need to teach his mother to reinforce positive attempts at speaking rather than attending to mute behaviors, a formal contingency contract was established between Charlie and his parents (see Table 10.7). Charlie was assigned each item to do at home. He continued to practice that item until it was completed with only minimal anxiety (no more than a rating of 1 on a 0–4 point rating scale). The outcome

TABLE 10.7 Charlie's Contract

I will try my best to do each step. If I try, I will get either
- a sticker that smells
- a popcorn snack

If I complete the step, I will get
- a small plastic dinosaur
- 15 minutes of cartoon watching
- an "extra" dessert

After I complete three items I will get to play miniature golf

After I complete three more items, I will get a walkie-talkie set

After I complete three more items, I will get a day at the water park

After all the items are completed, I will get an erector set of my choice

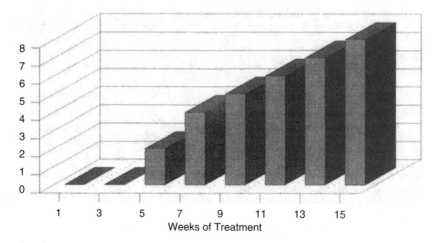

FIGURE 10.1 Number of new people spoken to each week.

measure selected to assess improvement and monitored daily by his parents was the number of "new" people that Charlie spoke to each day. For display, data are collapsed by week. Because of his age, his parents were in charge of monitoring his SUDS level and counting the number of new people to whom he spoke (see Figure 10.1 for an illustration of the outcome data). As depicted, the program was successful and at Week 14–15, Charlie was speaking to a wide variety of individuals across various settings.

SUMMARY

Social phobia is a prevalent and serious disorder and data are accumulating such that a comprehensive understanding of its clinical presentation is quite clear. Furthermore, there are data that attest to both its immediate and long-term implications for academic, social, and emotional functioning. With the recognition that this disorder can result in serious lifetime impairment, both pharmacological and psychosocial interventions are beginning to emerge. A recent survey of parents whose children were receiving treatment in a primary care setting indicated favorable attitudes toward psychological treatment for children with social anxiety whereas attitudes toward pharmacological treatment was "neutral" (Chavira, Stein, Bariley, & Stein, 2003). Despite these favorable attitudes, the literature on efficacious pharmacological and psychosocial treatments is still limited at this time, thus there is little parents can be told about the efficacy of these interventions. With respect to open trials of medication, improvement on SSRIs is superior to placebo. Similarly, most of the psychosocial treatment trials are controlled through the use of a wait-list control group and there is evidence of positive outcome. The next challenge for pharmacological and psychosocial treatment trials however, is to demonstrate that these interventions are efficacious (and superior to placebo) for children with social phobia as a distinct diagnostic entity (rather than examining efficacy across diagnostically different groups of children). For example, the few data that are available suggest that, in comparison to disorders such as GAD, social anxiety disorder may be one of the few conditions where SSRIs actually may be significantly superior to placebo (Birmaher et al., 2003; RUPP Anxiety Study Group, 2002). Similarly, although CBT interventions appear to be effective in reducing general anxiety, they may not be as effective in addressing the specific deficits of children with social anxiety disorder. Furthermore, even though current treatment outcomes indicate statistically significant improvement at posttreatment, many of these trials note that clinically significant symptoms remain at posttreatment and follow-up. Therefore, the question that remains is whether additional treatment sessions would produce an even more positive outcome or whether an alternative treatment strategy is necessary, or whether initial incomplete improvement results in complete remission over time.

Another area in need of further investigation is the relative contribution of specific treatment components in allowing greater efficiency in the delivery of these services. Currently, we do not know which component(s) are necessary or sufficient, although based on meta-analyses conducted with adult outcome studies, exposure in some form would appear to be the key ingredient (Beidel & Turner, 1998). Finally, there has been little attention given to developmental considerations, with regard to understanding the utility of specific psychosocial treatment components. Most studies include youth between the ages of 7 and 17, with few attempts to address developmental issues with respect to intervention or assessment of treatment outcome. Given the major developmental changes that occur across this age range, future studies may need to focus on restricted age ranges or examine outcomes separately for different developmental subgroups. Finally, long-term outcome data for psychosocial treatment are beginning to emerge and additional studies are underway. Pharmacological treatment trials lag behind in this regard but hopefully such data will be forthcoming.

CHAPTER 11

Obsessive-Compulsive Disorder and Trichotillomania

Anthony is a 16-year-old teen referred for evaluation of compulsive behaviors that include excessive hand washing, the need to enter a certain room in a specific fashion and the need to touch objects that he feels compelled to carry with him at all times. Although he had previous episodes of compulsive behaviors (showering for 45 minutes at a time), the current compulsions began about 2 years ago when his family moved from Maine to the southeast. At the time of the evaluation, he has intrusive thoughts that harm might come to him or his family. Most of the time, the thoughts are uncontrollable and repetitive behaviors designed to relieve them bring only temporary relief. The behaviors cause disruption in his schoolwork, family interactions, and peer socialization.

Angela is 9 years old. She has been anxious "her whole life" but her fears have increased in the past year. She has a myriad of negative thoughts and images, all with the underlying theme of harm or death to herself. Her fears include enclosed places, eating food without washing her hands, tornadoes, house fires, her house sinking into the ground, and her heart stopping. In response to these obsessions, Angela engages in numerous rituals and avoidance behaviors including reassurance seeking, hand washing (three times per hour with dishwasher detergent), and refusing to eat certain foods and/or without washing her hands first. As her fears have increased, her grades at school have decreased and there is increased family tension. Angela has been treated in the past, unsuccessfully, for specific phobias.

Anthony and Angela have Obsessive-Compulsive Disorder (OCD), one of the most severe and disabling of the anxiety disorders. Pediatric OCD was identified at the turn of the century (Janet, 1903), but only in the last 25 years has there been extensive study of this condition. Children with OCD suffer from intrusive, unwanted thoughts or feelings that create significant distress. To decrease that distress, children, like their adult counterparts, feel compelled to engage in rituals that appear to counteract their concerns and temporarily alleviate their anxiety. Children with OCD are at risk for impairment in their academic, social, and familial functioning (Adams, Wass, March, & Smith, 1994). Particularly challenging for clinicians is that the children often are not able to conceptualize or communicate their exact concerns, often stating that they feel compelled to do something until it "feels right." Furthermore, not all children with OCD feel that their behavior is unusual or dysfunctional, presenting further significant challenges for treatment compliance.

According to the *Diagnostic and Statistical Manual of Mental Disorders-Fourth Edition* (*DSM-IV*; APA, 1994; see Table 11.1 for the diagnostic criteria),

TABLE 11.1 *DSM-IV* Diagnostic Criteria for Obsessive-Compulsive Disorder

A. Either obsessions or compulsions:
Obsessions are defined as:

1. Recurrent and persistent thoughts, impulses, or images that are experienced, at some time during the disturbance, as intrusive and inappropriate and that cause marked anxiety or distress.

2. The thoughts, impulses, or images are not simply excessive worries about real-life problems.

3. The person attempts to ignore or suppress such thoughts, impulses, or images, or to neutralize them with some other thought or action.

4. The person recognizes that the obsessional thoughts, impulses, or images are a product of his or her own mind (not imposed from without as in thought insertion).

Compulsions are defined as:

1. Repetitive behaviors (e.g., hand washing, ordering, checking) or mental acts (e.g., praying, counting, repeating words silently) that the person feels driven to perform in response to an obsession, or according to rules that must be applied rigidly.

2. The behaviors or mental acts are aimed at preventing or reducing distress or preventing some dreaded event or situation; however, these behaviors or mental acts either are not connected in a realistic way with what they are designed to neutralize or prevent or are clearly excessive.

B. At some point during the course of the disorder, the person has recognized that the obsessions or compulsions are excessive or unreasonable. *Note:* This does not apply to children.

C. The obsessions or compulsions cause marked distress, are time consuming (take more than 1 hour a day), or significantly interfere with the person's normal routine, occupational (or academic) functioning, or usual social activities or relationships.

D. If another Axis I disorder is present, the content of the obsessions or compulsions is not restricted to it.

E. The disturbance is not due to the direct physiological effects of a substance (e.g., a drug of abuse, a medication) or a general medical condition.

Reprinted with permission from the *Diagnostic and Statistical Manual of Mental Disorders*. Copyright 2000. American Psychiatric Association.

children need not have insight into their disorder (Foa & Kozak, 1995; Geller et al., 1998).

> Michael had obsessional thoughts about dirt, germs, and contracting a disease. His mother did not wash his clothes to his satisfaction so Michael did his own laundry. He washed his clothes approximately 16 hours per day. In fact, he wore out three washing machines in 1 year, forcing his parents to replace each worn-out machine with a new one. Michael did not see this as a problem. He sincerely believed that his parents should just keep replacing the washing machines.

As with other disorders, children can suffer for many years before treatment is initiated (Last & Strauss, 1989; Thomsen, 1995). Like adults with OCD who often perform their rituals in secret, children also hide their rituals from their parents, sometimes for many months prior to parental awareness (Swedo, Rapoport, Leonard, Lenane, & Cheslow, 1989). Among a large epidemiological sample (Rapoport et al., 2000), 91% of OCD cases were diagnosed based on child report alone. In fact, only 16% of children with OCD had parents who had any awareness of their child's symptoms. These data are important for two reasons. First, it indicates that children can be very secretive regarding their symptoms (as is often the case with adults), allowing the disorder to become firmly entrenched. Second, it suggests that epidemiological data based on parental report alone may severely underestimate the prevalence of this disorder.

CLINICAL FEATURES

Like other anxiety disorders, symptoms of OCD extend along a continuum. Among high school students for example, 19% reported behaviors consistent with subclinical OCD (Valleni-Basile et al., 1994). Sub-clinical was defined as (a) having symptoms of OCD but insufficient for a diagnosis or (b) symptoms sufficient for a diagnosis but without functional impairment. In fact, whereas 10% of youth endorsed the presence of significant OCD symptoms, only 4.1% endorsed significant interference as a result of their symptoms (Thomsen, 1993). Among general outpatient clinic samples, 5% of children under 18 years of age had OCD symptoms (Honjo et al., 1989), although they did not meet full diagnostic criteria. What differentiates those with OCD from these subsyndromal conditions are the content, frequency, and severity of the behaviors (Leonard, Goldberger, Rapoport, Cheslow, & Swedo, 1990).

The current diagnostic criteria indicate that individuals with OCD may have either obsessions or compulsions. However, such a clinical presentation (i.e., only obsessions or compulsions) is usually the exception rather than the rule (Geller et al., 1998; Flament et al., 1988; Hanna et al., 1995; Last & Strauss, 1989; Riddle et al., 1990). When only one component is present, children, in comparison to adolescents, are more likely to present with compulsions only

(Geller et al., 1998; Last et al., 1989), although obsessions without rituals have been reported as well (Flament et al., 1988). Below, each component of the clinical presentation of OCD is reviewed.

Cognitive Symptoms

The hallmark cognitive symptoms of OCD are obsessional thoughts. However, obsessions can be in the form of thoughts, impulses, or images.

> Anthony had intrusive thoughts that something "bad" would happen to himself or his family (primarily become ill or be in an accident) if he did not engage in certain behaviors. Angela had intrusive images of her house sinking into the ground or a hurricane blowing her house away.

With respect to content, the most common obsessions include contamination fears and concerns about illness and disease (Barrett & Healy-Farrell, 2003; Flament et al., 1988; Hanna, 1995; Last & Strauss, 1989; Riddle et al., 1990; Swedo et al., 1989). Less frequent but also commonly reported are thoughts of aggression (inflicting harm on self or others), symmetry/exactness, hoarding or saving, magic, sex, and somatization. Specific obsessional thoughts appear to be more common among adolescents than younger children. Whereas 74% of adolescents with OCD reported the presence of specific obsessions (Valleni-Basile et al., 1994), among children, the most frequent reason for why they had to perform certain behavioral acts was that they "had no idea" (Swedo et al., 1989).

Overt Behaviors

Rituals are the overt manifestations of the distress experienced by a child with OCD. In most instances, rituals have some topographical relationship to the child's obsessional thoughts. Thus, washing and cleaning rituals are most often related to fears of contamination, and concern about harm to self or others is usually related to checking behaviors.

> Anthony engaged in a variety of behaviors designed to decrease his distress. This included washing his hands, carrying a rabbit's foot with him at all times and constantly checking to make sure it was there, checking that he did not harm himself or others, checking that he did not make a mistake, touching objects until it "feels right," and having to first turn around in a circle before entering a certain room in his home.

It is important to note that ritualistic behaviors alone do not automatically indicate the presence of OCD. For example, children with Crohn's disease and ulcerative colitis endorsed the presence of ritualistic behaviors but these behaviors appeared secondary to the demands of their illnesses (Burke et al., 1989). Also, repetitive behavior among unselected samples of young children actually is quite common (Evans et al., 1997; Zohar & Felz, 2001). For example, children between the ages of 2 and 4 years (mean age 39 months) exhibited approximately 10 ritualistic behaviors at any one time (e.g., preparing for bedtime by engaging in a certain routine, liking to eat food in a particular way, arranging objects or performing certain behaviors until they seem just right, collecting or storing objects; Zohar & Felz, 2001). However, over 98% of mothers denied worry about the behaviors. Thus, repetitive behaviors are common, at least among young children, and as discussed in chapter 1, developmental considerations are important when determining behavioral abnormalities. An important distinction in determining whether repetitive behaviors actually are OCD rituals is the motivating factor. Unlike "normal" rituals, compulsions develop at a later age, frequently persist into adulthood, and are incapacitating, distressing and interfere with normal development (King, Ollendick, & Montgomery, 1995).

The most prevalent rituals include checking, hand-washing, and cleaning (Barrett & Healy-Farrell, 2003; Flament et al., 1988; Hanna, 1995; Last & Strauss, 1989; Riddle et al., 1990; Swedo et al., 1989). Other common rituals include repeating, ordering/arranging, touching, counting and hoarding/saving.

> Henry was unable to throw away anything that he felt belonged to him—this included magazines, school papers, clothing that no longer fit him, and two-year-old school lunches. Often when walking down the street, he would feel compelled to pick something up and bring it home. His room was overflowing with items and because of the rotting food, had a terrible odor. By the time his parents sought treatment for Henry, they had been forced to rent a unit at the local self-storage facility because their house was no longer able to contain Henry's hoarded belongings.

Among Danish children hospitalized for OCD, repeating was the most commonly reported ritual although those with washing rituals were the most severely affected (Thomsen, 1995). Some children are able to control their ritualistic behaviors temporarily when in public settings. In addition to rituals, some children attempt to control their anxiety through behavioral avoidance (Swedo et al., 1989) and many children exhibit a combination of ritualistic and avoidant behaviors.

> When meeting Saundra, the first thing that one noticed was that she wore a pair of athletic socks on each hand. This was to prevent her hands from contamination. Saundra also refused to go to school because of potential contamination. If she accidentally came into contact with a contaminated object, an elaborate 4 hour bathing ritual ensued.

As illustrated by Anthony, the specific pattern of obsessions and compulsions often changes, with 90–100% of children changing ritualistic behaviors across time (Rettew, Swedo, Leonard, Lenane & Rapport, 1992; Swedo, Rapoport, Leonard, Lenane, & Cheslow, 1989). However, it is important to note that even though specific symptoms may change, and the disorder intensity may wax and wane, the disorder itself rarely remits without intervention.

Physical Symptoms

Although rarely discussed, children with OCD can present with the same constellation of symptoms that exist for children with other anxiety disorders. Furthermore, children, like adults, may experience panic attacks when faced with a feared object or situation (such as accidentally touching a contaminated object).

> When the intrusive thoughts occur, Anthony reported that his stomach "churns" and he suddenly became very warm. When Saundra was confronted by an object that she felt was contaminated, her hands sweated profusely. The reaction was so severe, it appeared that her hands were "raining" perspiration.

As noted above, OCD is a complex and chronic disorder. What data do exist on long-term outcome suggest that the majority of children with OCD continue to have symptoms into adulthood. Among adults treated for OCD as children, only 28% had no symptoms at follow-up (Thomsen & Mikkelsen, 1993) whereas 26% had "subclinical" OCD symptoms, 21% had phasic OCD (sometimes meeting diagnostic criteria and sometimes falling to sub-clinical levels) and 26% had a chronic, disabling course. There was no difference in outcome based on gender. Thus, even with available interventions, OCD presents a particular challenge for clinicians.

SOCIODEMOGRAPHIC INFLUENCES

Based on one epidemiological sample, the 1 year incidence rate for OCD among young adolescents was 0.7% (Valleni-Basile et al., 1996). With respect to prevalence, rates range from 1.9–4% of the general population (Flament et al., 1988; Geller et al., 1998; Valleni-Basile et al., 1994) and are consistent across samples collected in the United States and internationally. However, rates calculated via the use of symptom inventories are often higher than those based on a diagnostic interview. When diagnoses of OCD are determined by clinical interview rather than self-report, the prevalence rate is much lower, averaging 2.2% of the general population (Geller et al., 1998).

The average age of onset for OCD among children is approximately 9–10 years, but has been reported to range from 5–18 years (Flament et al., 1988;

Geller et al., 1998; Last & Strauss, 1989; Riddle et al., 1990; Swedo, Rapoport, Leonard, Lenane, & Cheslow, 1989; Thomsen, 1995). We have even seen frank OCD in a 3-year-old child who was the son of a patient in our clinic.

Unlike adults, children with OCD are predominantly male (3:2 male–female ratio; Geller et al., 1989; Last & Strauss, 1989) and boys have an earlier age of onset (Geller et al., 1998). However, gender disparity disappears as samples become older (Swedo et al., 1989; Valleni-Bassile et al., 1994). In addition to an earlier age of onset, boys are more likely to have a family member with OCD or Tourette's syndrome (March et al., 2004).

With respect to race or ethnicity, few studies have examined similarities and differences in the clinical presentation of OCD. One study from Australia (Barrett, Healy, & March, 2004) indicated that washing and cleaning rituals are the most common among Australian children and adolescents with OCD, as they are in the United States.

COMORBID AND DIFFERENTIAL DIAGNOSIS

The majority of children with OCD, perhaps as many as 74%, present with comorbid conditions (Flament et al., 1988; Last & Strauss, 1989; Swedo et al., 1989). Other anxiety disorders are most common (Flament et al., 1990; Last et al., 1989; Riddle et al., 1990; Swedo et al., 1989) and sometimes it is difficult to determine the primary condition. As presented earlier, Angela had been diagnosed previously with multiple specific phobias. Treatment directed toward her specific fears had been unsuccessful as the elimination of each specific fear was replaced by another concern. Treatment was successful only after her concerns were reconceptualized as an obsession about dying and behavioral interventions targeted that concern. In many instances, the primary disorder is the one that creates the greatest functional impairment and in most instances, particularly with respect to anxiety disorders, that would be OCD.

The incidence of comorbid depression among children with OCD is more controversial. Some samples found a very low incidence of comorbid depression (Last & Strauss, 1989; Riddle et al., 1990) whereas others reported high rates of comorbidity (Flament et al., 1988; Swedo et al., 1989; Valleni-Basile et al., 1994). It should be noted that this latter sample was screened initially for the presence of depression (rather than OCD), thus one would expect rates of depression to be higher than in a sample of those with primary OCD. Therefore, some of the differences in comorbidity rates might be due to different sampling strategies.

Disruptive behavior disorders also exist in children with OCD and again, the reported rates are quite variable. Whereas Flament et al. (1990) reported that only 8% of their follow-up sample had a lifetime diagnosis of conduct disorder, Geller et al. (1998) reported that 70% of children referred to a specialized OCD clinic had a disruptive disorder, including attention-deficit/hyperactivity disorder (ADHD) and oppositional defiant disorder. The specific rate of co-morbid ADHD among one population of children with OCD was 30%. In a separate sample of 121 children with primary ADHD (Geller et al., 2002), 55% were diagnosed with comorbid OCD based on diagnostic interview. The age of onset for ADHD (4 years) was earlier than the age of onset of OCD (6.4 years), and ADHD preceded the onset of OCD in 82% of the comorbid cases. There were no differences in ADHD symptomatology between children comorbid for OCD and those with ADHD alone. However, the study did not describe the type of obsessions or compulsions or compare the comorbid group to a group with OCD alone. Thus, it is unclear whether the clinical symptoms of OCD in the comorbid group were consistent with those usually characteristic of OCD. One difficulty interpreting these data is that it is clinically difficult to conceptualize the existence of these two disorders in one individual. That is, those with OCD usually are so fixated on one particular thought or idea that it is difficult, if not impossible, to distract them. The hallmark of ADHD however, is heightened distractibility. Thus, it is difficult to understand how these two opposing cognitive styles could co-exist within one individual.

Other disorders comorbid with OCD include tics and Tourette's syndrome (TS), although the strength of the relationship depends upon the manner in which the sample is recruited. Specifically, rates of comorbid TS are low when the sample consists of those with primary OCD (Flament et al., 1990; Last et al., 1989; Riddle et al., 1990; Swedo et al., 1989) whereas rates of OCD or OCD symptoms are high when the sample consists of individuals initially evaluated for TS (e.g., Grad, Pelcovitz, Olson, Mathews, & Grad, 1987). Interestingly, in a 2–7 year follow-up study of children with OCD (Leonard et al., 1992), 11% of children (all males) initially diagnosed with OCD had developed TS at follow-up. However, other than an earlier age of onset, there were no differences in the clinical presentation of those male children who later developed TS versus those who did not. Prior to determining that comorbid OCD exists among children with TS, it is important to carefully examine the behaviors that are termed ritualistic. In many instances, the behavior of those with TS or tics are characterized by small muscle movements, often appearing non-purposive. In contrast, the ritualistic behaviors of those with OCD are more complex, voluntary and directly related to the nature of the obsessions. Hence it is not clear that the behaviors referred to in some studies meet the usual criteria for compulsions. Trichotillomania, another repetitive behavior, also has been noted among children with OCD (March, Franklin, Leonard, & Foa, 2004) and this disorder is discussed in a later section of this chapter.

ETIOLOGY OF OCD

For 33–50% of adults with OCD, onset occurred during childhood (Rasmussen & Eisen, 1990). For some children, symptom onset can be gradual with no identifiable environmental stressors (Flament et al., 1988), but 55% of children hospitalized for OCD reported that onset occurred in conjunction with a precipitating event such as death or illness of the parents or a child's impending operation (Thomsen, 1995). Various theories regarding the etiology of OCD are reviewed here.

From a neurobiological perspective, Leonard and Rapoport (1989) hypothesized that OCD resulted from a basal ganglia dysfunction that in turn, resulted in the manifestation of thoughts and behaviors without the usual sensory triggers. Evidence for the hypothesis included an increased incidence of OCD in neurological illnesses of the basal ganglia (Tourette's syndrome, postencephalitic Parkinson's disease and Sydenham's chorea) as well as possible frontal lobe/basal ganglia dysfunction. Of course, the previous caveats regarding the need to examine the form and content of the repetitive behaviors and their relationship to obsessions is necessary. In fact, many of these early investigations were conducted on adult patients, and their relevance to child OCD is unclear.

More recently, several additional lines of evidence have been proposed to support a neurobiological basis for OCD (March, Franklin, Leonard, & Foa, 2004). First, with respect to familial relationships, 17–25% of parents of children with OCD also had OCD, either at the time of the assessment or at some point during their lifetime (Lenane et al., 1990; Riddle et al., 1990; Swedo et al., 1989; Thomsen, 1995). Fathers were almost three times more likely than mothers to be diagnosed with OCD or obsessive-compulsive personality disorder (Lenane et al., 1990). Furthermore, up to 52% of parents may have "subclinical" OCD (Riddle, Hardin, King, Scahill, & Woolston, 1990). Increased degree of familiality of OCD symptoms appears to be correlated with an earlier age of onset in the proband (Pauls, Alsobrook, Goodman, Rasmussen & Leckman, 1995).

In addition to parental psychopathology, OCD behaviors sometimes exist in siblings of those with OCD. The rates of OCD in siblings is approximately 5% (Pauls et al., 1995; Thomsen, 1995). Additionally, a child with OCD can impact sibling emotional status and behavior even when the sibling does not have OCD (Barrett, Rasmussen, & Healy, 2000). Specifically, when a child has OCD, siblings report higher rates of anxiety and depression when compared to a control group. Furthermore, they often accommodate to the child's disorder by providing reassurance, and helping with rituals and/or avoidance behaviors. Finally, sibling relationships are negatively impacted as a result of a child's OCD. Encouragingly, as children with OCD respond positively to cognitive-behavioral treatment, the quality of the sibling relationship improves as does the sibling's own level of anxiety and depression (Barrett et al., 2000).

Family studies also have examined the specific relationship between OCD and Tourette's Disorder. Several investigations (Pauls et al., 1995; Pauls, Towbin, Leckman, Zahner, & Cohen, 1986) documented that first-degree relatives of individuals with tics or Tourette's Disorder have a higher rate of both tic disorders and OCD. Similarly, there is an increased prevalence of tics and Tourette's

Disorder in relatives of those with OCD (Leonard et al., 1992) although the previous caveats regarding diagnosis remain a consideration. To reiterate, these relationships are highly dependent upon specific sample characteristics and the overt behaviors exhibited by those with Tourette's often are very different in form and content from the ritualistic behaviors of the child with OCD.

The second line of evidence for the neurobiological hypothesis are neuropsychological and neuroimaging studies that implicate abnormalities in the basal ganglia, the cortex, and the connecting pathways (Rosenberg, MacMillan, & Moore, 2001). Several investigations have documented neurological abnormalities that may be related to learning disabilities. For example, neuropsychological evaluation of one sample suggested that over 80% of children with OCD had results indicative of underlying frontal lobe-basal ganglia dysfunction (e.g., Denkla, 1989). Recently, childhood OCD has been conceptualized as a reversible glutamatergically mediated thalamo-cortical-striatal dysfunction (Rosenberg, MacMillan, & Moore, 2001). A full discussion of this issue is beyond the scope of this chapter and the interested reader is referred to Rosenberg et al. (2001). One aspect of this hypothesis deserves mention here, however. Unlike other theories that would suggest that these morphological characteristics are inflexible (e.g., increased thalamic volumes are fixed characteristics of those with the disorder), Rosenberg et al. (2001) hypothesized that identified structural abnormalities may be malleable to some forms of intervention. For example, thalamic volumes of treatment-naive children with OCD that were significantly larger than healthy controls prior to treatment significantly decreased in size after 12 weeks of successful treatment with paroxetine, and in fact, were no longer different in size from controls (Gilbert et al., 2000). However, in a followup investigation, there was no significant decrease in thalamic volume when children with OCD were treated with cognitive behavior therapy (Rosenberg, Benazon, Gilbert, & Sullivan, 2000). Furthermore, there was no decrease in glutamatergic neural activity in the caudate nucleus following successful treatment with cognitive-behavior therapy (Benazon, Moore, & Rosenberg, 2003) although decreased activity had been previously reported following successful treatment with SSRIs (Rosenberg et al., 2000). These results suggest that pharmacological and behavioral interventions may each work differently but achieve the same effect. An alternative hypothesis is that these morphological changes are side effects of the drug treatment and not causally related to treatment outcome. Furthermore, based on extant data, it appears that changes in anatomical structure and function are not necessary for successful treatment outcome. Finally, even if these neuroanatomical differences exist and can be changed by treatment, it is still necessary to emphasize that any initial group differences found in treatment-naive children could be a result, rather than a cause of OCD.

The third area identified by March et al. (2004) are neurotransmitter and neuroendocrine abnormalities in childhood onset OCD. Among one sample, boys with OCD were significantly shorter and thinner than a matched group of psychiatric controls and those with no disorder (Hamburger, Swedo, Whitaker, Davies, & Rapoport, 1989). Furthermore, their growth curve, although within the 95% confidence interval, was flatter than for the general male population. These differences suggest perhaps some subtle differences in neuroendocrine functioning but again, that difference could be a result of the disorder rather than its cause. In contrast, Flament et al. (1987) reported no neurotramsmitter abnormalities as assessed by platelet serotonin and monoamine oxidase activity, plasma epinephrine, or norepinephrine concentrations (Flament, Rapoport, Murphy, Berg, & Lake, 1987). Thus, results are not consistent across investigations and more importantly, the establishment of group differences once the disorder has developed cannot address etiology.

Over the last decade, there has been increased interest in a subset of children who appear to have a very sudden onset or acute exacerbation of OCD symptoms that follows a beta-hemolytic streptococcal infection. This acute exacerbation is known as Pediatric Autoimmune Neuropsychiatric Disorder Associated with Strep (PANDAS; Leonard & Swedo, 2001). Although a complete elaboration of this relationship is beyond the scope of our discussion here, the theory is that behaviors reminiscent of OCD often are seen in children with Sydenham's chorea, which is a variant of rheumatic fever. Furthermore, Sydenham's chorea is triggered by anti-streptococcal antibodies and results in an autoimmune inflammation of the basal ganglia (also hypothesized as a potential site of OCD). These data might suggest a biological model for OCD (Swedo et al., 1998) postulating that antineuronal antibodies formed after a strep infection cross react with tissue in the caudate nucleus and initiate OC symptoms (March et al., 2004). One limitation of the model is that the percentage of children with OCD whose symptoms follow a strep infection is quite small (22% of an initial screening sample responding to ads recruiting children with *sudden* onset of OCD). Therefore, although it may explain etiology in a few cases, at this time, it does not appear to account for the vast majority of children with OCD.

In summary, investigations examining a biological basis for OCD have benefited from the advanced assessment methods that have become available over the past decade. However, as is the case for the far more numerous adult investigations, the studies often are not theory-driven and current evidence is ambiguous. As noted in chapter 4, group differences seen in adult patients often are not replicated in children. Overall, the evidence for a biological etiology is limited and findings often are conflictual. To date, identified abnormalities do not appear to be unique to children with OCD and at the current time, there is insufficient evidence to view OCD simply as a neuropsychiatric disorder.

Behavioral theories of fear acquisition also may account for the etiology of OCD. These models were presented in chapter 4, and the reader is referred there for an extensive discussion. However, the issue of familial transmission also deserves mention when considering behavioral etiologies. Specifically, there is a higher prevalence of OCD among first degree relatives of a patient with OCD when compared to controls, but the pattern of rituals often is not the same for adults and their offspring (Lenane et al., 1990). Recall that in children, ritualistic behaviors change across time, therefore depending upon the time of the assessment, parent and child rituals may or may not match. Although some have indicated that lack of concordance with respect to ritualistic behavior argues against a simple modeling hypothesis (Lenane et al., 1990), it also argues against simple biological transmission. In fact, the data still are consistent with modeling strategies if one conceptualizes the modeled behavior as a general pattern of dealing with anxious distress (Henin & Kendall, 1997). Thus, what may be modeled is not a specific ritual but a pattern of behavioral rigidity and/or behavioral responses to anxious events.

There has been recent interest in a cognitive theory of the etiology of OCD, based on the notion that obsessions represent the extreme end of a continuum of normal, unwanted, intrusive cognitions (Parkinson & Rachman, 1981; Rachman and de Silva, 1978; Salkovskis & Harrison, 1984). Among adult samples, the form and content of "obsessional" thoughts do not differ between adults with OCD and those with no disorder. The difference is in terms of their frequency and the resultant interpretation (e.g., horrific, catastrophic). According to this model, for an intrusive thought to turn into a clinical obsession, the person must first have dysfunctional beliefs that involve blame or responsibility for harm occurring to self or others (Salkovskis, 1989). Rachman (1993) used the term thought-action fusion (TAF) to describe the cognitive process whereby thoughts of harm are equated with actually doing harm and those with OCD feel equally responsible for either thinking or acting on these thoughts. There are two specific TAF cognitive biases. First, there is a likelihood bias whereby thinking of an aversive event increases the likelihood that it will occur. Second, thoughts concerning immoral behavior are equal to acting immorally.

Although the distortions identified by these cognitive theories (inflated sense of responsibility, overestimates of harm probability and severity, self-doubt and lack of cognitive control, TAF) are sometimes detected in adults with OCD, they have not been demonstrated to be etiological in nature or unique to individuals with OCD. Furthermore, it is not clear how these "dysfunctional beliefs" differ from the primary characteristics of OCD or whether they exist independently of those who would meet clinical criteria for the disorder. In fact, the description of these cognitive factors appears to be nothing more than a description of the cognitive component of OCD. In other words, it has yet to be determined that these "cognitive processes" are independent of the disorder and therefore, etiological in nature. At this point, they appear to be epiphenomena.

However if they were etiological in nature, they should exist in children with OCD as well. Furthermore, to be useful as an etiological theory, it would be necessary to demonstrate that they are unique to OCD, rather than a reflection of general psychopathology. To examine this issue, children with OCD, those with other anxiety disorders, and those with no disorder were compared on the following variables: veracity of an obsessional statement (e.g., "If I think that I have germs on my hands and don't wash over and over, I will get really sick."), severity of the negative outcome, probability that the negative event would occur, and responsibility for the negative outcome. Self-doubt, and cognitive control also were assessed (Barrett & Healey, 2003). Although there were significant differences on all six variables when those with OCD were compared to normal controls, only the variables of veracity and cognitive control differentiated children with OCD from those with other anxiety disorders. These results present serious difficulties for cognitive etiological theories. Specifically, it suggests that many of the hypothesized cognitive elements may not be unique to children with OCD, but exist across children with various types of anxiety disorders. In a follow-up study (Barrett & Healy-Farrell, 2003) the effect of experimentally manipulated perceived levels of responsibility (child, parental, or experimenter responsibility) on perceptions of probability and severity of harm, distress, ritualizing, and avoidance behaviors related to the child's OCD were examined. There was no relationship between increased responsibility and ratings of distress, probability or severity of harm. In summary, these data also do not support a cognitive etiological model for OCD. Rather, they suggest that these "cognitive factors" are merely elements of the disorder (i.e., epiphenomenon), not separate cognitive processes that lead to its development.

IMPACT OF OCD UPON FAMILY FUNCTIONING

In addition to family influences on etiology, family interaction patterns are affected when a child has OCD. In laboratory settings, parents exhibit higher levels of criticism and/or over-involvement than parents of children without a disorder (Hibbs et al., 1991). Similarly, adolescents with OCD describe their family environment as significantly less warm, less emotionally supportive and more emotionally distant than children with no disorder (Valleni-Basile et al., 1995). Note, however, that it has not been demonstrated that these behaviors exist prior to the onset of OCD. Hence, they could be reactions to OCD rather than etiological factors. Only one study has demonstrated that some family characteristics are specific to children with OCD (Barrett, Shortt, & Healy, 2002). In comparison to parents of children with another anxiety disorder, an externalizing disorder, or no disorder, mothers and fathers of children with OCD were less confident in their child's ability to solve problems, less rewarding of independence, and less likely to use positive problem solving strategies with their children. Similarly, children with OCD showed significantly less positive problem solving, less confidence in their ability to solve problems, and were less warm in their social interactions than the other groups. However, because these children already had a disorder, these data do not address etiology. Nevertheless, the study highlights concerns about "lumping" all children with anxiety disorders into a single group for the purposes of studying psychopathology or treatment outcome. Children with various anxiety disorders have different symptoms and associated clinical parameters, and treatment outcome must be examined separately for the various diagnostic groups.

An important issue for clinicians is the role of the family in the perpetuation of rituals. Parents (perhaps as many as 70%) become intimately involved in ritualistic behavior, particularly the form of checking known as reassurance seeking (Allsopp & Verduyn, 1990; Geller et al., 1998). A smaller percentage of parents respond to rituals in a hostile fashion (Allsopp & Verduyn, 1990).

> Saundra's parents were extremely conflicted regarding her compulsions. They complained loudly and were quite verbally abusive toward her when she would engage in cleaning behaviors—telling her that if she only read the Bible more she could just "stop this nonsense." On the other hand, they assisted in her rituals, buying the "special soap" needed for washing and showering, and xeroxing material sent home from school so Saundra would not have to touch "contaminated" school papers.

ASSESSMENT OF OCD

In clinical settings, assessment strategies should be thorough but applied in a clinically sensitive and developmentally appropriate manner. Therefore, depending upon the child's age, diagnostic and clinical interviews might be conducted privately with adolescents but in the presence of parents for younger children. Self-monitoring strategies also should be tailored to age and developmental status. Various strategies for the assessment of OCD in children and adolescents are reviewed here.

Diagnostic Interviews

As noted in other chapters, assessment should always begin with a thorough diagnostic interview such as the Anxiety Disorders Interview Schedule for Children/Parent (Silverman & Albano, 1996) A description of this interview as well as its psychometric properties is presented in chapter 3.

Self-Report

The original Leyton Obsessional Inventory-Child Version was a 44 item assessment strategy that used a card-sort method to allow children to indicate the presence or absence of obsessions and compulsions (Berg, Rapoport & Flament, 1986). A shorter, 20 item, paper and pencil version now is commonly used. Obsessions and compulsions are rated using a 4-point Likert scale. Items load onto four factors: general-obsessive, dirt-contamination, numbers-luck, and school (Berg, Whitaker, Davies, Flament, & Rapoport, 1988). The scale has good psychometric properties (Berg et al., 1988; Roussos et al., 2002). Recently, a shorter 11 item screening version with three subscales (compulsions, obsessions/completeness, and cleanliness) has been developed. It appears to have good reliability and the ability to discriminate those with OCD from normal controls and those with depression (Bamber, Tamplin, Park, Kyte, & Goodyer, 2002).

Clinician Ratings

The Children's Yale-Brown Obsessive-Compulsive Scale (CY-BOCS; Scahill et al., 1997) is a clinician administered interview assessing a broad range of obsessions and compulsions as well as severity, interference, and ability to control/resist obsessions and compulsions. Scores range from 0–40; scores of 20 or higher indicate at least moderate severity, whereas scores of 10 or below indicate subclinical OCD. Few data on the reliability and validity of the CY-BOCS are available, although clinically it is a very useful interview for case conceptualization and treatment planning and it has become a mainstay of pharmacological research trials.

The NIMH Global Scale is a 15-point one-item clinician scale that rates OCD severity and impairment. Scores of 7 or greater are indicative of clinically significant OCD (Insel et al., 1983). The scale often is used in pharmacological studies of OCD treatment.

Behavioral Assessment

Behavioral avoidance tests (BAT) are commonly used, at least among behavior therapists, to provide an objective assessment of OCD symptoms. BATs have moderate convergent validity with self-report measures of OCD and are sensitive to the effects of treatment (Barrett, Healy, & March, 2003). Most BATs ask the child to approach and hopefully touch the "feared object" (e.g., contaminated object) and then measure the distance that the child is able to cover. In addition, rituals performed during the BAT are assessed (see Barrett et al., 2003 for a detailed description of how to conduct a BAT for OCD). BATs provide a much more objective assessment of psychopathology than self-report or clinician ratings. Even so, demand characteristics play a role, as children may feel pressure to do more than they normally would because of the assessment environment. An additional limitation is that BATs are most appropriate for obsessions and rituals involving contamination (washing) and in some cases, future events (checking). It is more difficult to construct BATs for covert behaviors (such as cognitive rituals).

Self-Monitoring

Self-monitoring can provide information on the daily frequency of obsessions and compulsions as well as daily information on emotional distress. A key issue for self-monitoring, particularly with children, is increasing compliance with the monitoring task. First, it is important that parents not be involved in forcing compliance. Given that familial relationships already are under some strain as a result of the child's disorder, creating more conflict by asking parents to enforce self-monitoring contingencies often is ill-advised. Instead, clinicians can increase compliance by constructing self-monitoring forms that are simple to use and require no more than 5 minutes a day to complete. Thus, asking for a daily rating of distress as well as for an estimate of the time spent carrying out obsessions and compulsions will provide needed information by which to gauge treatment success while at the same time not being overly burdensome to the child. Additionally, small, developmentally appropriate reinforcers also will increase compliance with self-monitoring procedures (Beidel, Neal, & Lederer, 1991).

TREATMENT OF OCD

Like assessment, treatment for OCD must be developmentally sensitive. Of course, medication dosages are different depending upon the age and weight of the child. Similarly, psychosocial interventions also must be adapted to the child's age (March et al., 2004). Thus, the goal of treatment is always the same, even if the manner in which that goal is achieved differs. By addressing developmental issues, children with OCD as young as age 5 can be treated with behavioral interventions (March et al., 2004).

Pharmacological Treatments

Several pharmacological agents have been used to treat childhood OCD. Initial investigations focused on clomipramine (Anafranil; DeVeaugh-Geiss et al., 1992; Flament et al., 1985; Leonard et al., 1989). Flament et al. (1985) reported that treatment with clomipramine was superior to placebo, with 75% having a moderate to marked improvement. Treatment outcome was positively correlated with high concentrations of platelet serotonin ($r = .73$)

at pretreatment and a greater decrease in serotonin concentration during treatment ($r = .78$; Flament et al., 1987). However, 16% of those treated with clomipramine were unchanged and even those judged as responders still had significant residual symptoms. In a double-blind cross-over design (Leonard et al., 1989), clomipramine was superior to desipramine for 48 children and adolescents with OCD. In a multi-center trial (DeVeaugh-Geiss et al., 1992), 60% of the clomipramine group were rated as much or very much improved. Mean reduction in CY-BOCS score was 37% for the clomipramine group and 8% for the placebo group. However, at posttreatment, the CY-BOCS score for the clomipramine group was 17.1, still indicative of mild to moderate OCD. In summary, although clomipramine appears effective in reducing (but not eliminating) OCD symptoms in children and adolescents, its side effects are more severe than those of the SSRIs to be reviewed below (see DeVeaugh-Geiss et al., 1992; Flament et al., 1985; Leonard et al., 1989). As a result, despite its apparent efficacy, clomipramine is not considered a first line pharmacological treatment for children with OCD.

In contrast, the SSRIs (fluoxetine, fluvoxamine, sertraline) are considered the pharmacological treatment of choice. In an open clinical trial (Riddle, Hardin, King, Scahill, & Woolston, 1990) 50% of the children were fluoxetine responders. Subsequent double-blind placebo controlled trials (Geller et al., 2001; Liebowitz et al., 2002) have yielded similar outcomes. Geller et al. (2001) reported that children treated with fluoxetine were significantly improved when compared to placebo (based on their final CY-BOCS score), a difference first evident at week 7. At posttreatment, CY-BOCS had decreased 9.5 points with fluoxetine (in comparison to 5.2 points with placebo), but children still reported mild to moderate OCD. Improvement rates were 55% for fluoxetine and 18.8% for placebo. Liebowitz et al. (2002) reported similar outcome. After 16 weeks of treatment, 57% were fluoxetine treatment responders compared to 27% placebo responders. Group differences were not detected until after 8 weeks of active treatment, suggesting that the drug's effect might take longer than 8 weeks to be apparent. Consistent with Geller et al. (2001), fluoxetine resulted in a 10 point decrement in CY-BOCS scores at posttreatment.

In a large multi-center randomized controlled trial (March et al., 1998), 156 children and adolescents were treated with either 12 weeks of sertraline or placebo. The sertraline group had significantly greater reductions on the CY-BOCS and the NIMH OC Scale. Between group differences were evident at week 3 and were maintained throughout the trial. At posttreatment, 42% of sertraline patients and 26% of placebo patients were rated as much or very much improved. Unfortunately, the data were presented only as change scores. The actual scores for the various instruments were not presented. Thus, it is impossible to determine what level of OCD severity remained at the end of the 12 week treatment trial.

The same conclusion can be drawn for a randomized, multicenter trial of paroxetine (Geller et al., 2004). After 10 weeks of treatment, CY-BOCS scores had decreased by 8.78 points for the paroxetine group compared to 5.34 points for the placebo group, a difference that was statistically significant. There also was a statistically significant group difference in the number of children who were judged to be treatment responders based on a greater that 25% reduction in CY-BOCS scores (64.9% for paroxetine vs. 41.8% for placebo). However, actual post-treatment scores on CY-BOCS were not provided, therefore it is not possible to determine the children's final clinical status. Finally, responders based on CGI-Improvement scores were not significantly different by group (46.9% vs. 33.3%). This last percentage suggests that less than 50% responded to paroxetine whereas one-third responded to placebo.

Until recently, SSRIs were presumed to have a good safety profile. Few changes in blood pressure, pulse, weight, or EKG were reported (e.g., Liebowitz et al., 2002; Riddle et al., 1990). Among children treated with fluoxetine or sertraline, the more common side effects when compared to placebo, include behavioral agitation, insomnia, nausea, heart palpitations, weight loss, drowsiness, tremors, nightmares, and muscle aches (Liebowtiz et al., 2002; March et al., 1998; Riddle et al., 1990). However, recent concerns about increased rates of suicidal ideation among depressed adolescents treated with SSRIs (when compared to those treated with placebo) have led the Food and Drug Administration to issue a "black box" warning and this undoubtedly will cause a re-evaluation of the safety of these medications.

These findings highlight important issues regarding pharmacological treatment for OCD. First, beneficial effects begin at 2–3 weeks and usually reach their peak by 3 months (March et al., 2004). Unlike older antidepressants, SSRIs do not have the potential for cardiac toxicity. A new meta-analysis (Abramowitz, Whiteside, & Deacon, 2005) indicates that children treated with SSRIs report reduced symptoms but in many instances still have obsessions and compulsions severe enough to meet most clinical trials entrance criteria, a finding also noted by March et al. (2004). Additionally, about 33% of patients fail to benefit from single pharmacotherapy. We agree with the conclusion of the meta-analysis that augmenting drug treatment with behavior therapy is a better option than augmenting with a second pharmacological treatment. Actually, we would go one step further, agreeing with King, Leonard, & March (1998) that behavior therapy should be the first line of treatment and medications used only in specific instances.

Psychosocial Treatment

It is generally agreed that psychoanalytic treatment is not effective for the treatment of OCD (Esman, 1989), whereas behavior therapy (exposure and response prevention) are the treatments of choice for children and adolescents (Expert Consensus Guidelines; March et al. 1997). Initial uncontrolled treatment trials of behavior therapy using small samples (Kozac, Foa, & McCarthy, 1994; March, Mulle, & Herbel, 1994) were very promising with 50–72% reduction in Y-BOCS scores at posttreatment and follow-up. Using a larger sample of children (n = 42; mean age of 11.8 years), in vivo and imaginal exposure, response prevention, and cognitive restructuring (March & Mulle, 1998) resulted in a treatment response rate of 79% (Piacentini, Bergman, Jacobs, McCracken, & Kretchman, 2002). Fifty-two percent of the children were on psychotropic medication during their participation in this trial. There were no significant differences in response rate between the children who were treated with CBT only (85%) and those who also received medication (73%).

A group adaptation of the March and Mulle's (1998) CBT program implemented with 18 adolescents with OCD (Thienemann, Martin, Cregger, Thompson, & Dyer, 2001) resulted in statistically significant changes on the CY-BOCS and on a global rating of OCD severity. However, the degree of improvement was substantially less than that reported for other CBT trials. Specifically, only 50% of patients achieved a 25% or greater improvement in symptoms, and although the 6.2 decrement in the average CY-BOCS score was statistically significant, the post-treatment mean of 18.6 is a score that would still qualify a child for entry into clinical trials. It may be that group treatment dilutes the amount of time required for efficacious exposure treatment, thereby attenuating treatment outcome.

Family members may play a role in treatment outcome, depending upon the type of family involvement (Waters & Barrett, 2000). For example, parents who participate in their child's rituals need instruction to cease any assistance and to provide encouragement for compliance with the treatment program. Parents who are hostile toward their children require education regarding the nature of OCD, what the child should be expected to be able to do and not do at various treatment phases, and how the parents can be active, positive participants in the treatment process. The need to formally address these issues has led some investigators to the development of behavioral treatments that include a family component, although given the diversity of family responses to a child's OCD, it is unclear that one intervention would work for all families. In an initial open trial (Waters, Barrett, & March, 2001), a parent skills training component was added to psychoeducation, anxiety management and cognitive training, and graduated exposure with response prevention. The parent skills training consisted of educating parents about OCD and its treatment, reducing parental involvement in the child's symptoms, encouraging family support of home-based exposure and response prevention, and increasing family problem-solving skills. Children reported significant improvement in OCD symptoms and there was significant decrease in family accommodation behaviors. However, contrary to expectations, there was no change in parental functioning as a result of the intervention. A follow-up controlled trial compared individual cognitive-behavioral family treatment (CBFT), group CBFT, and a 6 week wait-list control (Barrett, Healy, & March, in press). Again, significant improvement in OCD symptoms was evident for both active treatment conditions and treatment gains were maintained at 6 month follow-up. There was a 65% reduction in CY-BOCS scores for those treated individually, and 61% reduction for those treated in a group. At follow-up, 65% of those in the individual treatment and 87% of those in the group treatment did not meet criteria for a diagnosis. Sibling level of accommodation and depression also decreased across both treated groups. However, as with the pilot data, there was no significant change in parental functioning or parental distress and families scored in the unhealthy range of functioning at both pre and posttreatment. Thus, the intervention was efficacious for childhood OCD and in this case, group and individual interventions were equally efficacious. However, the family component did not affect family dysfunction and thus, its necessity as a treatment component for childhood OCD remains unclear, although it may be important for preventing relapse.

Combination and Comparison Treatment

In a combination treatment trial (Wever & Rey, 1997), 57 children with OCD received medication and exposure and response preventiont (ERP) (2 weeks of medication followed by the addition of daily ERP). The combination resulted in a 68% remission rate and a 60% mean reduction in OCD symptoms. A 12 week comparative trial examined the effect of ERP versus clomipramine in 22 children with OCD (de Haan, Hoogduin, Buitelaar, & Keisjers, 1998). Both treatments resulted in significant improvement but rates for ERP were significantly higher; 67% of those who received ERP were judged as treatment responders compared to 50% of those treated with clomipramine. Similarly, reduction in symptom severity was 60% for those treated with ERP and 33% for those treated with clomipramine.

Summary of Treatment Outcome

Overall, CBT that includes ERP is the most empirically supported intervention and the treatment of choice for childhood OCD (Expert Consensus Guidelines; March et al., 1997) just as it is for adults (Stanley & Turner, 1995). This conclusion is confirmed by data from the recently conducted meta-analysis examining pharmacological and psychosocial interventions (Abramowitz et al., 2005). Effect sizes were 0.88 for SSRIs, 0.84 for clomipramine, and 1.60 for ERP. In comparison, the effect size for placebo was 0.36. ERP was significantly more effective than either pharmacotherapy or placebo ($ps < .01$) but pharmacotherapy (all types of medications combined) was not more effective than placebo ($p < .10$). However, when considered alone, SSRIs were more effective than placebo ($p < .05$). In terms of clinical significance, at posttreatment children treated with pharmacotherapy scored at the lower end of the moderate range of symptoms. In contrast, those treated with ERP scored in the mild range; those in the placebo group were still in the moderate range. As with the effect size analysis, the CY-BOCS scores of those treated with ERP were significantly lower than those treated with pharmacotherapy or placebo and the two pill conditions were not significantly different. These data, in conjunction with the individual outcomes reviewed above, clearly indicate the superiority of ERP for the treatment of childhood OCD.

Predictors of Treatment Outcome

Among adults with OCD, those with washing and cleaning rituals are considered to have the best prognosis whereas cognitive rituals are considered the most difficult to address. Among children, however, consistent data are lacking with respect to any specific predictors of treatment outcome. Poorer treatment outcome has been associated with oppositionality and aggression (Wever & Rey, 1997), poorer initial response to medication, lifetime history of tics, a psychiatric disorder in the parent (Leonard et al., 1993), and more severe obsessions and greater academic impairment (Piacentini et al., 2002). However, in the largest examination of potential predictors of treatment outcome (Abramowitz et al., 2005), neither sample characteristics (age, gender, severity of illness, symptom duration, or comorbidity) or treatment characteristics (treatment duration, number of treatment sessions or number of sessions per week) were predictive of treatment outcome.

Treatment of OCD—Case Examples

Below are two examples of the behavioral treatment for children with OCD. Prior to presenting the specific treatment plans, a few general caveats are in order. First, among all of the anxiety disorders, OCD is the one that is most likely to create significant familial distress, a clinical impression recently confirmed by empirical data (e.g., Waters & Barrett, 2000). Therefore, it is necessary first to carefully consider the parent's role, if any, in the treatment program. In many instances, parents will need to actively participate by taking the child to places or situations necessary for homework completion. However, particularly with respect to response prevention, many parents might need to play a secondary role. That is, aspects of the response prevention program sometimes are contentious, at least initially (i.e., the child is not supposed to engage in activities that formerly reduced anxiety, therefore they are anxious and likely somewhat irritable). The role of the parent should be to remind the child that the response prevention program exists, but not try to be the therapist, or to police the child, or to badger him into compliance. Rather, parental participation should be in the form of positive support. In fact, rather than focusing on the child's pathology, parents should positively reinforce the child for compliance with the treatment program.

As discussed in previous chapters, use of contingency contracting to complete homework assignments is particularly relevant for the treatment of children with OCD. Children often do not understand the need for the intervention and are not always willing, at least initially, to comply with the program. Acknowledging that the program is difficult, can be stressful, and takes time away from other activities is an important part of therapeutic engagement. Furthermore, offering rewards as an acknowledgment of the time and effort needed to participate in the program increases compliance particularly among young children. In other words, a sound background in behavioral theory is necessary to implement behavioral programs effectively.

Anthony's Treatment Plan

The initial diagnostic interview confirmed the presence of OCD but did not indicate the presence of any other disorder. Further information on Anthony's specific pattern of obsessions and compulsions was collected with the Children's Yale-Brown Obsessive-Compulsive Disorder (CY-BOCS). Intrusive thoughts occurred 1–3 hours per day, were disturbing, resulted in moderate interference with social and school activities, and were only sometimes able to be controlled. Rituals also occupied 1–3 hours per day, and although they could be delayed, could not be prevented. As with the obsessions, the rituals impacted his academic and family functioning. Consistent with the diagnostic interview, scores on Anthony's self-report inventories indicated the lack of psychopathology

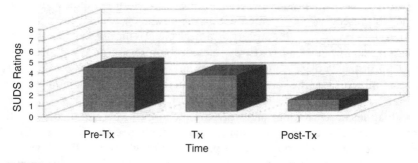

FIGURE 11.1 Anthony's distress experienced by obsessional thoughts.

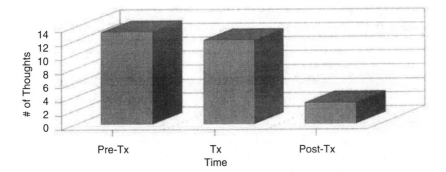

FIGURE 11.2 Anthony's number of obsessional thoughts per day.

other than OCD. His baseline self-monitoring data (see Figures 11.1 and 11.2) depict the presence of moderate distress and a significant number of intrusive thoughts per day.

His treatment plan included imaginal and in vivo exposure as well as response prevention. Imaginal sessions were conducted in the office (see Table 11.2) whereas the in vivo exposure and response prevention program occurred outside of the clinic sessions. Anthony was given a very detailed response prevention program (see Table 11.3) to assure that the instructions were implemented correctly. Treatment consisted of 11 clinic sessions and the accompanying homework assignments. At the end of the treatment, rituals were decreased to less than 5 minutes per day and obsessions to less than 10 minutes per day.

TABLE 11.2 Anthony's Imaginal Exposure Scene

I want you to imagine that you are at home with your younger sister alone. Your parents have gone out for the evening and you expect them to be arriving home sometime soon. It begins to get later and later and you are beginning to wonder where they are. They are now about an hour late and they have not called. More time passes and you begin to get concerned. You think, What if something has happened to them? As the thought comes into your mind, you begin to feel uncomfortable, your stomach churns, and you feel yourself becoming warm. These feelings grow more intense as it gets later and later. Suddenly, the phone rings. You go to answer, expecting it to be your parents. However, it is a doctor calling to tell you that your father has been hospitalized. He tells you that your father is in the hospital ill and that someone will be sent to pick you up. When you get to the hospital, you find that your mother is there and that your father is seriously ill. He is in great pain and they do not know what is wrong with him, nor whether he will live or die. When you see him and how bad he is, you panic and thoughts go through your head so fast you can't keep up with them. Your heart is pounding, you feel sick and overcome with fear.

TABLE 11.3 Anthony's Exposure and Response Prevention Program (Self-Delivered)

1. Put the box with the rabbit's foot in a room away from you for 3 hours each day. Do not check on the box, touch it or do anything with the rabbit's foot during that time.

2. Practice coming down the stairs, going into the kitchen through the family room without turning around. *Do this 10 times each evening.* Do not touch the box or its contents after having done this. Also, do not carry out the ritual (entering the kitchen by doing the turning behavior) after you have carried out the assignment.

3. When getting up in the AM, do not touch the box or the rabbit's foot. Go downstairs, enter the kitchen through the family room. Do not execute the turning behavior. Do not touch the box or the rabbit's foot after completing this.

4. When preparing to leave your house, you are allowed to touch the box and the rabbit's foot only once for a period not to exceed 15 seconds. Then leave the room and do not return.

Angela's Treatment Plan

The standard clinical interview did not reveal any psychiatric disorder other than OCD. A detailed analysis of her clinical presentation indicated that contact with specific situations and or images that triggered thoughts of harm to herself. These situations included enclosed places, heights, airplanes, eating food without washing her hands, tornadoes, house fires, her house sinking into the ground, vampires, death, her heart stopping, dirt, or germs. Rituals performed in response to the obsessions include reassurance seeking from her parents, monitoring weather reports for hurricanes or tornadoes, washing hands three times per hour with dishwasher detergent, and refusal to eat without washing her hands (even a small snack such as a cookie).

The decision was made to treat Angela with a combination of in vivo exposure and response prevention. In addition, a variant of imaginal exposure was incorporated to address her fear of dying. Prior to initiating treatment, Angela's obsessional thoughts were arranged in the following hierarchy (see Table 11.4). Each item was presented until Angela reported a SUDS rating of 0. Additionally, the following response prevention program was implemented by Angela and her parents (see Table 11.5).

TABLE 11.4 Angela's Exposure Hierarchy

Fear	SUDS Rating
Eating without washing hands	3
Riding in an elevator	4
Fire drills at school	5
Heights	6
Tornadoes or hurricanes	7
Heart stopping	8

TABLE 11.5 Angela's Response Prevention Program

1. You may wash your hands for 30 seconds with non-antiseptic hand soap only after using the bathroom or 30 minutes before you eat.

2. No washing your hands immediately before eating

3. Have a snack before bedtime—something you must eat with your fingers. You may not wash your hands first.

4. You cannot watch the weather report or the weather channel or read the weather report in the newspaper.

5. If you feel an urge to do any of these things, get someone to distract you until the urge goes away.

Figure 11.3 depicts the within session and between session habituation data for the task "eating without washing hands." For this task, Angela was presented with several of her favorite cookies and was asked to eat the cookies without first washing her hands. She had to remain in the situation (slowly eating cookies) until her anxiety regarding eating dissipated. As depicted in Figure 11.3, she habituated to this task over four sessions.

Although several of the items on Angela's hierarchy were able to be done in vivo, it obviously is not possible to overtly replicate items such as tornadoes or a child's heart stopping. With adolescents and adults, imaginal exposure would be the most appropriate intervention. Table 11.6 depicts Angela's imaginal scene. However, given Angela's age, typical imaginal flooding was not considered appropriate. As an alternative, Angela was asked to write out her obsessions in the form of stories. Standard exposure procedures were used. That is, she would write out the story and continue to write or read it aloud

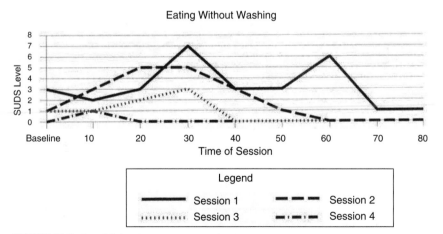

FIGURE 11.3 Angela's in vivo exposure session.

TABLE 11.6 Angela's Imaginal Exposure Story

All Nine-Year-Old Girls Go to Heaven

I am in the doctor's office. I had to wait 20 minutes. When the doctor came in, he says, "Angela, there is something wrong with your heart. Not enough blood is being pumped." I say, "Can you fix it?" He says, "Yes but you will be in the hospital." I say, "No way, how am I supposed to make up all that work?" He shakes his head. We go home and I start on my homework. I notice my heart is beating slower and slower. I put my hand on my heart and it has stopped. I know that you only have 5 minutes before you don't get any oxygen to your brain. I am very scared. And I wonder if I will die before I go to the hospital. I call for my mom and tell her, "My heart has stopped." My mom calls 911. And that is when I die. Everything just goes black. It is like I was shooting at warp speed back in time. I can hear my parents crying. But I can't do anything. I am dead.

until her anxiety habituated. In this way, it was not necessary for Angela to try and continuously imagine a scene, something that often is difficult for young children. However, by having to read the story over and over, she remained constantly engaged with the critical stimuli. Within and between session habituation data are presented in Figure 11.4. As depicted, use of this writing exposure task produced within and between session habituation consistent with other forms of imaginal and in vivo exposure. There were a total of 20 clinic sessions with response prevention implemented as homework. Treatment outcome was very successful with obsessions and rituals reduced to less than 5 minutes per day at posttreatment.

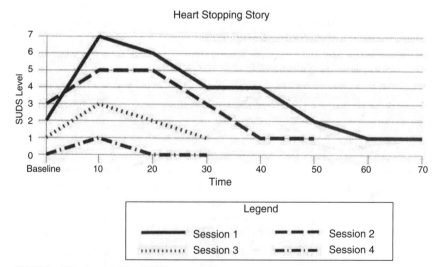

FIGURE 11.4 Angela's "imaginal exposure" scene.

TRICHOTILLOMANIA

Trichotillomania (TTM), or compulsive hair-pulling, was first identified by Hallopeau, a French dermatologist, in 1889 (Vitulano, King, Scahill, & Cohen, 1992). TTM is a frustrating condition both for the child who suffers from it and for the therapist who attempts to treat it. The repetitive nature of the pulling, the family history of OCD among many of those with TTM, the secretive nature of the behavior, and the response of pharmacological treatments have led many to suggest that this disorder is related to OCD (Jaspers, 1996; Swedo & Rapoport, 1991). However, there also are some clear differences between OCD and TTM (King, Ollendick, & Montgomery, 1995) and the treatment of this disorder is only rarely discussed in the literature. Thus, a brief discussion of the disorder and its treatment are included here.

Epidemiological data are scarce but perhaps up to eight million Americans suffer from TTM (Swedo & Rapoport, 1991). The hair-pulling often occurs in conjunction with: (a) negative emotions such as stress, irritation or doubt; (b) when the individual is sitting alone, perhaps doing homework, watching television, or reading; or (c) after significant life events (starting school, moving to a new city, automobile accident; Chang, Lee, Chiang, & Lu, 1991; Christenson, Ristvedt, & Mackenzie, 1993; Hanna, 1997; Reeve, Bernstein, & Christenson, 1992). Hair may be pulled from the head, eyebrows, eyelashes, or pubic area. Hair selected to be pulled is described as feeling different in some way (too kinky or straight, too short or long, or just odd in some way). In some instances, hairs are pulled only from areas where it is easy to cover the bald spot; in other cases the baldness may be so extensive that concealment is not possible. Some children eat the hair or at least the root and in certain instances, hair-pulling is related to thumb-sucking (Walsh & McDougle, 2001). As with anxiety disorders in general, some children have TTM alone whereas for others, a broader pattern of psychopathology is present (Hanna, 1997; Reeve et al., 1992; Swedo & Rapoport, 1991). Despite some similarities, the relationship of TTM and OCD remains unclear. In one study of 10 children with TTM, none had associated obsessions and compulsions (Reeve, Bernstein, Christenson, 1992). Similarly, only 13% of another sample of children with TTM also met criteria for OCD (King et al., 1995). However, 13–20% (King et al., 1995; Reeve et al., 1992) also met criteria for an affective disorder. Whereas Reeve et al. (1992) reported that 60% of their sample of children with overanxious disorder, King et al. (1995) reported that 90% of the sample met criteria for a disruptive behavior disorder, suggesting that the relationship of OCD to TTM is not unique.

The mean age of onset of some TTM samples was early adolescence (King et al., 1995; Swedo & Leonard, 1992). However, in other samples, approximately one-third of those with TTM had an onset prior to age 10 and 14% had an onset prior to age 7 (Muller, 1987 ; Walsh & McDougle, 2001). Among a sample of Chinese patients with TTM, the most prominent time of onset was during elementary school (Chang, Lee, Chiang, & Lu, 1991), and in a U.S. sample, the mean age was 8.5 years with a range of 2 to 13.5 years (Hanna, 1997). TTM sometimes remits spontaneously or with minimal intervention in the form of explanation, reassurance, and emotional support (Chang et al., 1991). However, adults may present with a childhood or adolescent age of onset, thus indicating a chronic or waxing and waning course for others (Chang et al., 1991; Cohen et al., 1995).

TTM can occur at very young ages. In one sample of infants and children (Swedo & Leonard, 1992), age on onset ranged from 11 to 54 months of age. Approximately 50% pulled hair while sleeping, 30% pull while sucking their thumb and 60% pulled while watching television. Other situations were associated with pulling but to lesser degrees. Among this very young sample, pulling was episodic in nature, with approximately one to three periods of remission per year. Two cases (20%) had relapses that occurred following streptococcal infections, reminiscent of the data on PANDAS presented earlier in this chapter.

There are few controlled trials of pharmacological treatment for children and adolescents with TTM. Clomipramine, fluoxetine, and lithium have been used but their utility remains unclear (Pomnoppadol & Todd, 1999; Vitulano et al., 1992) and data on the long-term efficacy of these medications suggest a high rate of relapse with discontinuation (see Walsh & McDougle, 2001). There also are few data examining the utility of psychosocial treatments. When pulling behavior occurs in conjunction with thumb-sucking, elimination of thumb-sucking often eliminates TTM (e.g., Watson & Allen, 1993). Additionally, traditional behavioral interventions such as self-monitoring, progressive muscle relaxation, habit interruption, prevention training and competing reaction training, overcorrection, awareness training, annoyance review, reinforcement and differential reinforcement of other behaviors have been reported as successful (e.g., Blum, Barone, & Friman, 1993; Vitulano et al., 1992). Some of these procedures (self-monitoring, progressive muscle relaxation, reinforcement) have been discussed in earlier chapters and will not be repeated here. With respect to the other procedures, *habit interruption, prevention training, and competing response training* refers to teaching engagement in an alternative, opposite movement when the child becomes aware of pulling or experiences an urge to pull. An easy opposite movement is clenching the fists when experiencing the urge to pull. *Overcorrection* usually has aversive connotations (Foxx & Bechtel, 1982) but in the case of children with TTM has been used as positive practice by having the children comb or brush their hair after a hair-pulling session (Vitulano et al., 1992). *Annoyance review* simply refers to having the children acknowledge the problematic nature of hair-pulling and their reasons for wanting to stop; probably most effective for preadolescents and adolescents rather than younger children. *Differential reinforcement of other behavior* means giving the child attention when pulling behavior is absent. Positive touches (in young children) and compliments (in older children and adolescents) are commonly used (Blum et al., 2001).

Obviously, the selection of the specific treatment components will be dependent upon the child's age. Several challenges treating children and adolescents with TTM have been identified (Vitulano et al., 1992). First are potential problems with compliance and motivation. Children sometimes find it difficult to adhere to self-monitoring procedures and can be embarrassed to collect their hairs and bring them to the therapist. As noted elsewhere, compliance with self-monitoring is a challenge faced by those who do behavioral interventions. Particularly with children and adolescents who are often reluctant to participate in treatment, two factors seem to increase the likelihood of compliance: (a) keeping the self-monitoring as simple as possible (no more than one page per day) and (b) small rewards for completion of self-monitoring and/or behavioral assignments.

A second challenge when treating children with TTM also has been mentioned with respect to children with OCD. That is, family conflict and parental frustration often confound treatment outcome (Vitulano et al., 1992). As noted earlier, helping the parents distance themselves from the treatment program and from the child's behavior may be necessary to reduce family conflict and enhance treatment compliance and outcome.

Case Example—Treatment of TTM

> Erica is 3.5 years old. Her mother requested treatment for chronic hair-pulling. At the time of the initial evaluation, Erica had pulled out all of the hair on her head. This behavior began about 12 months ago and was continuous since that time. Her mother sought treatment from Erica's pediatrician who prescribed clomipramine and then fluoxetine, both of which were unsuccessful. Currently, the pediatrician was recommending a trial of Haldol* but Erica's mother wanted to investigate behavioral treatment first.

Obviously, in this case, all of the information had to be collected from Erica's mother. At the time of the initial evaluation, Erica's family situation was quite chaotic and no doubt contributed to her emotional distress. Her older sister had a debilitating physical illness and there was a newborn infant in the family. Her parents were under some financial stress due to extensive medical bills. Finally, there was a grandmother who had OCD.

In addition to these family influences, several operant factors were identified that played a role in the maintenance of Erica's hair-pulling. Specifically, her parents and grandparents, distressed by her hair-pulling, spent much time trying to talk to Erica about why she should stop. Thus, there was substantial attention from both her parents and her grandmother for pulling her hair. In fact, Erica would seek attention from family friends and strangers by running up to them and saying, "I pull my hair." Finally, mother indicated that like other children with TTM, at night, Erica tended to suck her thumb and pull her hair.

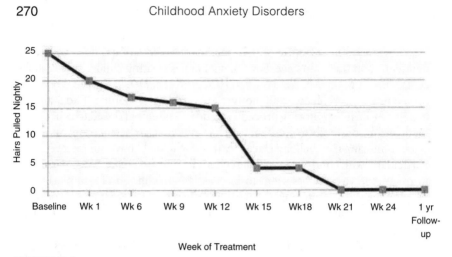

FIGURE 11.5 Erica's hair-pulling behavior.

Traditional interventions for TTM determine the outcome of treatment by counting the number of hairs daily. However, given Erica's age and the fact that parental attention appeared to be a maintaining factor for the behavior, a decision was made to use the number of hairs pulled at night as an indication of treatment outcome. Each morning, Erica's mother collected the hair on the pillow and each week, her mother brought the hairs to the clinic where they were counted and the total number graphed (see Figure 11.5).

The initial treatment program consisted of eliminating attention for hair-pulling. Parents were instructed to ignore Erica when she pulled her hair and provide positive attention when she was not pulling her hair. Furthermore, an hourly sticker program was implemented. Specifically, at the top of every hour, if Erica's hands were not near her face or head, she earned a sticker. After 5 weeks, there was a slight, but not substantial, decrease in nightly hair pulling (see Figure 11.5). One reason was that Erica's mother was not able to comply with the sticker program. Therefore, at week 6, relaxation-training was added to the treatment plan to reduce Erica's stress level. The child relaxation script by Koppen (1974) was used but modified for Erica's age. Additionally, both mother and Erica were taught the relaxation exercises and were instructed to do it at home together. Surprisingly, even given her young age, Erica participated fully in the relaxation exercises and by the third week, had actually memorized parts of the script. This phase of the intervention led to a further decrease in Erica's hair-puling and, by her mother's report, daytime hair-pulling was eliminated. However, she was still pulling her hair at night when she sucked her thumb (see Figure 11.5) and substances applied to her thumb to prevent sucking were ineffective.

To deal with the nighttime hair-pulling, a decision was made to attempt to prevent Erica from sucking her thumb and pulling her hair in her sleep.

TABLE 11.7 Pink Mittens and Cherry Ice Cream (Erica's Treatment Program)

A. Erica had a pair of pink mittens that she liked to wear.

B. Erica's favorite food was cherry ice cream.

C. If Erica wore her mittens all night (i.e., they were still on when she woke up in the morning), she could have cherry ice cream for breakfast.

D. Erica had no access to cherry ice cream or her pink mittens at any other time.

E. Erica got ice cream for breakfast no matter what else she might have done wrong (ice cream could not be withdrawn as a punishment).

The treatment program involved pink mittens and cherry ice cream. See Table 11.7 for the details of the contingency contract. As depicted in Figure 11.6, this contract was successful in eliminating the remaining hair-pulling behavior. Implementation of the contract was only necessary for a 5 week period. After that, Erica's newly growing hair and her pride in her new appearance negated the need for her "ice cream breakfast."

There are several reasons why this plan was successful. First, Erica lived in the southeastern United States and very rarely had opportunities to wear mittens. Erica viewed wearing her mittens at bedtime as exciting, not as a punishment. Second, it was imperative that Erica understand the contract contingencies. To help her remember, the contract was put to a tune of a child's song so that Erica could sing the words and remember the contract. Third, if a contract is to be effective, it must be implemented correctly. A major compliance concern would be whether Erica took her mittens off in order to pull her hair and then put her mittens back on in the morning. However, given her age, Erica was unable to put her mittens on correctly without help (she could not get her thumb correctly in the thumb "hole"). Therefore, it was very easy for her mother to determine whether she kept her mittens on all night. In summary, self-monitoring data was useful in determining the efficacy of the program and making alterations when the data indicated that ongoing strategies had reached maximal effectiveness.

SUMMARY

OCD is a chronic and disabling disorder that presents significant challenges for children and clinicians alike. Recent studies of psychopathology have clarified important aspects of the psychopathology of this disorder although its etiology remains unclear. ERP is clearly the treatment of choice for childhood OCD and results in positive treatment outcomes for a majority of patients. However, exactly which patients are most likely to benefit from ERP is still unknown and still more data are necessary on its long-term outcome. Similarly, TTM is a perplexing disorder and few data are available on effective treatments. In short, both OCD and TTM will continue to challenge researchers and clinicians for the foreseeable future.

CHAPTER 12

Panic Disorder

Angela is 17 years old. She has a history of "anxiety since childhood" and panic attacks since the age of 14. Her physical symptoms include breaking into a cold sweat, being chilled to the bone, feeling jittery, having a racing heart, and feeling like she wants to run away but does not know where to run. She has continued to go to school but often must go to the nurse's office to lie down because of the anxiety she experiences. She is reluctant to go places alone and has discontinued her social interactions and after school activities. She is seeking treatment now because she wants to attend an out-of-state college next year and is concerned that when the time comes, she will not be able to leave home.

PANIC ATTACKS

Panic attacks are discrete episodes of fear and anxiety sometimes experienced by those with various types of anxiety disorders. Unlike other anxiety disorders, however, one cannot meet criteria for panic disorder unless a panic attack has occurred. A panic attack is defined as an acute episode of anxiety that consists of somatic and sometimes cognitive symptoms. The somatic symptoms include heart palpitations, chest pain, tingling sensations, chills or hot flushes, dizziness, feelings of choking, nausea, sweating, trembling or shaking. Cognitive symptoms include fear of losing control or going crazy, feelings of unreality or detachment, and fear of dying. The symptoms usually peak in intensity within 5–10 minutes of onset and subside approximately 15–30 minutes later (DSM-IV, APA, 1994). When the symptoms occur out of the blue, the child may be concerned about the onset of future attacks, the possibility of an illness or the possibility of death.

The most recent *Diagnostic and Statistical Manual for Mental Disorders* (*DSM-IV*; APA, 1994) defines a panic attack as the simultaneous presence of at least four of the above symptoms (see Table. 12.1). Limited symptom attacks

TABLE 12.1 *DSM-IV* Criteria for Panic Attack and Panic Disorder
Without Agoraphobia

Panic Attack

A discrete period of intense fear or discomfort, in which four (or more) of the following symptoms developed abruptly and reached a peak within 10 minutes:

palpitations, pounding heart, or accelerated heart rate
sweating
trembling or shaking
sensations of shortness of breath or smothering
feeling of choking
chest pain or discomfort
nausea or abdominal distress
feeling dizzy, unsteady, lightheaded, or faint
derealization (feelings of unreality) or depersonalization (being detached from oneself)
fear of losing control or going crazy
fear of dying
paresthesias (numbing or tingling sensations)
chills or hot flushes

Panic Disorder

A. Both (1) and (2):

1. Recurrent unexpected Panic Attacks

2. At least one of the attacks followed by 1 month (or more) of one (or more) of the following: persistent concern about having additional attacks, worry about the implications of the attack or its consequences (e.g., losing control, having a heart attack, "going crazy"), or a significant change in behavior related to the attacks

B. Absence of Agoraphobia

C. The Panic Attacks are not due to the direct physiological effects of a substance (e.g., a drug of abuse, a medication) or a general medical condition (e.g., hyperthyroidism).

D. The Panic Attacks are not better accounted for by another mental disorder, such as Social Phobia (e.g., occurring on exposure to feared social situations), Specific Phobia (e.g., on exposure to a specific phobic situation), Obsessive-Compulsive Disorder (e.g., on exposure to dirt in someone with an obsession about contamination), Posttraumatic Stress Disorder (e.g., in response to stimuli associated with a severe stressor), or Separation Anxiety Disorder (e.g., in response to being away from home or close relatives).

are events that otherwise meet the criteria for a panic attack but consist of less than four symptoms. Additionally, panic attacks are categorized as one of three types: (1) uncued, (2) situationally bound, and (3) situationally predisposed. Uncued attacks are those that occur unexpectedly or perceived by the patient to come out of the blue. Situationally bound attacks are those that occur in the context of, or in anticipation of, a specific feared object, situation or event. Situationally predisposed attacks appear to fall somewhere between these two extremes-although triggered by specific events, situation or objects, situationally predisposed attacks do not always occur when in contact with the feared event.

The term "panic attack" has become part of everyday language and often is used to describe feelings of distress that might not meet the actual diagnostic criteria. Self-report of the presence and frequency of panic reveal that many individuals describe an anxiety response as "having had a panic attack." However, even when restricted to its actual *DSM-IV* definition, panic attacks appear to be quite common in the general child population. In one survey, 60–63% of 13 to 18-year-olds reported having at least one panic attack (Macaulay & Kleinknect, 1989;: Warren & Zgourides, 1988). Among African American adolescents, 26% reported panic attack symptoms (Ginsburg & Drake, 2002a). A close examination of adolescent self-report data (Warren & Zgourides, 1988) indicated that 28.1% of adolescents appeared to have experienced a panic attack consistent with diagnostic criteria and among those, 17.5% described uncued panic attacks, but only 1.5% had uncued attacks alone. In contrast to unselected samples, 47% of those with clinically diagnosed panic attacks reported that the attack was uncued (Essau et al., 1999).

Rather than self-report surveys, controlled investigations using structured diagnostic interviews and unselected samples of school students revealed a 5.3% prevalence rate for panic attacks among sixth and seventh graders (Hayward et al., 1992) whereas the rate was 8.7%-11.6% among samples of high school students (Hayward, Killen, & Taylor, 1989; Hayward, Wilson, Lagle, Killen, & Taylor, 2004). In each investigation, prevalence rates were based on the documented presence of at least one four-symptom attack. Interestingly, an additional 3.2% of ninth graders reported the existence of limited-symptom attacks (Hayward et al., 1989). Thus, panic attacks occur with some frequency, although the overall prevalence of panic attacks decreases substantially when trained interviewers and structured diagnostic interviews are used to determine the diagnosis. Another important consideration is that developmentally, the prevalence rate appears to increase with increasing age (see sociodemographic section).

PANIC DISORDER

Despite the fact that approximately 18% of adults with panic disorder endorsed the onset of panic attacks prior to the age of 10 (von Korff, Eaton, & Keyl, 1985), the incidence of panic disorder (as opposed to panic attacks) in young children appears to be quite rare. In one investigation, an analysis of the clinical narratives that accompanied structured diagnostic interviews of 903 adults were examined for the presence of uncued panic during the participant's childhood (Klein, Mannuzza, Chapman, & Fyer, 1992). The subjects consisted of 343 consecutive admissions to an anxiety disorders clinic and 560 first degree relatives of clinic patients. Among the patients and relatives, only 1% (9 individuals, 6 patients and 3 first degree relatives) reported spontaneous panic attacks prior to the age of 13. In only one case however, was there convincing evidence of early onset panic disorder. In the other instances, the "spontaneous panic" was determined not to be spontaneous but occurred in the context of other anxiety disorders such as separation anxiety disorder, social phobia, or specific phobia. Of course, these data are limited by all of the pitfalls of retrospective recollection even though the diagnostic interviews were conducted by, and diagnoses were assigned by, acknowledged experts in the area of anxiety disorders. These data illustrate the difficulty in determining the presence of panic attacks and panic disorder in young children. Self-report data are especially suspect as they appear to over-inflate the incidence of panic attacks and "spontaneous" panic attacks. Even when structured diagnostic interviews are conducted by trained experts, a subsequent careful examination of the case history often indicates that the attacks are not out of the blue even if described that way by the respondent. Rather, just as is the case for adults with this disorder panic attacks many occur within the context of another disorder or during the time of stressful life events (e.g., Faravelli & Pallanti, 1989; see section on etiology).

As indicated, there is substantial clinical evidence that panic disorder appears to be quite rare among children and adolescents, particularly pre-pubescent children (see sociodemographic section). However, the rate is higher among adolescent populations. Among unselected samples of high school students (Hayward et al., 1992; Warren & Zgourides, 1988), 4.7–5.3% met criteria for panic disorder (according to their self-report). When diagnostic interviews conducted by mental health professionals are used, the lifetime prevalence rate for panic disorder among adolescents ages 14–17 years drops to 0.6% (Whitaker et al., 1990). When the sample is further limited to those seeking treatment for psychiatric and behavioral problems, the prevalence rate for panic disorder ranges from 0.6–10.5% (Alessi, & Magen, 1988; Biederman et al., 1997; Last & Strauss, 1989; Masi, Favilla, Mucci, & Millipiedi, 2000; Vitiello, Behar, Wolfson & McLeer, 1990). The difference in prevalence rates can be explained at least in part by the nature of the sample. In some instances, the sample was composed entirely of anxiety patients. In other instances, the presenting problems were more mixed.

Even among those diagnosed with *DSM-IV* panic disorder, the frequency of panic attacks is variable. Forty-one percent of the children and adolescents had panic attacks that were more frequent than once per week, 15% had panic attacks more than once per month but less often than once per week, and 44% had panic attacks less than once per month (Bradley & Hood, 1993). Thus, similar to the adult literature, the rate and frequency of panic attacks probably is a function of many different variables, but in addition, physical and cognitive development likely play a role. Also, some cases of panic may be misdiagnosed as presented below.

HYPERVENTILATION SYNDROME

As we discussed in chapter 6, "Excessive Worry and Generalized Anxiety Disorder," the presence of physical distress in children usually leads parents to seek treatment from traditional medical professionals. Just as worry in children often is associated with gastrointestinal symptoms, and sometimes leads to a medical diagnosis of recurrent abdominal pain, children with panic attacks and/or panic disorder often received a medical diagnosis of "hyperventilation syndrome" (Herman, Stickler, & Lucas 1981; Joorabchi, 1977). In an early study (Enzer & Walker, 1967), 44 cases of childhood hyperventilation syndrome were identified among pediatric hospital records. The children were free of cardiac and respiratory disease and 70% of the sample was female. The children ranged in age from 5–16 years although most were 12 years and older. The most common symptoms included respiratory complaints, dizziness, paresthesias, and headaches. All of the children and their parents described an episodic nature of attacks, and children endorsed being anxious during the attacks. There also were a number of related fears such as fear of dying, worry about school, and concern about the possible death of parents or friends. Clearly, these cases of "hyperventilation syndrome" in pediatric clinics are highly similar to the psychiatric symptoms of panic. However, patients and parents are not always willing to see the relationship between physical symptoms and emotional distress. For example, reviewing all cases referred to one child psychiatric consultation service, four cases of panic disorder (one child, three adolescents) were identified (Garland & Smith, 1990). In three of these cases, referral to a psychiatry consultation service was made only after many months of medical tests and interventions. In some instances, the parents resented the implication of a psychiatric diagnosis, believing that it invalidated the severity of the child's physical distress. Thus, it is important to recognize that current prevalence rates for panic disorder may be an underestimate if some children are misdiagnosed with hyperventilation syndrome or other medical conditions. However, rates of that disorder also appear to be quite low, such that overall rates probably increase only slightly with the addition of those children.

CLINICAL FEATURES

As noted above, panic attacks consist of a variety of physical and cognitive symptoms that occur with sudden intensity. The physical symptoms most commonly reported by children and adolescents include heart palpitations, trembling and shaking, dizziness, sweating, hot or cold flushes, and shortness of breath (Alessi & Magen, 1988; Biederman et al., 1997; Bradley & Hood, 1993; Essau et al., 1999; Kearney, Albano, Eisen, Allan, & Barlow, 1997; Last & Strauss, 1989; Masi et al., 2000; Vitiello et al., 1990; Warren & Zgourides,

1988). Kearney et al. (1997) drew an interesting distinction between symptoms endorsed most frequently and symptoms reported as most severe. Whereas the most frequently reported symptoms included rapid heart beat, nausea, hot and cold flashes, and shaking/jitteriness, the symptoms reported as most severe included shortness of breath, feeling faint, rapid heart beat, and choking. Thus, the physical symptoms of panic attacks in youth appear to be very similar to those experienced by adults.

As presented in chapter 3, there has been a long-standing controversy regarding whether panic disorder exists in children. The cognitive model of panic is predicated on the premise that physiological symptoms such as heart palpitations, dizziness, and shortness of breath are misinterpreted as physically dangerous and that this misinterpretation increases anxiety and then leads to more physical sensations and more panic attacks (Clark, 1986). A cogent theoretical review by Nelles and Barlow (1988) argues that although children are capable of experiencing the physiological symptoms of panic, because of their limited cognitive abilities, they are not capable of making the catastrophic interpretations of "going crazy" or dying. This argument is reviewed in depth in chapter 3 and will not be repeated here. It should be noted however, that the cognitive "symptoms" of panic attacks are not necessary for one to meet the diagnostic criteria for panic attacks or panic disorder (Ollendick, Mattis, & King, 1994). Thus, even if children are incapable of making the cognitive attributions that does not necessarily discount the possibility that they might experience panic attacks, although it certainly discounts the possibility of a cognitive etiology

Even if the cognitive symptoms are not necessary for a diagnosis to be assigned, the data are quite mixed with respect to whether cognitive symptoms exist in children. Some studies report low frequency rates for cognitive symptoms (Biederman et al., 1997; Bradley & Hood, 1993; Kearney et al., 1997) whereas others suggest that these symptoms are quite frequent among child and adolescent populations (Last & Strauss, 1989; Vitiello et al., 1990). Of course, prior to determining whether panic attacks in children include cognitive symptoms, the first question is whether children have the capacity to formulate catastrophic internal attributions. In one of the few empirical studies to address this issue, children in the third, sixth, and ninth grade were assessed regarding their ability to conceptualize the causes of illness (in this case, panic symptoms; Mattis & Ollendick, 1997). Children in third grade were significantly less likely than those in the sixth or ninth grade to attribute somatic symptoms of panic to psychophysiological causes. However, there was no difference between the latter 2 groups. Over 90% of these children attributed panic symptoms to psychophysiological causes, suggesting that at least by age 12, most children/adolescents are capable of the cognitions included in the diagnostic criteria for panic attacks.

Mattis and Ollendick (1997) also examined children's attributions if actually experiencing a panic attack. Through the use of guided imagery to simulate a panic attack, attributions were classified as one of four types: external/noncatastrophic ("I'd think there were germs around that I had been exposed to"), external/catastrophic ("I'd think something or someone was trying to kill me."), internal/noncatastrophic ("I'd think I was worried about something."), internal/catastrophic ("I'd think that I must be dying."). Children listened to an audiotape describing a panic attack and then completed the attribution checklist. Across all three grades, both boys and girls gave more internal than external attributions in response to the panic imagery, thus there was no main effect for age. However, contrary to what would be expected from Beck's (1988) and Clark's (1996) cognitive models of panic, irrespective of grade level and gender, children gave more noncatastrophic than catastrophic attributions after listening to the panic imagery audiotape. These results indicate that children were able to make internal attributions, but they were of a noncatastrophic nature ("I'd think I was worried about something"). Thus, with respect to ages 8 through 14, there was no developmental progression of advanced cognitive functioning that might be expected from Nelles and Barlow's (1988) treatise. What is even more important, however, is that after imagining a panic situation, children were more likely to attribute the somatic arousal to noncatastrophic situations such as being sick, worried or scared rather than to dying. This calls into question the theory that panic disorder develops as a result of somatic symptoms that are catastrophically interpreted as indicative of a heart attack, dying, or going crazy. A few children at each age level did respond with catastrophic thoughts, thus indicating that at least some children did have the ability to generate catastrophic cognitions even if the preponderance of their thoughts were not in that domain. Furthermore, the authors noted that their sample did not consist of children who were diagnosed with panic disorder and thus results with a clinical sample might differ. However, cognitive models suggest that the disorder develops as a *result* of catastrophic misinterpretations of somatic symptoms. In contrast, these results suggest that the symptoms characteristic of panic disorder do not automatically result in cognitive misinterpretations. Thus, other etiological explanations must be considered. Indeed, one hypothesis is that these cognitive variables are metaphenomena and are merely secondary with no causal role; a hypothesis we fully support.

Similar to the behavioral avoidance exhibited by children with other disorders, those with panic attacks avoid a variety of situations due to concern about the onset of a panic attack. Among high school students with a history of panic attacks, social situations (parties, speeches, conflict with parents or friends, games/sports competitions, restaurants, public restrooms, and classes) were avoided by 44% of the sample (Warren & Zgourides, 1988). Agoraphobic situations (crowded places, being alone and movie theaters) were avoided by

37% of the sample. Fifteen percent avoided blood/injury situations (hospital, funeral, dentists), whereas avoidance of physically dangerous situations (icy roads, crossing highways) were endorsed by 5% of the sample. In a small sample of children and adolescents with clinically diagnosed panic disorder (Kearney et al., 1997), "typical" agoraphobic situations such as restaurants (35%), crowds (30%), small rooms (25%), auditoriums, elevators, parks, grocery stores, shopping malls, homes, and theaters (each 20%) were most commonly avoided. However, it is important to note that although some children and adolescents reported avoidance, these percentages were quite low, suggesting that behavioral avoidance was not characteristic of the entire sample.

Among those who are diagnosed with panic attacks in clinic or hospital settings, school refusal, aggression, depression, and somatic complaints often are the precipitating factors that lead parents to seek treatment for their children (Alessi & Magen, 1988; Vitiello et al., 1990). Furthermore, when compared to children who had a primary diagnosis of generalized anxiety disorder or depressive disorder, children with primary panic disorder had lower scores on the Children's Global Assessment Scale, indicating more severe functional impairment (Masi et al., 2000). In summary, physical symptoms of panic attacks/panic disorder include a variety of somatic complaints but most commonly heart palpitations, trembling and shaking, dizziness, and sweating. Behavioral avoidance is common but not characteristic of every child. With respect to cognitions, a subset of children as young as Grade 3 appear to have the capacity for catastrophic thinking, but the majority of children and adolescents do not react to the physical symptoms of panic with these types of thoughts. Thus, although cognitions may be reported by a subset of children, the disorder is more likely characterized as consisting primarily of physical symptoms.

SOCIODEMOGRAPHIC INFLUENCES

As noted, panic disorder rarely is diagnosed in preadolescent children. Among a sample of school age adolescents, no child age 12 or 13 met diagnostic criteria for panic disorder although 0.9% of 14 to 15-year-olds and 0.7% of 16 to 17-year-olds did so (Essau et al., 1999). Other authors, however, describe cases of panic disorder among prepubertal children (Ballenger, Carek, Steele, & Corning-McTighe, 1989; Last & Strauss, 1989; Vitiello, Behar, Wolfson, & McLeer, 1990). Among some samples (Last & Strauss, 1989), the percent of prepubertal cases was quite low (5.9%), but others report that cases are more evenly dispersed among children and adolescents (Masi et al., 2000). Among samples of adolescents, the age of onset for the first panic attack was 11.6–12.0 years of age (Bradley & Hood, 1993; Warren & Agourides, 1988) whereas the age of onset for prepubescent children ranged from 5–11 years. Children with the earliest age of onset were the most severely impaired in terms of daily functioning (Vitiello et al., 1990).

Hayward et al. (1992) noted that among their sample, there was a strong association between panic attacks and sexual maturity; none of their identified cases was a prepubescent child. In contrast, 8% of the girls who had completed puberty reported a history of at least one panic attack and at any given age between 11 and 13 years, a history of panic attacks was more common in those who were more sexually mature. As the authors noted, this study documented an intriguing association between panic attacks and pubertal stage but does not illuminate the stage of the physical maturity process when panic attacks are more likely to occur. Furthermore, the study used only a restricted age range (sixth and seventh graders), only one gender, and cannot rule out hormonal and/or psychosocial factors as contributory factors. Furthermore, important advances in cognitive development also take place during this time. In conclusion, the data from this study are interesting but many explanations other than simple changes in hormonal status may play a role in the onset of panic attacks.

Several investigations have reported that panic *disorder* appears to be more common among females (Bradley & Hood, 1993; Essau et al., 1999; Last & Strauss, 1989) although in one investigation, 61% of those diagnosed with panic disorder were male (Masi et al., 2000). Similarly, in one study, boys reported a greater frequency of panic *attacks* than did girls (Bradley & Hood, 1993) whereas in other investigations, there were no differences in prevalence of panic *disorder* based on gender (Essau et al., 1999; Hayward et al., 2000; King et al., 1993) or the attacks were more common among girls (Ginsburg & Drake, 2002). In summary, there is sufficient data to suggest that panic disorder is more common among adolescents than prepubertal children. The role of gender is less clear and may depend upon the specific sample characteristics.

The number of physical symptoms reported by youth with panic disorder averages 6.3 symptoms per attack (Masi et al., 2000). Age and gender also may play a role in the severity of the symptom picture. Panic attacks in adolescents (age 13 and older) averaged 6.6 specific panic symptoms versus 6.0 panic symptoms in children (ages 12 and younger). With respect to group differences across individual symptoms, only chills or hot flushes differentiated the two groups, with a significantly greater frequency of children more likely to report this symptom when compared to adolescents (80% vs. 23%; Masi et al., 2000). Also, panic symptoms appear to be more severe among females (Hayward et al., 1989; Hayward et al., 2000; Macaulay & Kleinknecht, 1989) although it is important to note, as we do throughout this book, that girls always endorse more frequent and more severe symptomatology when compared to boys. Thus, it is unclear if the greater severity reported by females is valid or merely reflects the tendency of males to under-report anxiety symptoms.

As noted, children in various countries have endorsed the presence of panic attacks and panic disorder (although the majority of the data to date are based on Caucasian samples). In addition to the rates established on samples in the United States cited above, similar prevalence rates of panic *attacks* have been reported for samples of Australian children (42.9%; King, Guillone, Tonge, & Ollendick, 1993) and German adolescents (18% of an epidemiological sample; Essau, Conradt, & Peterman, 1999). In contrast, the range of prevalence rates (0.6% to 5.3%) for children in the United States who meet criteria for panic *disorder*, are lower than that reported for a recent study with Italian children (10.4%; Masi et al., 2000), although the prevalence rate for German children in one large epidemiological sample (Essau et al., 1999) was 0.5%, matching the lowest rates reported in the United States.

COMORBID AND DIFFERENTIAL DIAGNOSIS

As is the case for most anxiety disorders in children, comorbidity is a common occurrence among children with panic attacks or panic disorder. In most instances, the comorbid condition is an anxiety or mood disorder. For example, ninth graders with panic attacks had significantly higher scores on a self-report measure of depression when compared to the group without a panic attack (Hayward et al., 1989). It is important to note, however, that the actual score for the panic attack group was in the mild to moderate range on the inventory, thus suggesting that those with panic attacks might be experiencing a moderate level of dysphoria but not necessarily severe depression.

Separation anxiety disorder, generalized anxiety disorder (overanxious disorder), and depressive disorders appear to be the most common comorbid conditions among children and adolescents with panic disorder with no difference in prevalence rate based on pubertal status. Among samples of children clinically diagnosed with panic disorder, 48–86% had comorbid separation anxiety disorder or a history of separation anxiety disorder (Alessi & Magen, 1988; Biederman et al., 1997; Masi et al., 2000; Vitiello et al., 1990). Similarly, 62–74% had comorbid generalized anxiety disorder (Biederman et al., 1997; Masi et al., 2000) and 43–80% had a depressive disorder, either major depression or dysthymic disorder (Alessi & Magen, 1988; Biederman et al., 1997; Essau et al., 1999; Masi et al., 2000). One hundred percent of a small sample of 6 children and adolescents with panic disorder had a history of depressive disorders (Black & Robbins, 1990). Based on a sample of 20 children and adolescents with panic disorder (with or without agoraphobia), 30% had a *DSM-IV* diagnosis of major depressive disorder/dysthymia, a significantly higher frequency (5%) of comorbid depressive diagnoses than that found in a group of matched anxiety disorder patients who did not have panic disorder (Kearney et al., 1997). In summary, although the data on comorbidity are not extensive, those that do exist suggest that comorbidity is common. However, it is not yet clear what role the comorbid condition plays in the clinical presentation of the disorder or if it affects treatment efficacy.

ETIOLOGY OF PANIC DISORDER

As noted by Klein et al. (1992), although the results of diagnostic interviews conducted by highly experienced clinicians suggested that a number of adults retrospectively reported the existence of panic attacks prior to the age of 13, only one had clearly documented panic disorder as a child. However, at least five others from this small sample experienced panic in the context of other disorders diagnosed in childhood (separation anxiety disorder, social phobia, or specific phobia) and went on to develop panic disorder as adults (Klein et al., 1992).

> Angela reported that as a young child she was "scared of so many things" including wars, earthquakes, being separated from her parents, and the dark. Even at age 17, she still sleeps with the lamp on her night stand turned on. Although she never experienced any event such as a war or an earthquake, she was exposed to them via the television and newspaper. For a period of time, she stopped watching the news and reading the newspaper.

Thus, early childhood anxiety, and perhaps the presence of situationally bound or predisposed panic attacks, may be one predispositional factor for the development of panic disorder. However, it is not established that the presence of a childhood anxiety disorder is either necessary or sufficient for the development of panic disorder.

Just as with adult-onset panic disorder, specific life events sometimes are associated with the first onset of panic attacks in children and adolescents (Bradley & Hood, 1993). Interpersonal conflicts (with parents, friends and teachers) were commonly reported associated events (Warren & Zgourides, 1988) as were loss related events (loss of someone cared about, parents separated or divorced, or moved to a different house or town; Hayward et al., 1989; Warren & Zgourides, 1988), academic difficulties (Warren & Zgourides, 1988), and physical events (such as medical illness or reaction to alcohol/drugs; Warren & Zgourides, 1988). One limitation of this latter study was that it was based solely on the adolescent's recall of events occurring 1 week to 6 months prior to the first panic attack. Six months prior to the attack is a long time frame and it is unclear if distress occurring that far in the past could continue to influence emotional behavior 6 months later. Furthermore, it was unclear if the items endorsed represented a singular event or a continuous source of conflict. However, the data represent an important reminder that panic attacks, even when perceived to occur out of the blue, most often occur within an environmental context.

In Angela's case, her parents were undergoing a period of marital distress. There were frequent verbal shouting matches and Angela witnessed many of these arguments. She stated that she began to get thoughts such as "I don't want to be here" and she felt restricted and confined. One day when she was having these thoughts she began to sweat, felt jittery, experienced heart palpitations, and wanted to run away. She did leave and go to a friend's house.

Family history also may represent an etiological factor in the onset of panic disorder in children. Among the studies that assessed family psychopathology, 53–100% of children with panic disorder had a family history of panic disorder or panic attacks severe enough to cause emotional distress/impairment (Bradley & Hood, 1993; Vitiello et al., 1990). In other samples, 68–90% of the children had at least one parent with an anxiety disorder (Bradley & Hood, 1993; Masi et al., 2000), and 33% had parents who had panic disorder and were being treated with medication (Masi et al., 2000). Of course, this was not a controlled trial and further studies examining family history of panic disorder among affected children and adolescents are necessary.

Hayward et al. (2004) interviewed parents of adolescents with panic attacks and reported several predictors of adolescent panic attacks. Characteristics of both the child and the parents were examined. Three factors, predictive of the onset of panic, identified 58% of the adolescents. Parental history of panic attacks was the highest risk factor identifying 24% of the adolescents with panic attacks. Among those without a positive family history, two other risk factors for those with panic attacks were identified: high childhood negative affect (14%) and a history of separation anxiety disorder (20%). Interestingly, when adolescents were assessed, childhood separation anxiety disorder was not a risk factor for panic disorder. Although negative affectivity was identified as a risk factor, it was not specific to panic disorder. Negative affectivity was also identified as a risk factor for major depression. The only factor that appears to be a specific risk factor and which predicted the presence of four symptoms of panic was anxiety sensitivity.

To summarize, there are few data examining the etiology of panic disorder in children and adolescents, probably due in part to the low prevalence of this condition in children and adolescents. Studies of etiology require large samples and thus are extremely difficult to conduct using only a single research center. A multi-center study, which is very costly, probably is necessary in order to understand the factors that contribute to the development of this disorder in children.

ASSESSMENT OF PANIC DISORDER

Consistent with the limited data on its psychopathology, the formalized assessment of panic disorder in children lags far behind what is available for use with other disorders. Although there are several well-validated self-report inventories to assess the physiological, cognitive, and behavioral aspects of panic disorder and agoraphobia in adults, these measures have not been validated for use with children. Clinician creativity is necessary to develop a valid assessment protocol. Generalized measures of fears and anxiety, such as the Fear Survey Schedule for Children (Ollendick, 1983; see chapter 7 for the specifics of its psychometric properties) may be helpful in identifying places or situations associated with panic attacks, which in turn may be useful in developing an exposure hierarchy. This instrument does not, however, assess symptoms or frequency of panic attacks. For children and adolescents, assessment of the frequency, severity and situations surrounding the onset of a panic attack is most easily assessed through the use of self-monitoring such as a daily diary. Although there is no specific format necessary to adequately collect data, one form that we have found useful is presented in Figure 12.1.

TREATMENT OF PANIC DISORDER

Although no clinical trials addressing the treatment of panic disorder in children and adolescents currently exist, a survey of high school students (Warren & Zgourides, 1988) indicated that adolescents tend to "deal' with their panic attacks in a variety of ways. Avoidance tactics (just forgot about it, forced self not to think about it, avoided situations where panic might occur, and used alcohol or drugs to reduce anxiety) were the most common method, endorsed by 98% of the sample. However, within this specific group of behaviors, only 13% of teenagers specifically endorsed the use of drugs/alcohol to reduce

| Name: _____ |
| Date: _____ |

Situation	Severity of Attack (0–8)	Severity of Anxiety (0–8)

FIGURE 12.1 Daily panic attack diary.

anxiety. Talking to a friend was endorsed by 30% of the sample, whereas 26% reported that they talked to a professional (doctor, counselor, teacher, hospital emergency room staffer, or pastor/rabbi). Finally, 3% of the sample sought information/education about panic attacks.

The literature on the pharmacological treatment of panic disorder in children is very limited. Ballenger and colleagues (Ballenger, Carek, Steele, & Cornish-McTighe, 1989) described the treatment of three children (ages, 8, 11, and 13) with panic disorder with agoraphobia. Two children were treated with imipramine and the third with alprazolam and imipramine. Two children were able to be withdrawn from their medications after a period of time without recurrence of their symptoms. Panic attacks for the third child were controlled with medication but recurred whenever the medication was withdrawn.

The literature on the psychosocial treatment of panic disorder is similarly sparse. Although there are data supporting the use of behavioral and cognitive-behavioral treatments, there are no controlled trials examining their utility in children and adolescents. The low prevalence rate for this disorder may prevent the collection of a sufficient sample such that a controlled trial with significant power may be conducted. In a recent review of panic disorder in children and adolescents (Ollendick, Birmaher, & Mattis, 2004), the authors noted that the primary cognitive-behavioral model is Panic Control Treatment (PCT; Barlow, 2002), a model that has been adapted for children (Mattis & Ollendick, 2002). Two single case studies have been published (Barlow & Seidner, 1983; Ollendick, 1995) and a controlled trial is ongoing (Mattis & colleagues, cited in Ollendick et al., 2004). In the initial publication (Barlow & Seidner, 1983), three adolescents diagnosed with agoraphobia were treated with an early version of PCT that consisted of 10 group sessions. Treatment included panic management procedures, cognitive restructuring, and in vivo exposure that was assigned as homework. Mothers were included in the intervention to assist in the exposure sessions and parents were educated about the nature of agoraphobia and procedures for dealing with their child's anxiety. Two of the three adolescents showed marked improvement at the end of the 10 week intervention whereas the third did not show any treatment response. The authors attributed the lack of improvement in the third adolescent to a conflictual parent–child relationship.

In the second study (Ollendick, 1995), four adolescents (aged 13–17) diagnosed with panic disorder with agoraphobia were treated with an adapted version of PCT. The average age of onset was 4 years prior to the decision to seek treatment, indicating a fair degree of chronicity for this sample. The treatment package consisted of psychoeducation, relaxation training and breathing retraining, cognitive restructuring, interoceptive exposure, participant modeling, in vivo exposure, and positive reinforcement. Treatment consisted of between 10 and 12 individual sessions and parents again participated in the treatment program. All four adolescents benefited from the intervention which resulted in elimination of panic attacks, reduced behavioral avoidance, decrease in negative mood and enhanced confidence in their abilities to handle future anxiety symptoms. Results were maintained at 6 month follow-up, suggesting some promise for this particular intervention. A controlled trial of a developmentally appropriate adaptation of PCT is underway and the results should reveal important information regarding the efficacy of this intervention for adolescents with panic disorder.

TREATMENT OF PANIC DISORDER—CASE EXAMPLE

Angela was interviewed with the Anxiety Disorders Interview Schedule for Children (ADIS-C; Silverman & Albano, 1996) and met diagnostic criteria for Panic Disorder with Agoraphobia and Generalized Anxiety Disorder. A battery of self-report instruments (the State-Trait Anxiety Inventory for Children, the Fear Survey Schedule for Children, and the Children's Depression Inventory) revealed high levels of state anxiety, trait anxiety, a plethora of specific fears, and a mild level of dysphoria. Thus, scores on the self-report inventories were consistent with her responses on the diagnostic interview. The self-monitoring data indicated an average of four panic attacks per week. In addition she was avoiding approximately five activities per week.

As indicated above, Angela was suffering from a high level of anxiety, many specific fears and 4 panic attacks per week. In addition, she was avoiding about five social activities per week. To address her panic attacks and associated avoidance, a treatment program of interoceptive exposure and in vivo exposure was developed. Interoceptive exposure (Barlow, 2002) is a procedure whose purpose is to disrupt or weaken associations between specific bodily cues and panic reactions. The full theoretical rationale underlying this procedure is beyond the scope of this chapter (see Barlow, 2002 for a full discussion) but is consistent with other forms of exposure (i.e., imaginal and in vivo). Specifically, if a child is to overcome a fear, there must be exposure to the object that elicits the fear response. In the case of panic attacks, the basis of the fear are the physical symptoms that comprises the attack. Thus, interoceptive exposure involves exposure to the physical symptoms of panic. Because panic attacks are sometimes considered to occur unexpectedly, the challenge for therapy is to elicit the physical symptoms so that the child has the opportunity to habituate to the fear associated with them (as happens in other forms of exposure). Interoceptive exposure is conducted by having the patient engage in exercises designed to produce panic-like physical sensations. Such exercises may include running up a flight of stairs (to increase heart rate), spinning in a chair (to elicit feelings of dizziness), or breathing through a straw (to mimic sensations of shortness of breath).

It should be noted that the following case material is not intended to provide all of the instructions necessary for Panic Control Therapy or Interoceptive Exposure to be implemented effectively. Rather, it is intended to provide the

TABLE 12.2 Angela's Interoceptive Exposure Assessment Results

Task	Severity of Sensation	Severity of Anxiety	Similarity to Panic
Shake head	6	2	0
Lifting head	3	2	0
Run in place for 1 minute	7	7	7
Spin in chair	8	8	0
Straw-breathing	6	6	7
Hold a push-up for 1 minute	3	5	5
Hyperventilate for 1 minute	5	6	5

reader with a sense of how the interventions are conducted. Clinicians interested in conducting interoceptive exposure should consult Barlow (2002).

Interoceptive exposure involves a structured assessment of somatic symptoms through a series of interoceptive exercises. The elicited sensations are rated by the patient for symptom intensity, anxiety intensity, and panic similarity. The results of Angela's interoceptive exposure assessment are presented in Table 12.2.

Items rated as moderately stressful or higher are arranged in a hierarchy (see Table 12.3) and the patient engages in the appropriate exercise in order to elicit the symptom. Presentation of the symptom is repeated until its elicitation results in none or only mild distress (fear rating of 0, 1, or 2 on a 9-point scale), but never more than five times in one session. Upon habituation the next item on the hierarchy is presented. In the case of adults, interoceptive exposure is coupled with cognitive restructuring procedures. However, as has been noted earlier in this chapter, cognitions often are not part of the clinical presentation of panic disorder in youth, and this was the case for Angela as well. Thus, her exposure plan did not include cognitive restructuring.

As noted, Angela avoided numerous situations because of her concern that if she had a panic attack, she might not be able to escape the situation. Angela avoided crowded situations such as shopping malls, buses, movie theaters as well as small places such as elevators. In vivo exposure sessions in the clinic included having Angela ride crowded buses and walk around a crowded shopping mall. Each exposure session was conducted for al least 90 minutes, longer

TABLE 12.3 Interoceptive Exposure Hierarchy

Item	SUDS Rating
Hold a push-up for 1 minute	3
Hyperventilate for 1 minute	5
Run in place for 1 minute	7
Breathe through a straw for 1 minute	7

TABLE 12.4 Angela's Homework
Exposure Hierarchy

Walk around the neighborhood
Go to the park
Go to the shopping mall
Go to a restaurant
Go to a movie theater
Go to church

if necessary for Angela to report her anxiety as a SUDS rating of "2" or less. Additionally, Angela was given homework exposure assignments that were to be carried out three times per week for 90 minutes each time. Angela's exposure homework is presented in Table 12.4.

Throughout treatment, Angela continued to monitor the number of panic attacks that she experienced and the number of situations that she avoided. Her progress is presented in Figure 12.2.

At 1 year follow-up, Angela's treatment gains were maintained and she was attending a small out-of-state college.

SUMMARY

In 1992, Kearney and Silverman reviewed the studies of panic disorder to date, noting that the majority used small inpatient samples, nonstandardized assessment procedures, evaluated few sources of information, and did not assess panic severity or differentiate between cued and uncued panic. Although some of these criticisms have been answered by more recent empirical studies,

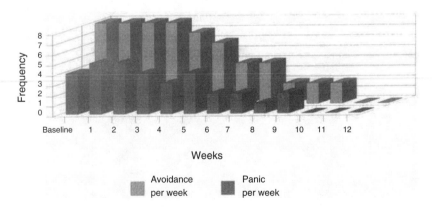

FIGURE 12.2 Angela's self-monitoring data.

others remain relevant over 10 years later. Several studies now have identified children and adolescents who suffer from panic disorder. Prevalence rates are fairly consistent but it is clear that the type of assessment used has a substantial effect on rates reported. Also, there now are substantial findings that adolescents more often suffer from panic disorder than preadolescent children, and that the physical symptoms expressed by children and adolescents are consistent with those found in adults. Children and adolescents do avoid situations typically associated with panic disorder and agoraphobia. However, children and adolescents rarely report the cognitive symptoms listed in the *DSM-IV* diagnostic criteria for panic disorder. As is the case with other disorders, cognitive symptoms may not emerge until children develop basic cognitive/metacognitive skills.

Although the past 10 years have illuminated at least some aspects of the psychopathology of panic disorder in children, the etiology of this disorder remains unclear. There are few studies addressing the development of panic disorder in children and adolescents although potential factors appear to be similar to those found for other disorders. Perhaps because of the limited number of children and adolescents with this disorder, assessment instruments and treatment data lag far behind the literature established for other conditions. Much work is needed to construct reliable, valid, and usable assessment instruments and to determine efficacious and effective intervention strategies. Given the chronic nature of these disorders, these efforts are sorely needed.

CHAPTER 13

Posttraumatic Stress Disorder

Marla is 17 years old. Her parents own a local tourist company and the family trains horses for carriage rides throughout the city. Marla helps train the horses after school and on the weekends. Her career goals include going to college, becoming a veterinarian's assistant, and returning to help run the family business. Last year, she was training a new horse that became frightened and suddenly bolted, severely injuring Marla. In addition to ongoing physical sequellae (headaches, blackouts, and stuttering), she has a high level of general arousal, sleep disturbance, startle reactions whenever she sees a horse or enters the training area, and intrusive thoughts and nightmares regarding the accident. In addition, she has withdrawn socially and refuses to go back to training the horses.

Marla is suffering from Posttraumatic Stress Disorder (PTSD), one of the most scientifically understudied anxiety disorders among children and adolescents. Although having many similarities to other anxiety disorders, PTSD differs in a number of respects. For example, unlike other anxiety disorders, the onset of PTSD always begins with an identifiable traumatic event (Koverola, 1995). However, the factors that determine who then goes on to develop PTSD are yet to be completely elucidated. In fact, in comparison to every other anxiety disorder, there are very few empirical data available for any aspect of PTSD, even though there is a voluminous clinical literature. Furthermore, even within the small empirical literature, few studies have used standardized diagnostic instruments when examining PTSD in children, although a number have used other types of structured procedures to assess PTSD symptoms (Lonigan, Philips, & Richey, 2003) Thus, in this chapter, available data are presented with a caveat that this is an anxiety disorder with a poorly developed scientific base.

STRESSFUL EVENTS, TRAUMATIC EVENTS, ACUTE STRESS DISORDER, AND POSTTRAUMATIC STRESS DISORDER

Events that could precipitate stress reactions in children appear to be quite common in the general population. For example, stabbings, shootings, and murder have been witnessed by 35%, 39%, and 25% of one sample of adolescents (Jenkins & Bell, 1994). Natural disasters (hurricanes, floods, lightning strikes), man-made disasters (airline disasters, boat sinkings), and events such as terrorism and war all may result in increased stress among those who are its victims. However, the mere experience of an event that has the potential to produce stress does not guarantee the subsequent emergence of PTSD.

Recent work on loss and trauma illustrate this assertion very well. Whereas 50–60% of the U.S. population is exposed to a traumatic event at some point in their lives, only 5–10% develop PTSD (Ozer, Best, Lipsey, & Weiss, 2003). These data illustrate the substantial empirical literature demonstrating although that many individuals exposed to traumatic events may show brief PTSD or subclinical stress, these reactions dissipate after a few months. Despite the often-made clinical predictions, relatively few individuals develop symptomatology severe enough to actually meet criteria for PTSD. In fact, in the face of traumatic events such as the September 11, 2001 terrorist attacks, the Oklahoma City bombing, or the Los Angeles riots, most individuals show *recovery* (threshold or subthreshold psychopathology for a few months followed by a return to pre-trauma levels) or *resilience* (those who maintain a stable equilibrium in the face of the traumatic event rather than experiencing the symptomatology of PTSD; Bonanno, 2004). As will be illustrated throughout this chapter, despite all of the clinical suppositions and clinical descriptions that attempt to pathologize the behavior of all individuals exposed to a traumatic event, the empirical data clearly indicate that recovery and resilience, not PTSD, is the more common behavioral response (Bonanno, 2004).

Theoretically related to PTSD is the newly introduced Acute Stress Disorder diagnostic category (ASD; APA, 1994). Like PTSD, ASD is precipitated by exposure to a traumatic event and is accompanied by or followed by dissociative symptoms that include three of the following: (a) a subjective sense of numbing or detachment, (b) a reaction in awareness of surroundings, (c) derealization, (d) depersonalization, and (e) dissociative amnesia (APA, 1994). Other PTSD symptom clusters (re-experiencing, avoidance, and hyperarousal) also are present. Presumed to be a predictor of future psychopathology including PTSD, ASD has received little attention with respect to its incidence in children except perhaps as a "first stage" of PTSD (McKnight, Compton, & March, 2004). However, the limited empirical data do not support this "first stage" hypothesis. For example, after automobile accidents where injuries requiring hospitalization were sustained, 8% of children met criteria for ASD and 14% met criteria for subsyndromal ASD (Kassam-Adams & Winston, 2004). However, only

14% of those with ASD went on to develop PTSD whereas 60% of those who developed PTSD did not have any earlier symptoms of ASD. Thus, initial data do not support the theoretical notion that ASD is a precursor of PTSD among children although the criteria delineated for this syndrome have poor empirical support. Indeed, in our view, this is a poorly supported diagnostic category as currently defined. Furthermore, because there is so little empirical literature on ASD, it will not be discussed further in this chapter.

Initially, as with anxiety disorders in general, there was skepticism that children could suffer from PTSD (American Academy of Child and Adolescent Psychiatry, 1998). However, studies of children traumatized by events such as the Chowchilla school bus kidnapping (Terr, 1979), the Buffalo Creek dam collapse (Green et al., 1991) and sniper attacks on the school yard (Pynoos et al., 1987) soon illustrated that certain events could produce traumatic stress in children. Traumatic events that might precipitate onset of PTSD have been conceptually and usefully divided into two distinct subgroups (Terr, 1991). Type I traumas are those that are unpredictable and sudden, and represent a single-incident event (that may be repeated). Type II traumas are chronic, expected and repeated stressors, usually childhood physical or sexual abuse. This classification delineates the different literatures and different treatment approaches (McKnight, Compton, & March, 2004). The Type II literature is voluminous, based primarily on clinical and descriptive reports rather than empirical data, and because of its largely nonscientific nature, will not be reviewed in this chapter. Those interested in the Type II category are referred to the excellent work by Cohen and Mannarino (e.g., Cohen, Mannarino, & Rogal, 2001) and Deblinger and colleagues (e.g., Deblinger & Heflin. 1996).

POSTTRAUMATIC STRESS DISORDER (PTSD)

Even when restricted to Type I events, the extant data are further limited by the lack of a standardized, or even consistent, system by which to determine the presence of a PTSD diagnosis. More recently, criteria established by the *Diagnostic and Statistical Manual of Mental Disorders–Fourth Edition* (*DSM-IV*; American Psychiatric Association, 1994) have become the diagnostic standard. The *DSM-IV* criteria are presented in Table 13.1.

As illustrated, there are four criteria necessary for a diagnosis of PTSD. First, of course, there must be exposure to a traumatic event and the perception that death or serious physical injury could result. As noted, a broad range of events such as natural disasters, man-made disasters, medical illnesses, war and combat, and personal injury could serve as a qualifying event for a diagnosis of PTSD. Since the diagnostic category's introduction in 1980 (*DSM-III*; APA, 1980), the definition of a triggering traumatic event has changed dramatically. In *DSM-III*, the event was defined as something outside the range of normal

TABLE 13.1 *DSM-IV* Criteria for Posttraumatic Stress Disorder

---

A. The person has been exposed to a traumatic event in which both of the following were present:
    (1) The person experienced, witnessed, or was confronted with an event or events that involved actual or threatened death or serious injury, or a threat to the physical integrity of self or others.
    (2) The person's response involved intense fear, helplessness, or horror. *Note:* In children, this may be expressed instead by disorganized or agitated behavior.

B. The traumatic event is persistently reexperienced in one (or more) of the following ways:
    (1) Recurrent and intrusive distressing recollections of the event, including images, thoughts, or perceptions. *Note:* In young children, repetitive play may occur in which themes or aspects of the trauma are expressed.
    (2) Recurrent distressing dreams of the event. *Note:* In children, there may be frightening dreams without recognizable content.
    (3) Acting or feeling as if the traumatic event were recurring (includes a sense of reliving the experience, illusions, hallucinations, and dissociative flashback episodes, including those that occur on awakening or when intoxicated). *Note:* In young children, trauma-specific reenactment may occur.
    (4) Intense psychological distress at exposure to internal or external cues that symbolize or resemble an aspect of the traumatic event.
    (5) Physiological reactivity on exposure to internal or external cues that symbolize or resemble an aspect of the traumatic event.

C. Persistent avoidance of stimuli associated with the trauma and numbing of general responsiveness (not present before the trauma), as indicated by three (or more) of the following:
    (1) efforts to avoid thoughts, feelings, or conversations associated with the trauma
    (2) efforts to avoid activities, places, or people that arouse recollections of the trauma
    (3) inability to recall an important aspect of the trauma
    (4) markedly diminished interest or participation in significant activities
    (5) feeling of detachment or estrangement from others
    (6) restricted range of affect (e.g., unable to have loving feelings)
    (7) sense of a foreshortened future (e.g., does not expect to have a career, marriage, children, or a normal life span)

D. Persistent symptoms of increased arousal (not present before the trauma), as indicated by two (or more) of the following:
    (1) difficulty falling or staying asleep
    (2) irritability or outbursts of anger
    (3) difficulty concentrating
    (4) hypervigilance
    (5) exaggerated startle response

E. Duration of the disturbance (symptoms in Criteria B, C, and D) is more than 1 month.

F. The disturbance causes clinically significant distress or impairment in social, occupational, or other important areas of functioning.

Specify if:
• Acute: if duration of symptoms is less than 3 months
• Chronic: if duration of symptoms is 3 months or more

Specify if:
• With Delayed Onset: if onset of symptoms is at least 6 months after the stressor

---

Reprinted with permission from the *Diagnostic and Statistical Manual of Mental Disorders*. Copyright 2000. American Psychiatric Association.

human experience (the classic notion regarding stimuli capable of producing PTSD). The fourth edition revision evolved from perceptions that certain events precipitating the development of PTSD (rape, child abuse, domestic violence, community violence, war) were not necessarily rare. Instead, under *DSM-IV*, the traumatic event must be considered "extreme." This has lead to a broadening of the class of traumatic events as well as to their definition: It must involve experiencing, witnessing, or confronting an event capable of causing death, injury, or threat to physical integrity to self or another person. The more subjective nature of the diagnostic criteria now allow the clinician to judge whether a particular stress is extreme, creating potential for great variability in judging qualifying events, and thus, a diagnosis of PTSD. This, in effect, introduces two levels of subjectivity into the diagnostic process: that of the patient and that of the clinician. Overall, in our view, the diagnostic category likely is too broad to be scientifically or clinically meaningful. Much work is needed to restore the clinical and scientific integrity of this diagnostic category and remove it from its political and economic arena.

As for other anxiety disorders, PTSD diagnostic criteria include developmental descriptors to increase its appropriateness for children. For example, among children, "recurrent and intrusive distressing recollections" may be repetitive play which may incorporate themes of the trauma. Similarly, for "recurrent distressing dreams of the event," frightening dreams with no recognizable content is considered a developmentally appropriate equivalent. Finally, instead of having the experience of acting or feeling as if the event were recurring (sense of re-living the experience, illusions, hallucinations or flashbacks), trauma-specific re-enactment may be present. Below, each symptom cluster is discussed in detail.

Clinical Features

> As the horse reared up, Marla felt helpless and thought that she was going to die.
> Every night she dreams of that moment and wakes up in a cold sweat.

Reexperiencing of the event in some fashion is a hallmark of PTSD. Reexperiencing may occur in the form of intrusive thoughts, dreams, or flashbacks, although the latter appears to be less common among children and adolescents (McKnight et al., 2004). Similar to obsessive-compulsive disorder, the intrusive thoughts associated with PTSD can occur spontaneously or in response to environmental events; sights, sounds, smells, people and/or places that are associated with or are reminiscent of the traumatic event. In addition, among young children, reexperiencing also may take the form of traumatic play (reenactment; McKnight et al., 2004). It is very important however, not to automatically interpret any behavior as indicative of trauma reenactment. For example, Gurwitch, Kees, and Becker (2002) noted that after the Oklahoma City bombing, children built and destroyed buildings made of blocks. However, many children who have never been victims of bombings will build block buildings or sandcastles and then delight in knocking them down. Without clear understanding of typical child play, and the ability to compare behaviors of those with PTSD to developmentally appropriate and normative data, the possibility exists that certain behaviors will be misinterpreted as indicative of PTSD. Thus, it is critical not to erroneously attribute every behavior as indicative of PTSD, even among those exposed to a traumatic event. To do so creates confusion in the empirical literature and delays the accumulation of scientific knowledge necessary to develop efficacious interventions.

Avoidance and numbing is another cluster of symptoms necessary for a diagnosis of PTSD. A child with PTSD may attempt to avoid situations, places, or people that precipitate the reexperiencing phenomena previously described.

> Despite all of her parents' efforts, Marla refused to go back to the stable where she was injured.

Thus, children may refuse to go to school if a violent event occurred there previously. Previous enjoyable activities now may be refused because of their association with a traumatic event. Some children may show behaviors typical of an earlier stage of development such as enuresis and thumb sucking (McKnight et al., 2004).

> Theresa was seriously injured in an automobile accident in which her two best friends were killed. Their automobile was struck by a drunk driver in a blue sedan. Now, whenever she sees a blue sedan, Theresa's heart races, she sweats, and she begins to cry.

The third cluster of behaviors (and the fourth necessary criterion for PTSD) are those that represent hyperarousal. Specific symptoms include sleep disturbances, difficulty concentrating, irritability, exaggerated startle responses, and hypervigilance (McKnight et al., 2004). Children may appear tense, scanning the environment for other potential threats or traumas. In addition to a general tonic increase in arousal, children and adolescents may experience panic attacks if they encounter stimuli that are associated with the traumatic event.

It has been suggested that the symptomatic expression of PTSD may differ depending upon the type of trauma (Type 1 vs. Type II). Sleep disturbances, autonomic hyperarousal, and reexperiencing have been hypothesized to occur more frequently among those who experienced a Type I traumatic event whereas dissociation, restricted affect, sadness and detachment are more characteristic of Type II (Famularo, Fenton, Kinscherff, & Augustyn, 1996; Terr, 1991), and at least one study (Cooley-Quille, Turner & Beidel, 1995) reported exposure to high levels of community violence was associated with externalizing, not internalizing, behaviors. As noted, these differences are based on clinical observation but to date, empirical data are lacking. Within Type I trauma, however, the symptoms with the highest degree of diagnostic efficacy (for example, identifying children with PTSD after exposure to Hurricane Hugo) were behavioral avoidance, bad dreams, emotional avoidance, and repetitive thoughts (Lonigan, Philips, & Richey, 2003). Similarly, after Hurricane Andrew, symptoms of reexperiencing were more frequent than those of avoidance and hyperarousal (Vernberg, La Greca, Silverman, & Prinstein, 1996).

Symptoms of PTSD can negatively affect school functioning. After Hurricane Hugo for example, the average decrease in school performance for children who met criteria for posttraumatic stress syndrome (not necessarily PTSD) was more than three times the decrease for children who did not meet full criteria for the syndrome (Shannon, Lonigan, Finch, & Taylor, 1994). The long-term sequella of trauma and PTSD can be extensive and quite complicated. Specifically, even though the actual event may last for only a short period of time, the resultant disruption in every day functioning often persists and continues to exert significant distress on those affected. For example, even 7 months after Hurricane Andrew, 27% of the children in a sample initially affected by the hurricane (but not necessarily meeting PTSD criteria) reported that most of the damage to their home was not yet fixed and 23% were still living in alternative housing. Forty-four percent were still experiencing two or more disaster-related sequellae (housing disruption, parent out of work). This type of ongoing stress may function to maintain or exacerbate PTSD symptomatology, although to date, empirical data examining this relationship are not available.

Sociodemographic Influences

As noted (McKnight et al., 2004), although events that might precipitate PTSD appear to be common among the general population, there are few epidemiological data. Those that exist suggest that its lifetime prevalence ranges from 1–14% (APA, 1994). However, it is difficult to calculate trends in prevalence rates because the defining event has been substantially expanded and often times, cases are included that do not meet the full criteria.

Among those experiencing a documented Type I traumatic event, rates of the development of PTSD range from 5.2–100% (see Table 13.2 for specific PTSD rates for different traumatic events). Furthermore, the absence of data makes it is difficult to determine the natural course of the disorder. However, the long-term follow-up of young adults who as adolescents survived the sinking of the cruise ship *Jupiter* are instructive (Yule et al., 2000). Across the 5–8 year follow-up period, 51.7% of survivors developed PTSD at some point during follow-up and 17.5% were still affected 5–8 years later. In 90% of the

TABLE 13.2 Rates of PTSD Among Children Subject
to Different Type 1 Traumatic Events

Study	Nature of Disaster	PTSD rate
Aaron et al. (1999)	Pediatric injury and hospitalization	23%
Daviss et al. (2000)	Pediatric injury and hospitalization	12.5%
Goenjian et al. (1995)	Spitak, Armenia earthquake (18 months later)	
	Epicenter	95%
	20 miles away	76%
	47 miles away	26%
Green et al. (1991)	Buffalo Creek Dam disaster	
	2 years later (probable PTSD)	37%
	17 years later (definite PTSD)	7%
Kassam-Adams & Winston (2004)	Motor vehicle accident	6%
LaGreca et al. (1996)	Hurricane Andrew	
	After 3 months	39.1%
	After 7 months	24.0%
	After 10 months	18.1%
McFarlane (1987)	Australian bush fire	
	After 8 months	29.5%
	After 26 months	26.3%
Pynoos et al. (1987)	School playground sniper attack	
	Overall prevalence	60.4%
	On the playground during shooting	77%
	In the school during shooting	67%
	Already left school for the day	26%
	Absent from school that day	17%
Shannon et al. (1994)	Hurricane Hugo	5.2%
Terr (1983)	School bus hijacking (4 years later)	100%
Udwin et al. (2000)	Sinking of the cruise ship *Jupiter*	51.5%
Yule et al. (2000)	Sinking of the *Jupiter* (5–8 years later)	34%

PTSD cases, onset occurred within the first 6 months postdisaster and for 30% of those affected, duration was less than 1 year. However, 34% of those with PTSD (as noted, 17.5% of the entire sample) still met criteria 5–8 years later. It is unclear whether recovery occurred as a result of therapeutic intervention or was a naturally occurring process. Furthermore, determining which variables may function to hasten or retard recovery have yet to be elucidated.

The role of gender in PTSD is unclear. Some investigations confirm the greater likelihood for the development of PTS symptoms and PTSD among females (Green et al., 1991; Gurwitch, Lefwich, Pfefferbaum, & Pynoos, 2000, cited in Gurwitch et al., 2002; Lonigan, Shannon, Taylor, Finch, & Sallee, 1994; Udwin, Boyle, Yule, Bolton, & Oryan, 2000). Even when exposed to the same trauma (i.e., sinking of the cruise ship Jupiter), 56.6% of the females and 32.6% of the males developed PTSD; Yule et al., 2000). However, other investigations do not report gender differences in rate of symptoms or the disorder (Kassam-Adams & Winston, 2004; Nader, Pynoos, Fairbanks, & Frederick, 1990; Pynoos et al., 1987).

Age may play a role in the frequency of some PTSD symptoms although the data remain conflictual (see Lonigan, Philips, & Richey, 2003). In a review summarizing the earlier literature (Fremont, 2004), younger children (aged 5 and under) were more likely to exhibit behaviors such as bed-wetting, thumb sucking or fear of the dark, as well as increased difficulties separating from parents. Latency age children were more likely to exhibit attentional problems, impaired school performance, school avoidance, somatic complaints, irrational fears, sleep problems, nightmares, irritability, and anger outbursts. Adolescents were more likely to express intrusive thoughts, hypervigilance, emotional numbing, nightmares, sleep disturbances and avoidance. Thus, as children mature, their symptomatology becomes more similar to that found for adults with PTSD.

Younger children also were more likely to report posttraumatic stress syndrome than early or late adolescents (9.2%, 4.2%, and 3.1%, respectively; Shannon et al., 1994). Repetitive thoughts and getting upset by the thoughts, bad dreams, fear of reoccurrence, anhedonia, emotional isolation, sleep difficulties, behavioral avoidance, upset at reminders of the hurricane, and reckless behaviors all were endorsed more frequently by children than adolescents (Shannon et al., 1994). In contrast, younger children are less likely to report amnesia for part of the trauma, less likely to have avoidance or numbing symptoms or visual flashbacks and because of their limited cognitive capabilities, may be less likely to perceive or understand the idea of a foreshortened future (see AACAP, 1998 for a review of this literature).

An important consideration when examining the role of age and gender is to carefully consider the assessment method used to determine the syndrome's presence. When data are based solely on self-report, there is a need to interpret these data carefully as overall, younger children and females tend to score higher on self-report measures of anxiety and fears. Thus, the finding that younger children and females reported higher levels of hurricane damage to their homes (Shannon et al., 1994) might be an artifact of reporting inasmuch as there is no rational reason why physical hurricane damage would vary by the age or gender of a child. Therefore, significantly higher rates of PTSD for females than males (6.9% vs. 3.8% for Hurricane Hugo victims; Shannon et al., 1994) also must be considered in light of the propensity for females to endorse a greater number of anxiety symptoms than males, as are younger children in comparison to older children or adolescents.

Judging the existence of PTSD symptoms among young children is particularly challenging and requires knowledge of basic child development. For example, it has been suggested that because the current diagnostic criteria rely primarily on verbal descriptions of internal experiences (Gurwitch et al., 2002), they are inappropriate for young, preverbal children because they exceed their verbal capabilities. However, rather than immediately concluding that prevalence rates among young children are therefore underestimated, it also is important to remember that basic cognitive abilities, like verbal abilities, also are under-developed in very young children. Therefore, it is necessary to consider whether very young children have the cognitive capacity to interpret the significance of certain traumatic events (such as the September 11, 2001, terrorist attacks) prior to determining that they have been affected by it but are not able to verbally express their symptomatology and distress.

After Hurricane Andrew, African American and Hispanic children reported more traumatic distress than white children (La Greca et al., 1996), but it is unclear whether rates of PTSD differ among children of different racial and ethnic groups (see AACAP, 1998 for a review). In certain natural disasters (such as hurricanes), socioeconomic factors may be related to the extensiveness of the physical damage that may result. For example, children from lower socioeconomic groups are more likely to live in housing more easily damaged from hurricane force winds. Thus, reported group differences based on racial or ethnic minority status need to be considered in terms of socioeconomic factors. In one investigation that did control for other demographic and exposure factors (Shannon et al., 1994), African American children still reported more symptoms of PTSD than non-African American children after exposure to Hurricane Hugo although there was no group difference in the percentage of children from each group who met criteria for the full PTSD stress syndrome (6.3% vs. 5.1% Shannon et al., 1994). Other investigations also conclude that group differences in rates of PTSD are inconsistent and need to be more concerned with controlling socioeconomic status (see Lonigan et al., 2003 for a review).

Comorbid and Differential Diagnosis

In addition to her frank PTSD symptoms, Marla is severely depressed.

Many children with PTSD also suffer from other comorbid conditions. In some instances, these comorbid disorders existed prior to the onset of PTSD (see section on etiology). In other instances, the onset of the comorbid disorder follows the diagnosis of PTSD. In these latter cases, depressive disorders appear to be the most common comorbid condition (AACAP, 1998; Brent et al., 1995; Goenjian et al., 1995; McKnight et al., 2004, Yule, 1994) although substance abuse, overanxious disorder, agoraphobia, separation anxiety disorder, and generalized anxiety disorder also has been reported (see AACAP, 1998). When comorbidity rates of children with PTSD are compared to rates for children without PTSD, 41% of adolescents with PTSD developed a comorbid major depressive disorder by the time they were 18 years old (Giaconia et al., 1995). In contrast only 8% of children without PTSD developed major depression by age 18. Rates of social phobia (33%), specific phobia (29%), alcohol and drug dependence (46% and 25% respectively) also were higher among children with PTSD, in most cases with onset occurring after PTSD. Other investigations also have reported higher rates of self-reported anxiety, depression and misconduct when compared to children with specific phobia or no psychiatric disorder (Saigh, 1989; Yule, Udwin, & Murdoch, 1990), but not different from children with other anxiety disorders. These differences were evident not only immediately after the event but were still there five months later (Yule et al., 1990).

Etiology

Behavioral perspectives form the basis of the majority of explanations for the development of PTSD and its etiology is in some ways very simple, yet in other ways, very complex. The simple part is that all instances of PTSD start with exposure to a traumatic event, although the definition of this event has changed n recent years. From there, the pathway to the disorder can become quite complex and not everyone who experiences a traumatic event develops PTSD. Overall, a conceptual model for predicting which children are most likely to develop posttraumatic stress or PTSD has been proposed (Green et al., 1991) and recently modified by LaGreca et al. (1996). Factors proposed to influence the development of posttraumatic reactions include: (a) characteristics of the stressor (e.g., severity, loss of life or property); (b) characteristics of the child (e.g., demographic characteristics and predisaster functioning); (c) characteristics of the postdisaster environment (e.g., social support and occurrence of major life stressors); (d) the child's efforts to process and cope with the disaster; and (e) intervening stressful life events. Evidence for these factors in the development of PTSD in children and adolescents are reviewed here.

Considered most important for the development of PTSD are concurrent disaster-related factors and include physical proximity to the event (Pynoos et al., 1987), actual injury or observation of injuries (Udwin et al., 2000), having to flee from the disaster site (Udwin et al., 2000), actual or perceived severity of the event (Green et al., 1991; Fremont, 2004; Lonigan et al., 1994), fears of dying, not being able to escape or becoming panicked, and feeling scared or alone (Lonigan et al., 1994; Udwin et al., 2000), all of which have predicted the onset of PTSD. Among all of the concurrent variables, data from the most well-controlled investigations (Goenjian et al., 1995; LaGreca, Silverman, Vernberg, & Prinstein, 1996; Udwin et al., 2000) indicate that primacy of exposure to the traumatic experience (direct injury or threat of injury as well as direct exposure to the sights and sounds of the event) is the factor most likely to predict the onset of PTSD. Other investigators have described this variable as proximity to the traumatic event (Pynoos et al., 1987). Higher rates of PTSD appear to occur among those within closest proximity (Goenjian et al., 1995; Pynoos et al., 1987). For example, even 18 months later, 95% of a sample of children at the epicenter of the devastating Spivak, Armenia earthquake (where the majority of buildings were destroyed and up to 50% of children in their schools were killed) still met criteria for PTSD. This compared to a rate of 71% of the children who lived in a city 20 miles away (where approximately 50% of the buildings were destroyed) and 26% of children who lived in a city 47 miles away (where there was only minimal damage and no loss of life; Goenjian et al., 1995). Rates of concurrent depression and separation anxiety disorder also covaried with respect to the distance from the earthquake's epicenter.

Predisaster factors associated with increasing the likelihood of developing PTSD included being female (Green et al., 1991; LaGreca et al., 1996; Udwin et al., 2000, see also the sociodemographic section above), mental health difficulties prior to the traumatic event (Daviss et al., 2000; Udwin et al., 2000), higher levels of premorbid trait anxiety (LaGreca et al., 1996; Lonigan et al., 1994; Pfefferbaum et al., 1999), and prior violence in the home (Udwin et al., 2000). By far, premorbid history is the most empirically supported factor within this group; anxiety level 15 months prior to Hurricane Andrew predicted higher levels of posttraumatic symptoms (PTS) 3 and 7 months after the hurricane (LaGreca et al., 1996). Whereas inattention levels 15 months prior to the hurricane predicted higher PTS levels at 3 months but not 7 months later, preexisting conduct problems did not predict higher symptomatology at ether time. These data suggest that it is preexisting levels of anxiety, and not psychopathology in general, that predicts onset of PTS after a traumatic event. Furthermore, these data suggest, as with other anxiety disorders, that those with what we have previously termed anxiety-proneness (Turner, Beidel, & Wolff, 1996) are more likely to develop PTSD. Thus, personal attributes likely contribute as much as the particular stimulus to the development of PTSD.

Postdisaster factors associated with the onset of PTSD include significant amnesia, feelings of guilt and intense fear (Udwin et al., 2000), home damage, displacement from home, and parental loss of job (Lonigan et al., 1994), high scores on self-report of psychopathology 5 months postdisaster (Udwin et al., 2000), increased numbers of subsequent major life events (La Greca et al., 1996), and extent of loss of family members (Goenjian et al., 1995).

Social support also has been related to higher levels of posttraumatic stress although not to the extent of the first three factors. For example higher support from parents and classmates was associated with lower levels of PTSD symptoms (AACAP, 1998; LaGreca et al., 1996). Consistent with receiving help and social support, a number of investigations have reported that family relationships and family pathology exert a significant impact on the development of PTSD.

Among those exposed to Australian bush fires, posttraumatic stress was more likely to occur among children whose parents had a negative response to the disaster (McFarlane, 1987). Other investigations (Daviss et al., 2000; Green et al., 1991; see also review by Fremont, 2004) also support the notion that parental distress, depression, and negative responses increase the likelihood of PTSD among offspring, whereas strong family relationships were protective even for children exposed to Type II stressors such as the Pol Pot regime (AACAP, 1989). Finally, with respect to specific coping variables, higher levels of positive coping, blame/anger, and social withdrawal were associated with more severe PTSD symptoms (La Greca et al., 1996). Among these three, blame/anger had the strongest effect.

In one of the few long-term follow-ups of the chronicity and severity of PTSD (Udwin et al., 2000), survivors of the cruise ship *Jupiter* disaster who had a premorbid history of poor social relationships and learning disabilities and postdisaster depression were the most likely to have PTSD that lasted 2 years or more. With respect to PTSD severity, retrospectively assigned premorbid diagnoses of separation anxiety and postdisaster depression were associated with more severe PTSD, whereas those who received help and social support in the disaster's aftermath had fewer PTSD symptoms (see also Fremont, 2004). This study illustrates the interplay of the various factors and also the complexity involved in predicting the onset, chronicity and severity of the disorder.

Assessment

Diagnostic Interviews

As noted above, one of the unique aspects of PTSD is that there are both semi-structured diagnostic interviews that include a PTSD module and distinct PTSD interviews. This latter group has been the most commonly used and although assessing the same symptoms, they do not always map directly on the current PTSD diagnostic criteria. Furthermore, these PTSD only interviews do not allow for the rule-out of other diagnostic conditions, thus making it more difficult to interpret the resultant data.

As noted numerous times throughout this volume, the semi-structured interview of choice for the diagnosis of anxiety disorders is the Anxiety Disorders Interview for Children-*DSM-IV* (Child/Parent; Silverman & Albano, 1996). This interview not only allows for a thorough assessment of PTSD symptomatology, but also assesses for the presence of other disorders that, as noted above, can sometimes coexist with PTSD.

Among specific PTSD interview schedules, a child version of a well-known adult PTSD diagnostic interview has been developed. The child version, the Clinician-Administered PTSD Scale-Child and Adolescent Version (CAPS-CA;

Nader, Blake, Kriegler, & Pynoos, 1994) combines both a quantifiable, dimensional approach to the assessment of PTSD, as well as allowing the assignation of both current and lifetime PTSD diagnoses. The scale has been described as detailed and allowing for reliable and valid diagnoses of PTSD although it may be a bit extensive for every-day clinical use (McKnight et al., 2004).

The Children's PTSD Inventory (Saigh et al., 2000) is keyed to *DSM-IV* criteria and was developed for use with children ages 7 to 18. The scale includes assessment of potential exposure to traumatic events, reaction to the events, an inventory of potential PTSD symptoms and questions regarding impairment in various areas of functioning. As noted (Lonigan et al., 2003), it is the most comprehensive diagnostic interview, has high internal consistency, good inter-rater and test–retest reliability, good convergent validity, and adequate sensitivity and specificity for the diagnosis of PTSD.

Clinician Ratings

With respect to PTSD-specific instruments, the one most often used is the Posttraumatic Stress Reaction Index (PTS-RI; Pynoos et al., 1987). This widely-used semi-structured interview does have moderate empirical support, although it does not adequately capture the diagnostic criteria (McKnight et al., 2004). Symptomatic cut-offs have been recommended to delineate those who are suffering from mild, moderate, severe, and very severe stress and its psychometric properties are quite good (Lonigan et al., 2003), with the exception of discriminant validity and specificity as an indicator of PTSD. Therefore, when diagnostic precision is necessary, interviews specifically developed for diagnostic purposes should be used.

Self-Report

In epidemiological investigations assessing a broad variety of potentially traumatic events, the PTS-RI has been used as a self-report measure of trauma but its psychometric properties have not been established for use in this format (McKnight et al., 2004). Better choices are the Child and Adolescent Trauma Survey (CATS; March, 1999) and the Child PTSD Symptom Scale (CPSS; Foa, Johnson, Feeny, & Treadwell, 2001). The CATS specifically assesses for the presence of DSM-IV diagnostic criteria. Normative data are available, the instrument is sensitive to change (March, Amaya-Jackson, Murray, & Schulte, 1998) and it includes stable indices of non-PTSD events and qualifying stressors (see McKnight et al., 2004 for additional information on the CATS). The CPSS uses a 5-point Likert scale (not at all to five times a week) to assess how often the child is affected by each of the 17 DSM-IV symptoms. Additionally, it assesses current functioning at school, with family and friends. The scale has good test-retest reliability as well as good convergent and divergent validity.

Behavioral Assessment

Constructing Behavioral Avoidance Tests (BAT) often is considered difficult to impossible to do for cases of PTSD inasmuch as it does not seem feasible to replicate hurricanes or automobile accidents in vivo. Such an assertion is incorrect; it ignores the fact that when conditioning occurs, it encompasses many specific stimuli (characteristics of the place where the event occurred, other people who were present, etc.). Thus, while it may not be possible to replicate the 140 mile per hour winds of a hurricane, it is still possible to construct BATs to the associated stimuli, for example, assessing approach/avoidance to objects (e.g., automobiles) or situations (place where the individual was standing when the dam broke/tornado touched down). Not only do BATs allow for an objective assessment of the ability to approach (or avoid) these objects or situations, but subjective distress or overt physiological response also can be determined. For example, a BAT constructed to assess treatment outcome for a 14-year-old boy previously abducted by the Lebanese militia for 48 hours consisted of a 10 minute walk where the teen "left his home, walked to the area where the abduction occurred, entered a shop, made a purchase, and returned by al alternate route" (Saigh, 1987, p. 148). The teen reported his progress (how far he was able to walk) and was unobtrusively observed by research assistants. Although not reported in this study, it would also be possible to rate subjective level of distress when attempting these tasks. With respect to assessing physiological response to stimuli associated with the trauma, sound effects records, movies, or videos may be used or virtual reality programs may be used to create feared situations such as hurricanes or automobile accidents. Patients could be asked to rate their level of distress while listening to or engaging in these tasks and overt physiological responses such as blood pressure, heart rate, or skin conductance could be assessed.

Self-Monitoring

Data collection through this modality could include number of times that the child attempts to approach or avoid a feared object or situation. Depending on the child's clinical presentation, other behaviors such as sleep difficulties, intrusive thoughts, flashbacks or general level of distress also might be monitored. As noted in other chapters, the keys to self-monitoring are simplicity and ease of completion.

Treatment

Prior to conducting any intervention, it is necessary to emphasize the importance of careful screening to distinguish normal, developmentally appropriate reactions to trauma from abnormal reactions (Fremont, 2004) that might require intervention. Suggested essential components for the treatment for children with PTSD include direct exploration of the trauma, stress management techniques, cognitive interventions to correct inaccurate attributions regarding the trauma, and the need to include parents in treatment (AACAP, 1998). However, there are few empirical data on the efficaciousness of these interventions, although what data do exist support the use of cognitive-behavior therapy, particularly the use of exposure procedures.

As noted (McKnight et al., 2004), the empirical database for the treatment of childhood PTSD is extremely sparse. Behavioral interventions that would appear to be relevant include imaginal and in vivo exposure, relaxation training, anger management training, and teaching coping skills (Fremont, 2004). Although conceptually, these interventions would prove appropriate, empirical data are lacking. In an early single-case design (Saigh, 1987), imaginal flooding was used to treat an adolescent abducted by the Lebanese militia. After six treatment sessions, state and trait anxiety had decreased by 32% and 37.5% respectively and most significantly, whereas the teen was only able to complete 33% of the BAT at pretreatment, he was able to complete the entire BAT (100%) at both posttreatment and four month follow-up. Interestingly, at follow-up, the teen reported considerable satisfaction with the intervention and felt the outcome was well worth the discomfort of the flooding sessions. This is important as many individuals who are not conversant with behavior therapy often express concern that those with PTSD will not be able to tolerate flooding treatment. Of course, this is not the case but this myth continues to exist and probably prevents many children with this disorder from being successfully treated. In fact, exposure is the one treatment recommended by the PTSD task force for the treatment of adults with this disorder.

An interesting variation in the delivery of treatment for children with PTSD is the concept of "pulsed" intervention. Following the initial intervention designed to help the child cope with the immediate aftermath of the traumatic event, treatment is suspended (or pulsed) until clinical issues dictate that continued intervention is necessary. This necessity may take the form of developmental transitions (starting to date, leaving for college) or clinical issues such as increases in anxiety or depression. The idea behind pulsed, rather than continuous intervention is to minimize feelings of ongoing helplessness in the child by minimizing dependence upon the therapist (McKnight et al., 2004). To date, there are no data suggesting that pulsed interventions are more efficacious than standard treatment and in effect, it is counter to behavioral theories of exposure intervention, which demonstrate that recovery of fear will occur if therapy is discontinued prior to achievement of habituation.

A conceptual model that incorporates both prevention and intervention (triage, coping responses for anticipated grief and trauma responses, treating the development of PTSD if it occurs and other disorders if they also occur) has been recommended by the American Academy of Child and Adolescent Psychiatry (1998). With respect to specific modes of intervention, cognitive-behavioral treatment has been recommended as the treatment of choice (Cohen, Berliner, & March, 2000). March et al. (1998) reported that a CBT intervention for PTSD, delivered in a school setting, was efficacious for children who had been exposed to a single incident stressor. The intervention, Multimodal Trauma Treatment (MMTT) is 18 weeks in length, combines psychoeducation, anxiety management training, anger coping, cognitive training, and exposure. In an initial open trial (Amaya-Jackson et al., 2003), 57% of the children no longer met criteria for PTSD at posttreatment and 86% were diagnosis free at 6 month follow-up. Symptoms were reduced by 40% at posttreatment and another 40% at follow-up and similar improvements were evident for measures of anxiety, depression and anger. In follow-up investigations using 14, rather than 18 sessions, outcome was consistent with the initial trial for both elementary and high school students (Amaya-Jackson et al., 2003). This intervention proved promising and what are needed now are randomized controlled trials, given that there are some data to indicate that even without intervention, rates of PTSD decrease across time (La Greca et al., 1996; Udwin et al., 2000; Yule et al., 2000).

In 1998, the Practice Parameters for the Assessment and Treatment of Children and Adolescents with Posttraumatic Stress Disorder concluded that despite prescribing practices, there was inadequate empirical support for the use of any particular medication to treat childhood PTSD (AACAP, 1998). More recently, SSRI medications have been recommended as the first line of pharmacological intervention, particularly when "treatment-responsive comorbid conditions are present" (Cohen et al., 2000, p. 251). Again, there are no controlled trials available confirming the efficacy of these medications for PTSD in children, although some data indicate some efficacy for anxiety and/or depression which often are associated conditions.

Treatment of PTSD–Case Example

Following Marla's initial assessment, several behaviors (general arousal, frequency of intrusive thoughts, and distance from the stable where the accident occurred) were selected as indicators of treatment efficacy. These variables were monitored for 1 week prior to treatment, during treatment, and for 1 week at 6 month follow-up (see Figures 13.1–13.3). Because Marla was 17 years old, imaginal exposure was selected for use. The imaginal scene is presented in Table 13.3. Treatment was conducted twice per week for the first 3 weeks and then once per week for an additional 8 weeks for a total of 14 weeks. During the first 3 weeks, two sessions per week were conducted in an effort to quickly decrease general levels of distress, begin to improve sleep hygiene, and also to closely monitor Marla's clinical condition. Other aspects of treatment implementation

TABLE 13.3 Marla's Imaginal Scene

I want you to imagine that you are in the stable. It is quiet and you are getting the new horse, Lucky, ready for his training session. Lucky is high spirited but you and your dad have had some success in training him so far. As you begin to lead Lucky out to the training grounds, a mouse runs across the stable floor. You jump and Lucky is startled. This scares you and you think, "I do not know this horse very well. What if he spooks in the stable?" You know this is dangerous because the stable is tight and there is little room to maneuver. As you try to calm Lucky, he begins to bolt even more and you are knocked to the ground. Your heart is racing, you feel dizzy and as you look up, you see Lucky's front hooves coming toward you. You move your head but Lucky's front hoof grazes the side of your head. You are very frightened and you think, "I am going to die." Your heart is racing, you can't breathe, and you can't move. Lucky continues to be out of control and when the hooves come crashing down again, they hit your arm and hand. Lucky rears up again and you realize that there is no room to escape. The horse is out of control and you cannot do anything about the situation. No one else is here to help you. You are in such pain that you cannot move out of the way. Lucky's hooves come toward you again and you think, "This is it. Now I am going to die." Then all you see is a blinding white light and you feel excruciating pain.

were conducted using the guidelines presented in chapter 10 on obsessive-compulsive disorder. Homework assignments included grooming other horses in the outdoor training area, cleaning bridles, and sitting in the empty tourist carriages. Treatment outcome is presented in Figures 13.1–13.3. As depicted, the treatment was effective in decreasing general arousal and intrusive thoughts, improving stuttering (not monitored on a daily basis), and allowing Marla to return to the stable and to resume her training activities.

SUMMARY

PTSD in children is an understudied disorder and little is known about its clinical presentation, etiology, or efficacious treatment strategies. To date, the research has been hampered by changing and subjective diagnostic criteria and

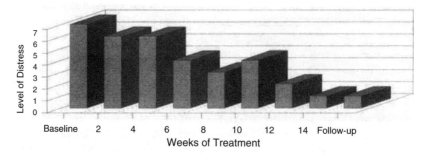

FIGURE 13.1 Marla's daily level of general arousal.

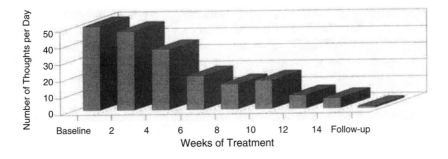

FIGURE 13.2 Marla's frequency of intrusive thoughts.

a myriad of events that might be considered as "traumatic" but do not meet the classic definition of a traumatic event. Furthermore, most of the available data have centered on child sexual abuse. There has been little attempt to merge this literature with findings from other types of traumatic events. Indeed, the separation of these types of abuse into Type I and Type II events and the resultant differing clinical presentations suggest that these indeed may be very different conditions, thereby questioning the validity of the Type I vs. Type II classification. With respect to Type I events, factors that may contribute to the onset of PTSD are beginning to be elucidated. Furthermore, assessment measures are becoming more sophisticated and this, in turn, should allow for the empirical assessment of pharmacological and psychosocial interventions. Currently, behavioral and cognitive-behavioral interventions appear to have the most (albeit still extremely limited) outcome data. The use of behavioral interventions theoretically makes sense inasmuch as PTSD can be conceptualized as a disorder that is acquired as a result of a traumatic conditioning event. One potential impediment to the implementation of behavioral treatment programs is the belief that those with PTSD are "too fragile" to handle exposure

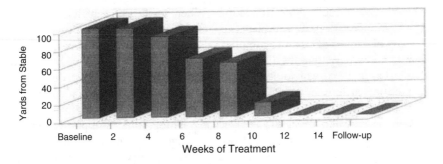

FIGURE 13.3 Distance Marla is able to comfortably stand and look at the stable.

interventions. Of course, there are no data to support this assumption but this view may hinder the examination of the efficacy of these interventions. To the contrary, what data we have show the opposite to be true. When conducted by qualified professionals using appropriate clinical guidelines, there is no reason to assert that behavioral interventions, so efficacious for other anxiety disorders, would be any less so for children and adolescents with PTSD.

CONCLUSIONS

PTSD in childhood can be a complex and severe condition involving the emotional response to a traumatic stimulus or event, now defined so broadly as to create confusion in the literature. Indeed, the classical conceptualization was a response to an event outside of usual human experience. In *DSM-IV*, this definition was broadened to include those events considered "extreme." This has opened the door to the inclusion of many stimuli as potential traumatic events such as natural disasters, motor vehicle accidents, and physical illness, among others. Expanding the category in this fashion has created a situation in which it is unclear if we are studying the same condition across categories. Perhaps even more problematic is the study of "PTSD symptoms" and reporting of these phenomena without clearly indicating that the condition did not constitute PTSD. One strategy to try and bring some order to the problem of different events involves the use of Type I and Type II designations. Type I traumas are t those resulting from unexpected events such as a motor vehicle accident. Type II PTSD results from chronic ongoing stress as in child abuse. It is not clear that this conceptualization clarifies the ambiguity associated with response to these various types of stimuli. *DSM-IV* also delineated a condition considered to be related to PTSD termed Acute Stress Disorder (ASD). However, it does not appear that these conditions are necessarily related and ASD appears to be related to dynamic theory and dissociation.

A primary difficulty for the area is that there are few empirically sound studies. Particularly problematic is the Type II area where virtually all data are retrospective and self-report from adults. When PTSD is present, it is clear that it can produce serious and enduring consequences. It is important to note that development of PTSD is more complicated than mere exposure to a certain type of stimulus a fact often not discussed in the literature. Available data indicate that just as is the case of adults, certain person characteristics may predispose one to the development of PTSD. As in adults, more children do not develop PTSD after exposure to a traumatic situation than those who do. In addition, in some circumstances factors such as sociodemographic, and perhaps racial ethnic variables, may be important. Also, younger children appear to be more vulnerable. Although there are many questions remaining related to the conceptualization and diagnosis of the condition, available data indicate that the condition is responsive to treatment. Based on the available scientific findings, those treatments that are rooted in behavioral and cognitive-behavioral theory are efficacious. In particular, treatments embodying principles of exposure are recommended.

Overall then, PTSD in general and PTSD in childhood in particular have become much broader conditions than they once were. Indeed, using current diagnostic criteria, any stimulus is capable of producing PTSD. The situation is such now that the scientific usefulness of the construct and the diagnostic category is threatened by what we judge to be gross overinclusiveness. Furthermore, the manner in which the mental health professions have portrayed a picture of children and adults as being extremely fragile, capable of developing PTSD in response to almost any emotionally arousing stimulus is problematic. This clearly is not the case and belies the rather extensive psychological literature on resiliency indicating the tremendous resiliency of the human species. This problem in general was discussed in a recent article appearing in the *American Psychologist* (Bonanno, 2004). In order to restore the integrity of the construct and diagnostic category, some clarifications and restrictions are needed, as well as some strengthening of the editorial process in reviewing scientific manuscripts for publication. This particularly is the case for the Type II category as the data here almost are all retrospective reports from adults. In all areas, better methodological approaches to assessment are needed. One problem is that the "trauma movement," and that is how we see it, largely has developed outside of the area of anxiety disorders. Hence, the rigor shown by researchers primarily interested in anxiety is not always evident in this area. This also likely explains the failure to fully incorporate scientific findings and methodological approaches used in the field.

References

Abramowitz, J. S., Whiteside, S. P., & Deacon, B. J. (2005). Treatment of pediatric obsessive-compulsive disorder: A comprehensive meta-analysis of the outcome research. *Behavior Therapy, 36,* 55–63.

Achenbach, T.M. (1985). Assessment of anxiety in children. In A. H. Tuma & J. D. Maser (Eds.), *Anxiety and the anxiety disorders* (pp. 707–734). Hillsdale, NJ: Erlbaum

Adams, G .B., Waas, G. A., March, J. S., & Smith, M. C. (1994). Obsessive compulsive disorder in children and adolescents: The role of the school psychologist in identification, assessment, and treatment. *School Psychology Quarterly, 9,* 274–294.

Agras, W. S. Sylvester, D., & Oliveau, D. (1969). The epidemiology of common fears and phobias. *Comprehensive Psychiatry, 10,* 151–156.

Agras, W. S., Chapin, H.N., & Oliveau, D. (1972). The natural history of phobias: course and prognosis. *Archives of General Psychiatry, 26,* 315–317.

Albano, A. M., Marten, P. A., Holt, C. S., Heimberg, R. G., & Barlow, D. H. (1995). Cognitive-behavioral group treatment for social phobia in adolescents: A preliminary study. *Journal of Nervous and Mental Disease, 183,* 649–656.

Alessi, N. E., & Magen, J. (1988). Panic disorder in psychiatrically hospitalized children. *American Journal of Psychiatry, 145,* 1450–1452.

Alfano, C. A., Beidel, D. C., & Turner, S. M. (2002). Considering cognition in childhood anxiety disorders: Conceptual, methodological and developmental considerations. *Clinical Psychology Review, 22,* 1209–1238.

Allsopp, M., & Verduyn, C. (1990). Adolescents with obsessive-compulsive disorder: A case note review of consecutive patients referred to a provincial regional adolescent psychiatry unit. *Journal of Adolescence, 13,* 157–169.

Amaya-Jackson. L., Reynolds, V., Murray, M. C., McCarthy, G., Nelson, A., Cherney, M. S., Lee, R., Foa, E., & March, J. S. (2003). Cognitive-behavioral treatment for pediatric posttraumatic stress disorder: Protocol and application in school and community settings. *Cognitive and Behavioral Practice, 10,* 204–213.

American Academy of Child and Adolescent Psychiatry. (1997). AACAP official action: Practice parameters for the assessment and treatment of children and adolescents with anxiety disorders. *Journal of the American Academy of Child and Adolescent Psychiatry, 36,* 9–20.

American Academy of Child and Adolescent Psychiatry. (1998). Practice parameters for the assessment and treatment of children and adolescents with posttraumatic stress disorder. *Journal of the American Academy of Child and Adolescent Psychiatry, 37*(Suppl.), 4S–26S.

American Psychiatric Association. (1980). *Diagnostic and statistical manual of mental disorders* (third edition). Washington, DC: Author.

American Psychiatric Association. (1987). *Diagnostic and statistical manual of mental disorders* (third edition, revised). Washington, DC: Author.

American Psychiatric Association. (1994). *Diagnostic and statistical manual of mental disorders* (fourth edition). Washington, DC: Author.

Andersson, C. B., & Thomsen, P. H. (1998). Electively mute children: An analysis of 37 Danish cases. *Norwegian Journal of Psychiatry, 52*, 231–238.

Andrews, G., Stewart, G., Allen, R., & Henderson, A .S. (1990). The genetics of six neurotic disorders: A twin study. *Journal of Affective Disorders, 19*, 23–29.

Anderson, J. C., Williams, S., McGee, R., & Silva, P. A. (1987). DSM-III disorders in preadolescent children: Prevalence in a large sample from the general population. *Archives of General Psychiatry, 44*, 69–77.

Andrews, G., Stewart, G., & Allen, r. (1990). The genetics of six neurotic disorders: A twin study. *Joural of Affective Disorders, 19*, 23-29.

Angelino, H., Dollins, J., & Mech, E. V. (1956). Trends in the "fears and worries" of school children as related to socioeconomic status and age. *Journal of Genetic Psychology, 89*, 263–276.

Anstendig, K. (198). Selective mutism: A review of the treatment literature by modality from 1980–1996. *Psychotherapy: Theory, Research, Practice, Training, 35*, 381–391.

Apley, J., & Naish, N. (1958). Recurrent abdominal pain: A field study of 1,000 schoolchildren. *Archives of Disease in Childhood, 34*, 165–170.

Argyropoulos, S. V., Bell, C. J., & Nutt, D. J. (2001). Brain function in social anxiety disorder. *The Psychiatric Clinics of North America, 4*, 707–722.

Armistead, L., Forehand, R. & Steele, R. (1998). Pediatric AIDS. In T.H. Ollendick & M. Hersen (Eds). *Handbook of child psychopathology* (3rd ed., pp. 463-481). New York: Plenum Press.

Aschenbrand, S. G., Kendall, P. C., Alicia Webb, A., Safford, S. M., & Flannery-Schroeder, E. (2003). Is childhood separation anxiety disorder a predictor of adult panic disorder and agoraphobia? A seven-year longitudinal study. *Journal of the American Academy of Child and Adolescent Psychiatry, 42*, 1478–1485.

Asendorpf, J. S. (1990). Development of inhibition during childhood: Evidence for situational specificity and a two-factor model. *Developmental Psychology, 26*, 721–730.

Ballenger, J. C., Carek, D. J., Steele, J. J., & Cornish-McTighe, D. (1989). Three cases of panic disorder with agoraphobia in children. *American Journal of Psychiatry, 146*, 922–924.

Bamber, D., Tamplin, A., Park, R. J., Kyte, Z. A., & Goodyer, I. M. (2002). Development of a short Leyton Obsessional Inventory for Children and Adolescents. *Journal of the American Academy of Child and Adolescent Psychiatry, 41*, 1246–1252.

Bandura, A. (1969). *Principles of behavior modification.* New York: Holt, Rinehart, & Winston.

Bandura, A., Blanchard, E. B., & Ritter, B. (1969). Relative efficacy of desensitization and modeling approaches for inducing behavioral, affective, and attitudinal changes. *Journal of Personality and Social Psychology, 13*, 173–199.

Bandura, A., Grusec, J. E., & Menlove, F. L. (1967). Vicarious extinction of avoidance behavior. *Journal of Personality and Social Psychology, 5*, 16–23.

Bandura, A., & Menlove, F. L. (1968). Factors determining vicarious extinction of avoidance behavior. *Journal of Personality and Social Psychology, 3*, 99–108.

Barabaz, A. F. (1973). Group desensitization of test anxiety in elementary school. *The Journal of Psychology, 83*, 295–301.

Barlow, D. H. (2002). *Anxiety and its disorders: The nature and treatment of anxiety and panic* (2nd ed.). New York: Guilford Press.

Barlow, D.H., & Seidner, A.L. (1983). Treatment of adolescent agoraphobics: Effects on parent-adolescent relations. *Behaviour Research and Therapy, 21*, 519-526.

Barrett, P. M. (1998). Evaluation of cognitive-behavioral group treatments for childhood anxiety disorders. *Journal of Clinical Child Psychology, 27*, 459–468.

Barrett, P. M., Dadds, M. R., & Rapee, R. M. (1996). Family treatment of childhood anxiety: A controlled trial. *Journal of Consulting and Clinical Psychology, 64,* 333–342.

Barrett, P. M., Duffy, A. L., Dadds, M. R., & Rapee, R. M. (2001). Cognitive-behavioral treatment of anxiety disorders in children: Long-term (6 year) follow-up. *Journal of Consulting and Clinical Psychology, 69*, 135–141.

Barrett, P. M., & Healy, L. J. (2003). An examination of the cognitive processes involved in childhood obsessive-compulsive disorder. *Behaviour Research and Therapy, 41*, 285–299.

Barrett, P., & Healy-Farrell, L. (2003). Perceived responsibility in juvenile obsessive-compulsive disorder: an experimental manipulation. *Journal of Clinical Child and Adolescent Psychology, 32*, 430–441.

Barrett, P., Healy, L., & March, J. S. (2003). Behavioral avoidance test for childhood obsessive-compulsive disorder. *American Journal of Psychotherapy, 57,* 80–100.

Barrett, P., Healy-Farrell, L., & March, J. S. (2004). Cognitive-behavioral family treatment of childhood obsessive-compulsive disorder: A controlled trial. *Journal of the American Academy of Child and Adolescent Psychiatry, 43*, 46–62.

Barrett, P. M., Johnson. S., & Turner, C. (in press). Developmental differences in universal preventive intervention for child anxiety. *Clinical Child Psychology and Psychiatry.*

Barrett, P. M., Moore, A. M., & Sonderegger, R. (2000). The FRIENDS program for young former-Yugoslavian refugees in Australia: A pilot study. *Behaviour Change, 17*, 124–133.

Barrett, P. M., Rasmussen, P., & Healy, L. (2001). The effects of childhood obsessive compulsive disorder on sibling relationships in late childhood and early adolescence: Preliminary findings. *The Australian Educational and Developmental Psychologist, 17*, 82–102.

Barrett, P. M., Rapee, R. M., Dadds, M. R., & Ryan, S. M. (1996). Family enhancement of cognitive style in anxious and aggressive children: Threat bias and the FEAR effect. *Journal of Abnormal Child Psychology, 24*, 187–203.

Barrett, P. M., Shortt, A. L., Fox, T. L., & Wescombe, K. (2001). Examining the social validity of the FRIENDS treatment program for anxious children. *Behaviour Change, 18*, 63–77.

Barrett, P. M., Shortt, A., & Healy, L. (2002). Do parent and child behaviours differentiate families whose children have obsessive-compulsive disorder from other clinic and non-clinic families? *Journal of Child Psychology and Psychiatry, 43*, 597–607.

Barrett, P. M., Sonderegger, R., & Sonderegger, N. L. (2001). Evaluation of an anxiety-prevention and positive coping programs (FRIENDS) for children and adolescents of non-English speaking background. *Behaviour Change, 18*, 78–91.

Barrett. P. M., Sonderegger, R., & Xenos, S. (2003). Using FRIENDS to combat anxiety and adjustment problems among young migrants to Australia: A national trial. *Clinical Child Psychology and Psychiatry, 8*, 241–260.

Barrett, P., & Turner, C. (2001). Prevention of anxiety symptoms in primary school children: preliminary results from a universal school-based trial. *British Journal of Clinical Psychology, 40*, 399–410

Barrios, B. A., Hartman, D. B., & Shigetomi, C. (1981). Fears and anxieties in children. In E. J. Mash & L. G. Terdal (Eds.), *Behavioral assessment of childhood disorders* (pp. 259–304). New York: Guilford Press.

Barton, L., Kearney, C. A., Eisen, A. R., & Silverman, W. K. (April 1993). *The relationship of school phobia to school refusal behavior: Not separate but not equal.* Symposium presented at the meeting of the Western Psychological Association, Phoenix, AZ.

Battaglia, M., Bajo, S., Strambi, L. F., Brambilla, F., Castronovo, C., Vanni, G., & Bellodi, L. (1997). Physiological and behavioral responses to minor stressors in offspring of patients with panic disorder. *Journal of Psychiatric Research, 31*, 365–376.

Battaglia, M., Bertella, S., Politi, E., Bernardeschi, L., Perna, G., Gabriele, A., & Bellodi, L. (1995). Age at onset of panic disorder: influence of familial liability to the disease and of childhood separation anxiety disorder. *American Journal of Psychiatry, 152*, 1362–1364.

Battaglia, M., Ogliari, A., Zanoni, A., Villa, F., Citterio, A., Binaghi, F., Fossati, A., & Maffel, C. (2004). Children's discrimination of expressions of emotions: Relationship with indices of social anxiety and shyness. *Journal of the American Academy of Child and Adolescent Psychiatry, 43*, 358–365.

Baxter, L. R., Jr. (1992). Neuroimaging studies of obsessive compulsive disorder. *Psychiatric Clinics of North America, 15*, 718–725.

Beck, A. T. (1988). Cognitive approaches to panic disorder: *Theory and therapy.* In S. Rachman and J. D. Maser (Eds.), *Panic: Psychological perspectives* (pp.91–109). Hillsdale, NJ: Lawrence Erlbaum Associates.

Bedi, R., Sutcliffe, P., Donnan, P. T., Barret, N., & McConnachie, J. (1992a). Dental care experience and prevalence of children afraid of dental treatment. *Community Dentistry and Oral Epidemiology, 20*, 368–371.

Bedi, R., Sutcliffe, P., Donnan, P. T., Barret, N., & McConnachie, J. (1992b). The prevalence of dental anxiety in a group of 13 and 14-year old Scottish children. *International Journal of Pediatric Dentistry, 2,* 17–24.

Beidel, D. C. (1991). Social phobia and overanxious disorder in school-aged children. *Journal of the American Academy of Child and Adolescent Psychiatry, 30,* 54–552.

Beidel, D. C., Christ, M. A. G., & Long, P. J. (1991). Somatic complaints in anxious children. *Journal of Abnormal Child Psychology, 19,* 659–670.

Beidel, D. C., Fink, C. M., & Turner, S. M. (1996). Stability of anxious symptomatology in children. *Journal of Abnormal Child Psychology, 20,* 257–269.

Beidel. D. C., Morris, T. L., & Turner, M. W. (2004). Social phobia. In T. L. Morris and J. S. March (Eds.), *Anxiety disorders in children and adolescents* (2nd ed.) (pp. 141–163). New York: Guilford Press.

Beidel. D. C., Neal, A. M., & Lederer, A. S. (1991). The feasibility and validity of a daily diary for the assessment of anxiety in children. *Behavior Therapy, 22,* 505–517.

Beidel, D. C., Silverman, W. K., & Hammond–Laurence, K. (1996). Overanxious disorder: Subsyndromal state or specific disorder? *Journal of Clinical Child Psychology, 25,* 25–32.

Beidel, D. C., & Stanley, M. A. (1993). Developmental issues in the measurement of anxiety. In C.G. Last (Ed.), *Anxiety across the lifespan: A developmental perspective* (pp. 167–203). New York: Springer Publishing.

Beidel, D. C., & Turner, S. M. (1997). At risk for anxiety: I. Psychopathology in the offspring of anxious parents. *Journal of the American Academy of Child and Adolescent Psychiatry, 36,* 918–925.

Beidel, D. C., & Turner, S. M. (1998). *Shy children, phobic adults: The nature and treatment of social phobia.* Washington, DC: American Psychological Association.

Beidel, D. C., Turner, S. M., Hamlin, K., & Morris, T. L. (2000). The Social Phobia and Anxiety Inventory for Children (SPAI-C): External and discriminative validity. *Behavior Therapy, 31,* 75–87.

Beidel, D. C., Turner, S. M.,& Morris, T. L. (1995). A new inventory to assess childhood social anxiety and phobia: The Social Phobia and Anxiety Inventory for Children. *Psychological Assessment, 7,* 73–79.

Beidel, D. C., Turner, S. M., & Morris, T. L. (1998). *Social Phobia and Anxiety Inventory for Children.* North Tonawanda, NY: Multi–Health Systems.

Beidel, D. C., Turner, S. M., & Morris T. L. (1999). Psychopathology of childhood social phobia. *Journal of the American Academy of Child and Adolescent Psychiatry, 38,* 643–650.

Beidel, D. C., Turner, S. M., & Morris, T. L. (2000). Behavioral treatment of childhood social phobia. *Journal of Consulting and Clinical Psychology, 68,* 1072–1080.

Beidel D. C., Turner, S.M., & Morris, T. L. (2003). Social Effectiveness Therapy for Children and Adolescents (SET-C): Therapist guide. Multi–Health Systems, Inc.

Beidel, D. C., Turner, S. M., Sallee, F. R., & Ammerman, R. A. (2000). Treatment of childhood social phobia. Unpublished manuscript, University of Maryland-College Park.

Beidel, D. C., Turner, S. M., Young, B., & Paulson, A. (in press). Social Effectiveness Therapy for Children: Three year follow-up. *Journal of Consulting and Clinical Psychology.*

Beidel, D. C., Turner, S. M., Young, B., Ammerman, R. A., & Sallee, F. R. (2004). Psychopathology of adolescent social phobia. Unpublished manuscript, University of Maryland-College Park.

Bell, C., Malizia, A., & Nutt, D. (1999). The neurobiology of social phobia. *European Archives of Psychiatry and Clinical Neuroscience, 249* (Suppl. 1), S11–S18.

Bell-Dolan, D. J., Last, C. G., & Strauss, C. C. (1990). Symptoms of anxiety disorders in normal children. *Journal of the American Academy of Child and Adolescent Psychiatry, 29,* 759–765.

Benazon, N. R., Moore, G. J., & Rosenberg, D. R. (2003). Neurochemical analyses in pediatric obsessive-compulsive disorder in patients treated with cognitive-behavioral therapy. *Journal of the American Academy of Child and Adolescent Psychiatry, 42,* 1279–1285.

Berg, C. J., Rapoport, J. L., & Flament, M. (1986). The Leyton Obsessional Inventory-Child Version. *Journal of the American Academy of Child Psychiatry, 25,* 84–91.

Berg, C. Z., Whitaker, A., Davies, M., Flament, M. F., & Rapoport, J. L. (1988). The survey form of the Leyton Obsessional Inventory—Child Version: Norms from an epidemiological study. *Journal of the American Academy of Child and Adolescent Psychiatry, 27,* 759–763.

Berg, I., Butler, A., & Pritchard, J. (1974). Psychiatric illness in the mothers of school-phobic adolescents. *British Journal of Psychiatry, 125,* 466–467.

Berg, I., Marks, I., McGuire, R., & Lipsedge, M. (1974). School phobia and agoraphobia. *Psychological Medicine, 4,* 428–434.

Berggren, U., & Meynert, G. (1984). Dental fear and avoidance: causes, symptoms, and consequences. *Journal of the American Dental Association, 109,* 247–251.

Bergman, R. L., Keller, M., Wood, J., Piacentini, J., & McCracken, J. (2001). Selective Mutism Questionnaire (SMQ): Development and findings. Presented at the Annual Meeting of the American Academy of Child and Adolescent Psychiatry, Honolulu, HI, October.

Bergman, R. L., Piacentini, J., & McCracken, J. T. (2002). Prevalence and description of selective mutism in a school-based sample. *Journal of the American Academy of Child and Adolescent Psychiatry, 41,* 938–946.

Berman, S. I., Weems, C. F., Silverman, W. K., & Kurtines, W. M. (2000). Predictors of outcome in exposure-based cognitive and behavioral treatments for phobic and anxiety disorders in children. *Behavior Therapy, 31,* 713–731.

Bernstein, G. A. (1991). Comorbidity and severity of anxiety and depressive disorders in a clinic sample. *Journal of the American Academy of Child and Adolescent Psychiatry, 30,* 43–50.

Bernstein, G. A., Borchardt, C. M., Perwien, A. R., Crosby, R.D., Kushner, M.G., Thuras, P.D., & Last, C.G. (2000). Imipramine plus cognitive –behavioral therapy in the treatment of school refusal. *Journal of the American Academy of Child and Adolescent Psychiatry, 39,* 276–283.

Bernstein, G. A., & Garfinkel, B. D. (1986). School phobia: The overlap of affective and anxiety disorders. *Journal of the American Academy of Child and Adolescent Psychiatry, 25* 235–241

Bernstein, G. A., & Garfinkel, B. D. (1988). Pedigrees, functioning, and psychopathology in families of school phobic children. *American Journal of Psychiatry, 145,* 70–74.

Bernstein, G. A., Garfinkel, B. D., & Borchardt, C. M. (1990). Comparative studies of pharmacotherapy for school refusal. *Journal of the American Academy of Child and Adolescent Psychiatry, 29,* 773–781.

Bernstein, G. A., Hektner, J. M., Borchardt, C. M., & McMillan, M. H. (2001). Treatment of school refusal: One year follow-up. *Journal of the American Academy of Child and Adolescent Psychiatry, 40,* 206–213.

Bernstein, G. A., Massie, E. D., Thuras, P. D., Perwein, A. R. Borchardt, C. M., & Crosby, R. D. (1997). Somatic symptoms in anxious-depressed school refusers. *Journal of the American Academy of Child and Adolescent Psychiatry, 36,* 661–668.

Bernstein, G. A., Svingen, P. H., & Garfinkel, B. D. (1990). School phobia: Patterns of family functioning. *Journal of the American Academy of Child and Adolescent Psychiatry, 29,* 24–30.

Bernstein, G. A., Warren, S. L., Massie, E D., & Thuras, P. D. (1999). Family dimensions in anxious–depressed school refusers. *Journal of Anxiety Disorders, 5,* 515–528.

Biederman, J., Farone, S. V., Marrs, A., Moore, P., Farcia. J., Ablon, S., Mick, E., Gershon. J., & Kearns, M. E. (1997). Panic disorder and agoraphobia in consecutively referred children and adolescents. *Journal of the American Academy of Child and Adolescent Psychiatry, 36,* 214–223.

Biederman, J., Hirshfeld-Becker, D. R., Rosenbaum, J. F., Friedman, D., Snidman, N., Kagan, J., & Faraone, S. V. (2001). Further evidence of association between behavioral inhibition and social anxiety in children. *American Journal of Psychiatry, 158,* 1673–1679.

Biederman, J., Rosenbaum, J. F., Bolduc-Murphy, E. A., Faraone, S. V., Charloff, J., Hirshfeld, D. R., & Kagan, J. (1993). A 3-year follow-up of children with and without behavioral inhibition. *Journal of the American Academy of Child and Adolescent Psychiatry, 32,* 847–850.

Bird, H. R., Canino, G., Rubio-Stipec, M., Gould, M. S., Ribera, J., Sesman, M., Woodbury, M., Huertas-Goldman, S., Pagan, A., Sanches-Lacay, A., & Moscoco, M. (1988). Estimates of the prevalence of childhood maladjustment in a community survey in Puerto Rico. *Archives of General Psychiatry, 45,* 1120–1126.

Bird, H. R., Gould, M. S., Yager, T., Staghezza, B., & Canino, G. (1989). Risk factors for maladjustment in Puerto Rican children. *Journal of the American Academy of Child and Adolescent Psychiatry, 28,* 847–850.

Birmaher, B., Axelson, D. A., Monk, K., Kalas, C., Clark, D. B., Ehmann, M., Bridge, J., Heo, J., & Brent, D. A. (2003). Fluoxetine for the treatment of childhood anxiety disorders. *Journal of the American Academy of Child and Adolescent Psychiatry, 42*, 415–423.

Birmaher, B., Brent, D. A., Chiappetta, L., Bridge, J., Monga, S., & Baugher, M. (1999). Psychometric properties of the Screen for Childhood Anxiety Related Emotional Disorders (SCARED): A replication study. *Journal of the American Academy of Child and Adolescent Psychiatry, 38*, 1230–1236.

Birmaher, B., Waterman, G. S., Ryan, N., Cully, M., Balach, L., Ingram, J., & Brodsky, M. (1994). Fluoxetine for childhood anxiety disorders. *Journal of the American Academy of Child and Adolescent Psychiatry, 33*, 993–998.

Black, B., & Robbins, D. R. (1990). Panic disorder in children and adolescents. *Journal of the American Academy of Child and Adolescent Psychiatry, 29*, 36–44.

Black, B., & Uhde, T. W. (1994). Treatment of elective mutism with fluoxetine: A double-blind placebo-controlled study. *Journal of the American Academy of Child and Adolescent Psychiatry, 33*, 1000–1006.

Blagg, N. R., & Yule, W. (1984). The behavioural treatment of school refusal: A comparative study. *Behaviour Research and Therapy, 22*, 119–127.

Blanchard, E. B., & Scharff, L. (2002). Psychosocial aspects of assessment and treatment of irritable bowel syndrome in adults and recurrent abdominal pain in children. *Journal of Consulting and Clinical Psychology, 70*, 725–737.

Blum, N. J., Barone, V. J., & Friman, P. C. (1993). A simplified behavioral treatment for trichotillomania: Report of two cases. *Pediatrics, 91*, 993–995.

Boey, C. C. M., & Goh, K. L. (2001). The significance of life-events as contributing factors in childhood recurrent abdominal pain in an urban community in Malaysia. *Journal of Psychosomatic Research, 51*, 559–562.

Bogels, S. M., van Oosten, A., Muris, P., & Smulders, D. (2001). Familial correlates of social anxiety in children and adolescents. *Behaviour Research and Therapy, 39*, 273–287.

Bogels, S. M., & Zigterman, D. (2000). Dysfunctional cognitions in children with social phobia, separation anxiety disorder, and generalized anxiety disorder. *Journal of Abnormal Child Psychology, 28*, 205–211.

Bonanno, G. A. (2004). Loss, trauma, and human resilience. *American Psychologist, 59*, 20–28.

Bondy, A., Sheslow, D., & Garcia, L. T. (1985). An investigation of children's fears and their mother's fears. *Journal of Psychopathology and Behavioral Assessment 7*, 1–12.

Borkovec, T. D. (1985). Worry: A potentially valuable concept. *Behaviour Research and Therapy, 23*, 481–482.

Bowen, R. C., Offord, D. R., & Boyle, M. H. (1990). The prevalence of overanxious disorder and separation anxiety disorder: Results from the Ontario Child Health Study. *Journal of the American Academy of Child and Adolescent Psychiatry, 29*, 753–758.

Bowlby, J. (1973). *Attachment and loss: Vol. 2. Separation anxiety and anger.* New York: Basic Books.

Boyd, R. C., Ginsburg, G. A., Lambert, S. F., Cooley, M. R., & Campbell, K. D. M. (2003). Screen for Child Anxiety Related Emotional Disorders (SCARED); Psychometric properties in an African-American parochial high school sample. *Journal of the American Academy of Child and Adolescent Psychiatry, 42*, 1188–1196.

Bradley S. J., & Hood, J. (1993). Psychiatrically referred adolescents with panic attacks: Presenting symptoms, stressors and comorbidity. *Journal of the American Academy of Child and Adolescent Psychiatry, 32*, 826–829.

Brady, E. U., & Kendall, P. C. (1992). Co-morbidity of anxiety and depression in children and adolescents. *Psychological Bulletin, 111*, 244-255.

Brent, D. A., Perper, J. A., Moritz, G., Liotus, L., Richardson, D., Canobbio. R., Schweers, J., & Roth, C. (1995).Posttraumatic stress disorder in peers of adolescent suicide victims: Predisposing factors and phenomenology. *Journal of the American Academy of Child and Adolescent Psychiatry, 34*, 209–215.

Bretherton, I., Fritz, J., Zahn-Waxler, C., & Ridgeway, D. (1986). Learning to talk about emotions: A functionalist perspective. *Child Development, 57*, 529–548.

Breton, J. J., Bergeron, L., Valla, J. P., Bertiaume, C., Gauder, N., Lambert, J., St.-Georges, M., Houde, L., & Lepine, S. (1999). Quebec child mental health survey: Prevalence of DSM-III-R mental health disorders. *Journal of Child Psychology and Psychiatry, 40*, 375–384.

Bromberg, A., Lamb, M. E., & Hwang, P. (1990). Inhibition: Its stability and correlates in sixteen to forty month old children. *Child Development, 61*, 1153–1163.

Broome, M. E., & Hellier, A. (1987). School-age children's fears of medical experiences. *Issues in Comprehensive Pediatric Nursing, 10*, 77–86.

Brown, J. B., & Lloyd, H. (1975). A controlled study of children not speaking at school. *Journal of the Association of Workers for Maladjusted Children, 3*, 49-63.

Bruch, M. A., & Heimberg, R .G., (1994). Differences in perceptions of parental and personal characteristics between generalized and nongeneralized social phobics. *Journal of Anxiety Disorders, 8*, 155–168.

Bruch, M. A., Heimberg, R. G., Berger, P., & Collins, T. M. (1989). Social phobia and perceptions of early parental and personal characteristics. *Anxiety Research, 2*, 57–63.

Bulik, C. M., Sullivan, P. F., Fear, J. L., & Joyce, P. R. (1997). Eating disorders and antecedent anxiety disorders: a controlled study. *Acta Psychiatrica Scandinavia, 96*, 101–107.

Bull, B. A., & Drotar, D. (1991). Coping with cancer in remission: Stressors and strategies reported by children and adolescents. *Journal of Pediatric Psychology, 16*, 767-782.

Burke, A. E. & Silverman, W. K. (1987). The prescriptive treatment of school refusal. *Clinical Psychology Review, 7*, 353–362.

Burke, P., Elliott, M., & Fleissner, R. (1999). Irritable bowel syndrome and recurrent abdominal pain. *Psychosomatics, 40*, 277–285.

Burke, P., Meyer, V., Kocoshis, S., Orenstein, D. M., Chandrea, R., Nord, D. J., Sauer, J., & Cohen, E. (1989). Depression and anxiety in pediatric inflammatory bowel disease and cystic fibrosis. *Journal of the American Academy of Child and Adolescent Psychiatry, 28*, 948–951.

Burke, P., Meyer, V., Kocoshis, S., Orenstein, D. M., Chandrea, R., & Sauer, J. (1989). Obsessive-compulsive symptoms in childhood inflammatory bowel disease and cystic fibrosis. *Journal of the American Academy of Child and Adolescent Psychiatry, 28*, 525–527.

Bush, J. P., & Melamed, B. G. (1983). Mother-Child Interactions During Medical Examinations. Paper presented at the 17th Annual Meeting of the Association for Advancement of Behavior Therapy, Washington, DC, December.

Bussing, R., Burket, R. C., & Kelleher, E. T. (1996). Prevalence of anxiety disorders in a clinic-based sample of pediatric asthma patients. *Psychosomatics, 37*, 108–115.

Buss, A. H., & Plomin, R. (1984). *Temperament: Early developing personality traits.* Hillsdale, NJ: Erlbaum.

Calhoun, J., & Koenig, K. P. (1973). Classroom modification of elective mutism. *Behavior Therapy, 4*, 700–702.

Campo, J. V., Perel, J., Lucas, A., Bridge, J., Ehmann, M., Kalas, C., Monk, K., Axelson, D., Birmaher, B., Ryan, N., DiLorenzo, C., & Brent, D. A. (2004). Citalopram treatment of pediatric recurrent abdominal pain and comorbid internalizing disorders: An exploratory study. *Journal of the American Academy of Child and Adolescent Psychiatry, 43*, 1234–1242.

Campos, J. J., Emde, R. N., Gaensbauer, T., & Henderson, C. (1975). Cardiac and behavioral interrelationships in the reaction of infants to strangers. *Developmental Psychology, 11*, 589–601.

Cantwell, D. P., & Baker, L. (1989). Stability and natural history of DSM-III childhood diagnoses. *Journal of the American Academy of Child and Adolescent Psychiatry, 28*, 691–700.

Caspi, A., Bem, D. J., & Elder, G. H. (1989). Continuities and consequences of interactional styles across the life course. *Journal of Personality, 57*, 375–406.

Caspi, A., Elder, G. H., & Bem, D. J. (1988). Moving away from the world: Life-course patterns of shy children. *Developmental Psychology, 24*, 824–831.

Caspi, A., & Silva, P. A. (1995). Temperamental qualities at age 3 predict personality traits in young adulthood; Longitudinal evidence from a birth cohort. *Child Development, 66*, 486–498.

Caster, J., Inderbitzen, H., & Hope, D. (1999). Relationship between youth and parent perceptions of family environment and social anxiety. *Journal of Anxiety Disorders, 13*, 237–251.

Chaan, M. (1962). School refusal. *British Journal of Educational Psychology, 32,* 201–207.

Chang, C. H., Leen, M. B., Chiang, Y. C., & Lu, Y. C. (1991). Trichotillomania: A clinical study of 36 patients. *Journal of the Formosan Medical Association, 90,* 176–180.

Chavira. D. A., & Stein, M. B. (2002). Combined psychoeducation and treatment with selective serotonin reuptake inhibitors for youth with generalized social anxiety disorder. *Journal of Child and Adolescent Child Psychopharmacology, 12,* 47–54.

Chavira, D. A., Stein, M. B., Bailey, K., & Stein, M. T. (2003). Parental opinions regarding treatment for social anxiety disorder in youth. *Journal of Developmental and Behavioral Pediatrics, 24,* 315–322.

Chazan, M. (1962). School phobia. *British Journal of Educational Psychology, 32,* 209–217.

Chen, X., Rubin, K. H., & Li, B. (1995). Social and school adjustment of shy and aggressive children in China. *Development and Psychopathology, 7,* 337–349.

Chorpita, B. F., Albano, A. M., & Barlow, D. H. (1996). Cognitive processing in children: Relation to anxiety and family influences. *Journal of Clinical Child Psychology, 25,* 170–176.

Chorpita, B. F., Tracey, S. A., Brown, T. A., Collica, T. J., & Barlow, D. H. (1997). Assessment of worry in children and adolescents: An adaptation of the Penn State Worry Questionnaire. *Behaviour Research and Therapy, 35,* 569–581.

Choudhury, M. S., Pimentel, S. S., & Kendall, P. C. (2003). Childhood anxiety disorders: Parent-child (Dis)Agreement Using a Structured Interview for the DSM-IV. *Journal of the American Academy of Child and Adolescent Psychiatry, 42,* 957–964.

Christensen, M. F., & Mortensen, O. (1975). Long-term prognosis in children with recurrent abdominal pain. *Archives of Diseases of Childhood, 50,* 110–115.

Christenson, G. A., Ristvedt, S. L., & Mackenzie, T. B. (1993). Identification of trichotillomania cue profiles. *Behaviour Research and Therapy, 31,* 315–320.

Clark, D. B. (1993). Assessment of social anxiety in adolescents. Presented at the Anxiety Disorders Association of America Annual Convention, Charleston, SC, March.

Clark, D. M. (1986). A cognitive approach to panic. *Behaviour Research and Therapy, 24,* 461–470.

Clark, D. M. (1996). Panic disorder: From theory to therapy. In P.M. Salkovskis (Ed.), *Frontiers of cognitive therapy* (pp. 318–344). New York: Guilford Press.

Cohen, J. A., Berliner, L., & March, J. (2000). Treatment of children and adolescents. In E. B. Foa, T. M. Keane, & M. J. Friedman (Eds.), *Effective treatments for PTSD* (pp. 106–138). New York: Guilford Press.

Cohen, J.A., Mannarino. A. P., & Rogal, S. (2001). Treatment practices for child posttraumatic stress disorder. *Child Abuse and Neglect, 25,* 123–135.

Cohen, L. L. (2001). Children's expectations and memories of acute distress: short-and long–term efficacy of pain management interventions. *Journal of Pediatric Psychology, 26,* 367–374.

Cohen, P., Cohen, J., & Brook, J. (1993). An epidemiological study of disorders in late childhood and adolescence. II: Persistence of disorders. *Journal of Child Psychology and Psychiatry, 34,* 869–877.

Cohen, L. J., Stein, D. B., Simeon, D., Spadaccini, E., Rosen, J. Aronowitz, B., & Hollander, E. (1995). Clinical profile, comorbidity, and treatment history in 123 hair pullers: A survey study. *Journal of Clinical Psychiatry, 56,* 319–326.

Compton, S. N., March, J. S., Brent, D, Albano, A. M., Weersing, R., & Curry, J. (2004). Cognitive-behavioral psychotherapy for anxiety and depressive disorders in children and adolescents: An evidence-based medicine review. *Journal of the American Academy of Child and Adolescent Psychiatry, 43,* 930–959.

Compton, S. C., Grant, P. J., Chrisman, A. K., Gammon, P. J., Brown, V. L. O., & March, J. S. (2001). Sertraline in children and adolescents with social anxiety disorder: An open trial. *Journal of the American Academy of Child and Adolescent Psychiatry, 40,* 564–571.

Cook, M., & Mineka, S. (1989). Observational conditioning of fear to fear-relevant versus fear-irrelevant stimuli in rhesus monkeys. *Journal of Abnormal Psychology, 98,* 448–459.

Cook, M., & Mineka, S. (1991). Selective associations in the origins of phobic fears and their implications for behavior therapy. In P. Martin (Ed.), *Handbook of behavior therapy and psychological science: An integrative approach* (pp. 413–434). Elmsford, NY: Pergamon Press

Cooley-Quille, M. R., Turner, S. M., & Beidel, D .C. (1995). Emotional impact of children's exposure to community violence: A preliminary study. *Journal of the American Academy of Child and Adolescent Psychiatry, 34,* 1362–1368.

Coolidge, J. C., Hahn, P.B., & Peck, A.L. (1957). School phobia: neurotic crisis or way of life. *American Journal of Orthopsychiatry, 27,* 296-306.

Cooper, M. (1996). Obsessive compulsive disorder: Effects on family members. *American Journal of Orthopsychiatry, 66,* 296–304.

Coplan, R. J., Prakash, K., O'Neil, K., & Armer, M. (2004). Do you "want" to play? Distinguishing between conflicted shyness and social disinterest in early childhood. *Developmental Psychology, 40,* 244–258.

Cornwall, E., Spence, S. H., & Schotte, D. (1997). The effectiveness of emotive imagery in the treatment of darkness phobia in children. *Behaviour Change, 13,* 223–229.

Costello, E. J., & Angold, A. (1995) Epidemiology. In J. S. March (Ed.) *Anxiety disorders in children and adolescents* (pp. 109–124). New York: Guilford Press.

Costello, E. J., Angold, A., Burns, B. J., Stangl, D. K., Tweed, D. L., Erkanli, A., & Worthman, C. L. (1996) The Great Smoky Mountains Study of Youth: Goals, design, methods, and the prevalence of DSM-III-R disorders. *Archives of General Psychiatry, 53,* 1129–1136.

Costello, E. J., Costello, A. J., Edelbrock, C., & Burns, B. J. (1988). Psychiatric disorders in pediatric primary care: Prevalence and risk factors. *Archives of General Psychiatry, 45,* 1107–1116.

Costello, A. J., Edelbrock, C., Kalas, R., Kessler, M., & Klaric, S. A. (1982). *Diagnostic Interview Schedule for Children (DISC).* Written under contract to the National Institute of Mental Health.

Costello, E. J., Stoudhamer–Loeber, M., & DeRosier, M. (1993). Continuity and change in psychopathology from childhood to adolescence. Paper presented at the Annual Meeting of the Society for Research in Child and Adolescent Psychopathology, Santa Fe, New Mexico. Cited in Costello, E. J., & Angold, A. (1995) Epidemiology. In J. S. March (Ed.) *Anxiety disorders in children and adolescents* (pp. 109–124). New York: Guilford Press.

Coupland, N. J. (2001). Social phobia: Etiology, neurobiology, and treatment. *Journal of Clinical Psychiatry, 62* (Suppl. 1), 25–35.

Craske, M. G., Poulton, R., Tsao, J. C. I., & Plotkin, D. (2001). Paths to panic disorder/agoraphobia: An exploratory analysis from age 3 to 21 in an unselected birth cohort. *Journal of the American Academy of Child and Adolescent Psychiatry, 40,* 556–563.

Creer, T. L. (1998). Childhood asthma. In T .H. Ollendick & M. Hersen (Eds.), *Handbook of child psychopathology* (3rd ed.) (pp.395–415.). Plenum Press: New York

Croake, J. W., & Knox, F. H. (1973). The changing nature of children's fears. *Child Study Journal, 3,* 91–105.

Crowe, R. R., Noyes, R., Persico, T., Wilson. A. F., & Elston, R. C. (1988). Genetic studies of panic disorder and related conditions. In D. L. Dunnel, E. S. Gershon, & J. E. Barrett, (Eds.), *Relatives at risk for mental disorders* (pp.73–85). New York: Raven Press.

Cunningham, C. E., Cataldo, M.F., Mallion, C., & Keyes, J. B. (1983). A review and controlled single case evaluation of behavioral approaches to the management of elective mutism. *Child and Family Behavior Therapy, 5,* 25–49.

Davey, G. C. L. (1989). Dental phobias and anxieties: Evidence for conditioning processes in the acquisition and modulation of a learned fear. *Behaviour Research and Therapy, 22,* 51–58.

Davey, G. C. L. (1997). A conditioning model of phobias. In G.C.L. Davey (Ed.), *Phobias: A handbook of theory, research and treatment* (pp.301–322). Chichester: Wiley.

Davidson, J. (1993). Childhood histories of adult social phobics. Presented at the Anxiety Disorders Association of America Annual Convention, Charleston, SC. March.

Daviss, W.B. Mooney, D., Racusin, R., Ford, J. D., Fleischer, A, & McHugo, G. J. (2000). Predicting posttraumatic stress after hospitalization for pediatric injury. *Journal of the American Academy of Child and Adolescent Psychiatry, 39,* 576–583.

De Bellis, M. D., Casey, B. J., Dahl, R. E., Birmaher, B., Williamson, D. E., Thomas, K. M., Axelson, D. A., Frustaqci, K., Boring, A. M., Hall, J. U., & Ryan, N. D. (2000). A pilot study of amygdala volumes in pediatric generalized anxiety disorder. *Biological Psychiatry, 48,* 51–57.

De Bellis, M. D., Keshavan, M., Clark, D. B., Casey, B. J., Giedd, J., Boring, A. M. Frustaci, K., & Ryan, N. D. (1999). A. E. Bennett Research Award. Developmental Traumatology Part II: Brain Development. *Biological Psychiatry, 45,* 1271–1284.

De Bellis, M. J. D., Keshavan, M., Frustaci, K., Shifflet, H., Lyengar, S. L., Beers, S. R., & Hall, J. (2002a). Superior temporal gyrus volumes in maltreated children and adolescents with PTSD. *Biological Psychiatry, 51,* 544–552.

De Bellis, M. D., Keshavan, M. S., Shifflett, H., Iyengar, S., Dahl, R. E., Axelson, D. A., Birmaher, B., Hall, J., Moritz, G., & Ryan, N. D. (2002b). Superior temporal gyrus volumes in pediatric generalized anxiety disorder. *Biological Psychiatry, 51,* 553–562.

De Haan, E., Hoogduin, K., Buitelaar, J., & Keisjers, G. (1998). Behavior therapy versus clomipramine for the treatment of obsessive-compulsive disorder. *Journal of the American Academy of Child and Adolescent Psychiatry, 37,* 1022–1029.

De Jong, P. J., Andrea, H., & Muris, P. (1997). Spider phobia in children: disgust and fear before and after treatment. *Behaviour Research and Therapy, 35,* 559–562.

DeVeaugh-Geiss, J., Moroz, G., Biederman, J., Cantwell, D., Fontaine, R., Greist, J. H., Reichler, R., Katz, R., & Landau, P. (1992). Clomipramine hydrochloride in childhood obsessive-compulsive disorder. *Journal of the American Academy of Child and Adolescent Psychiatry, 31,* 45–49.

De Wit, D. J., Macdonald, K., & Offord, D. R. (1999). Childhood stress and symptoms of drug dependence in adolescence and early adulthood. *American Journal of Orthopsychiatry, 69,* 61–72.

De Wit, D. J., Ogborne, A., Offord, D. R., & Macdonald, K. (1999). Antecedents of the risk of recovery from DSM-III-R social phobia. *Psychological Medicine, 29,* 569–582.

Deblinge, E., & Heflin, A.H. (1996). *Treating sexually abused children and their nonoffending parents: A cognitive behavioral approach.* Thousand Oaks, CA: Sage.

Delprato, D. J. & McGlynn, F. D. (1984). Behavioral theories of anxiety disorders. In S. M. Turner (Ed.), *Behavioral theories and treatment of anxiety* (pp. 1–49). New York: Plenum Press.

Denkla, M. B. (1989). The neuropsychological examination. In J. L . Rapoport (Ed.), *Obsessive-compulsive disorder in children and adolescents* (pp. 107–118). Washington, DC: American Psychiatric Press.

DeVeaugh-Geiss, J., Moroz, G., Biederman, J., Cantwell, D., Fontaine, R., Greist, J. H., Reichler, R., Katz, R., & Landau, P. (1992). Clomipramine hydrochloride in childhood and adolescent obsessive-compulsive disorder—A multicenter trial. *Journal of the American Academy of Child and Adolescent Psychiatry, 31,* 45–49.

DiNardo, P. A., Guzy, L. T., Jenkins, J. A., Bak, R.,M., Tomasi, S. F., & Copland, M. (1988). Etiology and maintenance of dog fears. *Behaviour Research and Therapy, 26,* 241–244.

Doogan, S., & Thomas, G. V. (1992). Origins of fear of dogs in adults and children: The role of conditioning processes and prior familiarity with dogs. *Behaviour Research and Therapy, 30,* 387–394.

Dong, Q., Yang, B., & Ollendick, T.H. (1994). Fears in Chinese children and adolescents and their relations to anxiety and depression. *Journal of Child Psychology and Psychiatry, 35,* 351–363.

Dow, S. P., Sonies, B. C., Scheib, D., Moss, S., & Leonard, H. L. (1995). Practical guidelines for the assessment and treatment of selective mutism. *Journal of the American Academy of Child and Adolescent Psychiatry, 34,* 836–845.

Drotar, D. (1981). Psychological perspectives in chronic childhood illness. *Journal of Pediatric Psychology, 6,* 211–228.

Dummit, E. S., Klein, R. G., Tancer, N. K., Asche, B., & Martin, J. (1996). Fluoxetine treatment of children with selective mutism: An open trial. *Journal of the American Academy of Child and Adolescent Psychiatry, 35,* 615–621.

Dummit, E. S., Klein, R. G., Tancer, N. K., Asche, B., Martin, J., & Fairbanks, J. A. (1997). Systematic assessment of 50 children with selective mutism. *Journal of the American Academy of Child and Adolescent Psychiatry, 36,* 653–660.

Durlak, J. A., Fuhrman, T., & Lampman, C. (1991). Effectiveness of cognitive-behavior therapy for maladapting children: A meta-analysis. *Psychological Bulletin, 110,* 204–214.

Eaves, L. J., Silberg, J. L., Meyer, J. M., Maes, H. H., Simonoff, E., Pickles, A., Rutter, M., Neale, M. C.,

Reynolds, C. A., Erikson, M. T., Heath, A. C., Loeber, R., Truett, K. R., & Hewitt, J. K. (1997). Genetics and developmental psychopathology:2. The main effects of genes and environment on behavioral problems in the Virginia Twin Study of Adolescent Behavioral Development. *Journal of Child Psychology and Psychiatry, 38*, 965–980.

Egger, H. L. Costello, E. J., & Angold, A. (2003). School refusal and psychiatric disorders: A community study. *Journal of the American Academy of Child and Adolescent Psychiatry, 42*, 797–807.

Ehrenreich, J. T., & Gross, A. M. (2001). Treatment of childhood generalized anxiety disorder/overanxious disorder. In Orvaschel, H. & Faust, J. *Handbook of conceptualization and treatment of child psychopathology* (pp. 211–238). Amsterdam, Netherlands: Elsevier Science Ltd.

Eisen, A. R., & Silverman, W. K. (1993). Should I relax or change my thoughts? *Journal of Cognitive Psychotherapy, 7*, 265–279.

Eisen, A. R., & Silverman, W. K. (1998). Prescriptive treatment for generalized anxiety disorder in children. *Behavior Therapy, 29*, 105–121.

Ekman, P., Roper, G., & Hager, J. C. (1980). Deliberate facial movement. *Child Development, 51*, 886–891.

Eli, I., Uziel, N., Baht, R., & Kleinhauz, M. (1997). Antecedents of dental anxiety: Learned responses versus personality traits. *Community Dentistry and Oral Epidemiology, 25*, 233–237.

Elizer, Y., & Perednik, R. (2003). Prevalence and description of selective mutism in immigrant and native families: A controlled study. *Journal of the American Academy of Child and Adolescent Psychiatry, 42*, 1451–1459.

Eme, R., & Schmidt, D. (1978). The stability of children's fears. *Child Development, 49*, 1277–1279.

Enzer, N. B., & Walker, P. A. (1967). Hyperventilation syndrome in childhood: A review of 44 cases. *Journal of Pediatrics, 70*, 521–532.

Esman, A. (1989). Psychoanalysis in general psychiatry: Obsessive-compulsive disorder as a paradigm. *Journal of the American Academy of Child and Adolescent Psychiatry, 37*, 319–336.

Essau, C. A. (2000). Frequency, comorbidity and psychosocial impairment of anxiety disorders in German adolescents. *Journal of Anxiety Disorders, 14*, 263–279.

Essau, C. A., Conradt, J., & Petermann, F. (1999). Frequency and comorbidity of social phobia and social fears in adolescents. *Behaviour Research and Therapy, 37*, 831–843.

Essau, C. A., Conradt, J., & Petermann, F. (1999). Frequency of panic attacks and panic disorder in adolescents. *Depression and Anxiety, 9*, 10–26.

Essau, C.A., Conradt, J., & Petermann, F. (2000). Frequency, comorbidity, and psychosocial impairment of specific phobia in adolescents. *Journal of Clinical Child Psychology, 29*, 221–231.

Evans, D. W., Leckman, J. F., Carter, A., Reznick, J. S., Henshaw, D., King, R. A., & Pauls, D. L. (1997). Ritual, habit and perfectionism: the prevalence and development of compulsive behavior in normal young children. *Child Development, 68*, 58–68.

Eysenck, H. J. (1976). The learning theory model of neurosis: A new approach. *Behaviour Research and Therapy, 14*, 251–267.

Eysenck, H. J. (1979). The conditioning model of neurosis. *Behaviour and Brain Sciences, 2*, 155–199.

Fairbanks, J. M., Pine, D. S., Tancer, N. K., Dummit, E. S., Kentgen, L. M., Martin, J., Asche, B. K., & Klein, R. G. (1997). Open fluoxetine treatment of mixed anxiety disorder in children and adolescents. *Journal of Child and Adolescent Psychopharmacology, 7*, 17–29.

Famularo, R., Fenton, T., Augustyn, M., & Zuckerman, B. (1996). Persistence of pediatric posttraumatic stress after two years. *Child Abuse and Neglect, 20*, 1245–1248.

Faravelli, C., & Pallanti, S. (1989). Recent life events and panic disorder. *American Journal of Psychiatry, 146*, 622–626.

Faust, J., & Melamed, B. G. (1984). Influence of arousal, previous experience, and age on surgery preparation of same day of surgery and in-hospital pediatric patients. *Journal of Consulting and Clinical Psychology, 52*, 359–365.

Feehan, M., McGee, R., & Williams, S. M. (1993). Mental health disorders from age15 to 18 years. *Journal of the American Academy of Child and Adolescent Psychiatry, 32*, 1118–1126.

Fergusson, D. M., Horwood. L. J., & Lynsky, M. T. (1993). Prevalence and comorbidity of DSM-III-R diagnoses in a birth cohort of 15 year olds. *Journal of the American Academy of Child and Adolescent Psychiatry, 31*, 243–263.

Ferrell, C., Beidel, D. C., & Turner, S. M. (2001). A scale to determine the effectiveness of treatment for childhood social phobia. Unpublished manuscript, University of Maryland-College Park.

Ferrell, C., Beidel, D. C., & Turner, S. M. (2004). Assessment and treatment of socially phobic children: A cross cultural comparison. *Journal of Clinical Child and Adolescent Psychology, 33*, 260–268.

Field, A. P., & Davey, G. C. L. (2001). Conditioning models of childhood anxiety. In W. K. Silverman and P. D. A. Treffers (Eds.), *Anxiety disorders in children and adolescents* (pp. 187–211). New York: Cambridge University Press

Finney, J. W., Lemanek, K. L., Cataldo, M. F., Katz, H. P., & Fuqua, R. W. (1989). Pediatric psychology in primary health care: Brief targeted therapy for recurrent abdominal pain. *Behavior Therapy, 20*, 283–291.

Flakierska, N., Lindstrom, M., & Gillberg, C. (1988). School refusal: A 15–20 year follow-up study of 35 Swedish children. *British Journal of Psychiatry, 152*, 834–837.

Flakierska–Praquin, N., Lindstrom, M., & Gillberg, C. (1997). School phobia with separation anxiety disorder: A comparative 20 to 29–year follow-up study of 35 school refusers. *Comprehensive Psychiatry, 38*, 17–22.

Flament, M. F., Koby, E., Rapoport, J. L., Berg, C. J., Zahn, T., Cox, C., Denckla, M., & Lenane, M. (1990). Childhood obsessive–compulsive disorder: a prospective follow–up study. *Journal of Child Psychology and Psychiatry, 31*, 363–380.

Flament, M. F., Rapoport, J. L., Berg, C. J., Sceery, W., Kilts, C., Mellstrom, B., & Linnoila, M. (1985). Clomipramine treatment of childhood obsessive–compulsive disorder: A double blind controlled study. *Archives of General Psychiatry, 42*, 977–983.

Flament, M. F., Rapoport, J. L., Murphy, D. L., Berg, C. J., & Lake, R. (1987). Biochemical changes during clomipramine treatment of childhood obsessive-compulsive disorder. *Archives of General Psychiatry, 44*, 219–225.

Flament, M. F., Whitaker, A., Rapoport, J. L., Davies, M., Zaremba Berg, C., Kalikow, K., Sceery, W., & Shaffer, D. (1988). Obsessive compulsive disorder in adolescence: An epidemiological study. *Journal of the American Academy of Child and Adolescent Psychiatry, 27*, 764–771.

Flannery-Schroeder, E. C., & Kendall, P. C. (2000). Group and individual cognitive-behavioral treatments for youth with anxiety disorders: A randomized clinical trial. *Cognitive Therapy and Research, 24*, 251–278.

Flavell, J. H., Flavell, E. R., & Green, F. L. (2001). Developments of children's understanding of connections between thinking and feeling. *Psychological Science, 12*, 430–432.

Flavell, J. H., Green, F. L., Flavell, E. R., & Grossman, J. B. (1997). The development of children's knowledge about inner speech. *Child Development, 68*, 39–47.

Foa, E. B., Johnson, K. M., & Treadwell, K. R. H. (2001). The child PTSD Symptom Scale: A preliminary examination of its psychometric properties. *Journal of Clinical Child Psychology, 30*, 376–384.

Foa, E. B., & Kozak, M. J. (1995). DSM-IV field trial: Obsessive-compulsive disorder. *American Journal of Psychiatry, 152*, 90–96.

Foley, D. L., Pickles, A., Maes, H. M., Silberg, J. L., & Eaves, L. J. (2004). Course and short-term outcomes of separation anxiety disorder in a community sample of twins. *Journal of the American Academy of Child and Adolescent Psychiatry, 43*, 1107–1114.

Foley, D., Rutter, M., Pickles, A., Angold, A., Maes, H., Silberg, J., & Eaves, L. (2004). Informant disagreement for separation anxiety disorder. *Journal of the American Academy of Child and Adolescent Psychiatry, 43*, 452–460.

Fonseca, A. C., & Perrin, S. (2001). Clinical phenomenology, classification, and assessment of anxiety disorders in children and adolescents. In W.K. Silverman and P.D.A. Treffers (Eds.), *Anxiety disorders in children and adolescents* (pp. 126–158). Cambridge, UK: Cambridge University Press

Fonseca, A. C., Yule, W., & Erol, N. (1994). Cross-cultural issues. In T. H. Ollendick, N. J. King, & W. Yule (Eds.), *International handbook of phobic and anxiety disorders in children and adolescents* (pp.67-84). New York: Plenum Press.

Fordham, K., & Stevenson-Hinde, J. (1999). Shyness, friendship quality and adjustment during middle childhood. *Journal of Child Psychology and Psychiatry, 40*, 757–768.

Foxx, R. M., & Bechtel, D. R. (1982). Overcorrection. *Progress in Behavioral Modification, 13*, 227–281.

Francis, G., Last, C. G., & Strauss, C. C. (1987). Expression of separation anxiety disorder: The roles of age and gender. *Child Psychiatry and Human Development, 18*, 82–89.

Freeman, J. B., Garcia, A. M., Miller, L. M., Dow, S. P., & Leonard, H. L. (2004). Selective mutism. In T. L. Morris & J. S. March (Eds.), *Anxiety disorders in children and adolescents* (2nd ed., pp. 280–301). New York: Guilford Press.

Fremont, W. P. (2004). Childhood reactions to terrorism–induced trauma: A review of the past 10 years. *Journal of the American Academy of Child and Adolescent Psychiatry, 43*, 381–392.

Freud, S. (1975). Analysis of a phobia in a five-year-old boy. In *The standard edition of the complete works of Sigmund Freud* (7th ed., Vol. 10, pp. 5–149). London: The Hogarth Press and the Institute of Psycho-analysis. (Original work published 1909)

Friedman, A. G., Latham, S. A., & Dahlquist, L. M. (1998). Childhood cancer. In T.H. Ollendick, & M. Hersen (Eds.), *Handbook of child psychopathology* (3rd ed., pp. 435–461). New York: Plenum Press.

Friedman, A. G., & Ollendick, T. H. (1989). Treatment programs for severe night-time fears: A methodological note. *Journal of Behavior Therapy and Experimental Psychiatry, 20*, 171–178.

Fung, D. S. S., Manassis, K., Kenny, A., & Fiksenbaum, L. (2002). Web based CBT for selective mutism. *Journal of the American Academy of Child and Adolescent Psychiatry, 39*, 721–726.

Fyer, A. J., Mannuzza, S., Chapman, T. F., Martin, L. Y., & Klein, D. F. (1995). Specificity in familial aggregation of phobic disorders. *Archives of General Psychiatry, 52*, 564–573.

Garber, J., Zeman, J., & Walker, L. S. (1990). Recurrent abdominal pain in children: Psychiatric diagnoses and parental psychopathology. *Journal of the American Academy of Child and Adolescent Psychiatry, 29*, 648–656.

Garcia-Coll, C., Kagan, J., & Reznick, J. S.(1984). Behavioral inhibition in young children. *Child Development, 55*, 1005-1019.

Garland, E. J., & Smith, D. H. (1990). Panic disorder in a child psychiatric consultation service. *Journal of the American Academy of Child and Adolescent Psychiatry, 29*, 785–788

Garrison, W. T., & Earls, F. J. (1987). *Temperamental and child psychopathology.* Newbury Park, CA: Sage.

Geller, D. A., Biederman, J., Faraone, S. V., Cradock, K., Hagermoser, L., Aman, N., Frazier, J. A., Coffey, B. J., & Spencer, T. J. (2002). Attention-deficit/hyperactivity disorder in children and adolescents with obsessive-compulsive disorder: Fact or artifact? *Journal of the American Academy of Child and Adolescent Psychiatry, 41*, 52–58.

Geller, D., Biederman, J., Jones, J., Park, K., Schwartz, S., Shapiro, S., & Coffey, B. (1998). Is juvenile obsessive-compulsive disorder a developmental subtype of the disorder? *Journal of the American Academy of Child and Adolescent Psychiatry, 37*, 420–427.

Geller, D. A., Hoog, S. L., Heiligenstein, J. H., Riadi, R. K., Tamura, R., Kluszynski, S., Jacobson, J. G., & the Fluoxetine Pediatric OCD Study Team (2001). Fluoxetine treatment for obsessive-compulsive disorder in children and adolescents: A placebo-controlled clinical trial. *Journal of the American Academy of Child and Adolescent Psychiatry, 40*, 773–779.

Geller, D. A., Wagner, K. D., Emslie, G., Murphy, T., Carpenter, D. J., Wetherhold, E., Perera, P., Machin, A., & Gardiner, C. (2004). Paroxetine treatment in children and adolescents with obsessive-compulsive disorder: A randomized, multicenter, double-blind, placebo-controlled trial. *Journal of the American Academy of Child and Adolescent Psychiatry, 43*, 1387–1396.

Gerull, F. C., & Rapee, R. M. (2002). Mother knows best: Effects of maternal modeling on the acquisition of fear and avoidance behaviour in toddlers. *Behaviour Research and Therapy, 40*, 279––287.

Gest, S. D. (1997). Behavioral inhibition: Stability and association with adaptation from childhood to early adulthood. *Journal of Personality and Social Psychology, 72*, 467–475.

Giaconia, R. M., Reinherz, H. Z., Silverman, A. B., Pakiz, B., Frost, A. K, & Cohen, E. (1995). Traumas and posttraumatic stress disorder in a community population of older adolescents. *Journal of the American Academy of Child and Adolescent Psychiatry, 34,* 1369–1380.

Gilbert, A. R., Moore, G. J., Keshavan, M. S., Paulson, L. A. D., Narula, V., MacMaster, F. P., Stewart, C. M., & Rosenberg, D. R. (2000). Decrease in thalamic volumes of pediatric patients with obsessive-compulsive disorder who are taking paroxetine. *Archives of General Psychiatry, 57,* 449–456.

Ginsburg, G. S., & Drake, K. L. (2002a). Anxiety sensitivity and panic attack symptomatology among low-income African-American adolescents. *Journal of Anxiety Disorders, 16,* 83–96.

Ginsburg, G. S., & Drake, K. L. (2002b). School-based treatment for anxious African–American adolescents: A controlled pilot study. *Journal of the American Academy of Child and Adolescent Psychiatry, 41,* 768–775.

Ginsburg, G .S., & Silverman, W. K. (1996). Phobic and anxiety disorders in Hispanic and Caucasian youth. *Journal of Anxiety Disorders, 10,* 517–528.

Gittelman, R., & Klein, D. F. (1984). Relationship between separation anxiety and panic and agoraphobic disorders. *Psychopathology, 17* (Suppl. 1), 56–65.

Goenjian, A. K., Pynoos, R. S., Steinberg, A. M., Najarian, L. M., Asarnow, J. R., Karaya, I., Ghurabi. M., & Fairbanks, L. A. (1995). Psychiatric comorbidity in children after the 1988 earthquake in Armenia. *Journal of the American Academy of Child and Adolescent Psychiatry, 34,* 1174–1184.

Gorman, J. M., & Gorman, L. F. (1987). Drug treatment of social phobia. *Journal of Affective Disorders, 13,* 183–192.

Graae, F., Milner, J., Rizzotto, L., & Klein, R. G. (1994). Clonazepam in childhood anxiety disorders. *Journal of the American Academy of Child and Adolescent Psychiatry, 33,* 372–376.

Grad, L. R., Pelcovitz, D., Olson, M., Matthews, M., & Grad, G. J. (1987). Obsessive-compulsive symptomatology in children with Tourette's Syndrome. *Journal of the American Academy of Child and Adolescent Psychiatry, 26,* 69–73.

Grannell de Aldez, E., Feldman, L., Vivas, E., & Gelfand, D. M. (1987). Characteristics of Venezualan school refusers: Toward the development of a high risk profile. *Journal of Nervous and Mental Disease, 175,* 401–407.

Graziano, A. M., DeGiovanni, I. S., & Garcia, K. A. (1979). Behavioral treatment of children's fears: A review. *Psychological Bulletin, 86,* 804–830.

Graziano, A. M., & Mooney, K. C. (1980). Family self-control instruction for children's nighttime fear reduction. *Journal of Consulting and Clinical Psychology, 48,* 206–213.

Graziano, A. M., & Mooney, K. C. (1982). Behavioral treatment of "Nightfears" in children: Maintenance of improvement at 2½–3-year follow-up. *Journal of Consulting and Clinical Psychology, 50,* 598–599.

Green, B. L., Grace, M. C., Vary, M. G., Kramer, T. L., Gleser, G. C., & Leonard, A. C. (1994). Children of disaster in the second decade: A 17-year follow-up of Buffalo Creek Survivors. *Journal of the American Academy of Child and Adolescent Psychiatry, 33,* 71–79.

Green, B. L., Korol, M., Grace, M. C., Vary, M. G., Leonard, A. C., Gleser, G. C., & Smitson-Cohen S. (1991). Children and disaster: Age, gender, and parental effects on PTSD symptoms. *Journal of the American Academy of Child and Adolescent Psychiatry, 30,* 945–951.

Greenbaum, P. E., Cook, E. W., Melamed, B. G., Abeles, L. A., & Bush, J. P. (1988) Sequential patterns of medical stress: Maternal agitation and child distress. *Child and Family Behavior Therapy, 10,* 9–18.

Grillon, C., Dierker, L., & Merikangas, K. R. (1998). Fear-potentiated startle in adolescent offspring of parents with anxiety disorders. *Biological Psychiatry, 44,* 990–997.

Grills, A. E., & Ollendick, T. (2002). Issues in parent-child agreement: The case of structured diagnostic interviews. *Clinical Child and Family Psychology Review, 5,* 57–83.

Grills, A. E., & Ollendick, T. H. (2003). Multiple informant agreement and the Anxiety Disorders Interview Schedule for Parents and Children. *Journal of the American Academy of Child and Adolescent Psychiatry, 42,* 30–40.

Gullone, E., & King, N. J. (1993). The fears of youth in the 1990s; Contemporary normative data. *Journal of Genetic Psychology, 154,* 137–153.

Gullone, E., & King, N. J. (2001). Self-reported anxiety in children and adolescents: A three year follow-up study. *Journal of Genetic Psychology, 162*, 5–20.

Gurwitch, R. H., Kees, M., & Becker, S. M. (2002). In the face of tragedy: Placing children's reactions to trauma in a new context. *Cognitive and Behavioral Practice, 9*, 286–295.

Guy, W. (1976). *ECDEU assessment manual for psychopharmacology.* Washington, DC: DHEW

Haggerty, R. (1986). The changing nature of pediatrics. In N. A. Krasnegor, J. D. Arateh, & M. F. Cataldo (Eds.), *Child health behavior: A behavioral pediatrics perspective* (pp. 9–16). New York: Wiley.

Hamburger, S. D., Swedo, S., Whitaker, A., Davies, M., & Rapoport, J.L. (1989). Growth rate in adolescents with obsessive–compulsive disorder. *American Journal of Psychiatry, 146*, 652–655.

Hamilton, M. (1959). The assessment of anxiety states by rating. *British Journal of Medical Psychology, 32*, 50–55.

Hanna, G. L. (1995). Demographic and clinical features of obsessive-compulsive disorder in children and adolescents. *Journal of the American Academy of Child and Adolescent Psychiatry, 34*, 19–27.

Hanna, G. L. (1997). Trichotillomania and related disorders in children and adolescents. *Child Psychiatry and Human Development, 27*, 255–268.

Hansen, C., Sanders, S.L., Massaro, S., & Last, C. G. (1998). Predictors of severity of absenteeism in children with anxiety–based school refusal. *Journal of Clinical Child Psychology, 27*, 246–254

Harter, S. (1990). Issues in the assessment of the self-concept of children and adolescents. In A.M. LaGreca (Ed.), *Through the eyes of the child: Obtaining self-reports from children and adolescents* (pp. 292–325). Boston: Allyn & Bacon.

Hayward, C., Killen, J. D., Hammer, L. D., Litt, I. F., Wilson, D., Simonds, B., & Taylor, C. B. (1992). Pubertal stage and panic attack history in sixth- and seventh-grade girls. *American Journal of Psychiatry, 149*, 1239–1243.

Hayward, C., Killen, J. D., Kraemer, H. C., & Taylor, C. B. (1998). Linking self–reported childhood behavioral inhibition to adolescent social phobia. *Journal of the American Academy of Child and Adolescent Psychiatry, 37*, 1308–1315.

Hayward, C., Killen, J. D., Kraemer, H. C., & Taylor, C. B. (2000). Predictors of panic attacks in adolescents. *Journal of the American Academy of Child and Adolescent Psychiatry, 39*, 207–214.

Hayward, C., Killen, J. D., & Taylor, C. B. (1989). Panic attacks in young adolescents. *American Journal of Psychiatry, 146*, 1061–1063.

Hayward, C., Varady, S., Albano, A.M., Thienemann, M., Henderson, L., & Schatzberg, A. F. (2000). Cognitive-behavioral group therapy for social phobia in female adolescents: Results of a pilot study. *Journal of the American Academy of Child and Adolescent Psychiatry, 39*, 721–726.

Hayward, C., Wilson, K. A., Lagle, K., Killen, J. D., & Taylor, C. B. (2004). Parent–reported predictors of adolescent panic attacks. *Journal of the American Academy of Child and Adolescent Psychiatry, 43*, 613–620.

Heimberg, R .G., Dodge, C. S., Hope, D. A., Kennedy, C. R., Zollo, R., & Becker, R. E. (1990). Cognitive-behavioral group treatment for social phobia: Comparison to a credible placebo control. *Cognitive Therapy and Research, 14*, 1–23.

Heiser, N. A., Turner, S. M., & Beidel, D. C. (2003). Shyness: Relationship to social phobia and other psychiatric disorders. *Behaviour Research and Therapy, 41*, 209–221.

Henin, A., & Kendall, P. C. (1997). Obsessive-compulsive disorder in childhood and adolescence. In T. H. Ollendick & R. J . Prins (Eds.), *Advances in Clinical Child Psychology, 19*, 75–131.

Henker, B., Whalen, C. K., & O'Neil, R. (1995). Worldly and workaday worries: Contemporary concerns of children and young adolescents. *Journal of Abnormal Child Psychology, 23*, 685–702.

Herman, S. P., Stickler, G. B., & Lucas, A.R. (1981). Hyperventilation syndrome in children and adolescents: Long-term follow-up. *Pediatrics, 67*, 183–187.

Heyne, D., King, N. J., Tonge, B., Rollings, S., Pritchard, M., Young, D., & Myerson, N. (1998). The Self-Efficacy Questionnaire for School Situations: Development and psychometric evaluation. *Behaviour Change, 15*, 31–40.

Hibbs. E. D., Hamburger, S. D., Lenane, M., Rapoport, J. L., Kruesi, M. J. P., Keysor, C. S., & Goldstein, M. J. (1991). Determinants of expressed emotion in families of disturbed and normal children. *Journal of Child Psychology and Psychiatry, 32*, 757–770.

Hill, J. H., Liebert, R. M., & Mott, D. E. W. (1968). Vicarious extinction of avoidance behavior through films: An initial test. *Psychological Reports, 22*, 192.

Hirshfeld, D. R., Biederman, J., Brody, L., Faraone, S. V., & Rosenbaum, J. F. (1997). Expressed emotion toward children with behavioral inhibition: Associations with maternal anxiety disorder. *Journal of the American Academy of Child and Adolescent Psychiatry, 36*, 910–917.

Hofmann, S. G., Albano, A. M., Heimberg, R. G., Tracey, S., Chorpita, B. F., & Barlow, D. H. (1999). Subtypes of social phobia in adolescents. *Depression and Anxiety, 9*, 15–18.

Hollingsworth, C., Tanguay, E., Grossman, L., & Pabst, P. (1980). Long-term outcome of obsessive-compulsive disorder in childhood. *Journal of the American Academy of Child and Adolescent Psychiatry, 19*, 134–144.

Honjo, S., Hirano, C., Murase, S., & Kaneko, T.(1989). Obsessive-compulsive symptoms in childhood and adolescence. *Acta Psychiatrica Scandinavia, 80*, 83–91.

Hotopf, M., Carr, S., Mayou, R., Wadsworth, M., & Wessely, S. (1998). Why do children have chronic abdominal pain, and what happens to them when they grow up? *British Journal of Medicine, 316*, 1196–2000.

Hudson, J. L., & Rapee, R. M. (2001). Parent-child interactions and anxiety disorders: An observational study. *Behaviour Research and Therapy, 39*, 1411–1427.

Hudson. K. L., & Rapee, R. M. (2002). Parent child interactions in clinically anxious children and their siblings. *Journal of Clinical Child and Adolescent Psychology, 31*, 548–555.

Hummel, R. M., & Gross, A. M. (2001). Socially anxious children: An observational study of parent-child interaction. *Child & Family Behavior Therapy, 23*, 19–41.

Hyams, P. E., Burke, G., Davis, P. M., Rzepski, B., & Andrulonis, P. A. (1996). Abdominal pain and irritable bowel syndrome in adolescents: A community-based study. *Journal of Pediatrics, 129*, 220–226.

Ingman, K. A., Ollendick, T. H., & Akande, A. (1999). Cross-cultural aspects of fears in African children and adolescents. *Behaviour Research and Therapy, 37*, 337–345.

Insel, T., Murphy, D., Cohen, R., Alterman, I. L., Kilts, C., & Linnoila, M. (1983). Obsessive-compulsive disorder in five US communities. *Archives of General Psychiatry, 40*, 605–612.

Izard, C. (1994). Intersystem connections. In P. Ekman & R. Davidson (Eds.), *The nature of emotion: Fundamental questions* (pp. 345–375). New York: Oxford University

Jackson, J. L., O'Malley, P. G., Tomkins, G., Balden, E., Santoro, J., & Kroenke, K. (2000). Treatment of functional gastrointestinal disorders with antidepressant medications: A meta-analysis. *American Journal of Medicine, 108*, 65–72.

Janet, P. (1903). *Les obsessions et la psychiasthenie*. Paris: Felix Arcan.

Jaspers, J. P. (1996). The diagnosis and psychopharmacological treatment of trichotillomania: A review. *Pharmacopsychiatry, 29*, 115–120.

Jay, S. M., Ozolins, M., Elliott, C. H., & Caldwell, S. (1983). Assessment of children's distress during painful medical procedures. *Health Psychology, 2*, 133–147.

Jenkins, E. J., & Bell, C. C. (1994). Violence among inner city high school students and posttraumatic stress disorder. In S. Friedman (Ed.), *Anxiety disorders in African Americans* (pp. 76–88). New York: Springer.

Jersild, A. T., & Holmes, F. B. (1935). Methods of overcoming children's fears. *Journal of Psychology, 1*, 75–104.

Jetty, P. V., Charney, D. S., & Goddard, A. W. (2001). Neurobiology of generalized anxiety disorder. *Psychiatric Clinics of North America, 24*, 75–97.

Johnson, A. M., Falstein, E. I., Szurek, S. A., & Svendsen, M. (1941). School phobia. *American Journal of Orthopsychiatry, 11*, 702–711.

Johnson, S. B. (1995). Insulin-dependent diabetes mellitus in childhood. In M. Roberts (Ed.), *Handbook of pediatric psychology* (2nd ed., pp. 263–285). New York: Guilford Press.

Johnson, S. B., & Melamed, B. G. (1979). The assessment and treatment of children's fear. In B. B. Lahey & A. E. Kazdin (Eds.), *Advances in Clinical Child Psychology*, (vol. 2; pp. 107–139). New York: Plenum Press.

Johnson, S. B., Riley, W., Hansen, C., & Nurick, M. (1990). Psychological impact of islet cell-antibody screening: Preliminary results. *Diabetes Care, 13*, 93–97.

Johnson, S. B., & Tercyak, K. (1995). Psychological impact of islet cell-antibody screening for IDDM on children, adults and their family members. *Diabetes Care, 18*, 1370–1372.

Jones, M. C., (1924). The elimination of children's fears. *Journal of Experimental Psychology, 7*, 382–390.

Jones, R. T., Ollendick. T. H., McLaughlin, K. J., & Williams, C. E. (1989). Elaborative and behavioral rehearsal in the acquisition of fire emergency skills and the reduction of fear of fire. *Behavior Therapy, 20*, 93–101.

Joorabchi, B. (1977). Expressions of the hyperventilation syndrome in childhood. *Clinical Pediatrics, 16*, 1110–1115.

Kagan, J., Reznick, J. S., Clarke, C., Snidman, N., & Garcia-Coll, C. (1984). Behavioral inhibition to the unfamiliar. *Child Development, 55*, 2212–2225.

Kagan, J., Reznick, J. S., & Snidman, N. (1988). Biological bases of childhood shyness. *Science, 240*, 167–171.

Kagan, J., Reznick, J. S., Snidman, N. Gibbons, J., & Johnson, M. O. (1988). Childhood derivatives of inhibition and lack of inhibition to the unfamiliar. *Child Development, 59*, 1580–1589.

Kahn, C., & Henderson, C. W. (2000). Venlafaxine significantly effective for children and adolescents. *Pain and Central Nervous System Week, June 10*, 11–14.

Kane, M. T., & Kendall, P. C. (1989). Anxiety disorders in children: A multiple-baseline evaluation of a cognitive–behavioral treatment. *Behavior Therapy, 20*, 499–508.

Kanfer, F. H., Karoly, P., & Newman, A. (1975). Reduction of children's fear of the dark by competence-related and situational threat–related verbal cues. *Journal of Consulting and Clinical Psychology, 43*, 251–258.

Kashani, J. H., Beck, N. C., Hoeper, E. W., Fallahi, C., Corcoran, C. M., McAllister, J. A., Rosenberg, T. K., & Reid, J. C. (1987). Psychiatric disorders in a community sample of adolescents. *American Journal of Psychiatry, 144*, 584–589.

Kashani, J. H., & Orvaschel, H. (1988). Anxiety disorders in mid-adolescence: A community sample. *American Journal of Psychiatry, 145*, 960–964.

Kashani, J. H., & Orvaschel, H. (1990). A community study of anxiety in children and adolescents. *American Journal of Psychiatry, 147*, 313–318.

Kassam-Adams, N., & Winston, F. K. (2004). Predicting child PTSD: The relationship between acute stress disorder and PTSD in injured children. *Journal of the American Academy of Child and Adolescent Psychiatry, 43*, 403–411.

Katz, E. R., Kellerman, J., & Siegel, S. E. (1980). Behavioral distress in children with cancer undergoing medical procedures: Developmental considerations. *Journal of Consulting and Clinical Psychology, 48*, 356–365.

Kearney, C. A. (1993). Depression and school refusal behavior: A review with comments on classification and treatment. *Journal of School Psychology, 31*, 267–279

Kearney, C. A. (1995). School refusal behavior. In A. R. Eisen, C. A. Kearney, & C. E. Shaeffer (Eds.), *Clinical handbook for treating fear and anxiety in children and adolescents* (pp. 19–52). Northvale, NJ: Jason Aronson.

Kearney, C. A. (2002). Identifying the function of school refusal behavior: A revision of the School Refusal Assessment Scale. *Journal of Psychopathology and Behavioral Assessment, 24*, 235–245.

Kearney, C. A., & Albano, A. M. (2004). The functional profiles of school refusal behavior. *Behavior Modification, 28*, 147–162.

Kearney, C. A., Albano, A. M., Eisen, A. R., Allan, W. D., & Barlow, D. H. (1997). The phenomenology of panic disorder in youngsters: An empirical study of a clinical sample. *Journal of Anxiety Disorders, 11*, 49–62.

Kearney, C. A., & Beasley, J. F. (1994). The clinical treatment of school refusal behavior : A survey of referral and practice characteristics. *Psychology in the Schools, 31*, 128–132.

Kearney, C. A., Eisen, A. R., & Silverman, W. K. (1995). The legend and myth of school phobia. *School Psychology Quarterly, 10*, 65–85.

Kearney, C. A., & Silverman, W. K. (1990). A preliminary analysis of a functional model of assessment and treatment for school refusal behavior. *Behavior Modification, 14*, 344–360.

Kearney, C. A., & Silverman, W. K. (1999). Functionally–based prescriptive and nonprescriptive treatment for children and adolescents with school refusal behavior. *Behavior Therapy, 30,* 673–695.

Kearney, C. A., Sims, K. E., Pursell, C. R., & Tillotson, C. A. (2003). Separation anxiety disorder in young children: A longitudinal and family analysis. *Journal of Clinical Child and Adolescent Psychology, 32,* 593–598.

Keller, M. B., Lavori, P. W., Wunder, J., Beardslee, W. R., Schwartz, C. E., & Roth, J. (1992). Chronic course of anxiety disorders in children and adolescents. *Journal of the American Academy of Child and Adolescent Psychiatry, 31,* 595–599.

Kendall, P. C. (1994). Treating anxiety disorders in children: Results of a randomized clinical trial. *Journal of Consulting and Clinical Psychology, 62,* 100–110.

Kendall, P. C., Brady, E. U., & Verduin, T. L. (2001). Comorbidity in childhood anxiety disorders and treatment outcome. *Journal of the American Academy of Child and Adolescent Psychiatry, 40,* 787–794.

Kendall, P. C., & Chansky, T. E. (1991). Considering cognition in anxiety-disordered children. *Journal of Anxiety Disorders, 5,* 167–185.

Kendall, P. C., Flannery-Schroeder, E., Panichelli-Mindel, S., Southam—Grow, M., Henin, A., & Warman, M. (1997). Therapy for youths with anxiety disorders: A second randomized clinical trial. *Journal of Consulting and Clinical Psychology, 65,* 366–380.

Kendall, P. C., Krain, A., & Treadwell, K. R. H. (1999). Generalized anxiety disorders. In R. T. Ammerman & M. Hersen (Eds.), *Handbook of prescriptive treatments for children and adolescents* (2nd ed., pp. 155–171). Boston: Allyn & Bacon.

Kendall, P. C., Safford, S., Flannery-Schroeder, E., & Webb, A. (2004). Child anxiety treatment: Outcomes in adolescence and impact on substance use and depression at 7.4-year follow-up. *Journal of Consulting and Clinical Psychology, 72,* 276–287.

Kendall, P. C. & Southam-Gerow, M. A. (1996). Long-term follow-up of a cognitive-behavioral therapy for anxious youth. *Journal of Consulting and Clinical Psychology, 62,* 724–730.

Kendler, K. S., Neale, M. C., Kessler, R. C., Heath, A. C., & Eaves, L. J. (1992). Generalized anxiety disorder in women: A population-based twin study. *Archives of General Psychiatry, 49,* 262–272.

Kendler, K. S., Neale, M. C., Kessler, R. C., Heath, A. C., & Eaves, L. J. (1993). Major depression and phobias: The genetic and environmental sources of comorbidity. *Psychological Medicine, 23,* 361–371.

Kendler, K. S., Walters, E. E., Neale, M. C., Kessler, R. C., Heath, A. C., & Eaves, L. J. (1995). The structure of the genetic and environmental risk factors for six major psychiatric disorders in women. *Archives of General Psychiatry, 52,* 374–383.

Kennedy, W. A. (1961). School phobia: Rapid treatment of fifty cases. *Journal of Abnormal Psychology, 70,* 285–289.

Kerr, M., Lambert, W., & Bem, D. J. (1996). Life course sequelae of childhood shyness in Sweden: Comparison with the United States. *Developmental Psychology, 32,* 1100–1105.

King, N. J., & Bernstein, G. A. (2001). School refusal in children and adolescents: A review of the past 10 years. *Journal of the American Academy of Child and Adolescent Psychiatry, 40,* 197–205.

King, N. J., Eleonora, G., & Ollendick, T. H. (1998). Etiology of childhood phobias: Current status of Rachman's three pathways theory. *Behaviour Research and Therapy, 36,* 297–309.

King. N. J., & Gullone, E. (1990). Fear of AIDS: Self-reports of Australian children and adolescents. *Psychological Reports, 66,* 245–246.

King, N. J., Gullone, E., Tonge, B. J., & Ollendick, T. H. (1993). Self-reports of panic attacks and manifest anxiety in adolescents. *Behaviour Research and Therapy, 31,* 111–116.

King, N. J., & Ollendick, T. H. (1989). School refusal: Graduated and rapid behavioral treatment strategies. *Australian and New Zealand Journal of Psychiatry, 23,* 213–233.

King, M. J., Ollendick, T. H., & Montgomery, I. M. (1995). Obsessive-compulsive disorder in children and adolescents. *Behaviour Change, 12,* 51–58.

King, N. J., Tonge, B. J., Heyne, D., Turner, S., Pritchard, M. K., Young, D., Rollings, S., Myerson, N., & Ollendick, T. H. (2001). Cognitive-behavioural treatment of school-refusing children: Maintenance of improvement at 3- to 5-year follow-up. *Scandinavian Journal of Behavior Therapy, 30,* 85–89.

King, R., Leonard, H., & March, J. (1998). Practice parameters for the assessment and treatment of children and adolescents with obsessive compulsive disorder. *Journal of the American Academy of Child and Adolescent Psychiatry, 37*, 27–45.

King, R. A., Scahill, L., Vituano, L. A., Schwab-Stone, M., Tercyak, K. P., & Riddle, M. A. (1995). Childhood trichotillomania: Clinical phenomenology, comorbidity, and family genetics. *Journal of the American Academy of Child and Adolescent Psychiatry, 34*, 1451–1459.

Klein, D. (1964). Delineation of two drug-responsive anxiety syndromes. *Psychopharmacologia, 5*, 397–408.

Klein, D. (1980). Anxiety reconceptualized: Early experience with imipramine and anxiety. *Comprehensive Psychiatry, 21*, 411–427.

Klein, D. F., Mannuzza, S., Chapman, T., & Fyer, A. J. (1992). Child panic revisited. *Journal of the American Academy of Child and Adolescent Psychiatry, 31*, 112–116.

Klein, R. G. (1995). Is panic disorder associated with childhood separation anxiety disorder? *Clinical Neuropharmacology, 18* (Suppl. 2), S7–S14.

Klein, R. G., Koplewicz, H., & Kanner, A. (1992). Imipramine treatment of children with separation anxiety disorder. *Journal of the American Academy of Child and Adolescent Psychiatry, 31*, 21–28.

Kleinhauz, M., Eli, I., Baht, R., & Shamay, D. (1992). Correlates of success and failure in behavior therapy for dental fear. *Journal of Dental Research, 71*, 1832–1835.

Klingberg, G., Berggren, U., Carlsson, S. G., & Noren, J. G. (1995). Child dental fear: Cause-related factors and clinical effects. *European Journal of Oral Science, 103*, 405–412.

Klingman, A. (1988). Biblioguidance with kindergartners: Evaluation of a primary prevention program to reduce fear of the dark. *Journal of Clinical Child Psychology, 17*, 237–241.

Klingman, A., Melamed, B. G., Cuthbert, M. I., & Hermecz, D. A. (1984). Effects of participant modeling on information acquisition and skill utilization. *Journal of Consulting and Clinical Psychology, 52*, 414–422.

Kondas, O. (1967). Reduction of examination anxiety and 'stage fright' by group desensitization and relaxation. *Behaviour Research and Therapy, 5*, 275–281.

Kopp, S., & Gillberg, C. (1997). Selective mutism: A population-based study: A research note. *Journal of Child Psychology and Psychiatry, 38*, 257–262.

Koppen, A. S (1974). Relaxation training for children. *Elementary School Guidance and Counseling, 9*, 14–21.

Korte, S. M. (2001). Corticosteriods in relation to fear, anxiety and psychopathology. *Neuroscience and Biobehavioral Research, 25*, 117–142.

Kovacs, M. J. (1998). Internalizing disorders in childhood. *Journal of Child Psychology and Psychiatry, 39*, 47– 63.

Kovacs, M., Brent, D., Steinberg, T., Paulauskas, S., & Reid, J. (1986). Children's self–reports of psychological adjustment and coping strategies during first year of insulin dependent diabetes mellitus. *Diabetes Care, 9*, 472–479.

Kovacs, M., Gatsonis, C., Paulauskas, S. L., & Richards, C. (1989). Depressive disorders in childhood: 4. A longitudinal study of comorbidity with and risk for anxiety disorders. *Archives of General Psychiatry, 46*, 776–782.

Koverola, C. (1995). Posttraumatic stress disorder. In R. T. Ammerman & M Hersen (Eds.), *Handbook of child behavior therapy in the psychiatric setting* (pp. 389–408). Oxford, UK: Wiley.

Kozak, M. J., Foa, E. B., & McCarthy, P. R. (1988). Obsessive-compulsive disorder. In C. G. Last & M. Hersen (Eds.), *Handbook of anxiety disorders* (pp. 87–108). New York: Pergamino Press.

Kratochvil, C., Kutcher, S., Reiter, S., & March, J. S. (1999). Pharmacotherapy of pediatric anxiety disorders. In S. W. Russ & T. Ollendick (Eds.), *Handbook of psychotherapies with children and families* (pp. 345–366). New York: Kluwer Academic.

Kristensen, H. (2000). Selective mutism and comorbidity with developmental disorder/delay, anxiety disorder, and elimination disorder. *Journal of the American Academy of Child and Adolescent Psychiatry, 39*, 249–256.

Kristjansdottir, G. (1996). Sociodemographic differences in the prevalence of self-reported stomach pain in schoolchildren. *European Journal of Pediatrics, 155*, 981–983.

Krysanski, V. L. (2003). A brief review of the selective mutism literature. *The Journal of Psychology, 137*, 29–40.

Kupst, M. J. (1992). Long-term family coping with acute lymphoblastic leukemia in childhood. In A. M. La Greca, L. J. Siegel, J. L. Wallander, & C. E. Walker (Eds.), *Stress and coping in child health* (pp. 242–261). New York: Guilford Press.

Kuroda, J. (1969). Elimination of children's fears of animals by the method of experimental desensitization: An application of learning theory to child psychology. *Psychologia, 12*, 161–165.

LaGreca, A. M., Silverman, W. K., Vernberg, E. M., & Prinstein, M. J. (1996). Symptoms of posttraumatic stress in children after Hurricane Andrew: A prospective study. *Journal of Consulting and Clinical Psychology, 64*, 712–723.

LaGreca, A. M., Silverman, W. K., & Wasserstein, S. B. (1998). Children's predisaster functioning as a predictor of posttraumatic stress following Hurricane Andrew. *Journal of Consulting and Clinical Psychology, 66*, 883–892.

La Greca, A. M., & Stone, W. L. (1993). Social Anxiety Scale for Children-Revised: Factor structure and concurrent validity. *Journal of Clinical Child Psychology, 22*, 17–27.

Lang, P. J. (1968). Fear reduction and fear behavior: Problems in treating a construct. In J. M. Shlien (Ed.), *The structure of emotion* (pp. 18–30). Seattle, WA: Hogrefe & Huber.

Langley, A. K., Bergman, R. L., & Piacentini, J. C. (2002). Assessment of childhood anxiety. *International Review of Psychiatry, 14*, 102–113.

Lapouse, R., & Monk, N. (1959). Fears and worries in a representative sample of children. *American Journal of Orthopsychiatry, 29*, 803–818.

Last, C. G. (1991). Somatic complaints in anxiety disordered children. *Journal of Anxiety Disorders, 5*, 125–138.

Last, C. G., Francis, G., Hersen, M., Kazdin, A. E., & Strauss, C. C. (1987). Separation anxiety and school phobia: A comparison using DSM-III criteria. *American Journal of Psychiatry, 144*, 653–657.

Last, C. G., Hansen, C., & Franco, N. (1998). Cognitive-behavioral treatment of school phobia. *Journal of the American Academy of Child and Adolescent Psychiatry, 37*, 404–411.

Last. C. G., Hersen, M., Kazdin, A. E., Finkelstein, R., & Strauss, C. C. (1987). Comparison of DSM-III separation anxiety and generalized anxiety disorders: Demographic characteristics and patterns of comorbidity. *Journal of the American Academy of Child and Adolescent Psychiatry, 26*, 527–531.

Last, C. G., Hersen, M., Kazdin, A., Orvaschel. H., & Perrin, S. (1991). Anxiety disorders in children and their families. *Archives of General Psychiatry, 49*, 928–934.

Last, C. G., & Perrin, S. (1993). Anxiety disorders in African–American and white children. *Journal of Abnormal Child Psychology, 21*, 153–164.

Last, C. G., Perrin, S., Hersen, M., & Kazdin, A.E. (1992). DSM-III-R anxiety disorders in children: Sociodemographic and clinical characteristics. *Journal of the American Academy of Child and Adolescent Psychiatry, 31*, 1070–1076.

Last, C. G., Perrin, S., Hersen, M., & Kazdin, A. E. (1996). A prospective study of childhood anxiety disorders. *Journal of the American Academy of Child and Adolescent Psychiatry, 35*, 1502–1510.

Last, C. G., & Strauss, C. C. (1989). Panic disorder in children and adolescents. *Journal of Anxiety Disorders, 3*, 87–95.

Last, C. G., & Strauss, C. C. (1989). Obsessive-compulsive disorder in childhood. *Journal of Anxiety Disorders, 3*, 295–302.

Last, C. G., & Strauss, C. C. (1990). School refusal in anxiety-disordered children and adolescents. *Journal of the American Academy of Child and Adolescent Psychiatry, 29*, 31–35.

Last, C. G., Strauss, C. C., & Francis, G. (1987). Comorbidity among childhood anxiety disorders. *Journal of Nervous and Mental Disease, 175*, 726–730.

Lautch, H. (1991). Dental phobia. *British Journal of Psychiatry, 119*, 405–412.

Lavigne, J., & Faier-Routman, J. (1992). Psychological adjustment to pediatric physical disorders: A meta-analytic review. *Journal of Pediatric Psychology, 17*, 133–157.

Layne, A. E., Bernstein, G. A., Egan, E. A., & Kushner, M. G. (2003). Predictors of treatment response in anxious-depressed adolescents with school refusal. *Journal of the American Academy of Child and Adolescent Psychiatry, 42*, 319–326.

Lazarus, A. A., & Abramowitz, A. (1962). The use of "emotive imagery" in the treatment of children's phobias. *Journal of Mental Science, 108*, 191–195.

LeBaron, S., & Zeltzer, L. (1984). Assessment of acute pain and anxiety in children and adolescents by self-reports, observer reports, and a behavioral checklist. *Journal of Consulting and Clinical Psychology, 52*, 729–738.

LeDoux, J. E., & Muller, J. (1997). Emotional memory and psychopathology. *Philosophical. Trans Royal Society of London, 352*, 1719–1726.

Legrand, L. N., McGue, M., & Iacono, W. G. (1999). A twin study of state and trait anxiety in childhood and adolescence. *Journal of Child Psychology and Psychiatry, 40*, 953–958.

Lehrer, P., Feldman, J., Giardino, N., Song, H. S., & Schmaling, K. (2002). Psychological aspects of asthma. *Journal of Consulting and Clinical Psychology, 70*, 691–711.

Leitenberg, H., & Calllahan, E. J., (1973). Reinforced practice and reduction of different kinds of fears in adults and children. *Behaviour Research and Therapy, 11*, 19–30.

Leckman, J. F., Weissman, M. M., Merikangas, K. R., Pauls, D. L., Prusoff, B. A., & Kidd, K. K. (1985). Major depression and panic disorder: A family study perspective. *Psychopharmacology Bulletin, 21*, 543–545.

Lenane, M. C., Swedo, S. E., Leonard, H., Pauls, D. L., Sceery, W., & Rapoport, J. L. (1990). Psychiatric disorders in first degree relatives of children and adolescents with obsessive compulsive disorder. *Journal of the American Academy of Child and Adolescent Psychiatry, 29*, 407–412.

Leonard, H. L., Goldberger, E. L., Rapoport, J. L., Cheslow, D. L., & Swedo, S. E. (1990). Childhood rituals: Normal development or obsessive-compulsive symptoms? *Journal of the American Academy of Child and Adolescent Psychiatry, 149*, 1244–1251.

Leonard, H. L., Lenane, M. C., Swedo, S. E., Rettew, D. C., Gershon, E. S., & Rapoport, J. L. (1992). Tics and Tourette's Disorder: A 2- to 7-year follow-up of 54 obsessive-compulsive children. *American Journal of Psychiatry, 149*, 1244–1251.

Leonard, H. L., & Rapoport, J. L. (1989). Pharmacotherapy of childhood obsessive-compulsive disorder. *Psychiatric Clinics of North America, 12*, 963–970.

Leonard, H. L., & Swedo, S. E. (2001). Paediatric autoimmune neuropsychiatric disorders associated with streptococcal infection (PANDAS). *International Journal of Neuropsychopharmacology, 4*, 191–198.

Leonard, H. L., Swedo, S. E., Rapoport, J. L., Koby, E. V., Lenane, M. C., Cheslow, D. L., & Hamburger, S. E. (1989). Treatment of obsessive-compulsive disorder with clomipramine and desipramine in children and adolescents: A double-blind crossover comparison. *Archives of General Psychiatry, 46*, 1088–1092.

Lewis, S. (1974). A comparison of behavior therapy techniques in the reduction of fearful avoidance behavior. *Behavior Therapy, 5*, 648–655.

Liddell, A. (1990). Personality characteristics versus medical and dental experiences of dentally anxious children. *Journal of Behavioral Medicine, 13*, 183–194.

Liddell, A., & Murray, P. (1989). Age and sex differences in children's reports of dental anxiety and self-efficacy relating to dental anxiety. *Canadian Journal of Behavioral Science, 21*, 270–279.

Lieb, R., Wittchen, H. U., Höfler, M., Fuetsch, M., Stein, M. B., & Merikangas, K. R. (2000). Parental psychopathology, parenting styles, and the risk of social phobia in offspring. *Archives of General Psychiatry, 57*, 859–866.

Liebowitz, M. R., Turner, S. M., Piacentini, J., Beidel D. C., Clarvit, S. R., Davies, S. O., Graae, F., Jafer, M., Lin, S. H., Sallee, F. R., Schmidt, A. B., & Simpson, H. B., Fluoxetine in children and adolescents with OCD: A placebo-controlled trial. *Journal of the American Academy of Child and Adolescent Psychiatry, 41*, 1431–1438.

Linton, S. J. (1986). A case study of the behavioural treatment of chronic stomach pain in a child. *Behaviour Change, 3*, 70–73.

Liossi, C. (1999). Clinical hypnosis versus cognitive behavioral training for pain management with pediatric cancer patients undergoing bone marrow aspirations. *International Journal of Clinical and Experimental Hypnosis, 47*, 104–116.

Lipsitz, J. D., Martin, L. Y., Mannuzza, S., Chapman, T. F., Liebowitz, M. R., Klein, D. F., & Fyer, A. J. (1994). Childhood separation anxiety disorder in patients with adult anxiety disorders. *American Journal of Psychiatry, 151*, 927–929.

Lonigan, C. J., Phillips, B. M., & Richey, J. A. (2003). Posttraumatic stress disorder in children: Diagnosis, assessment, and associated features. *Children and Adolescent Psychiatric Clinics of North America, 12*, 171–194.

Lonigan, C. J., Shannon, M. P., Taylor, C. M., Finch, A. J., & Sallee, F. R. (1994). Children exposed to disaster: II. Risk factors for the development of post-traumatic symptomatology. *Journal of the American Academy of Child and Adolescent Psychiatry, 33*, 94–105.

Lowry-Webster, H. M., Barrett, P. M., & Dadds, M. R. (2001). A universal prevention trial of anxiety and depressive symptomatology in childhood: Preliminary data from an Australian study. *Behaviour Change, 18*, 36–50.

Lowry-Webster, H.M ., Barrett, P. M., & Lock, S. (2003). A universal prevention trial of anxiety symptomatology during childhood: Results at one year follow-up. Unpublished manuscript, Griffith University.

Lumley, M. A., Melamed, B. G., & Abeles, L. A. (1993). Predicting children's presurgical anxiety and subsequent behavior change. *Journal of Pediatric Psychology, 18*, 481–497.

Macaulay, J. L., & Kleinknecht, R. A. (1989). Panic and panic attacks in adolescents. *Journal of Anxiety Disorders, 3*, 221–241.

MacFarlane, J. W., Allen, L., & Honzik, M. P. (1954). A developmental study of the behavior problems of normal children between twenty-one months and fourteen years. In *University of California Publications in Child Development*, (vol. 21, p. 61–87). Berkeley: University of California Press.

Magni, G., Pierri, M., & Donzelli, F. (1987). Recurrent abdominal pain in children: A long term follow-up. *European Journal of Pediatrics, 146*, 72–74.

Manassis, K., Bradley, S., Goldberg, S., Hood, J., & Swinson, R. (1995). Behavioural inhibition, attachment and anxiety in children of mothers with anxiety disorders. *Canadian Journal of Psychiatry, 40*, 87–92.

Manassis, K., Fung, D., Tannock, R., Sloman, L., Fiksenbaum, L., & McInnes, A. (2003). Characterizing selective mutism: Is it more than social anxiety? *Depression and Anxiety, 18*, 153–161.

Manassis, K., & Kalman, E. (1990). Anorexia resulting from fear of vomiting in four adolescent girls. *Canadian Journal of Psychiatry, 35*, 548–550.

Manassis, K., Mendlowitz, S. L., Scapillato, D., Avery, D., Fiksenbaum, L., Freire, M., Monga, S., & Owens, M. (2002). Group and individual cognitive-behavioral therapy for childhood anxiety disorders: A randomized trial. *Journal of the American Academy of Child and Adolescent Psychiatry, 41*, 1423–1430.

Mancini, C., Van Ameringen, M., Oakman, J. M., & Farvolden, P. (1999). Serotonergic agents in the treatment of social phobia in children and adolescents: A case series. *Depression and Anxiety, 10*, 33–39.

Mancini, C., Van Amerigen, M., & Szatmari, P.(1996). A high-risk pilot study of the children of adults with social phobia. *Journal of the American Academy of Child and Adolescent Psychiatry, 35*, 1511–1517.

Manicavasagar, V., & Silove, D. (1997). Is there an adult form of separation anxiety disorder? A brief clinical report. *Australian and New Zealand Journal of Psychiatry, 31*, 299–303.

Manicavasagar, V., Silove, D., & Curtis, J. (1997). Separation anxiety in adulthood: A phenomenological investigation. *Comprehensive Psychiatry, 38*, 274–282.

Manicavasagar, V., Silove, D., Curtis, J., & Wagner, R. (2000). Continuities of separation anxiety from early life into adulthood. *Journal of Anxiety Disorders, 14*, 1–18.

Mann, J., & Rosenthal. T. L. (1969). Vicarious and direct counter-conditioning of test anxiety through individual and group desensitization. *Behaviour Research and Therapy, 7*, 359–367.

Manne, S. L., Bakeman, R., Jacobsen, P. B., Forfinkle, K., Bernstein, D., & Redd, W. H. (1994). An analysis of a behavioral intervention for children undergoing venipuncture. *Health Psychology, 11*, 241–249.

Manne, S., Bakeman, R. Jacobsen, P., Gorfinkle, K., & Redd, W. (1994). An analysis of a behavioral intervention for children undergoing venipuncture. *Health Psychology, 13*, 556–566.

March, J. S. (1997). *Multidimensional anxiety scale for children.* Toronto: Multi-Health Systems, Inc.

March, J. S. (1999). Assessment of pediatric posttraumatic stress disorder. In P. Saigh & D. Bremner (Eds.), *Post-traumatic stress disorder* (pp. 199–218). Washington, DC: American Psychological Press.

March, J. S., Amaya-Jackson, L., Murray, M. C., & Schulte, A. (1998). Cognitive-behavioral psychotherapy for children and adolescents with post-traumatic stress disorder following a single-incident stressor. *Journal of the American Academy of Child and Adolescent Psychiatry, 37*, 585–593.

March, J. S., Biederman, J., Wolkow, R., Safferman, A., Mardekian, J., Cook, E. H., Cutler, N. R., Dominguez, R., Ferguson, J., Muller, B., Riesenberg, R., Rosenthal, M., Sallee, F. R., & Wagner, K. D. (1998). Sertraline in children and adolescents with obsessive-compulsive disorder. *Journal of the American Medical Association, 280*, 1752–1756.

March, J. S., Franklin, M. E., Leonard, H. L., & Foa, E. B. (2004). Obsessive-compulsive disorder. In T. L. Morris, & J. S. March (Eds.) *Anxiety disorders in children and adolescents* (pp. 212–240). New York: Guilford Press.

March, J. S., & Mulle, K. (1998). *OCD in children and adolescents: A cognitive-behavioral treatment manual.* New York: Guilford.

March, J. S., Mulle, K., & Herbel, B. (1994). Behavioral psychotherapy for children and adolescents with obsessive-compulsive disorder: An open trial of a new protocol-driven treatment package. *Journal of the American Academy of Child and Adolescent Psychiatry, 33*, 333–341.

March, J. S., Parker, J. D. A., Sullivan, K., Stallings, P., & Conners, K. (1997). The Multidimensional Anxiety Scale for Children (MASC): Factor structure, reliability and validity. *Journal of the American Academy of Child and Adolescent Psychiatry, 36*, 554–565.

Marks, I. M. (1969). *Fears and phobias.* New York: Academic Press.

Marks, I. M. (1970). The classification of phobic disorders. *British Journal of Psychiatry, 116*, 377–386.

Marks, I. M. (1985). Behavioral psychotherapy for anxiety disorders. *Psychiatric Clinics of North America, 8*, 25–35.

Martin, C., Cabrol, S., Pierre-Bouvard, M., Lepine, J. P., & Mouren-Simeoni, M. C. (1999). Anxiety and depressive disorders in fathers and mothers of anxious school-refusing children. *Journal of the American Academy of Child and Adolescent Psychiatry, 38*, 916–922.

Masi, G., Favilla, L., Mucci, M., & Millepiedi, S. (2000). Depressive comorbidity in children and adolescents with generalized anxiety disorder. *Child Psychiatry and Human Development, 30*, 205–215.

Masi, G., Favilla, L., Mucci, M., & Millepiedi, S. (2001). Anxiety comorbidity in referred children and adolescents with dysthymic disorder. *Psychopathology, 34*, 253–258.

Masi, G., Millepiedi, S., Mucci, M., Poli, P., Bertini, N., & Milantoni, L. (2004). Generalized anxiety disorder in referred children and adolescents. *Journal of the American Academy of Child and Adolescent Psychiatry, 43*, 752–760.

Masi, G., Mucci, M., Favilla, L., Romano, R., & Poli, P (1999). Symptomatology and comorbidity of generalized anxiety disorder in children and adolescents. *Comprehensive Psychiatry, 40*, 210–215.

Masia, C. L., Hofmann, S. G., Klein, R. G., & Liebowitz, M. R. (1999). *The Liebowitz Social Anxiety Scale for Children and Adolescents (LSAS-CA).* Unpublished manuscript, NYU Child Study Center.

Masia, C. L., Klein, R. G., Storch, E. A., & Corda, B. (2001). School-based behavioral treatment for social anxiety disorder in adolescents: Results of a pilot study. *Journal of the American Academy of Child and Adolescent Psychiatry, 40*, 780–786.

Masia, C. L., Storch, E. A., Dent, H. C., Adams, P., Verdeli, H., Davies, M., & Weissman, M. W. (2003). Recall of childhood psychopathology more than 10 years later. *Journal of the American Academy of Child and Adolescent Psychiatry, 42*, 6–12.

Masia-Warner, C., Klein, R., Dent, H., Albano, A. M., & Guardino, M. (2003). *School-based intervention for social anxiety disorder: Results of a wait-list control trial.* Presented at the Anxiety Disorders Association of America Annual Convention, Toronto, Ontario.

Mattis, S. G., & Ollendick, T. H. (1997). Children's cognitive responses to the somatic symptoms of panic. *Journal of Abnormal Child Psychology, 25*, 47–57.

Mattis, S. G., & Ollendick, T. H. (2002). *Panic disorder and anxiety in adolescents.* London: British Psychological Society.

Mauer, A. (1965). What children fear. *Journal of Genetic Psychology, 106,* 265–277.

McCathie, H., & Spence, S. H. (1991). What is the revised Fear Survey Schedule for Children measuring? *Behaviour Research and Therapy, 29,* 495–502.

McClure, E. B., Brennan, P. A., Hammen, C., & Le Brocque, R. M. (2001). Parental anxiety disorders, child anxiety disorders, and the perceived parents-child relationship in an Australian high-risk sample. *Journal of Abnormal Child Psychology, 29,* 1–10.

McDonald, A. S. (2001). The prevalence and effects of test anxiety in school children. *Educational Psychology, 21,* 89–102.

McFarlane, A. C. (1987). Posttraumatic phenomena in a longitudinal study of children following a natural disaster. *Journal of the American Academy of Child and Adolescent Psychiatry, 26,* 764–769.

McGee, R., Feehan, M., Williams, S. & Anderson, J. (1992). DSM-III disorders from age 11 to age 15 years. *Journal of the American Academy of Child and Adolescent Psychiatry, 31,* 51–59.

McGee, R., Feehan, M., Williams, S., Partridge, F., Silva, P. A., & Kelly, J. (1990). DSM-III disorders in a large sample of adolescents. *Journal of the American Academy of Child and Adolescent Psychiatry, 29,* 611–619.

McKnight, C. D., Compton, S. N., & March, J. S. (2004). Posttraumatic stress disorder. In T. L. Morris and J. S. March (Eds.), *Anxiety disorders in children and adolescents* (2nd ed., pp. 241–262). New York: Guilford Press.

McMurray, N. E., Bell, R. J., Fusillo, A. D., Morgan, M., & Wright, F. (1986). Relationship between locus of control and effects of coping strategies on dental stress in children. *Child and Family Behavior Therapy, 8,* 1–17.

Melamed, B. G. (1998). Preparation for medical procedures. In R. T. Ammerman & J. V. Campo (Eds.), *Handbook of pediatric psychology and psychiatry* (vol. 2, pp. 16–30). Needham Heights, MA: Allyn & Bacon.

Melamed, B. G., Bennertt, G., Jerrell, G., Ross, S. L., Bush, J. P., Hill, C., Courte, F., & Ronk, S. (1983). Dentists' behavior management as it affects compliance and fear in pediatric patients. *Journal of the American Dental Association, 106,* 324–330.

Melamed, B. G., Dearborn, M., & Hermecz, D. A. (1983). Necessary considerations for surgery preparation: Age and previous experience with the stressor. *Psychosomatic Medicine, 45,* 517–525.

Melamed, B. G., & Fogel, J. (2000). The psychologist's role in the treatment of dental problems. In D. I. Mostofsky & D. H. Barlow (Eds.) *The management of stress and anxiety in medical disorders* (pp. 268–281). Needham Heights, MA: Allyn & Bacon.

Melamed, B.G., Meyer, R., Gee, C., & Soule, L. (1976). The influence of time and type of preparation of children's adjustment to hospitalization. *Journal of Pediatric Psychology, 1,* 31–37.

Melamed, B. G., & Ridley-Johnson, R. (1988). Psychological preparation of families for hospitalization. *Journal of Developmental and Behavioral Pediatrics, 9,* 96–102.

Melamed, B. G., & Williamson, D. J. (1991). Programs for the treatment of dental disorders. In J. J. Sweet & R. Rozensky (Eds.), *Handbook of clinical psychology in medical settings* (pp. 539–565). New York: Plenum Press.

Melamed, B. G., Yurcheson, R., Fleece, E. L., Hutcherson, S., & Hawes, R. (1978). Effects of film modeling on the reduction of anxiety-related behaviors in individuals varying in level of previous experience in the stress situation. *Journal of Consulting and Clinical Psychology, 46,* 1357–1367.

Menzies, R. G., & Clarke, J. C. (1993). A comparison of in vivo and vicarious exposure in the treatment of childhood water phobia. *Behaviour Research and Therapy, 31,* 9–15.

Merckelbach, H., de Jong, P. J., Muris, P., & van den Hout, M. A. (1996). The etiology of specific phobias: A review. *Clinical Psychology Review, 16,* 337–361.

Mesman, J., & Koot, H. M. (2000). Child-reported depression and anxiety in preadolescence: I. Associations with parent- and teacher-reported problems. *Journal of the American Academy of Child and Adolescent Psychiatry, 39,* 1371–1378.

Milgrom, P., Fiset, L. Melnick, S., & Weinstein, P. (1988). The prevalence and practice management consequences of dental fear in a major U.S. city. *Journal of the American Dental Association, 116,* 641–647.

Milgrom, P., Manci, L., King, B., & Weinstein, P. (1995). Origins of childhood dental fear. *Behaviour Research and Therapy, 33,* 313–319.

Milgrom, P., Vignehsa, H., & Weinsten, P. (1992). Adolescent dental fear and control: prevalence and theoretical implications. *Behaviour Research and Therapy, 30,* 367–373.

Miller, A. J., & Kratochwill, T. R. (1979). Reduction in frequent stomachache complaints by time out. *Behaviour Change, 3,* 70–73.

Miller, L. C. (1983). Fears and anxieties in children. In C. E. Walker & M. C. Roberts (Eds.), *Handbook of clinical child psychology* (pp. 337–380). New York: Wiley.

Miller, L. C., Barrett, C. L., Hampe, E., & Noble, H. (1971). Revised anxiety scales for the Louisville Behavior Checklist. *Psychological Reports, 29,* 503–511.

Miller, L. C., Barrett, C. L., Hampe, E., & Noble, H. (1972). Comparison of reciprocal inhibition, psychotherapy, and waiting list control for phobic children. *Journal of Abnormal Psychology, 79,* 269–279.

Mineka, S. (1987). A primate model of phobic fears. In H. Eysenck & I. Martin (Eds.), *Theoretical foundations of behavior therapy* (pp. 87–111). New York: Plenum Press.

Mineka, S., & Cook, M. (1988). Social learning and the acquisition of snake fear in monkeys. In T. Zentall & G. Galef (Eds.), *Comparative social learning* (pp. 51–73). Hillsdale, NJ: Erlbaum.

Mineka, S., & Öhman, A. (2002). Born to fear: Non-associative vs associative factors in the etiology of phobias. *Behaviour Research and Therapy, 40,* 173–184.

Mineka, S., Gunnar, M., & Champoux (1986). Control and early socioemotional development: Infant rhesus monkeys reared in controllable versus uncontrollable environments. *Child Development, 57,* 1241–1256.

Mineka, S., Suomi, S. J., & Delizio, R. D. (1981). Multiple separations in adolescent monkeys: An opponent–process interpretation. *Journal of Experimental Psychology: General, 110,* 56–85.

Mizuta, I. M., Zahn-Waxler, C., Cole, P. M., & Hiruma, N. (1996). A cross–cultural study of preschooler's attachment: Security and sensitivity in Japanese and US dyads. *International Journal of Behavioral Development, 19,* 141–159.

Monk, C., Lovelenko, P., Ellman, L. M., Sloan, R .P., Bagiella, E., Gorman, J. M., & Pine, D. S. (2001). Enhanced stress reactivity in paediatric anxiety disorders: Implications for future cardiovascular health. *International Journal of Neuropsychopharmacology, 42,* Special Issue, 199–206.

Moore, R., Brodsgaard, I., & Birn, H. (1991). Manifestations, acquisition and diagnostic categories of dental fear in a self-referred population. *Behaviour Research and Therapy, 33,* 313–319.

Morris, T. L., Hirshfeld-Becker, D. R., Henin, A., & Storch, E. A. (2004). Developmentally sensitive assessment of social anxiety. *Cognitive and Behavioral Practice, 11,* 13–28.

Mowrer, O. H. (1947). On the dual nature of learning: A re-interpretation of "conditioning" and "problem–solving". *Harvard Educational Review, 17,* 102–148.

Mrazek, D. A. (1992). Psychiatric complications of pediatric asthma. *Annals of Allergy, 69,* 285–290.

Mufson, L., Weissman, M. M., & Warner, V. (1992). Depression and anxiety in parents and children: A direct interview study. *Journal of anxiety disorders, 6,* 1–13.

Muller, S. A. (1987). Trichotillomania. *Dermatology Clinic, 5,* 595-601

Muris, P., Meesters, C., Merckelbach, H., Sermon, A., & Zwakhalen, S. (1998). Worry in normal children. *Journal of the American Academy of Child and Adolescent Psychiatry, 37,* 703–710.

Muris, P., Merckelbach, H., Gadet, B., & Moulaert, V. (2000). Fears, worries, and scary dreams in 4–12 year old children: Their content, developmental pattern, and origins. *Journal of Clinical Child Psychology, 29,* 43–52.

Muris, P., Merckelbach, H., Ollendick, T. H., King, N. J., Meesters, C., & van Kessel, C. (2002). What is the Revised Fear Survey Schedule for Children measuring? *Behaviour Research and Therapy, 40,* 1317–1326.

Muris, P., Schmidt, H., & Merckelbach, H. (1999). The structure of specific phobia symptoms among children and adolescents. *Behaviour Research and Therapy, 37,* 863–868.

Muris, P., Steerneman, P., Merckelbach, H., & Meesters, C. (1996). The role of parental fearfulness and modeling in children's fear. *Behaviour Research and Therapy, 34*, 265–268.

Murphy, C. M., & Bootzin, R. R. (1973). Active and passive participation in the contact desensitization of snake fear in children. *Behavior Therapy, 4*. 203–211.

Murphy, D. L., Pickar, D, & Alterman, I. D. (1982). Methods for the quantitative assessment of depressive and manic behavior. In E. L. Burdock & S. Gershon (Eds), *The behavior of psychiatric patients* (pp. 355–392). New York: Marcel Dekker.

Murray, P., Liddell, A., & Donohue, J. (1989). A longitudinal study of the contribution of dental experience to dental anxiety in children between 9 and 12 years of age. *Journal of Behavioral Medicine, 12*, 309–320.

Nader, K., Blake, D., Kriegler, J., & Pynoos, R. (1994). *Clinician Administered PTSD Scale for Children (CAPS–C), Current and Lifetime Diagnosis Version, and Instructional Manual.* Los Angeles: UCLA Neuropsychiatric Institute and National Center for PTSD.

Nalvern, F. B. (1970). Manifest fears and worries of ghetto versus middle class suburban children. *Psychological Reports, 27*, 25–286.

Nauta, M. H., Scholing, A., Emmelkamp, P. M. G., & Minderaa, R. B. (2001). Cognitive-behavioural therapy for anxiety disordered children in a clinical setting: Does additional cognitive parent training enhance treatment effectiveness? *Clinical Psychology and Psychotherapy, 8*, 330–340.

Nauta, M. H., Scholing, A., Emmelkamp, P. M. G., & Minderaa, R. B. (2003). Cognitive-behavioral therapy for children with anxiety disorders in a clinical setting: No additional effect of a cognitive parent training. *Journal of the American Academy of Child and Adolescent Psychiatry, 42*, 1270–1278.

Naylor, M. W., Staskowski, M., Kenney, M. C., & King, C. A. (1994). Language disorders and learning disabilities in school refusing adolescents. *Journal of the American Academy of Child and Adolescent Psychiatry, 35*, 1331–1337.

Neal, A. M., Lilly, R. S., & Zakis, S. (1993). What are African American children afraid of? *Journal of Anxiety Disorders, 7*, 129–139.

Nelles, W. B., & Barlow, D. H. (1988). Do children panic? *Clinical Psychology Review, 8*, 359–372.

Newman, D. L., Moffitt, T. E., Caspi, A., Magdol, L., Silva, P. A., & Stanton, W. R. (1996). Psychiatric disorder in a birth cohort of young adults: Prevalence, comorbidity, clinical significance, and new case incidence from ages 11 to 21. *Journal of Consulting and Clinical Psychology 64*, 552–562.

Obler, M., & Terwilliger, R. F. (1970). Pilot study on the effectiveness of systematic desensitization with neurologically impaired children with phobic disorders. *Journal of Consulting and Clinical Psychology, 34*, 314–318.

Olafsdottir, E., Ellertsen, B., & Fluge, G. (2001). Personality profiles and heart rate variability (vagal tone) in children with recurrent abdominal pain. *Acta Paediatrica, 90*, 632-637.

Olivares, J., Garcia-Lopez, L. J., Beidel, D. C., Turner, S. M., Albano, A. M., & Hidalgo, M. D. (2002a). Results at long-term among three psychological treatments for adolescents with generalized social phobia (I): Statistical significance. *Psicologia Conductual, 10*, 147–164.

Olivares, J., Garcia-Lopez, L. J., Turner, S. M., Beidel, D. C., Albano, A. M., & Sanchez-Meca, J. (2002b). Results at long-term among three psychological treatments for adolescents with generalized social phobia (II): Clinical significance and effect size. *Psicologia Conductual, 10*, 371–385.

Ollendick, T. H. (1979). Fear reduction techniques with children. In M. Hersen, R. M. Eisler, & P. M. Miller (Eds.), *Progress in Behavior Modification*, (Vol. 8, pp. 127–168). New York: Academic Press.

Ollendick, T .H. (1983). Reliability and validity of the Revised Fear Survey Schedule for Children (FSSC–R). *Behaviour Research and Therapy, 21*, 685–692.

Ollendick, T. H., Birmaher, B., & Mattis, S. G. (2004). Panic disorder. In T.L. Morris and J. S. March (Eds), *Anxiety disorders in children and adolescents* (pp.189–211). New York: Guilford Press.

Ollendick, T. H., & King, N. J. (1991). Origins of childhood fears: An evaluation of Rachman's theory of fear acquisition. *Behaviour Research and Therapy, 29*, 117–123.

Ollendick, T. H., & King, N. J. (1994). Diagnosis, assessment and treatment of internalizing problems in children: The role of longitudinal data. *Journal of Consulting and Clinical Psychology, 62,* 918–927.

Ollendick, T. H., & King, N. J. (1998). Empirically supported treatments for children with phobic and anxiety disorders: Current status. *Journal of Clinical Child Psychology, 27,* 156–167.

Ollendick, T. H., King, N. J., & Frary, R. B. (1989). Fears in children and adolescents: Reliability and generalizability across gender, age and nationality. *Behaviour Research and Therapy, 27,* 19–26.

Ollendick, T. H., King, N. J. & Muris, P. (2004). Phobias in children and adolescents. In M. Maj, H. S. Akiskal, J. J. Lopez-Ibor, & A. Okasha (Eds.), *Phobias* (pp. 245–279). London: Wiley.

Ollendick, T. H., Matson, J. L., & Helsel, W. J. (1985). Fears in children and adolescents: Normative data. *Behaviour Research and Therapy, 23,* 465–467.

Ollendick, T. H., Mattis, S. G., & King, N. J. (1994). Panic in children and adolescents: A review. *Journal of Child Psychology and Psychiatry, 35,* 113–134.

Ollendick, T. H., & Mayer, J. A. (1984). School phobia. In S. M. Turner (Ed.) *Behavioral theories and treatment of anxiety* (pp. 367–411). New York: Plenum Press.

Ollendick, T. H., & Meador, A. E. (1981). Behavioral assessment of children. In G. Goldstein, & M. Hersen (Eds.), *Handbook of psychological assessment* (pp. 351–368). New York: Pergamino.

Ortega, A. N., Huertas, S. E., Canino, G., Ramirez, R., & Rubio-Stipee, M. (2002). Childhood asthma, chronic illness, and psychiatric disorders. *Journal of Nervous and Mental Disease, 190,* 275–281.

Orton. G. L. (1982). A comparative study of children's worries. *Journal of Psychology, 110,* 153–162.

Öst, L. G. (1985). Ways of acquiring phobias and outcomes of behavioral treatments. *Behaviour Research and Therapy, 23,* 683–689.

Öst, L. G. (1987). Age of onset in different phobias. *Journal of Abnormal Psychology, 96,* 223–229.

Öst, L. G., Fellenius, J., & Sterner, U. (1991). Applied tension, exposure in vivo, and tension-only in the treatment of blood phobia. *Behaviour Research and Therapy, 29,* 561–574.

Öst, L. G., & Hugdahl, K. (1985). Acquisition of blood and dental phobia and anxiety response patterns in clinical patients. *Behaviour Research and Therapy, 23,* 27–34.

Öst, L. G., Svensson, L., Hellstrom, K., & Lindwall, R. (2001). One-session treatment of specific phobias in youths: A randomized clinical trial. *Journal of Consulting and Clinical Psycholog,y 69,* 814–824.

Ozer, E. J., Best, S. R., Lipsey, T. L., & Weiss, D. S. (2003). Predictors of posttraumatic stress disorder and symptoms in adults: A meta-analysis. *Psychological Bulletin, 129,* 52–71.

Park, S. Y., Belsky, J. U., Putnam, S., & Crnic, K. (1997). Infant emotionality, parenting and 3–year inhibition: Exploring stability and lawful discontinuity in a male sample. *Developmental Psychology, 33,* 218–227.

Parkinson, L., & Rachman, S. (1981). Part II. The nature of intrusive thoughts. *Advances in Behavioural Research and Therapy, 3,* 101–110.

Partridge, J. M. (1939). Truancy. *Journal of Medical Science, 85,* 45–81.

Pauls, D. L., Alsobrook, J. P., Goodman, W., Rasmussen, S., & Leckman, J. F. (1995). A family study of obsessive compulsive disorder. *American Journal of Psychiatry, 152,* 76–84.

Pauls, D. L., Towbin, K., Leckman, J., Zahner, G., & Cohen, D. (1986). Gilles de la Tourette syndrome and obsessive-compulsive disorder: Evidence supporting a genetic relationship. *Archives of General Psychiatry, 43,* 1180–1182.

Pavlov, I. P. (1994). The conditioned reflex. *Psychopathology and psychiatry* (pp. 378–397). Piscataway, NJ: Transaction Publishers.

Perrin, S., & Last, C. G. (1992). Do childhood anxiety measures measure anxiety? *Journal of Abnormal Child Psychology, 20,* 567–578.

Perrin, S., & Last, C. G. (1993). Comorbidity of social phobia and other anxiety disorders in children. Paper presented at the Anxiety Disorders Association of America Annual Convention, Pittsburgh.

Perrin, S., & Last, C. G. (1997). Worrisome thoughts in children clinically referred for anxiety disorder. *Journal of Clinical Child Psychology, 26,* 181–189.

Pfefferbaum, B., Nixon, S. J., Tucker P. M., Tivis, R. D., Moore, V. L., Gurwitch, R. H., Pynoos, R. S., & Geis, H. K. (1999). Posttraumatic stress responses in bereaved children after the Oklahoma City bombing. *Journal of the American Academy of Child and Adolescent Psychiatry, 38,* 1372–1379.

Piacentini, J. (1999). Cognitive behavior therapy of childhood OCD. *Child and Adolescent Psychiatric Clinics of North America, 8,* 599–616.

Piacentini, J., & Bergman, R. L. (2001). Developmental issues in cognitive therapy for childhood anxiety disorders. *Journal of Cognitive Psychotherapy: An International Quarterly, 15,* 165–182.

Piacentini, J., Jaffer, M., Bergman, R. L., McCracken, J., & Keller, M. (2001, October). *Measuring impairment in childhood OCD: Psychometric properties of the COIS.* Paper presented at the Annual Meeting of the American Academy of Child and Adolescent Psychiatry, Honolulu, HI.

Piacentini. J., Vergman, R. L., Jacobs, C., McCracken, J. T., & Kretchman, J. (2002). Open trial of cognitive-behavior therapy for childhood obsessive-compulsive disorder. *Journal of Anxiety Disorders, 16,* 207–219.

Pina, A. A., Silverman, W. K., Fuentes, R. M., Kurtines, W. M., & Weems, C. F. (2003). Exposure-based cognitive-behavioral treatment for phobic and anxiety disorders: Treatment effects and maintenance for Hispanic/Latino relative to European-American youths. *Journal of the American Academy of Child and Adolescent Psychiatry, 42,* 1179–1187.

Pina, A. A., Silverman, W. K., Weems, C. F., Kurtines, W. M., & Goldman, M. L. (2003). A comparison of completers and noncompleters of exposure-based cognitive and behavioral treatment for phobic and anxiety disorders in youth. *Journal of Consulting and Clinical Psychology, 71,* 701–705.

Pine, D. S., Coplan, J. D., Papp, L. A., Moreau, D., Tancer, M., Dummitt, E. S., Shaffer, D., Gorman, J. M., & Klein, D. F. (1995). *Noradrenergic function in youth and adults with anxiety disorders.* Published in Scientific Proceedings of the 42 annual meeting of the American Academy of Child and Adolescent Psychiatry, Washington, DC.

Pine, D. S., & Grun, J. B. S. (1998). Anxiety disorders. In T. B. Walsh (Ed.), *Child Psychopharmacology* (1st ed.) (Vol. 17, pp. 115–144). Washington, DC: American Psychiatric Press.

Pine, D. D., Klein, R. G., Coplan, J. D., Coplan. J. D., Papp, L. A., Hoven, C. W., Martinez, J., Kovalenko, P., Mandell, D. J., & Moreau, D. (2000). Differential carbon dioxide sensitivity in childhood anxiety disorders and non-ill comparison group. *Archives of General Psychiatry, 57,* 960–967.

Plafsdottir, E., Ellerstsen, B., Berstad, A., & Fluge, G. (2001). Personality profiles and heart rate variability (vagal tone) in children with recurrent abdominal pain. *Acta Paediatrica, 90,* 632–637.

Pomnoppadol, C., & Todd, R. D. (1999). Trichotillomania responds to lithium therapy in a 13-year-old girl. *Journal of the American Academy of Child and Adolescent Psychiatry, 38,* 1470–1471.

Potts, N. L., Davidson, J. R., Krishnan, K. R. R., & Doraiswamy, P. M. (1994). Magnetic resonance spectroscopy in social phobia: Preliminary findings. *Psychiatric Research, 52,* 35–42.

Poulton, R., & Menizes. R. G. (2002). Non-associative fear acquisition: a review of the evidence from retrospective and longitudinal research. *Behaviour Research and Therapy, 40,* 127–149.

Poulton R., Thomson, W. M., Brown, R. H., & Silva, P. A. (1998). Dental fear with and without blood–injection fear: implications for dental health and clinical practice. *Behaviour Research and Therapy, 36,* 591–597.

Poulton, R., Trainor, P., Stanton, W., McGee, R., Davies, S., & Silva, P. (1997). The (in)stability of adolescent fears. *Behaviour Research and Therapy, 35,* 159–163.

Powell, M. B., & Oei, T. P. (1991). Cognitive processes underlying the behavior change in cognitive behavior therapy with childhood disorders: A review of experimental evidence. *Behavioural Psychotherapy, 19,* 247–265.

Prins, P. J. M. (2001). Affective and cognitive processes and the development and maintenance of anxiety and its disorders. In W. K. Silverman & P. D. A. Treffers (Eds.), *Anxiety disorders in children and adolescents* (pp. 23–44). Cambridge, UK: Cambridge University Press.

Prior, M., Smart, D., Sanson, A., & Oberklaid, F. (2000). Does shy-inhibited temperament in childhood lead to anxiety problems in adolescence? *Journal of the American Academy of Child and Adolescent Psychiatry, 39,* 461–468.

Pruis, A., Lahey, B. B., Thyer, B. A., Christ, M. A. G., Loeber, R., & Loeber, M. (1990). Separation anxiety disorder and overanxious disorder: How do they differ? *Phobia Practice and Research Journal, 3,* 51–59.

Pynoos, R. S., Frederick, C., Nader, K., Arroyo, W., Steinberg, A., Eth, S., Nunez, F., & Fairbanks, L.

(1987). Life threat and posttraumatic stress in school-age children. *Archives of General Psychiatry, 44*, 1057–1063.

Rachman, S. (1977). The conditioning theory of fear acquisition: A critical examination. *Behaviour Research and Therapy, 15*, 375–387.

Rachman, S. (1990). The detriment and treatment of simple phobias. *Advances in Behaviour Research and Therapy, 12*, 1–30.

Rachman, S. (1993). Obsessions, responsibility, and guile. *Behavioural Research and Therapy, 16*, 233–238.

Rachman, S., & de Silva (1976). Abnormal and normal obsessions. *Behaviour Research and Therapy, 14*, 223–248.

Rapee, R. M. (2000). Group treatment of children with anxiety disorders: Outcome and predictors of treatment response. *Australian Journal of Psychology, 52*, 125–129.

Rapee. R. M. (2003). The influence of comorbidity on treatment outcome for children and adolescents with anxiety disorders. *Behaviour Research and Therapy, 41*, 105–112.

Rapoport, J. L. (1986). Childhood obsessive compulsive disorder. *Journal of Child Psychology and Psychiatry, 27*, 289–296.

Rapoport, J. L., Weissman, M. M., Greenwald, S., Narrow, W., Jensen, P. S., Lahey, B. B., & Canino, G. (2000). Childhood obsessive-compulsive disorder in the NIMH MECA study: Parent versus child identification of cases. *Journal of Anxiety Disorders, 14*, 535–548.

Rasmussen, S. A., & Eisen, J. L. (1990). Epidemiology of obsessive compulsive disorder. *Journal of Clinical Psychiatry, 53*, 4–10.

Reeve, E. A., Bernstein, G. A., & Christenson, G. A. (1992). Clinical characteristics and psychiatric comorbidity in children with trichotillomania. *Journal of the American Academy of Child and Adolescent Psychiatry, 31*, 132–138.

Reid, A. R. (1988). Some suggested techniques for dental anxiety in children. *Australian Journal of Clinical Hypnotherapy & Hypnosis, 9*, 85–88.

Research Units on Pediatric Psychopharmacology Anxiety Study Group (2002). The Pediatric Anxiety Rating Scale (PARS): Development and psychometric properties. *Journal of the American Academy of Child and Adolescent Psychiatry, 41*, 1061–1069.

Rettew, D. C., Swedo, S. E., Leonard, H. L., Lenane, M. C., & Rapoport, J. L. (1992). Obsessions and compulsions across time in 79 children and adolescents with obsessive-compulsive disorder. *Journal of the American Academy of Child and Adolescent Psychiatry, 31*, 1050–1056.

Reynolds, C. R., & Richmond, B. O. (1978). What I Think and Feel: A revised measure of children's manifest anxiety. *Journal of Abnormal Child Psychology, 6*, 271–280.

Reznick, J. S., Kagan, J., Snidman, N., Gersten, M., Boak, K., & Rosenberg, A. (1986). Inhibited and uninhibited children: A follow-up study. *Child Development, 57*, 660-680.

Riddle, M. A., Hardin, M. T., King, R., Scahill, L., & Woolston, J. L. (1990). Fluoxetine treatment of children and adolescents with Tourette's and obsessive-compulsive disorders: Preliminary clinical experience. *Journal of the American Academy of Child and Adolescent Psychiatry, 29*, 45–48.

Riddle, M. A., Scahill, L., King, R., Hardin, M. T., Tobin, K. E., Ort, S. I., Leckman, J. F., & Cohen, D. J. (1990). Obsessive compulsive disorder in children and adolescents: Phenomenology and family history. *Journal of the American Academy of Child and Adolescent Psychiatry, 29*, 766–772.

Ritter, B. (1968). The group desensitization of children's snake phobias using vicarious and contact desensitization procedures. *Behaviour Research and Therapy, 6*, 1–6.

Roberson-Nay, R., & Turner, S. M. (2002). Behavioral treatment of emetophobia (fear of vomiting): A single case study. Presented at the Association for Advancement of Behavior Therapy Annual Convention, Reno, NV, November.

Robinson, J. O., Alverez, J. H., & Dodge, J. A. (1990). Life events and family history in children with recurrent abdominal pain. *Journal of Psychosomatic Research, 34*, 171–181.

Rosenbaum, J. F., Biederman, J., Gersten, M., Hirshfeld, D. R., Meminger, S. R., Herman, J. B., Kagan, J., Reznick, J. S., & Snidman, N. (1988). Behavioral inhibition in children of parents with panic disorder and agoraphobia: A controlled study. *Archives of General Psychiatry, 45*, 463–470.

Rosenbaum, J. F., Biederman, J., Hirshfeld–Becker, D. R., Kagan, J,, Snidman, N., Friedman, D., Nineberg, A., Gallery, D. J., & Faraone, S. V. (2000). A controlled study of behavioral inhibition in children of parents with panic disorder and depression. *American Journal of Psychiatry, 157,* 2002–2010.

Rosenberg, D. R., & Keshavan, M. S. (1998). A.E. Bennett Research Award: Toward a neurodevelopmental model of obsessive–compulsive disorder. *Biological Psychiatry, 43,* 623–640.

Rosenberg, D. R., MacMaster, F. P., Keshavan, M. S., Fitzgerald, K. D., Stewart, K. D., Stewart, C. M., & Moore, G. J. (2000). Decrease in caudate glutamatergic concentrations in pediatric obsessive-compulsive disorder patients taking paroxetine. *Journal of the American Academy of Child and Adolescent Psychiatry, 39,* 1096–1103.

Rosenberg, D. R., MacMillan, S. N., & Moore, G. J. (2001). Brain anatomy and chemistry may predict treatment response in paediatric obsessive-compulsive disorder. *International Journal of Neuropsychopharmacology, 4,* 179–190.

Roussos, A., Francis, K., Koumoula, A., Richardson, C., Kabakos, C., Kiriakidou, T., Karagianni, S., & Karamolegou, K. (2003). The Leyton Obsessional Inventory-Child version in Greek adolescents. *European Child & Adolescent Psychiatry, 12,* 58–66.

Rubin, K. H., & Asendorpf, J. B. (1993). *Social withdrawal, inhibition, and shyness in childhood.* Hillsdale, NJ: Erlbaum.

Rubin, K. H., Hastings, P. D., Stewart, S. L., Henderson, H. A., & Chen, X. (1997). The consistency and concomitants of inhibition: Some of the children, all of the time. *Child Development, 68,* 467–483.

RUPP Anxiety Study Group (2001). Fluvoxamine treatment of anxiety disorders in children and adolescents. *New England Journal of Medicine, 344,* 1279–1285.

RUPP Anxiety Study Group (2002). Treatment of pediatric anxiety disorders: An open-label extension of the Research Units on Pediatric Psychopharmacology Anxiety Study. *Journal of Child and Adolescent Psychopharmacology, 12,* 175–188.

RUPP Anxiety Study Group (2003). Searching for moderators and mediators of pharmacological treatment effects in children and adolescents with anxiety disorders. *Journal of the American Academy of Child and Adolescent Psychiatry, 42,* 13–21.

Ryan, N. D., Puig–Antich, J., Ambrosini, P., Rabinovich, H., Robinson, D., Nelson, B., Iyengar, S., & Twomey, J. (1987). The clinical picture of major depression in children and adolescents. *Archives of General Psychiatry, 44,* 854–861.

Rynn, M. A., Siqueland, L., & Rickels, K. (2001). Placebo-controlled trial of sertraline in the treatment of children with Generalized Anxiety Disorder. *American Journal of Psychiatry, 158,* 2008–2013.

Saigh, P. A. (1987). *In vitro* flooding of an adolescent's posttraumatic stress disorder. *Journal of Clinical Child Psychology, 16,* 147–150.

Saigh, P. A., (1989). A comparative analysis of the affective and behavioral symptomatology of traumatized and nontraumatized children. *Journal of School Psychology, 27,* 247–255.

Salkovskis, P. M. (1989). Cognitive behavioural factors and the persistence of intrusive thoughts in obsessional problems. *Behaviour Research and Therapy, 27,* 677–682.

Salkovskis, P. M., & Harrison, J. (1984). Abnormal and normal obsessions: A replication. *Behaviour Research and Therapy, 22,* 1–4.

Sallee, F. R., & March, J. S. (2001). Neuropsychiatry of anxiety disorders. In W. K. Silverman and P. D. A. Treffers (Eds.) *Anxiety disorders in children and adolescents* (pp. 90–125). Cambridge: Cambridge University Press.

Sallee, F. R., Richman, H., Sethuraman, G., Dougherty, D., Sine, L., & Altman–Hamamdzic, S. (1998). Clonidine challenge in childhood anxiety disorders. *Journal of the American Academy of Child and Adolescent Psychiatry, 37,* 655–662.

Sallee, F. R., Sethuraman, G., Sine, L., & Liu, H. (2000). Yohimbine challenge in children with anxiety disorders. *American Journal of Psychiatry, 157,* 1236–1242.

Sanders, M. R., Rebgetz, M., Morrison, M., Bor, W., Gordon, A., Dadds, M., & Shepherd, R. (1989). Cognitive-behavioral treatment of recurrent nonspecific abdominal pain in children: An analysis of generalization, maintenance, and side effects. *Journal of Consulting and Clinical Psychology, 57,* 294–300.

Sanders, M. R., Shepherd, R. W., Cleghorn, G., & Woolford, H. (1994). The treatment of recurrent abdominal pain in children: A controlled comparison of cognitive-behavioral family intervention and standard pediatric care. *Journal of Consulting and Clinical Psychology, 62,* 306–314.

Sank, L. I., & Biglan, A. (1974). Operant treatment of a case of recurrent abdominal pain in a 10-year-old boy. *Behavior Therapy, 5,* 677–681.

Scahill, L., Riddle, M. A., McSwiggin–Hardin, M., Ort, S. I., King, R. A., Goodman, W. K., Cicchetti, D., & Leckman, J. F. (1997). Children's Yale-Brown Obsessive Compulsive Scale: Reliability and validity. *Journal of the American Academy of Child and Adolescent Psychiatry, 36,* 844–852.

Scharff, L. (1997). Recurrent abdominal pain in children: A review of psychological factors and treatment. *Clinical Psychology Review, 17,* 145–166.

Schniering, C. A., Hudson, J. L., & Rapee, R. M. (2000). Issues in the diagnosis and assessment of anxiety disorders in children and adolescents. *Clinical Psychology Review, 20,* 453–478.

Schwartz, A. N., Campos, J. J., & Baisel, E. J., Jr. (1973). The visual cliff: Cardiac and behavioral responses on the deep and shallow sides at five and nine months of age. *Journal of Experimental Child Psychology, 35,* 239–243.

Schwartz, C. E., Snidman, N., & Kagan, J. (1999). Adolescent social anxiety as an outcome of inhibited temperament in childhood. *Journal of the American Academy of Child and Adolescent Psychiatry, 38,* 1008–1015.

Seligman, L. D., Ollendick, T. H., Langley, A. K., & Baldacci, H. B. (2004). The utility of measures of child and adolescent anxiety: A meta-analytic review of the Revised Children's Manifest Anxiety Scale, the State-Trait Anxiety Inventory for Children, and the Child Behavior Checklist. *Journal of Clinical Child and Adolescent Psychology, 33,* 557–565.

Seligman, M. E. P. (1971). Phobias and preparedness. *Behavior Therapy, 2,* 307–320.

Shannon. M. P., Lonigan, C. J., Finch, A. J., Jr., & Taylor, C. M. (1994). Children exposed to disaster: I. Epidemiology of post-traumatic symptoms and symptom profiles. *Journal of the American Academy of Child and Adolescent Psychiatry, 33,* 80–93.

Sherer, M. W., & Nakamura, C. Y. (1968). A fear survey schedule for children (FSS-FC): A factor analytic comparison with manifest anxiety (CMAS). *Behaviour Research and Therapy, 6,* 173–182.

Sheslow, D. V., Bondy, A. S., & Nelson, R. O. (1983). A comparison of graduated exposure, verbal coping skills, and their combination in the treatment of children's fear of the dark. *Child and Family Behavior Therapy, 4,* 33–45.

Shirk, S. R., & Karver, M. (2003). Prediction of treatment outcome from relationship variables in child and adolescent therapy: A meta-analytic review. *Journal of Consulting and Clinical Psychology, 71,* 452–464.

Shortt, A. L., Barrett, P. M., & Fox, T. L. (2001). Evaluating the FRIENDS program: A cognitive-behavioral group treatment for anxious children and their parents. *Journal of Clinical Child Psychology, 30,* 525–535.

Silverman, W. K., & Albano, A. M. (1996). *The Anxiety Disorders Interview Schedule for Children DSM–IV Child and Parent Version.* San Antonio: Psychological Corporation.

Silverman, W. K., & Berman, S. L. (2001). Psychosocial interventions for anxiety disorders in children: Status and future directions. In W. K. Silverman & P. D. A. Treffers (Eds.), *Anxiety disorders in children and adolescents* (pp. 313–334). Cambridge, UK: Cambridge University Press.

Silverman, W. K., & Dick-Niederhauser, A. (2004). Separation anxiety disorder. In T. L. Morris & J. S. March (Eds.), *Anxiety disorders in children and adolescents* (pp.164–188).

Silverman, W. K., & Eisen, A. R. (1992). Age differences in the reliability of parent and child reports of child anxious symptomatology using a structured interview. *Journal of the American Academy of Child and Adolescent Psychiatry, 31,* 117–124.

Silverman, W. K., & Hicks–Carmichael, D. (1999). Phobic disorders. In R. Ammerman, C. G., Last, & M. Hersen (Eds.), *Handbook of prescriptive treatments for children and adolescents* (2nd ed., pp. 172–192). Needham Heights, MA: Allyn & Bacon.

Silverman, W. K., & Kurtines, W. M. (1996). *Anxiety and phobic disorders: A pragmatic approach.* New York: Plenum Press.

Silverman, W. K., Kurtines, W. M., Ginsburg, G. S., Weems, C. F., Lumpkin, P. W., & Carmichael, D. H. (1999a). Treating anxiety disorders in children with group cognitive-behavioral therapy: A randomized clinical trial. *Journal of Consulting and Clinical Psychology, 67,* 995–1003.

Silverman, W. K., Kurtines, W. M., Ginsburg, G. S., Weems, C. F., Rabian, B., & Serafini, L. T. (1999b). Contingency management, self-control, and education support in the treatment of childhood phobic disorders: A randomized clinical trial. *Journal of Consulting and Clinical Psychology, 67,* 675–687.

Silverman, W. K., La Greca, A. M., & Waserstein, S. B. (1995). What do children worry about? Worries and their relations to anxiety. *Child Development, 66,* 671–686.

Silverman, W. K., & Nelles, W. B. (1988). The Anxiety Disorders Interview Schedule for Children. *Journal of the American Academy of Child and Adolescent Psychiatry, 27,* 772–778.

Silverman, W. K., Saavedra, I. M., & Pina, A. A. (2001). Test-retest reliability of anxiety symptoms and diagnoses with the Anxiety Disorders Interview Schedule for DSM-IV-child and parent versions. *Journal of the American Academy of Child and Adolescent Psychiatry, 40,* 937–944.

Simeon, J. G., & Ferguson, H. B. (1987). Alprazolam effects in children with anxiety disorders. *Canadian Journal of Psychiatry, 32,* 570–574.

Simeon, J. G., Ferguson, H. B., Knott, V., Roberts, N., Gauthier, B., Dubois, C., & Wiggins, D. (1992). Clinical, cognitive, and neurophysiological effects of alprazolam in children and adolescents with overanxious and avoidant disorders. *Journal of the American Academy of Child and Adolescent Psychiatry, 31,* 29–33.

Simonian, S. J., Beidel, D. C., Turner, S. M., Berkes, J. L., & Long, J. H. (2001). Recognition of facial affect by social phobic children. *Child Psychiatry and Human Development, 32,* 137–145.

Siqueland, L., Kendall, P. C., & Steinberg, L. (1996). Anxiety in children: Perceived family environments and observed family interaction. *Journal of Clinical Child Psychology, 25,* 225–237.

Skinner, H. A., Steinhauer, P. D., & Santa-Barbara, J. (1983). The Family Assessment Measure. *Canadian Journal of Community Mental Health, 2,* 91–105.

Southam-Gerow, M. A., & Kendall, P.C . (2000). A preliminary study of the emotional understanding of youths referred for treatment of anxiety disorders. *Journal of Clinical Child Psychology, 29,* 319–327.

Southam-Gerow, M. A., Weisz, J. R., & Kendall, P. C. (2003). Youth with anxiety disorders in research and service clinics: Examining client differences and similarities. *Journal of Clinical Child and Adolescent Psychology, 32,* 375–385.

Spence, S. H., & McCathie, H. (1993). The stability of fears in children: A two-year prospective study. *Journal of Psychiatry and Psychology, 34,* 379–385.

Spence, S. H., Donovan, C., & Brechman-Toussaint, M. (1999). Social skills, social outcomes, and cognitive features of childhood social phobia. *Journal of Abnormal Psychology, 108,* 211–221.

Spence, S. H., Donovan, C., & Brechman-Toussaint, M. (2000). The treatment of childhood social phobia: The effectiveness of a social skills training-based, cognitive-behavioral intervention, with and without parental involvement. *Journal of Child Psychology and Psychiatry, 41,* 713–726.

Sroufe, L. A., & Waters, E. (1977) Heart rate as a convergent measure in clinical and developmental research. *Merrill-Palmer Quarterly, 23,* 3–27.

Sroufe, L. A., Waters, E., & Matas, L. (1974). Contextual determinants of infant affective response. In M. Lewis & L. Rosenblum (Eds.), *The origins of behavior Vol. 2: Fear* (pp. 49–51). New York: Wiley.

Stallard, P., Velleman, R., & Baldwin, S. (1998). Prospective study of post-traumatic stress disorder in children involved in road traffic accidents. *British Medical Journal, 317,* 1619–1923.

Stanley, M. A., & Turner, S. M. (1995). Current status of pharmacological and behavioral treatment of obsessive-compulsive disorder. *Behavior Therapy, 26,* 163–186.

Stavrakaki, C., Bargo, B., Goodsingh, L., & Roberts, N. (1987). The relationship between anxiety and depression in children: Rating scales and clinical variables. *Canadian Journal of Psychiatry, 32,* 433–439.

Stein, M. B. (1998). Neurobiological perspectives on social phobia: From affiliation to zoology. *Biological Psychiatry, 44,* 1277–1285.

Steinhausen, H. C., & Juzi, C. (1996). Elective mutism: An analysis of 100 cases. *Journal of the American Academy of Child and Adolescent Psychiatry, 35*, 606–614.

Steinhausen, H. C., Metzke, C. W., Meier, M., & Kannenberg, R. (1998). Prevalence of child and adolescent psychiatric disorders: The Zurich epidemiological study. *Acta Psychiatrica Scandinavica, 98*, 262–271.

Stemberger, R. T., Turner, S. M., Beidel, D. C., & Calhoun, K. S. (1995). Social phobia: An analysis of possible developmental factors. *Journal of Abnormal Psychology, 104*, 526–531.

Stevenson, J., Batten, N., & Cherner, M. (1992). Fears and fearfulness in children and adolescents: A genetic analysis of twin data. *Journal of Child Psychology and Psychiatry, 33*, 977–985.

Steward, M., & Steward, D. (1981). Children's conceptions of medical procedures. In R. Bibace & N. Walsh (Eds.), *Children's conceptions of health, illness and bodily function* (pp. 67–84). San Francisco: Jossey-Bass.

Stickler, G. B., & Murphy, D. B. (1979). Recurrent abdominal pain. *American Journal of Diseases of Childhood, 133*, 486–489.

Strauss, C. C. (1988). Behavioral assessment and treatment of overanxious disorder in children and adolescents. *Behavior Modification, 12*, 234–251.

Strauss, C.C., Lahey, B. B., Frick, P., Frame, C. L., & Hynd, G. W. (1988). Peer social status of children with anxiety disorders. *Journal of Consulting and Clinical Psychology, 56*, 137–141.

Strauss, C. C., & Last, C. G. (1993). Social and simple phobias in children. *Journal of Anxiety Disorders, 7*, 141–152.

Strauss, C. C., Last, C. G., Hersen, M., & Kazdin, A. E. (1988). Association between anxiety and depression in children and adolescents with anxiety disorders. *Journal of Abnormal Child Psychology, 16*, 57–68.

Strauss, C. C., Lease, C. A., Last, C. G., & Francis, G. (1988). Overanxious disorder: An examination of developmental differences. *Journal of Abnormal Child Psychology, 16*, 433–443.

Striker, G., & Howitt, J. W. (1965). Physiological recording during simulated dental appointments. *New York State Dental Journal, 31*, 204–206.

Suomi, S. J. (1986). Anxiety in young nonhuman primates. In R. Gittelman (Ed.), *Anxiety disorders of childhood* (pp. 1–23). New York: Guilford Press.

Svensson, L., Larsson, A., & Öst, L. G. (2002). How children experience brief-exposure treatment of specific phobias. *Journal of Clinical Child and Adolescent Psychiatry, 31*, 80–89.

Swedo, S. E., & Leonard, H. L. (1992). Trichotillomania: An obsessive compulsive spectrum disorder? *Psychiatric Clinics of North America, 15*, 777–790.

Swedo, S. E., Leonard, H. L., Garvey, M., Mittleman, B., Allen, A.J., Perlmutter, S., Lougee, L., Dow, S., Zamkoff, J., & Dubbert, B. K. (1998). Pediatric autoimmune neuropsychiatric disorders associated with streptococcal infections: Clinical description of the first 50 cases. *American Journal of Psychiatry, 155*, 264–271.

Swedo, S. E., & Rapoport, J. L. (1991). Trichotillomania. *Journal of Child Psychology and Psychiatry, 32*, 401–409.

Swedo, S. E., Rapoport, J. L., Leonard H., Lenane, M., & Cheslow, D. (1989). Obsessive-compulsive disorder in children and adolescents. *Archives of General Psychiatry, 46*, 335–341.

Szajnberg, N., Krall, V., Davis, P., Treem, W., & Hyams, J. (1993). Psychopathology and relationship measures in children with inflammatory bowel disease and their parents. *Child Psychiatry and Human Development, 23*, 215–232.

Tal, A., & Miklich, D. R. (1976). Emotionally induced decreases in pulmonary flow rates in asthmatic children. *Psychosomatic Medicine, 39*, 190–200.

Terr, L. (1983). Chochilla revisited: The effects of psychic trauma four years after a school-bus kidnapping. *American Journal of Psychiatry, 140*, 1543–1550

Terr, L. C. (1991). Childhood traumas: An outline and overview. *American Journal of Psychiatry, 148*, 10–20.

Thapar, A., & McGuffin, P. (1995). Are anxiety symptoms in childhood heritable? *Journal of Child Psychology and Psychiatry, 36*, 439–447.

Thienemann, M., Martin, J., Cregger, B., Thompson, H. B., & Dyer-Friedman, J. (2001). Manual-driven group cognitive-behavioral therapy for adolescents with obsessive-compulsive disorder: A pilot study. *Journal of the American Academy of Child and Adolescent Psychiatry, 40*, 1254–1260.

Thomsen, A. H., Compas, B. E., Colletti, R. B., Stanger, C., Boyer, M. C., & Konik, B. S. (2002). Parent reports of coping and stress responses in children with recurrent abdominal pain. *Journal of Pediatric Psychology, 27*, 215–226.

Thomsen, P. H. (1993). Obsessive-compulsive disorder in children and adolescents: Self-reported obsessive-compulsive behaviour in pupils in Denmark. *Acta Psychiatrica Scandinavia, 88*, 212–2217.

Thomsen, P. H. (1995). Obsessive-compulsive disorder in children and adolescents: A study of parental psychopathology and precipitating events in 20 consecutive Danish cases. *Psychopathology, 28*, 161–167.

Thomsen, P. H. (2000). Obsessions: The impact and treatment of obsessive-compulsive disorder in children and adolescents. *Journal of Psychopharmacology, 14*(2 Suppl. 1), S31–S37.

Thomsen, P. H., & Mikkelsen, H. U. (1993). Development of personality disorders in children and adolescents with obsessive-disorder. *Acta Psychiatrica Scandinavia, 87*, 456–462.

Thyer, B. A., Nesse, R. M., Cameron, O. G., & Curtis, G. C. (1985). Agoraphobia: A test of the separation anxiety hypothesis. *Behaviour Research and Therapy, 23*, 75–78.

Topolski, T. D., Hewitt, J. K., Eaves, L. J., Silberg, J. L., Meyer, J. M. J., Rutter, M., Pidkles, A., & Simonoff, E. (1997). Genetic and environmental influences on child reports of manifest anxiety symptoms and symptoms of separation anxiety and overanxious disorders: A community-based twin study. *Behavior Genetics, 27*, 15–28.

Torgersen, S. (1983). Genetics of neurosis: The effects of sampling variation upon the twin concordance ratio. *British Journal of Psychiatry, 142*, 126–132.

Toto, J., Cervera, M., Osejo, E., & Salamero, M. (1992). Obsessive compulsive disorder in childhood and adolescence: A clinical study. *Journal of Child Psychology and Psychiatry and Allied Disciplines, 33*, 1025–1037.

Townend, E., Dimigen, G., & Fung, D. (2000). A clinical study of child dental anxiety. *Behaviour Research and Therapy, 38*, 31–46.

Tracey, S. A., Chorpita, B. F., Douban, J., & Barlow, D. H. (1997). Empirical evaluation of DSM-IV Generalized Anxiety Disorder criteria in children and adolescents. *Journal of Clinical Child Psychology, 26*, 404–414.

Tracey, S. A., Mattis, S. G., Chorpita, B. F., Albano. A. M., Heimberg, R. G., & Barlow, D. H. (1998). *Cognitive-behavioral group treatment of social phobia in adolescents: Preliminary examination of the contribution of parental involvement.* Presented at the Annual Meeting of the Association for Advancement of Behavior Therapy, Washington, DC, November.

Tramer, M. (1934). Elektiver mutismus im Kindes alter. *Zeitschrift für Kinderpsychiatrie, 30–35.*

Treadwell, K. R., & Kendall, P. C. (1996). Self-talk in youth with anxiety disorders: States of mind, content specificity, and treatment outcome. *Journal of Consulting and Clinical Psychology, 64*, 941–950.

Treffers, P. D. A., & Silverman, W. K. (2001). Anxiety and its disorders in children and adolescents before the twentieth century. In W. K. Silverman & P. D. A. Treffers (Eds.), *Anxiety disorders in children and adolescents* (pp. 1–22). Cambridge, UK: Cambridge University Press.

Turner, B. G., Beidel, D. C., Hughes, S., & Turner, M. W. (1993). Test anxiety in African American school children. *School Psychology Quarterly, 8*, 140–152.

Turner, S. M., Beidel, D. C., & Costello, A. (1987). Psychopathology in the offspring of anxiety disordered patients. *Journal of Consulting and Clinical Psychology, 55*, 229–235.

Turner, S. M., Beidel, D. C., Dancu, C. V., & Stanley, M. A. (1989). An empirically derived inventory to measure social fears and anxiety: The Social Phobia and Anxiety Inventory. *Psychological Assessment, 1*, 35–40.

Turner, S. M., Beidel, D. C., & Jacob. R. G. (1994). Social phobia: A comparison of behavior therapy and atenolol. *Journal of Consulting and Clinical Psychology, 62*, 350–358.

Turner, S. M., Beidel, D. C., & Larkin, K. T. (1986). Situational determinants of social anxiety in clinic and non-clinic samples: Physiological and cognitive correlates. *Journal of Consulting and Clinical Psychology, 54,* 523–527.

Turner, S. M., Beidel, D. C., Roberson-Nay, R., & Tervo, K. (2003). Parenting behaviors in parents with anxiety disorders. *Behaviour Research and Therapy, 41,* 541–554.

Turner, S. M., Beidel, D. C., & Wolff, P. L. (1996). Is behavioral inhibition related to the anxiety disorders? *Clinical Psychology Review, 16,* 157–172.

Twenge, J. M. (2000). The age of anxiety? Birth cohort change in anxiety and neuroticism, 1952–1993. *Journal of Personality and Social Psychology, 79,* 1007–1021.

Udwin, O., Boyle, S., Yule, W., Bolton, D., & Oryan, D. (2000). Risk factors for long-term psychological effects of a disaster experienced in adolescence: Predictors of Post Traumatic Stress Disorder. *Journal of Child Psychology and Psychiatry, 41,* 969–979.

Ultee, C. A., Griffioen, D., & Shellekens, J. (1982). The reduction of anxiety in children. A comparison of the effects of "systematic desensitization in vitro" and "systematic desensitization in vivo". *Behaviour Research and Therapy, 20,* 61–67.

Valleni-Basile, L. A., Farrison, C. Z., Jackson, K. L., Waller, J. L., McKeown, R. E., Addy, C. L., & Cuffe, S. P. (1995). Family and psychosocial predictors of obsessive compulsive disorder in a community sample of young adolescents. *Journal of Child and Family Studies, 4,* 193–206.

Valleni-Basile, L., Garrison, C. Z., Jackson, K. L., Waller, J. L., McKeown, R. E., Addy, C. L., & Cuffe, S. P. (1994). Frequency of obsessive-compulsive disorder in a community sample of young adolescents. *Journal of the American Academy of Child and Adolescent Psychiatry, 33,* 782–791.

Valleni-Basile, L. A., Garrison, C. Z., Waller, J. L., Ady, C. L., McKeown, R. E., Jackson, K. L., & Cuffe, S. P. (1996). Incidence of obsessive-compulsive disorder in a community sample of young adolescents. *Journal of the American Academy of Child and Adolescent Psychiatry, 35,* 898–906.

Vandenberg, B. (1993). Fears of normal and retarded children. *Psychological Reports, 72,* 473–474.

Vasa, R. A., & Pine, D. S. (2004). Neurobiology. In T. L. Morris, & J. S. March (Eds.) *Anxiety disorders in children and adolescents* (2nd ed., pp. 3–26). New York: Guilford Press.

Vasey, M. W. (1993). Development and cognition in childhood anxiety: The example of worry. *Advances in Clinical Child Psychology, 15,* 1–39.

Vasey, M. W., Crnic, K. A., & Carter, W. G. (1994). Worry in childhood: A developmental perspective. *Cognitive Therapy and Research, 18,* 529–549.

Vasey, M. W., & Daleiden, E. L. (1994). Worrying in children. In G. C. L. Davey & F. Tallis, (Eds.), *Worrying: Perspectives on theory, assessment and treatment* (pp. 185–207). Chichester, England: Wiley.

Velez, C. N., Johnson, J., & Cohen, P. (1989). A longitudinal analysis of selected risk factors of childhood psychopathology. *Journal of the American Academy of Child and Adolescent Psychiatry, 28,* 861–864.

Velosa, J. F., & Riddle, M. A. (2000). Pharmacologic treatment of anxiety disorders in children and adolescents. *Psychopharmacology, 9,* 119–133.

Velting, O. N., & Albano, A. M. (2001). Current trends in the understanding and treatment of social phobia in youth. *Journal of Child Psychology and Psychiatry, 42,* 127–140.

Venham, L., Bengston, D., & Cipes, M. (1977). Children's response to sequential dental visits. *Journal of Dental Research, 56,* 454–459.

Verduin, T. L., & Kendall, P. C. (2003). Differential occurrence of comorbidity within childhood anxiety disorders. *Journal of Clinical Child and Adolescent Psychology, 32,* 290–295.

Verhulst, F. C., van der Ende, J., Ferinand, R., & Kasius, M. C., (1997). The prevalence of DSM-III-R diagnoses in a national sample of Dutch adolescents. *Archives of General Psychiatry, 54,* 329–336.

Vernberg, E. M., La Greca, A. M., Silverman, W. K., & Prinstein, M. J. (1996). Prediction of post-traumatic stress symptoms in children after Hurricane Andrew. *Journal of Abnormal Psychology, 105,* 237–248.

Vila, G., Nollet-Clemencon, C., DeBlic, J., Falissard, B., Mouren-Simeoni, M. C., & Scheinmann, P. (1999). Assessment of anxiety disorders in asthmatic children. *Psychosomatics, 40,* 404–413.

Vitiello, B., Behar, D., Wolfson, S., & McLeer, S. V. (1990). Diagnosis of panic disorder in prepubertal children. *Journal of the American Academy of Child and Adolescent Psychiatry, 29,* 782–784.

Vitulano. L. A., King, R. A., Scahill, L., & Cohen, D. J. (1992). Behavioral treatment of children and adolescents with trichotillomania. *Journal of the American Academy of Child and Adolescent Psychiatry, 31*, 139–146.

Von Korff, M. R., Eaton, W. W., & Keyl, P. M. (1985). The epidemiology of panic attacks and panic disorder. *American Journal of Epidemiology, 122*, 970–981.

Wagner, K. D., Berard, R., & Stein, M. B. A multicenter, randomized, double-blind, placebo-controlled, trial of paroxetine in children and adolescents with social anxiety disorder. *Archives of General Psychiatry, 61*, 1153-1162.

Walker, L. S., Garber, J., Smith, C. A., Van Slyke, D. A., & Claar, R. L. (2001). The relation of daily stressors to somatic and emotional symptoms in children with and without recurrent abdominal pain. *Journal of Consulting and Clinical Psychology, 69*, 85–91.

Walker, L. S., Garber, J., Van Slyke, D. A., & Greene, J. W. (1995). Long-term health outcomes in patients with recurrent abdominal pain. *Journal of Pediatric Psychology, 20*, 233–245.

Walker, L. S., & Greene, J. W. (1989). Children with recurrent abdominal pain and their parents: More somatic complaints, anxiety and depression than other patient families? *Journal of Pediatric Psychology, 14*, 231–243.

Walsh, K. H., & McDougle, C. J. (2001). Trichotillomania: Presentation, etiology, diagnosis and therapy. *American Journal of Clinical Dermatology, 2*, 327–333.

Wamboldt, M. Z., Schmitz, S., & Mrazek, D. (1998). Genetic association between atropy and behavioral symptoms in middle childhood. *Journal of Child Psychology and Psychiatry, 39*, 1007–1016.

Warren, R., & Zgourides, G. (1988). Panic attacks in high school students: Implications for prevention and intervention. *Phobia Practice and Research Journal, 1*, 97–113.

Warren, S. L., Schmitz, S., & Emde, R. N. (1999). Behavioral genetic analyses of self-reported anxiety at 7 years of age. *Journal of the American Academy of Child and Adolescent Psychiatry, 38*, 1403–1408.

Warren, W. (1948). Acute neurotic breakdown in children who refuse to go to school. *Archives of Disease in Childhood, 23*, 266–272.

Waters, T. L., & Barrett, P. M. (2000). The role of the family in childhood obsessive-compulsive disorder. *Clinical Child and Family Psychology Review, 3*, 173–184.

Waters, T. L., Barrett, P. M., & March, J. S. (2001). Cognitive-behavioral family treatment of childhood obsessive-compulsive disorder. *American Journal of Psychotherapy, 55*, 372–387.

Watson, J. B., & Rayner, R. (1920). Conditioned emotional reactions. *Journal of Experimental Psychology, 3*, 1–14.

Watson, T. S., & Allen, K. D. (1993). Elimination of thumb-sucking as a treatment for severe trichotillomania. *Journal of the American Academy of Child and Adolescent Psychiatry, 32*, 830–834.

Weems, C. F., Silverman, W. K., & La Greca, A. M. (2000). What do youth referred for anxiety problems worry about? *Journal of Abnormal Child Psychology, 28*, 63–72.

Weems, C. F., Silverman, W. K., Saavedra, L. M., Pina, A. A., & White-Lumpkin, P. (1999). The discrimination of children's phobias using the revised Fear Survey Schedule for Children. *Journal of Child Psychology and Psychiatry, 40*, 941–952.

Weinstein, P. (1990). Breaking the worldwide cycle of pain, fear and avoidance: Uncovering risk factors and promoting prevention for children. *Annals of Behavioral Medicine, 12*, 141–147.

Weinstein, P., Getz, T., Ratener, P.,& Domoto, P. (1982a). Dentists' response to fear- and non- fear- related behaviors in children. *Journal of the American Dental Association, 104*, 38–40.

Weinstein, P., Getz, T., Ratener, P., & Domoto, P. (1982b). The effect of dentists' behaviors on fear-related behaviors in children. *Journal of the American Dental Association, 104*, 32–38.

Weinstein, P., Milgrom, P., Hoskuldsson, O., Gelletz, D., Jeffcot, E., & Koday, M. (1996). Situation-specific child control: A visit to the dentist. *Behaviour Research and Therapy, 34*, 11–21.

Weissman, M. M., Leckman, J. F., Merikangas, K. R., Gammon, G. D., & Prusoff, B. A. (1984). Depression and anxiety disorders in parents and children: Results from the Yale family study. *Archives of General Psychiatry, 41*, 845–852.

Weisz, J. R., Donenberg, G. R., Han, S. S., & Weiss, B. (1995). Bridging the gap between lab and clinic in child and adolescent psychotherapy. *Journal of Consulting and Clinical psychology, 63*, 688–701.

Werry, J. S. (1991). Overanxious Disorder: A review of its taxonomic properties. *Journal of the American Academy of Child and Adolescent Psychiatry, 30*, 533–544.

Westenberg, P. M., Siebelink, B. M., Warmenhoven, N. J. C., & Treffers, P. D. A. (1999). Separation anxiety and overanxious disorders: Relations to age and level of psychosocial maturity. *Journal of the American Academy of Child and Adolescent Psychiatry, 38*, 1000–1007.

Wever, C., & Rey, J. (1997). Juvenile obsessive-compulsive disorder. *Australian and New Zealand Journal of Psychiatry, 31*, 105–113.

Whaley, S. E., Pinto, A., & Sigman, M. (1999). Characterizing interactions between anxious mothers and their children. *Journal of Consulting and Clinical Psychology, 67*, 826–836.

Whitaker, A., Johnson, J., Shaffer, D., Rapoport, J. L., Kakikow, K., Walsh, B. T., Davies, M., Braiman, S., & Dolinsky, A. (1990). Uncommon troubles in young people: Prevalence estimates of selected psychiatric disorders in a nonreferred adolescent population. *Archives of General Psychiatry, 47*, 487–496.

Wilens, T. E., Spencer, T. J., Frazier, J., & Biederman, J. (1998). Child and adolescent psychopharmacology. In T. Ollendick & M. Hersen (Eds.), *Handbook of child psychopathology* (pp. 603–636). New York: Plenum Press.

Williams, C. E., & Jones, R. T. (1989). Impact of self-instructions on response maintenance and children's fear of fire. *Journal of Clinical Child Psychology, 18*, 84–89.

Williams, J. M., Murray, J. J., Lund, C. A., Harkiss, B., & DeFranco, A. (1985). Anxiety in the child dental clinic. *Journal of Child Psychology and Psychiatry and Allied Disciplines, 26*, 305–310.

Wittchen, H. U., Nelson, C. B., & Lachner, G. (1998). Prevalence of mental disorders and psychosocial impairments on adolescents and young adults. *Psychological Medicine, 28*, 109–126.

Wittchen, H. U., Stein, M. B., & Kessler, R. C. (1999). Social fears and social phobia in a community sample of adolescents and young adults: Prevalence, risk factors and co-morbidity. *Psychological Medicine, 29*, 309–323.

Woodruff-Borden, J., Morrow, C., Bourland, S., & Cambron, S. (2002). The behavior of anxious parents: Examining mechanisms of transmission of anxiety from parent to child. *Journal of Clinical Child and Adolescent Psychology, 31*, 364–374.

Wolpe, J. (1958). *Psychotherapy by reciprocal inhibition*. Stanford, CA: Stanford University Press.

Wood, J. J., Piacentini, J. C., Bergman, R. L., McCracken, J., & Barrios, V. (2002). Concurrent validity of the Anxiety Disorders Section of the Anxiety Disorders Interview Schedule for DSM-IV: Child and Parent version. *Journal of Clinical Child and Adolescent Psychology, 31*, 335–342.

Woodward, L. J., & Fergusson, D. M. (2001). Life course outcomes of young people with anxiety disorders in adolescence. *Journal of the American Academy of Child and Adolescent Psychiatry, 40*, 1086–1093.

Wright, F., A. C., Lucas, J., & McMurray, N. E. (1980). Dental anxiety in 5–9-year-old children. *The Journal of Pedodontics, 4*, 99–115.

Yeganeh, R., Beidel, D. C., Turner, S. M., Pina, A. A., & Silverman, W. K. (2003). Clinical distinctions between selective mutism and social phobia: An investigation of childhood psychopathology. *Journal of the American Academy of Child and Adolescent Psychiatry, 42*, 1069–1075.

Yule, W., Bolton, D., Udwin, O., Boyle, S., O'Ryan, D., & Nurrish, J. (2000). The long-term psychological effects of a disaster experienced in adolescence: I: The incidence and course of PTSD. *Journal of Child Psychology and Psychiatry, 41*, 503–511.

Yule, W., & Canterbury, R. (1994). The treatment of posttraumatic stress disorder in children and adolescents. *International Review of Psychiatry, 6*, 141–151.

Yule, W., Udwin, O., & Murdoch, K. (1990). The "Jupiter" sinking: Effects on children's fears, depression and anxiety. *Journal of Child Psychology and Psychiatry, 31*, 1051–1061

Zitrin, C. M., & Ross, D. C. (1988). Early separation anxiety and adult agoraphobia. *Journal of Nervous and Mental Disease, 176*, 621–625.

Zohar, A. H., & Felz, L. (2001). Ritualistic behavior in young children. *Journal of Abnormal Child Psychology, 29*, 121–128.

Index

Page numbers in italics refer to tables or figures.

351